BUILDING CHILDREN'S WORLDS

Children are the future architects, clients and users of our buildings. The kinds of architectural worlds they are exposed to in picturebooks during their formative years may be assumed to influence how they regard such architecture as adults.

Contemporary urban environments the world over represent the various stages of modernism in architecture. This book reads that history through picturebooks and considers the kinds of national identities and histories they construct.

Twelve specialist essays from international scholars address questions such as: Is modern architecture used to construct specific narratives of childhood? Is it taken to support 'negative' narratives of alienation on the one hand and 'positive' narratives of happiness on the other? Do images of modern architecture support ideas of 'community'? Reinforce 'family values'? If so, what kinds of architecture, community and family? How is modern architecture placed vis-à-vis the promotion of diversity (ethnic, religious, gender etc.)? How might the use of architecture in comic strips or the presence of specific kinds of building in fiction aimed at younger adults be related to the groundwork laid in picturebooks for younger readers?

This book reveals what stories are told about modern architecture and shows how those stories affect future attitudes towards and expectations of the built environment.

Torsten Schmiedeknecht is a Reader in Architecture at the University of Liverpool. His research interests include the representation of architecture in print media, rationalism in architecture and architectural competitions. He is the co-editor of *Modernism and the Professional Architecture Journal, The Rationalist Reader, Rationalist Traces, An Architect's Guide to Fame* and *Fame and Architecture*. In 2016 he was the recipient of an RIBA Research Trust Award for his project *The representation of Modern Architecture through illustrations in postwar British Children's Literature*, which resulted in a co-authored paper ('Absent Architectures: Post-War Housing in British Children's Picture Books') with Emma Hayward, and the exhibition Building Children's Worlds at RIBA North in Liverpool in Spring 2019.

Jill Rudd is a Professor of Literature in the English Department at the University of Liverpool, where, amongst other things, she teaches medieval literature and children's literature. Chiefly a medievalist with an interest in eco-criticism, her publications include *Greenery: Ecocritical Readings of Late Medieval English Literature* (MUP, 2007) and various articles and chapters on mice, clouds, flowers and plants. She has also written on *Sir Gawain and the Green Knight* and *The Secret Garden* and in the past, on Charlotte Perkins Gilman's short stories. She has supervised postgraduate theses on issue-led children's literature written for older children readers and young adults.

Emma Hayward is a secondary school English teacher and Honorary Research Fellow at the University of Liverpool. Her research interests include curriculum design and 20th- and 21st-century literature – in particular, the relationship between literature and the built environment, verbal-visual narratives and postmodernism/late postmodernism. She has published on children's literature and the built environment. Her publications include 'Absent Architectures: Post-War Housing in British Children's Picture Books, 1960–present' and '"Horrible muddy English places": Downriver, Swandown, and the Mock-Heroic Tradition'.

BUILDING CHILDREN'S WORLDS

The Representation of Architecture and Modernity in Picturebooks

Edited by
Torsten Schmiedeknecht, Jill Rudd
and Emma Hayward

Routledge
Taylor & Francis Group

LONDON AND NEW YORK

Cover image: Henri Schmiedeknecht (Power and Conflict)
Cover design: Torsten Schmiedeknecht

First published 2023
by Routledge
4 Park Square, Milton Park, Abingdon, Oxon OX14 4RN

and by Routledge
605 Third Avenue, New York, NY 10158

Routledge is an imprint of the Taylor & Francis Group, an informa business

British Library Cataloguing-in-Publication Data
A catalogue record for this book is available from the British Library

ISBN: 9780367675479 (hbk)
ISBN: 9780367675486 (pbk)
ISBN: 9781003131755 (ebk)

DOI: 10.4324/9781003131755

Typeset in Bembo
by codeMantra

In memory of
Charles Rattray
Architect and Teacher
1956–2022

CONTENTS

List of Contributors   *ix*

Introduction   1
Torsten Schmiedeknecht, Jill Rudd and Emma Hayward

PART ONE
Modernity   **9**

1 Building for the future – children as future citizens in Swedish
   picturebooks of the 1930s   11
   Elina Druker

2 A modern utopia: Architecture, modernity and Ladybird books in
   post-war Britain   29
   Torsten Schmiedeknecht and Jill Rudd

3 Reading as building: Modernist architecture and book space in
   picturebooks   49
   Honglan Huang

4 Representations of modern architecture and urbanism in Colombian
   children's literature from the mid-20th century onwards   68
   Carolina Rodríguez, Roberto Londoño and Antonio Manrique

PART TWO
Domestic space 93

5 Domestic architecture and environmental design in
Australian picturebooks 95
John Stephens

6 The house, where everything begins 111
Christophe Meunier

7 Architecture and interior design in Italian picturebooks: A case study
of Bruno Munari 125
Marnie Campagnaro

8 Representations of architecture in children's picturebooks in
Australia, Singapore and China 143
Sabine Tan, Xinchao Zhai, Lyndon Way and Kay L. O'Halloran

9 Building diversity in British and American children's picturebooks
(2000 to present) 166
Emma Hayward

PART THREE
Urban space 185

10 Highly modern ideal homestead 187
Lucie Glasheen

11 Architecture and magic – mapping the London of children's
fantasy fiction 201
Madison McLeod

12 Ordinary cityscapes and architecture in Jörg Müller's
picturebook oeuvre 219
Jörg Meibauer

Index *235*

CONTRIBUTORS

Marnie Campagnaro, PhD, is an Assistant Professor at the University of Padova and didactic co-ordinator of a postgraduate course in Children's Literature (https://www.childrensliterature-unipd.it/). Her main research fields include picturebooks, fairy tales, architecture, object-oriented literary criticism, sustainability and Italian children's writers. She has lectured as a visiting professor at several European universities and been an invited speaker at numerous international conferences. Her most recent publications include *Stepping into the World of Houses. Children's Picturebooks on Architecture* (in Goga, Iversen & Teigland [eds], 2021), *Materiality in Bruno Munari's Book Objects: The Case of Nella notte buia and I Prelibri* (Libri & Liberi, 2019) and *Narrating homes and objects: images of domestic life in Italian picturebooks since the mid-20th century* (*RPD Journal*, 2019).

Elina Druker is a Professor of Comparative Literature at Stockholm University, Sweden. Her research area covers children's literature, picturebooks, illustration history and intermedia studies. She has published and edited several publications dealing with *radical* writing for children, avant-garde and modernism and is author of *Images of Modernism* (2008) and co-editor for *Children's Literature and the Avant-Garde* (2015). Druker is a jury member for the Astrid Lindgren Memorial Award and co-edits the John Benjamin series 'Children's Literature, Culture and Cognition'.

Lucie Glasheen is a Teaching Fellow in Human Geography at the University of Southampton and Honorary Research Fellow in the School of Languages, Linguistics and Film, where she has been Co-Investigator on the British Academy-funded project Childhood heroes: storytelling survival strategies and role models of resilience to COVID-19 in the UK. She is an Early Career Representative on the Steering Group of the Centre for Childhood Cultures and Conference Organiser for the Literary London Society. Lucie is currently in the early stages of a book project on play spaces, urban redevelopment and child citizenship in 1930s East London based on PhD research and has published in *The London Journal* and *The Materiality of Literary Narratives* edited by Jason Finch, Lieven Ameel, Richard Dennis and Silja Laine (London: Routledge, 2020).

Emma Hayward is a secondary school English teacher and Honorary Research Fellow at the University of Liverpool. Her research interests include curriculum design and 20th- and 21st-century literature – in particular, the relationship between literature and the built environment, verbal-visual narratives and postmodernism/late postmodernism. She has published on children's literature and the built environment. Her publications include 'Absent Architectures: Post-War Housing in British Children's Picture Books, 1960-present' and '"Horrible muddy English places": Downriver, Swandown, and the Mock-Heroic Tradition'.

Honglan Huang is a PhD candidate in Comparative Literature at Yale University, USA. Her current dissertation project focuses on books as sites for material encounter and embodied performance. She is also a participant artist in the Chicago Puppet Lab, and her puppetry project uses books as performing objects to explore reading as a process of animation.

Roberto Londoño is an architect from the University of Los Andes (1990), with a Master's degree from the Polytechnic University of Cataluña (UPC-ETSAB 1993) and a PhD from the University of Buenos Aires (UBA-FADU 2013). He was associate professor at the University of Los Andes (2001–2015) where he was involved in the project *Children and Architecture*. He is the author of *El Observatorio astronómico de Bogotá* (2008); *Edificio Francisco Camacho. Un momento, un lugar y una arquitectura* (2012); and has published papers in several international journals such as *DEARQ, Cadernos Pro-arq, BJET, V!rus* and *Módulo*. Currently, he is a teacher and researcher at the National University of La Matanza, the University of Buenos Aires – Catedra Speranza, and the Virtual Network Workshop linked to the ARQUISUR organisation and the UNESCO Chair, City and Project.

Antonio Manrique is an architect from the Javeriana University (1978). He has practised at various firms (1977–2018) and has been a fellow of the Fulbright Commission (1978), a consultant to the United Nations Development Program (UNDP), a supervisor of the Central Housing Unit of the United Nations for Human Settlements (HABITAT, 1993–1994) and a visiting professor at Mackintosh School of Architecture, Glasgow (1995). He was associate professor at University of Los Andes (1995–2015), where he coordinated the School of Architecture for Children (2008–2012). Gutiérrez has been invited to present his work at international events, including *Soundings for Architecture* (2006) at the Alvar Aalto Academy, *Taking Playce*, Gothenburg, Sweden (2007), and *Transmitting Architecture*, Turin (2008). He is a member of the Architecture & Children Group of the International Union of Architects (2009).

Madison McLeod completed her MA in English (1850s to present) at King's College London in 2017 and her PhD in Children's Literature at the University of Cambridge in 2022. Her research interests centre around the digital mapping of protagonists in children's fantasy literature, mythology in children's literature and the intersection of feminist studies and children's literature.

Jörg Meibauer is a Professor Emeritus of German Language and Linguistics at the Johannes Gutenberg Universität Mainz, Germany. His recent linguistic fields of research include lying, bullshitting and insulting. He has published numerous articles on children's literature, often in tandem with Bettina Kümmerling-Meibauer. Currently, he researches the visual culture of picturebooks from the German Democratic Republic, with a focus on architecture, design and photography. He is the editor of *The Oxford Handbook of Lying* (2019) and the co-editor of *Learning from picturebooks. Perspectives from Child Development and Literacy Studies* (2015) and *Pragmatikerwerb und Kinderliteratur* (Pragmatic Acquisition and Children's Literature, 2021).

Christophe Meunier teaches history and geography at the Institut National Superieur du Professorat et de l'Education, University of Orleans. His doctoral dissertation, *Quand les albums pour enfants parlent d'espace*, was published in 2016 and entitled *Space in Children's Books*. His research in cultural geography leads him to work on representations of space and spatiality in iconotexts (bande dessinée, children's picturebooks). Since 2010, he has been the webmaster of the blog *Les Territoires de l'album* (lta.hypotheses.org).

Kay L. O'Halloran is Chair Professor and Head of Department of Communication and Media in the School of the Arts at the University of Liverpool. She is an internationally recognised leading academic in the field of multimodal analysis, involving the study of the interaction of language with other resources in texts, interactions and events. A key focus of her work is the development of digital tools and techniques for multimodal analysis. Kay is developing mixed methods approaches that combine multimodal analysis, data mining and visualisation for big data analytics within and across media platforms.

Carolina Rodríguez is an architect from the National University of Colombia (2000) with doctoral studies at the University of Nottingham, UK (2006), and a Certificate of Professional Studies from the University of Liverpool, UK (2009). She is a Registered Senior Researcher (Minciencias) with more than 20 years of experience as a practitioner and in teaching, research and administration at the Universities of Nottingham, Liverpool, Los Andes and currently at the Universidad Piloto de Colombia. Her research interests focus on architectural education, architecture and children and building technology. Her academic production includes various Q1, Q2 and Q3 articles, books and book chapters, other journal articles and conference proceedings. She has received international awards and distinctions, supervises PhD and Master´s thesis and has acquired external funding for research projects. Carolina currently leads the environment and sustainability research group GUIAS and takes part in the process of updating Colombian regulations on sustainable construction.

Jill Rudd is a Professor of Literature in the English Department at the University of Liverpool. where, amongst other things, she teaches medieval literature and children's literature. Chiefly a medievalist with an interest in eco-criticism, her publications include *Greenery: Ecocritical Readings of Late Medieval English Literature* (MUP, 2007) and various articles and chapters on mice, clouds, flowers and plants. She has also written on *Sir Gawain and the Green Knight* and *The Secret Garden* and in the past, on Charlotte Perkins Gilman's short stories. She has supervised postgraduate theses on issue-led children's literature written for older children readers and young adults.

Torsten Schmiedeknecht is a Reader in Architecture at the University of Liverpool. His research interests include the representation of architecture in print media, rationalism in architecture and architectural competitions. He is the co-editor of *Modernism and the Professional Architecture Journal, The* Rationalist *Reader, Rationalist Traces, An Architect's Guide to Fame* and *Fame and Architecture.* In 2016 he was the recipient of an RIBA Research Trust Award for his project *The Representation of Modern Architecture through Illustrations in Postwar British Children's Literature,* which resulted in a co-authored paper ('Absent Architectures: Post-War Housing in British Children's Picture Books') with Emma Hayward and the exhibition *Building Children's Worlds* at RIBA North in Liverpool in Spring 2019.

John Stephens is an Emeritus Professor at Macquarie University, Australia. He is author or co-author of five books and editor of four collections. *Language and Ideology in Children's Fiction* (1992) introduced many concepts to children's literature criticism and has remained a constantly cited reference for over 25 years. He has also authored over 100 articles and book chapters. He was founding Editor (2008–2016) of *International Research in Children's Literature.* In 2007 he received the 11th International Brothers Grimm Award and in 2014 the Anne Devereaux Jordan Award, both in recognition of his contribution to research in children's literature.

Sabine Tan is currently a Senior Research Fellow at Curtin University, Western Australia. She has a background in critical multimodal discourse analysis, social semiotics and visual communication. She has applied multidisciplinary perspectives for the analysis of institutional discourses involving traditional and new media. She has worked on interdisciplinary projects involving the development of interactive software for the multimodal analysis of images, videos and 360-degree videos for research and educational purposes. She has also worked on projects to develop mixed methods approaches which combine multimodal analysis, data mining and visualisation for big data analytics in areas such as violent extremism, news discourse and 360-degree video.

Lyndon Way is a Senior Lecturer in Communication and Media at the University of Liverpool. He analyses political discourses in (digital) popular culture, popular music and news through the lens of multimodal critical discourse studies. He has published extensively in academic journals and in edited collections, co-edited/edited a number of publications, and written monographs on music and politics (Bloomsbury 2018) and digital popular culture and politics (2021).

Xinchao Zhai is currently a PhD student in the School of the Arts at the University of Liverpool. She has a background in Systemic-Functional Linguistics (SFL) and multimodal discourse studies. Her research interests lie in the intersection areas between discourse semantics, metaphor studies and multimodal analysis. She investigates the semantic structure of multimodal discourses, especially the metaphorical multimodal discourses. She also publishes papers in critical multimodal discourse analysis.

INTRODUCTION

Torsten Schmiedeknecht, Jill Rudd and Emma Hayward

'Picturebooks', as Perry Nodelman puts it, 'are a significant means by which we integrate young children into the ideology of our culture' (Nodelman, 2004, p.157). In part, this is due to the fact that 'the intended audience of picturebooks is by definition inexperienced – in need of learning how to think about their world, how to see and understand themselves and others' (Nodelman, 2004, p.157). Part of the world those young children necessarily think about is the built environment, so what they encounter through stories and information books and also what they don't will inevitably shape their attitudes towards different kinds of architecture and design. This book reflects upon that and the idea for it emerged some years ago: in 2014 Julia Chance, a painter originally trained as an architect, who had up to this point also been running architecture workshops in schools, decided to work on an architecture themed picturebook for children. For some time, Chance had been discussing with Torsten Schmiedeknecht of Liverpool University's Architecture department, why it is that modern architecture in the UK is still not very well received by the general public, with both agreeing that, as Alan Powers put it, 'the lack of widespread popular acceptance of Modernism in Britain since its inception cannot simply be ignored or dismissed as the stupidity of the unenlightened' (Powers, 2007, p.1).

Their discussion led to debate over how children, via the means of architectural images, are introduced to various societal norms, conventions, and ideologies, all of which subsequently resulted in the paper 'Absent Architectures: post-war housing in British children's picturebooks (1960–present)' (Hayward and Schmiedeknecht, 2019) and the exhibition 'Building Children's Worlds' at RIBA North in Liverpool, curated by Schmiedeknecht. In turn, the paper and the RIBA exhibition prompted further research, leading us to wonder how architecture is represented in picturebooks in different countries across the globe. The following collection of 12 essays by authors originating from Sweden, Germany, USA, Colombia, Australia, France, Italy, Singapore, China and the UK, covering work from North and South America, Europe, Asia and Australia, addresses questions such as: Is modern architecture used to construct specific narratives of childhood? Is it taken to support 'negative' narratives of alienation on the one hand and 'positive' narratives of happiness

DOI: 10.4324/9781003131755-1

on the other? Do images of modern architecture support ideas of 'community'? Do they reinforce 'family values'? If so, what kinds of architecture, community and family? How is modern architecture placed vis-à-vis the promotion of ethnic, sexual, gender or other diversity? How is architecture used in related forms, such as the comic strip or fiction aimed at younger adults?

The result is a volume which reveals what stories are told about modern architecture and show how those stories affect future attitudes towards and expectations of the built environment, particularly in relation to Modernity, Domestic Space and Urban Space, which are the three constituent parts of this book. Part I, Modernity, sets the context, looking at the broader scope of how modern architecture and ideas of modernity have been represented in picturebooks. The sections on Domestic Space and Urban Space then take a more focussed look at the home and the city, respectively. Throughout, we are reminded that children are the future architects, clients and users of our buildings. The kinds of architectural worlds they are exposed to in picturebooks during their formative years may be assumed to influence how they regard such architecture as adults. Indeed, as Kimberly Reynolds argues, this assumption gave rise to books such as Badmin's *Village and Town* in 1942 (Reynolds, *Left Out: The forgotten tradition of radical publishing for children in Britain 1910–1949*, Oxford, 2016). Our book builds on Reynold's work, expanding beyond Britain to reflect upon the representation of modern architecture in children's books internationally and consider how the portrayal of (modern) architecture varies between different countries and continents. Contemporary urban environments the world over represent the various stages of modernism in architecture. Very much conceived as a multidisciplinary effort from the beginning, this book reads that history through picturebooks and considers the kinds of national identities and histories they construct. Housing may be assumed to address those concerns directly, as Reynolds has already demonstrated (see Reynolds *Left Out*, Chapter 2); her arguments are expanded upon and added to here, but they are also addressed indirectly through illustrations to stories not overtly concerned with housing at all, such as pictures in which other forms of architecture serve as the backdrop to adventures or books that offer information about the world beyond the home.

In this, our collection joins other work already done in the field of picturebook research and endorses the description of how picturebooks work offered by Maria Nikolajeva and Carole Scott, who point out that although 'pictures in picturebooks are complex iconic signs, and words are complex conventional signs; however, the basic relationship between the two levels is the same. The function of pictures, iconic signs, is to describe or represent'. They go on to elaborate on the difference between the typically linear nature of the conventional sign (word) which is thus linked to narrative and that of the iconic sign which, in their view, is not to be linear and so does not give 'direct instruction about how to read them'. Importantly, the 'tension between the two functions creates unlimited possibilities for interaction between word and image' (Nikolajeva and Scott, 2006, p.1). Other work, too, such as that by Marnie Campagnaro (2019), Teresa Colomer, Bettina Kümmerling-Meibauer and Cecilia Silva-Díaz (eds, 2010) and John Stephens (ed, 2017) demonstrate that picturebooks are highly influential in moulding the opinions, social beliefs and expectations of children, showing this to be internationally the case, regardless of what those beliefs and expectations might be. In short, the humble picturebook is now recognised as not only one of the most appealing but also one of the most important kinds of book we encounter during the course of our lives.

Picturebook/picture book

Throughout this volume, we have used the term 'picturebook' rather than the two-word phrase 'picture book'. Up until fairly recently, the two were interchangeable, but increased attention has created nuanced appreciation of the different ways words and images act and interact within this form of literature. Uri Shulevitz has been particularly forthright on the difference between a work in which the pictures are entirely and solely at the service of the words – a form he prefers to call 'illustrated texts' – and those in which the pictures carry a narrative which may or (as many of the essays in this collection demonstrate) may not be the same as the one conveyed by the words (Shulevitz, 1996). Kimberley Reynolds, in her highly informative and very useful *Children's Literature: A Very Short Introduction*, clarifies the distinction by detecting an emerging trend in the use of the two available terms, thus in picturebooks, the written text and the images repeat information. This is so regardless of whether the image is used to show what the word means (such as in early learner readers where the word 'apple' is accompanied by the picture of the fruit, apple) or the words explain what the picture is showing (a picture of a house is accompanied by the words 'this is a house' or perhaps 'this is Alex's house'). In contrast, in picturebooks the words and the images are 'interdependent', that is, they are linked, and indeed frequently focus on the same topic, incident or object, but each offers something the other does not (see Reynolds, 2011, p.57). That linked yet simultaneously independent relation offers much room for critical analysis and debate, as the essays in this volume amply demonstrate.

It is also worth noting that since its inception with Comenius's *Orbis Sensualum Pictus* (published in 1658 and often cited as the first book primarily aimed at children), the picturebook format has been used as much for conveying factual information, as for storybooks. Academic discussion, however, has tended to keep these two categories apart, focusing on either fact or, more often, fiction; a tendency Nina Goga, Sarah Hoem Iversen and Anne-Stefi Teigland comment upon, attributing the relative paucity of studies of non-fiction picturebooks to 'the unwillingness to include the many verbal and visual strategies of nonfiction within the concept of children's literature' (Goga, Iversen and Teigland, 2021, p.1). The aim of Goma, Iversen and Teigland is to provide theoretical frameworks for discussion of non-fiction picturebooks; a by-product is to increase awareness of the variety of non-fiction picturebooks that exist. While our aim is different, in that we focus specifically on the presence of modern architecture in picturebooks (mainly those aimed at children under 12 years of age, but including also some consideration of comic strips and graphic books), this volume, too, draws attention to the great variety of form, content and purpose to be found in between their pages.

Part One – Modernity

In Chapter 1, Elina Druker examines how modernist ideas were communicated in children's literature in Sweden through the use of images of, for example, the 1930 Luma Factory. Conjuring up attributes such as hygiene and speed, the Factory stood a representative of technical innovation on the one hand, and of ideas of the welfare state and children as its future citizens – and consumers – on the other. Employing Mitchell's concept of 'imagetext' in her analysis of the illustrations of the Luma Factory in the popular Per and Lisa picturebooks, Druker specifically asks 'how these books exhibit an interdisciplinary convergence between children's literature, commercialism, and high-modernist architecture'.

Following on, Torsten Schmiedeknecht and Jill Rudd in Chapter 2 examine Ladybird books from the late 1950s, the 1960s and the early 1970s, concluding that there are plenty of illustrations of modern architecture to be found, almost all of which are associated with positive aspects of progress and the modern world. The 'Ladybird Book of Achievements' Series 601, illustrated by John Berry and Robert Ayton, amongst others, and the 'People at Work' Series 606B, with illustrations by Robert Ayton, are cases in point. The chapter sets out the 'typology' of Ladybird books in the context of post-war children's literature, followed by an analysis of what kind of modern architecture was represented in the books and how this architecture was used to support a particular narrative of modernity.

In Chapter 3, Honglan Huang posits that 'Like architectural books, picturebooks for children pay particular attention to generating meaning through non-verbal means'. Examining three books – El Lissitzky's *About Two Squares* (1922), David Macaulay's *Unbuilding* (1980) and Fanny Millard's *Upside Down* (2019) – and drawing on similarities between architectural books and picturebooks for children in 'generating meaning through non-verbal means', she demonstrates how picturebooks can not only contain and represent ideas on architecture, but become architecture themselves by turning 'reading into an exercise of building, whether metaphorically or literally'.

In the final chapter in this section (Chapter 4) on modernity, Carolina Rodríguez, Roberto Londoño and Antonio Manrique investigate how 'imaginaries of the modern city and its ideal architecture' are represented in Colombian picturebooks from the middle of the 20th century to the present day, reviewing 'the events, narratives, and adaptations that affected their emergence, development, demise, and legacy'. The authors base their findings on a study of seven illustrations, which were also subjected to a survey by a group of 5–13-year-old children as to their perceived messages and meaning, and show that fiction and reality are mingled via the use of imaginaries, thus extending the influence of pictures in these books beyond simple depiction into affecting 'the construction of utopias and dystopias regarding our connection with the built environment'.

Part Two – Domestic space

Despite domestic buildings in Australian picturebooks being 'seldom represented as the central theme of a book', John Stephens in Chapter 5 points out their importance in 'narratives of Australian childhoods'. And while 'exteriors appear mainly as settings or as background fragments', he posits that 'elements of design: a collection of artefacts, especially items of furniture' often carry more significance, particularly with regards to their metonymic function, than we might expect. Stephens's analysis of Australian picturebooks therefore 'needs to include more than the fabric of buildings but also embrace design and contents' before taking into account broader settings such as suburban landscapes and houses, which are 'underpinned' by 'notions of well-being in Australian communities'.

In Chapter 6, Christophe Meunier traces the evolution of the representation of the house in children's picturebooks published in France since the 1930s. Initially, the home was depicted in a way that emphasised its elementary functions, communicating narratives of safety and security. However, the 1950s saw an increased interest in the psychology of the home, particularly the role it plays in the complex processes of identification. Drawing on ideas developed by a range of French philosophers and thinkers, including Gaston Bachelard, Gilles Deleuze and Félix Guattari, and Pierre Bourdieu, Meunier examines the ways in which Modernist architecture is evoked and deployed by authors and illustrators to represent the psychology of its users. Like Druker, Meunier also shows how Modernist domestic architecture assumes a preparatory function in children's picturebooks, becoming not just a machine for living in, but also 'a machine for dwelling the world'.

Marnie Campagnaro turns her attention towards Italian interior design after the Second World War, in Chapter 7. Following the Second World War, the city was no longer considered safe for children: 'From being assiduous and wandering flaneurs of open spaces outdoors, children were forced to spend much more time at home and become more permanent inhabitants of domestic spaces'. As a result, the structure of the home changed to accommodate the presence of children, and Italian interior designers created children's furniture that could meet their needs for play and creativity within the restricted space of the home. Examining two children's picturebooks by the pioneering Italian artist, designer and writer Bruno Munari, Campagnaro explores the ways in which furniture, indoor objects and Modern and historic architecture are used to convey and challenge social and cultural values of the period.

In Chapter 8, Sabine Tan, Xinchao Zhai, Lyndon Way and Kay L. O'Halloran examine representations of architecture from three different cultural regions and environments, namely Australia (low to medium density dwellings), Singapore (high-density dwellings) and China (traditional low rise and high-density buildings), looking at 'how they function to socialise children in different social and cultural contexts in a modern, globalised world'. Arguing that architectural representations are also indicators of how different societies might reflect on their own development regarding 'the pressures of modernity', the authors used purpose-built software for multimodal image analysis investigating 'the role of representations of architecture and how the social practices depicted in various spaces defined through modern architectural design function to instil core values in relation to the individual, family, community and society'.

Focusing on a selection of British and American picturebooks published since 2000, Emma Hayward concludes this section of the book in Chapter 9 by responding to a growing critical discourse on diversity in children's picturebooks. In particular, she considers to what extent depictions of modern domestic architecture – including American suburbia and post-war, high-rise British housing estates – can be seen to authenticate narratives which engage with issues of diversity, such as sexual diversity and economic diversity, and to what extent they can be seen to threaten the authenticity of these narratives. Hayward argues that verbal-visual representations which draw attention to the protean nature of architecture – its fluidity and adaptability – give material form to a range of family types, and in so doing, go some way to validating their identity and experiences.

Part Three – Urban space

In the first chapter on Urban Space (Chapter 10), Lucy Glasheen shifts the focus away from picturebooks to consider the comic strip form. Looking at three 'Casey Court' cartoons published between 1936 and 1939 which focused on the *Daily Mail* Ideal Home Exhibition, Glasheen demonstrates how the 'Exibishun' presented in 'Casey Court' mimics and satirises key aspects, such as innovation and spectacle, allowing the cartoon to represent and challenge 'the aspirational community' that the Ideal Home exhibition constructed. Glasheen further examines the ways in which the cartoons consider children as an audience for modern architecture as well as positioning them as subjects of narratives about modern architecture.

Following on from Glasheen, in Chapter 11 Madison McLeod directs her attention to the kinds of literature children go on to read beyond their early years – specifically, novels. Drawing on the digital humanities, McLeod adopts a unique approach to analysing the significance of 'geographic specificity' in children's fantasy books set in London. Her combination of Geographic Information Systems, binary coding, literary mapping software, close reading and children's literature scholarship sheds new light on London's architectural landmarks and their role in children's fantasy fiction published between 1990 and 2021. McLeod notes that modern buildings are largely neglected in youth fantasy literature and asks to what extent children's picturebooks set in London have contributed to this absence. Discussing the picturebook form, Nikolajeva and Scott suggest that the interplay between iconic signs (pictures) and conventional signs (words) 'creates unlimited possibilities for interaction between word and image'. Not only is this true of children's picturebooks but true also of academic literary scholarship, which can, as McLeod's maps show, be enriched by visual interpretation of textual narratives.

The final chapter (Chapter 12) returns to the picturebook form with Jörg Meibauer introducing the work of Swiss illustrator Jörg Müller and how he used images of architecture and cityscapes to support narratives of 'ideological criticism' directed towards the flaws of modernity, in particular modern urban environments. Drawing on samples from across Müller's oeuvre, Meibauer highlights the illustrator's technique of creating generic modern cityscapes based on the photographic documentation of existing cities.

Concluding thoughts

Taken individually, each essay in this book offers a new way into the varied world of children's picturebooks and at the same time demonstrates how attitudes towards and conversations around modern architecture are played out within their pages. One result of gathering together such an international collection is that it demonstrates the extent to which the forms and fate of modern architecture differs from country to country. In each case, modernism's optimistic desire for a fresh start and cleaner, less cluttered lines and lives has made its mark, but while the optimism may be seen to continue, for instance in Singapore and Columbia, disappointment or disillusion may be seen in the books discussed from Britain and Switzerland. That said, picturebooks published in Britain in more recent years can be seen to recuperate the optimism associated with post-war modernism.

Taken as a whole, though, certain themes emerge – such as class, civicism, family values, the relationship between 'reality' and representation and interior design – as children are shown to be astute observers of their environment, and while they may be as susceptible as adults to the influences of illustrations encountered in early childhood, they are also more enquiring and open to alternative responses than we perhaps give them credit for. The optimism and positivity, so easily associated with early years of both Modern architecture and childhood, are revealed to sit alongside associations with middle- and upper-class living, which is beyond the personal experience of many of the target readership of children up to age nine. That fact is variously suppressed or addressed by the works considered here. At the same time, by drawing in their audience, through both words and images, and giving them space to reflect and respond, the books discussed in this volume all ensure that their readers engage with (modern) architecture, one way or another, whether as child or adult.

This collection also serves to remind us of the variety of ways in which we all encounter representations of architecture: in early learner readers, in stories, in activity books and in cartoons. Both fact and fiction are discussed here, allowing readers to consider the two modes side by side in a way that seems to be found only rarely in scholarly work on children's picturebooks to date. Above all, we hope that the separate and cumulative effect of the chapters offered here will go some way to demonstrate how rich the field of architecture and children's literature is and how diverse and interesting its products may be.

Acknowledgements

The work for this book was generously supported by various funding initiatives from the University of Liverpool's School of Architecture, its Department of English and Liverpool University's School of the Arts. Our thanks are due to Fran Ford at Routledge, who, as always, was extremely supportive and helpful. We'd also like to thank Hannah Studd, editorial assistant at Routledge and Sashivadana, project manager at Codemantra. Our particular thanks go to all the contributors for their chapters (and for their patience) - it has been a real joy working with all of you.

References

Campagnaro, M. (2019). 'Narrating' Homes and Objects: Images of Domestic Life in Italian. *Theories and Research in Education*, 14 (2), 9–48. https://doi.org/10.6092/issn.1970-2221/10030

Colomer, T., Kümmerling-Meibauer, B., and Silva-Díaz, C. (2010). *New Directions in Picturebook Research*. New York. Routledge.

Goga, N., Iversen, S. H. and Teigland, A.-S. (eds) (2021). *Verbal and Visual Strategies in Nonfiction Picturebooks: Theoretical and Analytical Approaches*. Oslo: Scandinavian University Press.

Hayward, E. and Schmiedeknecht, T. (2019). Absent Architectures: Post-War Housing in British Children's Picture Books (1960–Present). *The Journal of Architecture*, 24 (4), 487–511. https://doi.org/10.1080/13602365.2019.1641736

Nikolajeva, M. and Scott, C. (2006). *How Picturebooks Work*. New York: Routledge. First published in 2001 by Garland Press.

Nodelman, P. (2004). Picture Books and Illustrations. In P. Hunt (ed), *International Companion Encyclopedia of Children's Literature*. Abingdon: Routledge.

Powers, A. (2007). *Britain - Modern Architectures in History*. London: Reaktion Books.

Reynolds, K. (2011). *Children's Literature: A Very Short Introduction*. Oxford: OUP.

Shulevitz, U. (1996). What Is a Picture Book? Reprinted in S. Egoff, G. Stubbs, R. Ashley and W. Sutton (eds), *Only Connect: Readings on Children's Literature*. Toronto and Oxford: Oxford University Press, pp. 238–241.

Stephens, J. (2017). *The Routledge Companion to International Children's Literature*. London and New York: Routledge.

PART ONE
Modernity

1

BUILDING FOR THE FUTURE – CHILDREN AS FUTURE CITIZENS IN SWEDISH PICTUREBOOKS OF THE 1930S

Elina Druker

During the 1930s and 1940s, hundreds of grocery stores in functionalist style were built in Sweden by the Cooperative Union retail group. They sold everything from tableware and shoes to food items and canned goods. One of the few toys sold in Cooperative stores during the 1930s was a set of building blocks called *Bygg upp* [Build up]. The set could be constructed in two ways: it could either form a model of a Cooperative grocery store or it could be shaped as a factory. When using the blocks to build a factory, the green, black and white blocks formed a strikingly modernist building with sleek horizontal lines. In fact, it formed a miniature of an existing modernist building, the Luma Light Bulb Factory in Stockholm, built in 1930 and considered to be Sweden's first functionalist industrial facility.

A set of building blocks that form two highly emblematic modernist buildings can be seen as an expression of a period where new industries were rapidly developing at the same time as ideas of functionalist architecture emerged throughout Scandinavia. But while manufacturing building blocks that form a play grocery store can hardly be considered an unusual subject for a toy, the choice of a functionalist industrial facility raises some questions. The building blocks are connected to progressive educational ideas of the time, where simple, wooden toys with elemental shapes and colours were seen as pedagogically and aesthetically beneficial; but the toy also expresses notions of childhood and modern design and architecture.

The Luma Factory was a flagship in the Cooperative Union's operations and quickly became a well-known symbol for modernist ideas about architecture, industrial innovation and engineering. On the roof of the facility, a distinctive, rectangular glass tower was constructed, which was used for testing light bulbs. The tower created a striking, luminous cube on the top of the building. Images of the building with the light tower were reproduced in a range of different contexts and media, in advertising, window displays and films as well as in novels, picturebooks and toys for children. How should we, then, understand the images and narratives constructed in this context? And what ideas are communicated through modern architecture and children who interact with modern design in children's literature?

DOI: 10.4324/9781003131755-3

FIGURE 1.1 Set of building blocks, *Bygg upp*, Cooperative Union, ca 1930.
Source: © private collection.

Using literary and visual depictions of the Luma Factory and other industrial buildings from the 1930s and 1940s, this chapter will examine how ideas about modernist architecture and technology were explored in books for children during the period. Applying concepts from childhood studies and consumer research as well as theories about modernism and modernity in children's literature, I will discuss how selected picturebooks and toys and their advertisements communicate particular narratives about children as future citizens and consumers. Using W. J. T. Mitchell's concept 'imagetext', which proposes a level of meaning which is not medium specific and in which word and image complement, reinforce, and sometimes contradict each other in complex ways (Mitchell, 1986), I will specifically study the use of the Luma Factory and other industrial buildings in a series of picturebooks about Per and Lisa, published in Sweden from the early 1930s to the 1950s, and will discuss how these books exhibit an interdisciplinary convergence between children's literature, commercialism and high-modernist architecture.

As well as prevailing ideas about children and childhood, which are fundamental for the development of children's literature during the 1930s and 1940s, the aim of this chapter is to study representations of children in multiple narratives of modernity.

'Folkhemmet'—the idea of the Swedish people's home—was introduced in 1928. Marked by democracy and equality, the concept proposed that the country should strive to become a 'good home' for its citizens and revealed its greatest idealism in its view of children. Children's development, education and welfare was considered particularly important for building the new society and large investments were made towards welfare reforms, especially after World War II (Sandin, 2012, p. 68). The state also promoted consumerist habits amongst children, for example, through a general child-allowance which was launched in 1948 and aimed at all children under 16 years of age (Sandin, 2012, p. 65).

The picturebooks about the two children Per and Lisa were published by The Swedish Cooperative Union, one of the leading Swedish retailers. For several decades, the Cooperative Union was also a powerful and influential actor in the Swedish political landscape. It had a vast influence on marketing, architecture, design and consumer policies, and became an important participant in the development of the Swedish welfare state and the people's home idea (Mattsson, 2012, p. 65). From the early 1930s to the mid-1950s, the company published a series of branded picturebooks which were free of charge, printed in very large editions—up to 250,000 copies—and written and illustrated by established authors and illustrators. These publications consisted of children's books with embedded marketing, incorporating products by different manufacturers in the narratives. Product placement was implemented by including different commodities in the illustrations and by explicitly mentioning the trademarks in the text. The Cooperative Union was not the only retailer who frequently used this marketing method; branded picturebooks or pamphlets with stories can be found in different countries during the first half of the 20th century, their publishers ranging from candy manufacturers to producers of hygiene products, shoes, toys, even types of insurance (Hallberg, 1996, pp. 48–51, Druker, 2014, pp. 167–180).

The introduction of the branded books coincides with new marketing strategies and platforms aimed at children. Previous researchers like Viviane Zelizer (1985) and Daniel Thomas Cook (2000, 2004) have shown that a general commercialisation of children's daily life took place during the first four decades of the 20th century. The construct of the child as a 'little consumer' replaced previous ideas which saw children as 'unfinished' persons in need of socialisation. This meant that children were now considered a key market for advertisers (Cook, 2000, p. 501). In Sweden, by the 1930s, advertisements frequently included representations of children as competent consumers who make decisions about their purchases and act in the commodity society (Berggren Torell & Brembeck, 2001, pp. 76–77). These kinds of images multiplied during the 1940s and 1950s.

Modern architecture and space travel

The set of building blocks from the Cooperative Union can primarily be seen as a way to market the Cooperative brand. But it can also be seen as an effort to influence the child's taste and sense for architecture, design and form. As Kimberley Reynolds shows, children's literature with radical design aesthetics or images of modernist architecture was used to introduce 'new aesthetic codes, sensibilities, and vocabularies' during the 1930s and 1940s, to develop new patterns and new kinds of behaviour and thus 'to build with the future in mind' (Reynolds, 2016, p. 181).

The Luma Factory, which was designed by Artur von Schmalensee and Eskil Sundahl, the latter founder and manager of the Cooperative Union's in-house architecture office, had a distinctive shape and was characterised by bold straight lines, which contributed to its minimalistic, austere appearance. The Cooperative Union stood for radical, functionalist objectivity, where social commitment was paired with a strong sense of form, and it influenced Swedish architecture for decades. In fact, as Lisa Brunnström suggests, the kind of stripped-down, rational and objective modernism that the Cooperative architectural firm aimed for shaped modern Sweden's view of itself (Brunnström, 2004). The Luma brand was very successful and facilities were built even outside Sweden, for example, in Glasgow, where a modern Luma light factory—including a protruding, rounded light bulb tower—was built in 1938 in art deco style.[1] Modern architecture was seen as an important part of marketing and Eskil Sundahl proposed that all the Cooperative's business buildings would have a uniform style 'from an advertising point of view' (Eriksson, 2001, p. 425). Radically, modern architecture was used not only for commercial purposes but was seen as part of a cultural effort. Sundahl was also one of the authors of the seminal debate book *acceptera* (1931) that embraced a new, functionalist idiom. In its introduction, a drastic break from old styles and ideas is formulated:

> We have no need for ancient forms of old cultures to maintain our self-esteem. We cannot sneak back from our own time. Nor can we elude something that is difficult and uncertain in a utopian future. We can only face reality and accept it in order to master it.[2]
>
> *acceptera (1931), p. 203*

The sense of liberation that characterises the ideas in *acceptera* can be seen as the result of an attitude unrestricted by history, which includes a radical break from old styles and ideas. How is then the ambition to break from traditional architecture expressed in toys and books for children?

A fascination not only with modernist architecture but also with the latest technology is apparent in the picturebook *Per och Lisas luftfärd med Lampe Rör* [*Per and Lisa's journey with Lampe the tube*, 1933] by Nils Jerring and Aina Stenberg-Masolle.[3] On the cover we see the children travelling in a spaceship. Beneath them, the cloud-covered earth can be seen with trees, lakes, tiny buildings and a factory with the sign 'Luma'.

At the beginning of the story, the two children are listening to a tube radio. Their father, who usually uses the radio, isn't home and the children toggle its knobs offhandedly, which causes a very irritated figure, a radio tube called Lampe, to emerge. He is described as 'a funny little character, no bigger than a man's finger, with a shiny, silvery head, the same size as his body'.[4] He scolds the children for meddling with the electrical signals, shrieking until he almost loses his voice. The children manage to calm him down by offering him throat pastilles and he decides that he needs a vacation. Per and Lisa prepare to join him by shrinking to a miniature size and flying away on radio waves in Lampe's spaceship constructed from radio tubes. Before climbing into the spaceship, the children mention that they are covered by insurance and Lampe brings some chocolate with him. The throat pastilles, the chocolate bar, and the insurance are of Cooperative brand and are mentioned in the text. During their journey, the children and their companion visit the man in the moon and travel to different foreign countries. The episodic narrative is centred around different food items, beverages and convenience goods, which are also mentioned in the text and displayed in the illustrations.

The tone of the story throughout is cheerful, optimistic and affirmative of modernity. It expresses enthusiasm for modern technology, transportation and consumerism. The plot is simple and straightforward with short, rhyming advertising jingles included in the text.

FIGURE 1.2 Nils Jerring, Aina Stenberg-Masolle, *Per and Lisa's journey with Lampe the tube*, 1933, Cooperative Union.

Source: © Reproduction by Swedish Children's Literature Institute, Stockholm.

In addition to the pure advertising slogans incorporated in the text, the author Nils Jerring, a well-known film director and actor, uses expressions and stylistic devices that relate to the tube radio's technical vocabulary. Words like vacuum tubes, regenerative circuits and feedback amplifiers are used in the text. In the end, Lampe, who has gained some extra weight because of all the sweets he has eaten, is afraid that he might not fit in his radio anymore and decides to exercise. He takes part in a bicycle race, which he wins. In this section of the text, the narrator uses genre expressions from contemporary sports journalism, which further highlights the fascination with speed and rapid transportations in the story (Hallberg, 1996, p. 50).

The scene with the bicycle race in *Per and Lisa's journey with Lampe the tube* is noteworthy in several ways. Not only is the personified radio tube here associated with speed and energy, but Jerring also creates immediate connections to the rapid, pattering vocal style in radio and short film during this time. Radio quickly became a central part of lives in many families in the Western world during the 1930s, and the era has often been described as the golden age of the radio. Jerring's narrative style thus heightens the association with innovation, new techniques, and science, and helps to differentiate the brand from its competitors. The fact that an established and well-known film director is the author for a commercial picturebook can be seen as an example of the rapid development of advertising during the 1930s. The method can be compared with the use of celebrities in present-day commercials, where a celebrity's status and image are used to endorse the brand. However, Jerring's involvement also suggests a wider targeted audience, which includes the parents. The central position of the radio in the story can also be seen in relation to ideas in many European and North American countries during the era, where radio was seen as a medium that gathered families together and became important for national unity (Björck, 2010, p. 33).

Stylistically, the scene where Lampe attends a bicycle race can be compared to the quick and over-enunciated style of radio speech of the 1930s. In fact, the style of the entire story is characterised by constant shifting in style and rhythm. The text is saturated with sudden advertising jingles; the brand names are included in the dialogue and mention a range of products from the Luma light bulb to shoe polish and bananas. Furthermore, the short, rhymed jingles are often replicated in the illustrations, as if to repeat them in order to create easy-to-remember hooks. A connection to early radio marketing is apparent, where the short advertising jingle became common during the 1930s as a way to avoid prohibitions concerning direct advertising of products.

The use of technical novelties like the radio and electricity as well as a futuristic motif like the spaceship (almost 20 years prior to the first rocketsonde being sent to space) conveys an aura of innovation and novelty. It is also significant that Lampe is a personified radio tube. Similar kind of anthropomorphic characters, like personified light bulbs, were popular in advertising in both Europe and North America during the first half of the 20th century. In an attempt to spread awareness about electricity, it was often personified or given an anthropomorphic form to 'domesticate' the new devices and to demonstrate that electricity was helpful and useful rather than something to be feared. As Graeme Gooday shows, visual depictions of electricity as female characters like fairies, angels or even an infant child were used as early as the 1880s to inform the public and market electricity. These characters guided its users and answered questions concerning electricity and its use in homes (Gooday, 2008, p. 199, p. 208). Lampe the radio tube has a similar function, demonstrating that the radio is not a dangerous intruder, but on the contrary, opens up a home to new experiences and unknown parts of the world.

Embracing electricity and new techniques not only reflects a new, modern era, but makes modernisation and innovation the core subject of the picturebook. The technical and electrical culture that is presented in the story is furthermore supported by and made attractive through narratives of joyful consumption. While anthropomorphic objects and animals is a common motif in children's literature, it is noteworthy that the traditional anthropomorphic characters have here been replaced by personified commodities, like talking radio tubes and other animated products. These animated objects bring the advertising concept beyond product placement and instead let the children interact with them.

Around the world in eight days

In Marie Walle's *Per och Lisa. Jorden runt på 8 dagar* [*Per and Lisa. Around the world in 8 days*, 1931] the children travel around the world and visit foreign countries where they meet with anthropomorphic commodities once more. The cover image depicts the two children standing on a flying carpet, carrying an abundance of Cooperative items. Below them, the Luma Factory is visible.

FIGURE 1.3 Marie Walle, *Per and Lisa. Around the world in 8 days*, 1931, Cooperative Union.
Source: © Reproduction by Swedish Children's Literature Institute, Stockholm.

When the Luma Factory, the personified Luma light bulbs, radio tubes or the trademark of the product are depicted, the product is connected to speed and technical innovation. The children are portrayed travelling around the world using a range of transportation systems and encountering different consumer artefacts and exotic food items like bananas or cacao beans. For the general consumer of the time, these products were still associated with novelty and indulgence as was travelling abroad. The images suggest that the children are part of the modern world, and playfully and confidently use its technical innovations and merchandise.

Stinas märkliga födelsedagsresa [*Stina's Peculiar Birthday Journey*] published in 1928 by the candy manufacturer Mazetti, is a small colour-illustrated book promoting cacao, which demonstrates how exoticism is used within the genre. Through a daydream, the main character Stina experiences a journey to Africa and learns how her favourite beverage, hot cocoa, is produced. The book describes the production of cocoa powder from colourful images of cocoa trees to harvesting and transporting the beans to harbours for shipping to Europe. The different phases of the transportation process are described in detail. Both the exotic origin of the product and the modernised process of shipping and transportation is used to endorse the quality of the product as 'sweet and healthy'.[5]

Describing the transformation of raw materials such as wool, cotton, gold or rubber is a common topic in many non-fiction picturebooks from the era. In these books, repetitive attention is often given to the transportations of the goods as well as the machines and tools used to process them, a fact that Natalie op de Beeck sees as an expression of a fear that the modern child would be alienated from the origins of the products (op de Beeck, 2010, p. 129). In her study of the modern picturebook of the interwar era, she proposes that these kinds of books for children were describing modern industry and trade in the child's modern context: 'Children were to be armed with practical understandings of the modern world so that they might become active engineers of the future, as opposed to passive victims of industry' (p. 129). Op de Beeck's example shows similarities with the process of domestication of new techniques through narratives that present and familiarise the new phenomena to people. Introducing children to stories about how the global trade world is structured can be seen as an effort to explain and normalise the fundamental changes taking place in the world during the first decades of the 20th century, where machines, new information

FIGURE 1.4 *Stina's Peculiar Birthday Journey*, 1928, Mazetti.
Source: Reproduction by National Library of Sweden, Stockholm.

FIGURE 1.5 *A little song about Per and Lisa,* 1930, Cooperative Union.
Source: Reproduction by Swedish Children's Literature Institute, Stockholm.

technology and imported and commercially manufactured goods successively entered children's everyday lives.

However, depictions of other countries and cultures in the studied material were not always factual. Instead, these narratives about the origins of cocoa beans, tea, or bananas are often based on highly stereotypical and even inaccurate representations of the countries or products. In *Per and Lisa. Around the world in 8 days*, this concept is taken even further. The book's title is a play on Jules Verne's *Around the World in Eighty Days*; the allusion is further emphasised at the beginning where Verne's protagonist Phileas Fogg is explicitly mentioned. The story then is a mix of different literary motifs, characters and fairy tales. And while some segments describe the collecting of raw materials like tea leaves in India in a factual manner, the children also visit the imaginary country of Macaronia, where pasta and macaroni grow everywhere and can be picked and eaten. Again, the text can be described as fragmentary, consisting of disparate contexts and images, fact and fiction.

In the final illustration of *Stina's Peculiar Birthday Journey*, the chocolate factory is illustrated and described in detail. The machines in the factory are described as 'modern and practical' and the interior of the facility is portrayed in detail: 'The production is based on meticulous cleanliness and observance. The walls of the factory are covered with white glazed tiles, which are easy to clean'.[6] What is noteworthy is that the origins of the products are described with terms connected to natural resources and the African climate and nature, where the cocoa beans are produced with the help of 'sun, warmth and careful attention'.[7] And while natural resources and sunlight are here directly connected to the claim that the product is healthy, it is significant that the final process of the production in Sweden is associated with modern design, industrial progress, hygiene and effectiveness.

Architectural elements included in the stories also illustrate the ongoing development and ideas within architecture. In *Stina's Peculiar Birthday Journey*, the company's pride, the Mazetti Factory, built in 1888, is depicted. Just a couple of years later, a modern, functionalist architecture is included in the book *En liten visa om Per och Lisa* [*A little song about Per and Lisa*], published by the shoe manufacturer Svenska Skoindustri in 1930.

Hygiene and cleanliness are also evoked in advertising for the Luma light bulb. As discussed previously, Lampe the radio tube personifies technological innovation, communication and futurist dreams. Advertising for the Luma brand (the name derived from Latin *lumen*, light) evokes images of light, electricity and modernisation. The fact that the Luma Factory in Stockholm is so frequently depicted in the advertisement also places this specific industrial building in the middle of a vibrant, rapidly evolving urban milieu at the beginning of the 1930s. As a result of new electric lighting devices, such as the neon sign, the light advertisement, illuminated shop windows, and the movie theatre marquees, the urban environment was transformed. Spectacular lighting was used to attract visitors but also to signal innovation and modernity. Electricity, lighting and inventions like the elevators, escalators and modern window displays were also used in marketing new department stores, where the amount of electricity used daily was sometimes particularly mentioned in advertisements, signalling technological innovation (Husz, 2004, p. 62).

It is therefore no coincidence that the Cooperative Union's light bulb prototypes were tested in a glass tower at the top of the facility even during the night. The light emitted from the glass tower lit up the surrounding area at night and was visible throughout the southern parts of Stockholm—an image used frequently in Cooperative propaganda and produced in many different publications and films. The illuminated glass tower symbolises the idea of enlightenment and transparency towards the Cooperative consumers (Brunnström, 2004, p. 145). The visually striking placement of the facility also reflects the leading position this single modernist building had in the urban landscape. Modernist architecture thus became a central part of the product's brand. The way Luma Factory is described as a landmark and a symbol for modern architecture, industrial innovation, and commerce is repeated in both *Per and Lisa. Around the world in 8 days* and *Per and Lisa's journey with Lampe the tube*. In the latter book, the idea is developed even further, as it is indicated that the building with its glass tower was visible even from space.

The child consumer

The two main characters, Per and Lisa, appear in the book series over a time span of about 40 years and can thus be seen as a general representation of an 'ideal' childhood from the era. Per is the older of the two, and is portrayed as active, fearless and sturdy, while Lisa is usually depicted with a more cautious posture and has a slightly more passive role in their interactions with their surroundings. Gendered stereotypes are generally common in advertising, but at the same time, neither Per nor Lisa hesitate to leave their home and to abandon its safe, domestic sphere. They both actively take part in adventurous episodes in different countries and even in space; they shop in grocery stores, meet different personified commodities and use different transportation methods. They are depicted as energetic, curious and competent.

Several scholars have suggested that advertising during this era was often aimed at house-wives and mothers. They serve as keys to consumer life, both presently and historically (Cook, 2004). Accordingly, the choice of merchandise in the Cooperative picturebooks—convenience goods like food items, cleaning products, shoes and kitchen utensils—suggest a twofold target group: children and their parents (possibly mainly the mothers). Interestingly, during this era, women were the main consumers of electrical home appliances, lamps and light bulbs, products that were also associated with health, hygiene and cleanliness (Gooday, 2008, p. 6).

It is, however, significant that by specifically launching picturebooks for children, the manufacturers also viewed the child as a consumer. It is plausible that the branded books were developed as a form of long-term marketing and were used to familiarise children with Cooperative products in order to establish credibility and brand familiarity during childhood. The general idea of educating individuals to become 'modern' members of the society, and to thus make them better functioning, healthier and happier members of society, was wide-ranging in the interwar and post-war eras. Part of this idea was also to improve the knowledge and thus the taste of the consumer in modern design and materials as well as prefabricated modern housing (Reynolds, 2016, pp. 184–185). Similar ideas were expressed in children's books created by high-profile architects and designers in the United Kingdom during the 1940s (Reynolds, 2016, p. 179).

In Sweden, analogous ideas were expressed in various programme declarations, housing projects, public art, evening classes and guidebooks for adults—but also in advertising and different kinds of commercial materials aimed for different age groups. Even within the advertising industry of the 1930s, there was a strong belief that advertising could be bene-ficial for society and could improve people's lives and public health, for example, through knowledge about hygiene, health and better eating habits (Dahlgren, 2007, p. 136). The way the characters, Per and Lisa, are depicted in the books suggests that children were not only an important component in the modern society but were also seen as an essential part of the emerging consumer culture and could be educated about modern architecture, new technology and consumerism. Thus, as the next generation, the children would be provided with knowledge and skills needed in the future.

Collage and branding

The branded picturebooks were free of charge, printed in large editions and aimed at a wide target group from different socio-economic standings. While their illustration style is rather conventional, the books often include collage-like insertions of products and build-ings in the illustrations. Sometimes photographic reproductions of the products or facto-ries are included in the otherwise traditional illustrations, creating collages that seem to have connections to both popular culture and product catalogues, a marketing method that was introduced for the general public during the late 19th century. Using photograph or photo-realistically drawn detailed image is a way to ensure that the products and brands are easily recognisable. This concept can be found in department store catalogues and mail order catalogues, which quite early on included photographic illustrations or realistic drawings of the products. However, while the text-image relations in these picturebooks to some extent resemble early mail order catalogues, I would like to suggest that the collage technique and photographic (or photorealistic drawings) that are used function in a slightly different way.

While most mainstream children's books during the 1930s and 1940s were still occupied with fairy tales and idyllic rural landscapes, what we see in the branded picturebooks are depictions of contemporary urban and commercial society, and most importantly, of children who are portrayed not only as consumers but also as active participants in modern society. Furthermore, the collage-like construction of text and image places the books in a modern context. The style can be described as a meeting of motifs and structures from children's literature on the one hand and advertising vocabulary on the other (Hallberg, 1996, p. 49). Although the examples of collage in the studied children's books seem far from the modernist collage or montage art from the time period, the photographic or photorealistic images included here are not simply used to make the products easily recognisable; instead, the choice of the photographic image and collage signals novelty and modernity. The choice of style also has a certain shock value or is used comically or even ironically in the stories. At the same time, the overall visual and narrative style expresses innovation and modernity, an aura of novelty that is closely connected to the consumer experience and identity.

Within arts, advertising, graphic design and picturebooks alike, breaking with the past involves a renegotiation of how pictures are constructed. Collage, montage and other combination techniques have traditionally been used in the search for new modes of expression, sometimes as a means of shocking or surprising, questioning representation or the nature and value of art itself (Taylor, 2004, pp. 38–39). The use of collage leads to new possibilities of communication in a world that is quickly and dramatically transforming. Advantages and disadvantages of using photographic versus drawn illustrations within advertising was a topic of debate during the 1930s. While photographic images were seen as 'alive' and more objective, drawings could depict the products with clarity, sharp contours and colours (Dahlgren, 2007, p. 135).

In this context, the photographic image was seen as reliable and factual, 'a rational, true and correct image medium' (Dahlgen, p. 139). Within advertising, illustrations of modern industrial plants were often used to create associations with technical innovation and engineering, but also with the modernisation of the urban environment. Detailed drawings and engravings as well as photographic images of industrial buildings or department stores can be found in most of the children's books studied in this chapter. Besides the already discussed Luma Light Bulb Factory, industrial buildings for different trademarks, like the Chocolate Factory by Mazetti in Malmö or The Cooperative Union's Shoe Factory in Örebro, are included in the illustrations.

Even here, photographs or photo-realistically drawn illustrations are used, as if to strengthen the connection to actual buildings. The text-image relationship is noteworthy as well. Like the names of the brands and the short advertising jingles embedded in the text, images of industrial facilities and department stores are incorporated in the illustrations, as if creating a collage of elements from both reality and fiction. The technique to insert surprising or strange elements in the text and illustrations can, in both cases, be seen as a collage method, applied to both visual and verbal modes. New forms of image-texts, to use W.J.T. Mitchell's term, are thus created in children's literature, depicting the modern, urban society as a combination of technical innovation, dreams and fairy tales.

Images of the modern spectacle

How then, should we describe the connection between the wooden set of building blocks in the form of a modernist factory, discussed initially in this chapter, and the other examples of marketing for children? Why is modern architecture used in these narratives for children

FIGURE 1.6 Cooperative window display, *Kooperativa Skyltfönstret*, nr 26, December 1932.
Source: © Reproduction: National Library of Sweden, Stockholm.

and what is their function in the stories? As already discussed, the use of certain recurring motifs in the Cooperative campaigns points to a systematic use of images associated with modernity and new technologies. During the 1930s, Cooperative laid the foundation for systematic and effective campaigns that took place simultaneously in different advertising media. The importance of co-ordinating and utilising different types of marketing channels and media, from packaging and posters to shop windows and publications for children, became increasingly important. Besides advertising in magazines and other marketing publications, Cooperative retailers could order readymade advertising material like posters and cardboard signs to their stores and window displays. Also, handbooks for retailers in successful storekeeping and advertising were common. One of these was the monthly magazine called the *Kooperativa Skyltfönstret* [*Cooperative Window Display*], which offered guidance in the composing of window displays and in-store product placement.

One of the suggestions in this magazine from 1931 depicts a window display promoting the Luma brand, with the Luma Factory dramatically illuminated in the background, surrounded by cars, an airplane and a row of light bulb packages.

The composition is typical for its time. Inspired by constructivist aesthetics, arrangements with consumer articles were often used to form stylised shapes like circles, arcs, squares and semicircles (Dahlgren, 2010, p. 150). But the window display is also interesting because it is constructed of both three-dimensional and flat elements, and composed and lit in a way that is evocative of a theatre stage. The concept of the window display as a stage was widespread during the 1920s and 1930s. Dramatic lighting that drew attention to the display was common and the products were often arranged to form a narrative or a dramatic scene (Dahlgren, 2010, p. 147).

Depicting modernist architecture and technical inventions in different kinds of marketing can be seen as a means of equipping children with knowledge of their urban surroundings, but the method also identifies children as an integral part of the vision of a modern existence and sees children as future citizens and consumers. The use of a collage technique—both

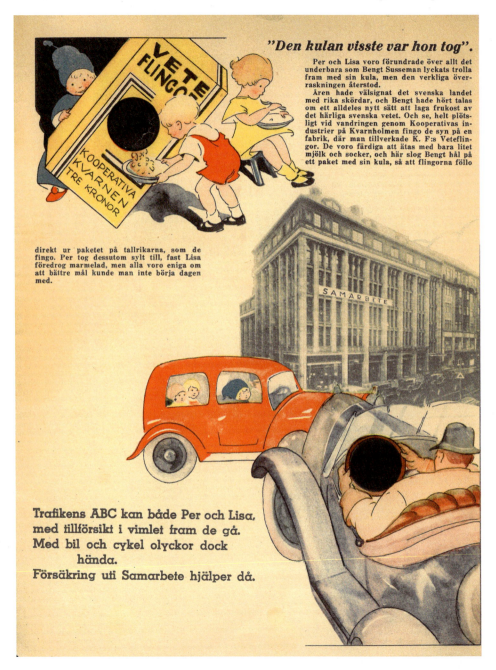

FIGURE 1.7 Per och Lisa: en julbok med hål i, 1934. Cooperative Union.

Source: © Reproduction: Swedish Children's Literature Institute, Stockholm.

in the text and the images of the picturebook—creates a strange fluidity between reality, fantasy and advertising, between exotic, foreign locations and realistic depictions of the urban environment. In *Per och Lisa: en julbok med hål i* [*Per and Lisa: A Christmas book with holes*, 1934], a book actually perforated with small round holes through the pages, the children are once again visiting different fantastic places. In its final scene, the children are depicted travelling in a red car in the middle of a city centre, a slightly chaotic illustration depicting a busy intersection. The reader is reminded of caution in traffic and of the importance of insurance.

The illustration captivates an urban scene of the 1930s, a city centre filled with traffic, high buildings and window displays. In the background, the building for the insurance company 'Samarbete' is included as a photographic image.

While the layout of the page follows a linear left to right reading order, the composition of the illustration is unstable and chiasmatic, and the movement and direction of the car in the bottom right-hand corner is directed towards the children in a threatening way. This kind of movement from right to left with diagonal directions creates a visual pattern that is usually perceived as disharmonious (Nikolajeva & Scott, 2006, p.155). The cautionary message of importance of traffic safety—one of the few negative images of technology and transportation in the book series—is generated through a jarring, chiastic arrangement that emphasises movement and vulnerability.

How then should we understand the combination of image, text, trademarks and advertising applied in these books? According to the postmodern theorist Jean Baudrillard (2001), the increasing proliferation of products, advertising, marketing strategies, mass media and entertainment multiplied the number of signs created in the beginning of the 20th century. This created new *spectacles*, images of display and performance. In line with scholars like Foucault and Baudrillard, Jonathan Crary has argued that with the shift into modernity, the traditional notion of the spectacle as a theatrical and visual medium should rather be understood through its relationship to the spectator. Crary describes the spectacle as something that is 'not primarily concerned with a looking at images but rather with the construction of conditions that individuate, immobilise, and separate subjects, even within a world in which mobility and circulation are ubiquitous' (Crary, 1999, pp. 73–73). These understandings of the spectacle can be seen as a basis for Op de Beeck's study of the modern picturebook, where she suggests that books for children signalled 'a change in reading subjects' awareness of themselves as spectators and as parts of the grand modern spectacle' (op de Beeck, 2010, p. 162).

Despite a superficial focus on marketing products and more or less fragmentary narratives, the branded picturebooks studied in this chapter aim to capture a sense of modernity, innovation and change. They describe a commercial and technological world in the young reader's modern context. But it is not merely a practical understanding of the modern world and its commodities that is offered; instead, what is established is a mixture of signs, text and images, fantasies and fairy tales, consumer items and urban environments. Children are described as spectators but also as modern (or postmodern) subjects, taking part in a grand modern spectacle that seems to be constantly changing and developing.

The concept of collage is relevant even here. In his study *Collage: The Making of Modern Art*, Brandon Taylor suggests that the development of collage should be understood in the context of the growth of mass media and advertising and that the visual and verbal construction of advertising changed the reception and understanding of narratives.

According to Taylor, collage 'had a special and even profound part to play in the expression of modern sensibility: a sensibility attuned to matter in the modern city, matter under the regime of capital' (p. 8). A similar mixture is created in the picturebooks discussed here, where consumer items, advertising jingles and industrial facilities are included in both the text and the images. Even here, the term 'domestication' could be applied. Not only are new products introduced to the child through the picturebook, but also new techniques, contexts and *spectacles*. What we witness in these books are contradictory impulses of modernity.

With their intermingling of actual, branded products, personified merchandise, and fairy tale characters, these books can be seen as early examples of media crossover where multi-directional interaction between children's picturebooks, advertising and nation building is taking place. Printed in large editions and distributed free to their target groups, they engage with the modern society in ways that regular children's literature seldom did during the interwar era. Their method can be described as a collage of disparate contexts and interests or as a modern spectacle, an ideologically charged construction of images from different spheres. The child as a reader, as a future citizen and as a consumer is introduced to a variety of messages, images and fantasies.

When creating the set of painted wooden building blocks, the Cooperative Union made direct reference to modern functionalist architecture and design, but what is also applied are contemporary educational ideas that advocated cognitive and visual development through play which could give the child an awareness of form, structure and design. The motif of children building houses and towns is common in children's literature during the era, and there is even an example of this within the Per and Lisa series. In Åke Löfgren and Carl-Einar Borgström's *Per och Lisa bygger en snabbköpsbutik* [*Per and Lisa build a grocery store*, ca. 1948] the children decide to build a store of their own filled with Cooperative commodities. It is suggested that not only constructing a miniature grocery store but playing shop, making shopping lists and choosing and organising different goods in the store develop skills that are useful for the child.

The set of building blocks and the idea of the child constructing modernist buildings, stores and factories places the child in the centre of the Swedish welfare project. Inseparable connections between visions of modernity, consumerism and ideas of national identity are expressed here. The child is seen as a symbol for a better future, as someone who can be educated and shaped to become a competent member of the 'people's home', but who will also actively take part in building this future society.

Notes

The illustrators in the images used in this chapter are unknown. The location of the rights holder for these works has been unsuccessful after a diligent search. Copyright claims to this work are welcomed and should be addressed to the publisher.

1 The Luma light bulb factory in Glasgow, Renfrew Road, Shieldhall (1936–1938), was designed by Cornelius Armour and functioned as the headquarters of the British Luma Co-Operative Electric Lamp Society Ltd. It was built by Co-Operative Wholesale Society and the Swedish Cooperative Union. Brunnström (2004), p. 145.
2 My translation.

Vi har inte behov av en gammal kulturs urvuxna former för att uppehålla vår självaktning. Vi kan inte smyga oss ur vår egen tid bakåt. Vi kan inte heller hoppa förbi något som är besvärligt och oklart in i en utopisk framtid. Vi kan inte annat än att se verkligheten i ögonen och acceptera den för att behärska den.

acceptera (1931), p. 203.

3 The picturebooks discussed in the chapter are unpaginated.
4 My translation. *Per och Lisas luftfärd med Lampe Rör:* 'en lustig liten figur, inte större än ett finger och med ett silverglänsande huvud, som var lika stort som den övriga kroppen'.
5 My translation. *Stinas märkliga födelsedagsresa:* 'Undra inte på att cacaon är så god och hälsosam, Karin, när den fått så mycket sol, värme och fin behandling. Och nu vet jag, varför John och jag blivit så rödblommiga och friska'.
6 My translation. *Stinas märkliga födelsedagsresa:* 'de mest moderna och praktiska maskiner', 'Tillverkningen är baserad på den mest minutiösa renlighet och omsorgsfullhet. Väggarna i fabrikslokalerna äro beklädda med vita glaserade kakelplattor, vilka äro lätta att rengöra'.
7 My translation. *Stinas märkliga födelsedagsresa:* 'sol, värme och fin behandling'.

References

Asplund, G. (ed) (1931). *acceptera.* Stockholm: Tiden.

Baudrillard, J. (2001). *Selected writings.* (Second edition, rev. and expanded). Stanford: Stanford University Press.

Berggren Torell, V. & Brembeck, H. (2001). *Det konsumerande barnet: representationer av barn och konsumtion i svensk dags- och veckopress under 1900-talet med utgångspunkt i reklamannonser.* Göteborg: Etnologiska fören. i Västsverige

Björck, A. (2010). *Höra hemma: familj och social förändring i svensk radioserieteater från 1930-talet till 1990-talet.* Diss. Göteborg: Makadam.

Brunnström, L. (2004). *Det svenska folkhemsbygget: om kooperativa förbundets arkitektkontor.* Stockholm: Arkitektur.

Cook, D.T. (2000). The other 'child study': Figuring children as consumers in market research, 1910s–1990s. In *The sociological quarterly* 41, no 3. Carbondale, IL: Southern Illinois University Press.

——— (2004). *The commodification of childhood: the children's clothing industry and the rise of the child consumer.* Durham: Duke University Press.

Crary, J. (1999). *Suspensions of perception: attention, spectacle, and modern culture.* Cambridge, MA: MIT Press.

Dahlgren, A. (2007). Commercial realism: concepts on photography in advertising in the 1930s. *Konsthistorisk tidskrift.* 3(76), pp. 135–146.

——— (2010). Butiken som ansikte: Skyltning som visuell kultur. In Nordiska Museet (2010). *Burkar, påsar och paket: förpackningarnas historia i vardagens konsumtionskulturer.* Stockholm: Nordiska Museets Förlag.

Druker, E. (2014). *Eva billow: bilderbokskonstnär och författare.* Göteborg: Makadam.

Eriksson, E. (2001). *Den moderna staden tar form: arkitektur och debatt 1910–1935.* Stockholm: Ordfront.

Gooday, G. (2008). *Domesticating electricity. Technology, uncertainty and gender, 1880–1914.* Pittsburgh, PA: University of Pittsburgh Press.

Hallberg, K. (1996). *Den svenska bilderboken och modernismens folkhem.* Lic.avh. Stockholm: Stockholm University

Husz, O. (2004). *Drömmars värde: varuhus och lotteri i svensk konsumtionskultur 1897–1939.* Diss. Stockholm: Stockholm University. Hedemora.

Jerring, N. & Stenberg-Masolle. A. (1933). *Per och Lisa luftfärd med lampe rör.* Stockholm: Kooperativa förbundet.

Kooperativa förbundet (1932–1958). *Kooperativa skyltfönstret.* Stockholm: Kooperativa förbundet.

Löfgren, Å. & Borgström, C-E. (undated, ca 1948). *Per och Lisa bygger en snabbköpsbutik.* Stockholm: Kooperativa förbundet.

Mattsson, H. (2012). Designing the 'consumer in infinity': The Swedish co-operative Union's new consumer policy, c. 1970. In Fallan, K. (ed), *Scandinavian design: alternative histories*. London and New York: Bloomsbury Academic, pp. 65–82.

Mitchell, W.J.T. (1986). *Iconology: image, text, ideology*. Chicago: University of Chicago Press.

Nikolajeva, M. & Scott, C. (2006). *How picturebooks work*. (First pbk. edition). New York: Routledge.

Op de Beeck, N. (2010). *Suspended animation: children's picture books and the fairy tale of modernity*. Minneapolis: University of Minnesota Press.

Reynolds, K. (2016). *Left out: the forgotten tradition of radical publishing for children in Britain 1910–1949*. (First edition). Oxford: Oxford University Press.

Sandin B. (2012). More children of better quality. Pricing the child in the welfare state. In Sparrman, A., Sandin, B. & Sjöberg, J. (eds), *situating child consumption: rethinking values and notions of children, childhood and consumption*. Lund: Nordic Academic Press.

Stenberg-Masolle, A. (1934). *Per och Lisa: en julbok med hål i*. Stockholm: Kooperativa förbundet.

Stinas märkliga födelsedagsresa (1928). Malmö: Mazetti.

Svenska Skoindustri AB (1930). *En liten visa om Per och Lisa*. Örebro: Svenska Skoindustri AB.

Taylor, B. (2004). *Collage: the making of modern art*. London: Thames & Hudson.

Walle, M. (1931). *Per och Lisa. Jorden runt på 8 dagar*. Stockholm: Kooperativa förbundet.

Zelizer, V.A.R. (1985). *Pricing the priceless child: the changing social value of children*. New York: Basic Books.

2

A MODERN UTOPIA

Architecture, modernity and Ladybird books in post-war Britain

Torsten Schmiedeknecht and Jill Rudd

Utopia and nostalgia

> [...] The more both adults and children realise the degree to which all representations misrepresent the world, the less likely they will be to confuse any particular representation with reality, or to be unconsciously influenced by ideologies they have not considered.
>
> *(Nodelman, 1999, p. 138)*

For many who were children in the 1960s and 1970s, the Ladybird books are treasured icons of their childhood, whose bright colours and user-friendly format helped create a sense of positive outlook and trust in the modern age and its new materials and knowledge. New industries and new ways of living, learning and working were presented as beneficial, for the main part without reservation. *The Story of Houses and Homes* (1963) is a case in point. The book is discussed in detail later, but here it is useful to note two things, as they epitomise much of both the attitudes promulgated by the Ladybird series and the fondness and reactions to them today.

First, the narrative of *The Story of Houses and Homes* follows the expected chronological trajectory from early to contemporary human living. The book begins with 'Man's first home' which is presented as 'a rock shelter' that 'may not seem very comfortable to us' (p. 4). Although the Old Stone Age family presented is suspiciously clean and well fed and their surroundings pristine, as all surroundings are in the Ladybird world, there is no doubting the sense of physical labour involved in this way of life. An open-air fire is being coaxed into flame in the foreground in order to cook the fish held by a weary male, while in the background a younger figure chips at a rock with a mallet. There is precious little architecture here: a wickerwork panel supported by sticks creates a partial roof under which clothes (surely intended to be skins) drape over unseen props. This structure is pushed into the background of the picture, indicating that architecture has hardly begun. By the end of the book, 'modern methods and materials' always governed by 'careful planning' ensures that 'the maximum use can now be made of even the most limited space' (p. 50). Space, of course, was not an issue in the Stone Age, and nor, it appears, is it an issue in the modern age, as the picture indicates. The illustration is uncluttered, as befits modern life, and the representative family is no longer made up of three figures (we might presume parents and

DOI: 10.4324/9781003131755-4

child) but an affluent middle-class couple who are to be seen in the foreground with their sailing boat on their private jetty, their bespoke modern country house on the rise behind them. Words and picture seem of one accord, the message the same, regardless of whether one reads the words and then looks at the picture or vice versa.[1]

The second element is easily overlooked but is perhaps more indicative of the way this book tacitly promotes the aspirational and above all sleek and modern lifestyle, which is so much a part of the Ladybird image. This element is the familiar device of a simple drawing on the title page. In this case that drawing is of the same modern house with which the book ends. Intriguingly, however, this is not simply a reduced, monochrome version of the full-page colour illustration of the book's final page. Instead, the picture offers a wider view of the house, showing that its design includes that essential of Modern life, a garage, whose raised door reveals the back of a typical family car.[2] Today, and quite plausibly even in 1963, the combination of these illustrations as representing a kind of typical family life may elicit a rather wry smile. Even in 1963, not every middle-class couple had a country home with lawns down to a river, a car and a sailing dingy. Most readers would find themselves accommodated in houses illustrated elsewhere in the book, in the 'better homes' of the Victorian terrace, the semi-detached of the 1930s, in the council estate or the high-rise flats, all of which are portrayed with unbelievably clean streets and almost equally unbelievable sunshine.

A LADYBIRD 'ACHIEVEMENTS' BOOK

THE STORY OF

HOUSES AND HOMES

by
RICHARD BOWOOD

with illustrations by
ROBERT AYTON

Publishers: Wills & Hepworth Ltd., Loughborough
First published 1963   ©   *Printed in England*

FIGURE 2.1   Title page from *THE STORY OF HOUSE AND HOMES*
© Ladybird Books Ltd, 1963.

However, even at the time of original publication, there seems to have been something of a disconnect between the society and the environments depicted by some of the books describing the modern post-war world and the world desired by those who would grow up to inhabit it. This difference is particularly marked where the built environment is concerned. Readers who revisit the classic Ladybirds produced between 1950 and 1975 find themselves reacting with a mixture of nostalgia and amusement, perhaps cynicism, as they detect in both the prose and the illustrations details that, even at the time of first publication, may have struck an astute reader as suggesting an element of doubt over the seamless positivism regarding the clean and shiny modern world presented within the covers of a Ladybird book. Lawrence Zeegen, whose book in general endorses the view that the imprint took a predominantly optimistic outlook on the world, suggests the possibility of reservations when he remarks, 'the pace of change would probably have been felt quite acutely by a generation of commercial artists who had lived through the Second World War and were now witnessing the relative prosperity of the late 1950s and the 1960s' (Zeegen, 2015, p. 64).[3] 'Acute' feelings and 'relative prosperity' hint at a less rosy response to times of accelerated and, in some cases, heedless change. As he goes on to remark, in these books, 'little mention was made of any social problems, such as the impact of the 1970s recession or the oppression of the Cold War' (Zeegen, 2015, p. 64).

Jeremy Burchardt's article 'Ladybird landscapes: or, what to look for in the What To Look For Books', makes the point that these books quietly accept and, in his view, celebrate the advent of the modern world by including modern machinery in their illustrations of rural life. As the century advanced and ecological concerns began to register, such celebrations became more muted and are opened to question, but in general the books put down that marker of a positive attitude and occasionally, even deliberately, suppress any hint of discord within the scenes they present, as, for example, where foxhunting is concerned (Burchardt, 2020, p. 83). Similarly, in our example above, the mention of the efficient use of space being an advantage in a house depicted within a generous garden with no sign of other houses or buildings close by silences any concerns of over-crowding that might have been suggested by the facing words, which caution that 'As our towns become more crowded, land on which to build becomes more and more scarce and valuable' (p. 50). Here, it seems words and image not only collude in the kind of misrepresentation to which Nodelman alerts us, but also conspire to ensure readers do not consider too deeply the ideologies these pages present. It is a testament to the influence of these little books, the affection in which they are held and our associated reluctance to disturb their quiet waters, that most readers still nod in agreement with Zeegen's assertion that, 'Ladybird's relentless optimism remained steadfast' (Zeegen, 2013, p. 65), despite the tacit acknowledgement detected by Burchardt that not quite everything was perfect in the modern world.

Steadfast, but not utterly without question. The hints underlying Zeegen's comments are more fully expressed elsewhere, and in general, it might be said that the critical response to the books mirrors that of an individual reader. First, either as child or as adult new to the series, one feels one has entered a kind of utopian world in which all progress is good, life is essentially clean and benign and, to use one of the titles from their keywords reading scheme, *We Have Fun* (1964). Returning later, sometimes not much later, that sense of an ideal world mutates into the nostalgia so often associated with books encountered in childhood, ours or our children's. Pat on the heels of such nostalgia, indeed often a part of it, is a critique which renders ironic the joyful assertions of the books or detects an undercurrent of unease, sometimes located in a disparity between what the words assert and what the illustration depicts, sometimes felt in the tone of the main text or its frontmatter. This chapter forms part of that final critique stage, discussing examples drawn from three of the main areas of concern for the Ladybird series: homes and houses, education, the world of work. Inevitably, we have had to be selective, even within these topics, and are even more conscious of the wide range of what is left out: the retelling of fairy tales, nursery rhymes and Biblical stories; the history series; the books on nature; the series on composers; the story of cultural aspects such as ballet and art; books on engineering, mechanics, knitting, original stories such as the animal tales and later the Garden Gang; and we only touch upon the Key Word Reading Scheme, better known perhaps by its unofficial title of 'the Peter and Jane books'. It's a wide world to be covered by such a small insect, but in what follows, our focus is on the way the treatment of architecture, in some of its pages at least, both reflects and reflects upon the atmosphere of the 'modern' world of the two and a half decades from 1950 to 1975 which Ladybirds themselves did so much to create.

The critique of Bowood's words and Ayton's image for *The Story of Houses and Homes*, offered above, broadly worked with the relation of word and image described by Perry Nodelman in his essay 'Decoding the images: how picture books work' and endorses his summative remark:

> The pictures 'illustrate' the texts – that is, they purport to show us what is meant by the words, so that we come to understand the objects and actions the words refer to in terms of the qualities of the images that accompany them – the world outside the book in terms of the images within. And the world as they show it is not necessarily the world all viewers would agree to seeing.
>
> *(Nodelman, 1999, p. 131)*

Nodelman's remarks and our critique take for granted that the words serve the pictures and also assume they are read first, but as William Moebius, amongst others, has pointed out, this is not invariably the case.[4] In common with Philip Pullman, Sonia Sandes and Uri Shulevitz, Moebius prefers the concept of these books offering a counterpoint in which words and pictures each offer a narrative, which then intertwine and comment upon each other. While more easily applied to fiction than factual books, our discussion here will show that even in books whose primary aim is to offer clear information, an element of such contrapuntal relation between words and image may be detected. In what follows, we were looking for what is explicitly said in the text accompanying the illustrations, what is directly expressed through the images and more importantly, the implicit messages conveyed in the images of these different environments. How thus do the Ladybird books we analyse 'integrate young children into the ideology of our culture' (Nodelman, 2004, p. 157) but also how may the 'irony' that is 'inevitable' between words and picture provide space for dissent or scepticism on the part of the readers, including the child reader (Nodelman, 1990, p. 172)?[5] In other words, how are images of (modern) architecture used to support the narratives presented on modernity and progress in post-war Britain and, in turn, what kind of ideas of modernity and progress are promoted in the books?[6]

We have chosen to interrogate three environments represented in Ladybird books in relation to modern architecture relevant to a child's life and development and with which they are likely to be able to identify either from experience or from expectation: the home, the school and the world of work. We selected 14 original Ladybird books, seven from the Ladybird Easy Reading Book 'People at Work' series, three additional titles from the Ladybird

'Achievements' Books, one Ladybird Learning To Read Book and three Ladybird Leaders. A 15th title, *The Hangover* (2015), which is part of the satirical Series 999, is also briefly discussed, as it contains an image from the 'People at Work' book *The Builder* (1965).[7] In most cases, the books follow the format of the left-hand page carrying the words, the right hand a facing, full-page picture. An exception is *homes*, where the pictures work across both sides of the spread, with the words running beneath. Both these formats fit Barbara Bader's concept of the 'opening', whereby each double-page spread is a complete and *completed* unit (Bader, 1976, pp. 155, 316). In this model, the pictures serve to clarify, sometimes elaborate, the ideas or individual examples contained within each opening, but also, as Moebius remarks, to close off the topic as the reader turns the page: 'implied, of course, is a closing, a deliberate shutting out of what came before' (Moebius, 1986, p. 141). In many ways, this suits information books designed to present facts in easily digestible form rather than convey a story's narrative,[8] but if a reader chooses to dwell on a particular opening, it can also allow for a thoughtful appraisal of how the combination of words and picture may comment on each other, reciprocally. As we demonstrate in what follows, the words may draw attention to the 'fact' that junks are dirty or that buildings take up land, just as the pictures indicate the secondary roles held by women in a work place or reveal their absence altogether. In other places, words and pictures unite to literally silence the noisy world of the railway terminus or the active construction site. Lacunae such as these have become material for a parody series, which provide new words to original pictures, satirising but also acknowledging the very sunny optimism and cosy assumptions that make the Ladybird books as a whole such firm favourites for those who, as children, were doubtless indoctrinated by them to some extent.

Although we focus on factual books, the first books published by Wills and Hepworth in 1914 as 'the Ladybird Series' were *Hans Andersen's Fairy Tales* and *Tiny Tots Travels*, which were followed by various others, predominantly saccharine stories about animals, simple adventures, retellings of familiar fairy tales or ABC books aimed at a very young audience. The appearance of an 'Uncle Mac' series in 1945 (series 455) heralded a move into non-fiction, building on the popularity of the wartime radio persona adopted by Derek McCulloch for his broadcasts to children. While his is often assumed to be the voice addressing the child reader in these books, Johnson and Alderson point out that for all the books in this series, the words are clearly secondary to the pictures (Johnson and Alderson, 2014, pp. 45–47). In general, they are directed at young children being shown the world they are likely to encounter, without being invited to do more than observe and absorb the information offered. That changed in 1953 when *British Birds and their Nests* was published, with a clear shift in target audience signalled on its cover: this is 'A Ladybird Senior'. The implied older child is then addressed directly in the words printed on the inside front fold-over of the dust jacket, creating a connection to the readership that held good in the third of the series (1956), where a similar address begins cheerily 'Hullo children! Thank you very much for all your letters' and is concluded by Vesey-Fitzgerald's signature. While such direct address is not a consistent feature of the Ladybird books, it is fair to say that they all have the child reader very much in mind. Thus, *The Story of Houses and Homes* (1963) is identified as 'Another Ladybird "Achievements" Book' specially planned for children who want to know 'How, when, where and why', while *The Story of Our Churches and Cathedrals* (1964) notes that 'With simple text and superb full-colour illustrations it describes the many interesting and beautiful features of the various periods of architecture, and will add greatly to your understanding and pleasure'. Interestingly, *The Builder* (1965), which is both 'A Ladybird

"Easy-Reading" Book' and part of the 'People at Work' series, leaves open the possibility of an adult reader, asserting that 'In this carefully planned reference book, interesting and accurate information is given about the various skills, materials and equipment involved in modern building' before going on to consider a child reader in the next paragraph, even one 'whose reading experience is limited'.

Whether addressing early readers developing language skills or mature adults in search of knowledge on Scott of the Antarctic or nuclear reactors, Ladybirds thus gained and retain a reputation for being go-to books for succinct and professional information; a reputation that survives into the recent parody series, such as *The Ladybird Book of the Hangover*, of which more anon. However, it is worth noting that the accuracy of information emphasised in *The Builder*'s self-description, which is an accepted and indeed integral part of the Ladybird reputation, is not the same as realistic portrayal. As Nodelman asserts:

> Because we assume that pictures, as iconic signs, do in some significant way actually resemble what they depict, they invite us to see objects *as* the pictures depict them – to see the actual in terms of the fictional visualisation of it.
>
> *(Nodelman, 1999, p. 131)*

Place this next to Reynold's demonstration of the 'radical determination to provide the next generation with the knowledge, skills, and ideas necessary for joining in the rebuilding of Britain' (Reynolds, 2016, pp. 180–181) and we arrive at the tension between the idealisation of the modern world and the lived experience of those inhabiting it. A relevant example of this is the change in house architecture from 1930s suburban semi to modern 1970s terrace that provides the backdrop to the *I Like to Write* workbook (Johnson and Alderson, 2014, p. 99). While the change in setting surely reflects a desire to ensure the books remain up-to-date, feeling fresh and modern to their readership (and likely adult purchasers), it also sustains the domestic narrative carried by the pictures here and elsewhere in the various Ladybird series, which promotes a sense that everyone with access to the Ladybird world lives a happy, comfortable life in clean, modern houses with easy access to safe places to play, shop for sweets and go to school. Generally speaking, the press thus established and then maintained its place as part of the modern world, reflecting the optimism for the future and love of clean lines, clarity, space and communal benefit that is broadly associated with the post-war reconstruction of the 1950s and 1960s.

House and home

In *The Story of Houses and Homes* (1963), *The Builder* (1965) and *homes* (1975), there are noteworthy illustrations of high-rise domestic buildings, pertinent to this discussion because of the time of their publication. In 1963, there was perhaps still some faith in high-rise tower blocks as a remedy for the housing crisis, and as Glendinning and Muthesius stated, 'Before the mid-1960s, to praise Victorian terraces or tenements and attack the Modern dwelling, […], could only have seemed sophistic, if not incomprehensible' (Glendinning and Muthesius, 1994, p. 326). But by 1975, the appetite for this kind of housing type had somewhat waned and it is possible to detect some of that diminishing enthusiasm in *homes*, as we shall see below.[9]

One illustration by Robert Ayton in *The Story of Houses and Homes* shows a happy couple – him in dark jumper and trousers, her in a pink knee length dress – on an immaculate lawn, between a tree and some shrubs, in front of a white 12-storey residential tower block.

At some distance in the background, the reader can spot the building site of another high-rise block. On the opposite page, without being explicit, the accompanying text makes reference to some of CIAM's principles and Le Corbusier's ideas about the 'tapis vert', describing the benefits of 'extra space, sunlight and fresh air' and how building high 'means that more ground can be left free for lawns, flowers, trees and shrubs, for tennis courts and playgrounds'. Considering that many post-war estates suffered precisely from the poor design of the public space between high-rise blocks, the text reads, in hindsight, as wishful thinking. Referring to the book's nature as a collection of houses and homes starting from the 'Old Stone Age', the author remarks of high-rise residential buildings that 'when carefully planned and sited, they can be as beautiful in their way as were the best homes of the past'. 'Public dining and recreation rooms' in blocks of flats are mentioned, as a further reference to modernist ideals and buildings such as Le Corbusier's 1952 Unité d'Habitation in Marseille, which included a series of public facilities of a kind that in reality were rarely incorporated in tower blocks in the UK. Another issue repeatedly raised by critics of high-rise housing, namely the tendency of lifts to fail, is here brushed over, as 'electric lifts' are mentioned in the words as convenient elements of tower block design and are invisible in the accompanying illustration.

In similar vein, two years after the publication of *The Story of Houses and Homes*, *The Builder* is more concerned with building technology, illustrating the virtues of both steel and concrete frame construction without any positive or negative reference to the nature of high-rise buildings as a type. And yet, as in the example cited above, John Berry's illustrations, with their flat blocks of colour reminiscent of posters, have jolly and positive connotations; they depict progress and in some sense, hope and trust in technology.[10]

homes, illustrated by Bernard Robinson, Martin Aitchison and Brian Price Thomas, contains three page spreads depicting high-rise buildings in a broader urban context and a single image of another very tall housing block. As a 'Ladybird Leader', this book is one of the 'carefully planned *first information books* that instantly attract inquiring minds and stimulate reluctant readers' (our italics), an ambition somewhat reflected in the first of the three images of high-rise buildings. Showing a perspective of a tower block in which neither the building's base nor its top can be seen, this image is accompanied by a short text reminding the reader that 'All blocks of flats need space below where children can safely play'. The intention is there and is in line with the arguments brought forward by modernist architects and planners, but there is no child or playground to be seen in the predominantly hard landscape (or perhaps carpark) the viewer is looking down onto in the picture. The question of irony and intention arises here: is the text an ironic commentary on what is displayed by the image, implying that it is the lack of connection between site and building that is the problem for many high-rise blocks? Or is the illustration a sardonic depiction of what was actually built as opposed to what the architects (and modernist principles) might have proposed? Or perhaps it is mere accident and something went missing in the editing process. Whatever the reason, image and text do not form a coherent narrative in this case, leaving plenty of scope for the 'inquiring mind' to speculate.

In *The Architectures of Childhood* Roy Kozlovsky offers a comment that reflects the somewhat jaded view of the high-rise that began in the mid-1960s and dominated the 1970s attitudes:

> [...] The high-rise housing block preferred by modernist planners was criticised by sociologists and child advocates as being detrimental to children's emotional and social development.
>
> *(Kozlovsky, 2013, p. 175)*

Looking back from the vantage point of Kozlovsky's remarks, it is interesting to note that two of the three page spreads in *homes* use dense high-rise urban settings as backdrops for dwellings that the accompanying text suggests are undesirable. The first is a view of Hong Kong, seen from the bay and across floating homes or 'junks'. 'In Hong Kong, many Chinese live on them. They have nowhere else to live', we are told. Despite the page spread being titled 'Homes on water', contrasting the houseboats with the high-rise city beyond strongly suggests that the latter is the environment the reader should aspire to. In this case, text and illustration encourage the same conclusion: that the 'many Chinese' only stay in these 'homes on water' because 'they have nowhere else to live', not because they are desirable abodes. The same contrast is set up in a more extreme way on a spread titled 'The world needs more homes', where a shanty town kept in dark colours in the foreground is set against a shiny white high-rise city in the distance. Referring to the shanty town (although not by that term), the accompanying text once again leaves the reader in no doubt: 'Many people have to live in huts like these. Their homes are small, ugly and hard to keep clean'.

The third page spread showing a high-rise development is, however, a little ambiguous in its message and could be interpreted in different ways. It is composed of two views of the same stretch of landscape, one showing a rural and agricultural area by a river and the other depicting the same area after development, with a series of what looks like domestic tower blocks in the foreground and a neighbouring dense low rise stretch of buildings towards and beyond the river. The page is titled 'Homes use up land' and the text below the images informs the reader that 'To grow food, good land is needed. [...] When homes are built, good farmland is often used up. More homes may mean less food'. The ambiguity created here becomes more evident when taking into consideration that the text and images are from 1975, that is, after the 1973 oil crisis

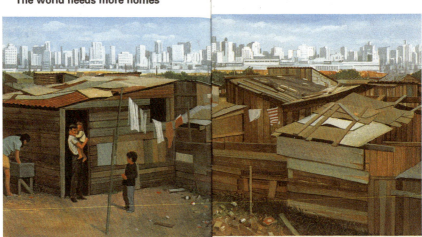

The world needs more homes

Each year there are more and more people in the world.
More and more homes are needed.

42

Many people have to live in huts like these.
Their homes are small, ugly and hard to keep clean.

43

FIGURE 2.2 Illustrations and text from *homes* © Ladybird Books Ltd, 1975.

and at a time when the wisdom of high-rise dwellings had already been in question for some time in the UK. What is not clear though is whether what is being implied is that if all the flats contained in the high-rise towers depicted here had been built as low-rise dwellings, the use of land would have been even greater or that development in general is in question. Noteworthy in this regard is John Boughton's assertion that 'tower blocks did not offer higher-density housing than lower-rise alternatives, precisely because of the "open character" of the space that encircled the blocks' (Boughton, 2018, p. 112). But it was on the mistaken assumption that high-rise housing would achieve higher densities, that 'the 1956 subsidy regime [...] incentivised high-rise' (Boughton, 2018, p. 113). So the narrative created by image and text in *homes* challenges the reader to make up their own mind and to alert them to the problems of population expansion and its consequences for the environment, food sufficiency and the viability of farming.

This is also where the different page layout used by *homes* becomes significant. Rather than words on the left facing full-page picture on the right, the Ladybird Leader series, of which *homes* was a part, used pictures on both left and right pages, with the quite few words placed either at top or bottom, and so above or beneath the image. Each opening in *homes* also carries a brief title in bold font, top left, summing up the theme that links the various images on its double page spread. This change in design reflects that these books were aimed at 'less able readers' or 'reluctant' readers of any age, but arguably also invites a more fluid relation between words and image, as the opening now accommodates a mini narrative between the pictures as well as between the picture and the words that explain it. A 'modern' tent, for example, shares a page with a 'Lapland home', both facing 'an Indian wigwam' and Bedouin-style tent, identified merely as 'a home in the desert'; while three of these are 'homes', the modern tent is specifically associated with (Western) holidaying (pp. 8–9). This book offers many opportunities to criticise the optimistic assumptions of Modern life: the comparison between the Georgian pile on p. 16 exemplifying a home that has many rooms with the facing 1970s interior, illustrating that 'sometimes, home is only one room' (p. 17) speaks volumes. The words, however, maintain a neutral stance, and later in the book, we are encouraged to associate the word 'home' more with the people inside the building than the kind of building itself.[11]

Overall, despite having been published over a span of 12 years during which attitudes to modernism dramatically changed in the public eye and the profession, the message conveyed relating to high-rise dwellings and development in general in *The Story of Houses and Homes, The Builder* and *homes*, now seems astoundingly uncritical. Only *homes*' last spread, 'Homes use up land', openly hints at any disadvantages, and even then only gently, as discussed above. Beyond that, and despite the noticeably dour tone of *homes*' written text, these three books on the whole echo some of the principles of Le Corbusier's 1924 *Ville Radieuse* and its perceived benefits – light, air, space between buildings – and of the functional city propagated by CIAM in the Athens Charter, particularly the division of housing, work, recreation and traffic. Paradoxically, they do this at a time, 1963 onwards, when it was becoming evident that the application of the principles of the functional city had also often destroyed aspects of the traditional city which by 1975 had been deemed worthy again, such as the mixing of functions rather than their separation. It is thus possible to detect in the illustrations of the high-rise on which we have concentrated a combination of clinging on to the modern dream of clean, convenient and often communal living with a sense that the architecture of this particular modern habitat often did not live up to its ideals – for reasons that have been fully rehearsed, amongst others, by Glendinning and Muthesius (1994), Bullock (2002), Gold (2007), Grindrod (2013) and Boughton (2018).

Going to school

The dual interest in education and in modern building makes the school building itself a relevant focus for our discussion. It is worth noting that the 1944 Education Act is credited with increasing social mobility by encouraging more working-class children and more girls from any background to remain in education for longer. More children to educate inevitably required more school buildings in which to teach them and this, in turn, may account for why the few school buildings shown in the Ladybird books are newly built, apparently brightly lit, airy and by implication open to all; a far cry from the adapted Victorian mansions which housed (and continue to house) many actual schools, particularly smaller-scale junior and country schools.

Modern housing and schools are treated with equal optimism and admiration in the earlier Ladybird books considered in this study. However, this is perhaps not an entirely realistic reflection of how modern architecture was perceived, and in some respects conceived, in the post-war years. A point in case may be Andrew Saint, who described 'a particular attitude of mind, an approach towards [modern] architecture which bore most fruit in educational building' (Saint, 1987, p. viii). Saint explains the difference between the success of the relatively privileged and more professionalised, post-war school building programme and its acceptance by the general population compared to the problems and criticism public housing experienced at the same time:

> We all live in dwellings, we all have opinions about them and therefore we are all housing experts. Council committees wish to scrutinise housing plans in detail, and tenants too must have their say. We also went to school, many of us have children, yet few of us feel that we authoritatively understand a teacher's or a child's educational needs.
>
> *(Saint, 1987, p. 228)*

Nicholas Bullock makes a similar observation regarding the difference in the acceptance by the general public of non-traditional post-war housing and non-traditional post-war schools (and modern commodities for that matter):

> But those [houses] that looked as inescapably unconventional as their construction or could not be disguised were generally viewed askance. Those who lived in them might welcome the benefits of their comfort and their equipment and even come to view them with affection, but they never came to be valued for their newness and their otherness. Unlike the Airstrem caravan or the Citroen 2cv they never established a new canon, an acceptance of a 'machine for living in'.
>
> *(Bullock, 2002, p. 193)*

Bullock further points out that 'With non-traditional schools the position was different' (Bullock, 2002, p. 193), as arguably for both teachers and parents new school design represented the generally positively received reform of the education system. Although Bullock refers to low-rise housing built in non-traditional ways with (then) innovative and new construction methods rather than to the type of high-rise housing discussed in this chapter, his comment may be used to reflect upon the difference in attitude to and the acceptance of modern architecture and technology when applied to public buildings as opposed to when applied to the home. It is, as we have seen, in stark contrast to the images of modern housing in Ladybird books such as *The Story of Houses and Homes* (1963), *The Builder* (1965) and *homes* (1975) where text and image provide a powerful narrative of a brave new world of modern dwellings.

Perhaps surprisingly, given their focus on child readers and the scale of the post-war school building programme, there are relatively few modern school buildings portrayed in Ladybird books; some of the most notable ones can be found in *Going to School* (1959) and *The Builder* (1965). While in the former, school interiors dominate the pictures as the book takes us through a day in school chronologically, the two images of schools shown in *The Builder* are used first as backdrop to illustrate groundworks (p. 39) and later to demonstrate the virtues of prefabrication (p. 49). The first image shows what we may presume is a school building, typified by its dimensions, repetitive façade, fenestration pattern and the materials depicted for the elevation. Here, the building really just serves as the background to a large building site, including a digger in action (p. 39). School and building site dominate the picture, whereas to the left of the school and set further back, we can identify what look like Victorian houses, a detail which bears out Bullock's point about there being greater tolerance for modern design in public buildings rather than housing. In this image, then, modern architecture is synonymous with technology and progress, but also with modern education. The accompanying text only refers to the building site, but the building forms an important element of the composition.

FIGURE 2.3   Illustration from *People at Work: THE BUILDER* © Ladybird Books Ltd, 1965.

Latter-day scepticism finds its echo in the reuse of this illustration from *The Builder* in *The Hangover* (2015), which is part of the parody series 999.[12] Here, the same picture of the building site is used but this time, rather than leaving the function of the building whose foundations are being laid unspecified, we are told that they are for a new hospital, leaving the reader to appreciate the irony of the construction noise that mirrors the drilling headache of the hangover sufferer. In each case, the school building in the background is barely noticed, but nevertheless silently provides a modern framework for the construction work being done and, in the later book, the hangover being endured. In contrast, on the page spread pp. 48–49 of *The Builder*, the text and image form a more explicit relationship, as the text refers directly to the fact that we see a prefabricated school building in the picture. This picture resembles the type of temporary classrooms that eventually became permanent and which can still be found on many school grounds in the UK, and the text makes a virtue of the flexibility of prefabrication as 'The architect and the builder can make buildings of different shapes by adding more prefabricated units'(p.48).

While the two schools in *The Builder* are reminiscent of the kind of commercialised and compromised version of modern architecture that would plague much of post-war housing—borne out of the scarcity of resources, time constraints and need for efficiency—the school

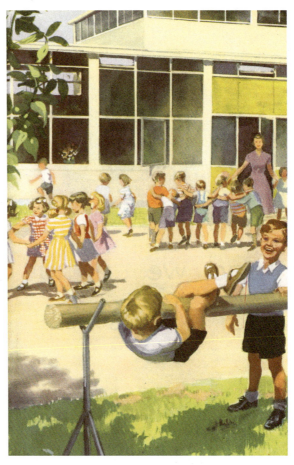

FIGURE 2.4 Illustration and text from *GOING TO SCHOOL* © Ladybird Books Ltd, 1975.

building in *Going to School* not only still bears some stylistic traces of the more socially progressive interwar modernism, but also carries echoes of the positive and educationally driven attempts at school construction in the post-war period, which emphasised the importance of the school building as a place in which children spend a lot of time growing up and becoming social beings. The depiction of the large windows and the use of colour are a case in point.

These two books thus reflect the attitudes of their respective dates: 1959 (*Going to School*) when the excitement of modern concepts was still evident, and 1965 (*The Builder*) by which time those same concepts were beginning to become a little tarnished by the experience of substandard execution. Yet, despite the difference in the schools depicted, the implicit messages on modernity in all three external representations of school buildings are broadly positive, and are supported by interiors in which large windows flood rooms with light and the concomitant desired affirmative outlook. Thus, modern schools are variously associated with different aspects of optimistic progress, be it technological in *The Builder* (big machines, technology, prefabrication) or social in *Going to School* (1944 Education Act). Even the parodic use of the modern building in *The Hangover* signals that by 2015, this kind of architecture had become a familiar, accepted and indeed expected part of what a school is.[13]

The world of work

The world of work is manifestly presented in the Ladybird series 'People at Work', in which books like *The Policeman* (1962), *The Nurse* (1963), *The Builder* (1965), *The Road Makers* (1967), *The Car Makers* (1968), *In A Hotel* (1972) and *On The Railways* (1972) were published, each categorised as 'A Ladybird "Easy Reading" Book'. In total, 20 titles were published in the series between 1962 and 1973, all illustrated by John Berry, with an additional book *The Milkman* published 'hors série' (Johnson and Alderson, 2014, p. 175) in 1987 (written by Tina Hook, illustrated by Jim Clark).[14] When looking at this series, one of the questions arising is: are images of modern architecture and modernity in the Ladybird 'People at Work' books used to support the status quo characterised by the prevailing gender divisions or does this very status quo paradoxically support images and ideas of modernity and progress, including those of modern architecture?

In a lecture given during the symposium *God is in the Detail* at the Architectural Association, Professor Christine Wall presented some interesting findings from her research on the building processes of the Queen Elizabeth Hall on London's South Bank in London and the Barbican Centre in the City of London.[15] Wall's research, also published as a book chapter (Wall, 2019) and based on interviews with the very people who built both schemes, that is, the builders and craftsmen on the respective building sites, highlighted the differences in how both sites were run and managed and what that meant for the people involved. The project for the Queen Elizabeth Hall was presented as a positive example in which there was a certain autonomy and inventiveness on behalf of the craftsmen in order to build a complex scheme. The Barbican building site, much larger in scope, was, however, regarded less favourably, partly because of the working conditions the builders had to endure. For our purposes here what is interesting is the difference between the clean, tidy and seemingly very well-organised building sites depicted in *The Builder* and the reality of both the sites discussed by Wall and evident in her visual material. The pictures in the Ladybird book show working environments that seem, by and large, dust, dirt and sweat free, with neatly arranged building materials and tools, and builders who effortlessly perform what under any circumstances is hard physical work. These images are in stark contrast to those shown by Wall, in particular of the Barbican site (1965–1976) but also of the Queen Elizabeth Hall site, both of which were depicted as being a lot more chaotic, dirty, noisy and at times cold, wet and dangerous. The exclusively white male workforce of the Ladybird world – Wall elaborates on the fact that building sites in the 1960s were also sites of immigration, something blissfully (and woefully) ignored in *The Builder* – thus perform their heroic actions in front of a backdrop of a modern world, clearly apparent in the pictures of this modern built environment.

Building sites are still predominantly male arenas, so the all-male workforce of *The Builder* might not raise a question even today. That is less true of other jobs presented in the 'People at Work' series, but the affection with which Ladybird books as a whole are regarded means that criticism of the sexism depicted within their pages is often gentle and understanding. Lawrence Zeegen is a case in point:

> At a time when men and women still had very defined, stereotypical gender roles, women seldom feature in the series, and where they do we are reminded of their supporting role. […] Only in *The Policeman* do we learn that 'policewomen are trained in the same way as the men and they can do the same jobs.'
>
> *(Zeegen, 2015, p. 152)*

There is, however, only one image of policewomen in the entire book (p. 21), showing two female officers taking notes questioning three people sitting at a table.[16] Women may be in the force, but the pictures and the shutting down of the topic enacted when one turns the page (Moebius, 1986, p. 141) betray how difficult it was to conceive of them as anything other than, essentially, secretaries.

In contrast, the third page spread of *The Policeman* unmistakably combines male heroism and modern architecture. From the text on the left-hand side to the illustration, we learn that 'Some policemen live in the village where they work […]. The chief policeman is called Chief Constable. His office is at Police Headquarters' (I. & J. Havenhand, 1962, p. 8). The image itself shows a policeman, identified in the text as the chief constable, standing tall on the steps in front of his police headquarters, which are housed in what looks like a purpose-built modern edifice, featuring a gridded façade and a modernist canopy on slender steel columns. The chief constable's posture and his being positioned at the top of the steps radiate authority. At the same time, the image composition, the perspective chosen and the architecture itself are, in keeping with modernist principles, void of centrality and symmetry. So while, perhaps, in this page spread of text and image, modernism and male authority are married to reinforce each other, in some of the other spreads of *The Policeman* the message on modernism is a little more ambiguous. It is noticeable that while for much of the book only minor law violations (traffic related for example) occur or police uniforms and clerical sides of the job are described, the story is different for the two other images showing modern buildings. The text in both instances is related to more serious crimes – 'a house has been broken into'; 'robbery' – here modern buildings are identifiable as either the backdrop or the actual scene of a crime. As opposed to the heroic modernism of the police headquarters, here modern architecture is associated with the site of unlawfulness. What remains, however, is the all-male cast: a police officer in the role of the saviour chasing the (male) offender in front of a modern building site (p. 15), and another one driving a police car, possibly to see to the robbers (p. 25), with what looks like a modern office block as a backdrop. In *The Policeman*, then, modern architecture plays a supporting role as the setting for a policeforce that retains gender bias and sexist attitudes; this does not cast modern architecture in the most positive light. Rather, modern architecture, when it is shown, generally helps to reinforce images of white male dominance and vice versa, resulting in a particular and probably accurate portrayal of the link between modernity and society in 1960s and 1970s Britain.

Unsurprisingly, then, one of the most extreme examples of this male modernity is to be found in the 1968 Ladybird book *The Car Makers* written by I & J Havenhand. Here, women are respectively relegated to the role of car passenger (p. 5) and dinner ladies serving the car makers (p. 49). The rest of the book contains no images of women involved in the process of car production, although there is another, unillustrated, token mention of 'girls [...] taking in orders for cars and planning the work in the factories' whose 'work is just as important as that of the men who make the cars' (p. 8). The book, however, contains several images of modern architecture supporting the effort of designing and producing one of the 20th century's most significant symbols of individual freedom and mobility. Among other things, we see men leaning over drawing boards in a large open-plan office with modern clerestory glazing; a close-up of a draughtsman or engineer in a white coat in front of a large expanse of glazed façade; several images of a modern assembly line ('girls' mentioned again here in the text for their clerical support role, but not depicted); men 'put oil in the engine'; and 'A man gets into the driving seat, presses the starter and the car starts' in a light-filled hall with a large modern glass façade; and finally we read that 'men and women go to one of the canteens where they can buy dinners', although the only women shown in the accompanying image are the above-mentioned dinner ladies: women serve the meals, they don't eat them. Text and images in *The Car Makers* combine to show car production as being a clean and logical process, one which is carried out by men in light-filled modern spaces.

Two other books in the 'People at Work' series have modern transport environments, hallmarks of modernity, as their subject: *The Road Makers* (I. & J. Havenhand, 1967) and *On The Railways* (Forbes, 1972). In *The Road Makers*, we again encounter the familiar draughtsmen in a well-lit environment. The orderly, neatly arranged large open-plan office is illuminated both via a grid of overhead lamps and repetitive floor to ceiling glazing, typical of the layout of post-war office buildings. Similar to the building sites shown in *The Builder* and just like the office where the roads are designed, the actual roadworks as well as the finished roads and bridges on display are generally clean, tidy and well organised. One particular absence to note is that of noise – neither the actual noise created from building roads and bridges, be it on the roadworks or the production of the materials needed, like cement, nor the noise created by traffic finds any mention in the text. This creates a picture of surreal silence for what in reality would be high decibel environments. On the final page spread, we see cars passing on a large system of flyovers and underpasses, and although the text states that '[...] the Ministry of Transport have to think about traffic in towns as well as on motorways. Better roads are needed in towns to keep traffic moving', the scene is similarly tranquil – relatively few cars populate the illustration and they seem to almost serenely float by. It is perhaps worth mentioning Colin Buchanan's *Traffic in Towns*, commissioned in 1960 by the then Transport Minister Ernest Marples and published in 1963, which acknowledged that the motorcar was here to stay for the foreseeable future, but which also pointed out the potential problems caused by increased car ownership and thus traffic (Buchanan, 1963). Neither in *The Road Makers* (1967), nor in *The Car Makers* (1968) does this seem to have been of any concern, as in both books text and images paint a thoroughly positive picture of cars and their associated infrastructure. By 1974, however, Ladybird's outlook in this respect had shifted. The Ladybird Leaders *man and his car* (p. 26) and *roads* (pp. 48–49) contain references to air pollution, 'Engine fumes can spoil the air we breathe', and land use, 'Land used for roads can no longer grow crops for food'.

On The Railways contains surprisingly few images of modern buildings, but three of those featured seem to be modelled on the architecture of the rebuilding of London's Euston Station, which was completed in 1968. While fewer passengers passed through Euston in 1972 than today, the illustration of the station hall interior (p. 9), showing only a small number of exclusively male passengers (bar one figure that might perhaps be a woman), bears no relation to what normally, at any time of the day, is a space packed with people waiting for or rushing to and from trains.

FIGURE 2.5 Illustration from *People at Work: ON THE RAILWAYS*
© Ladybird Books Ltd, 1972.

As in *The Road Makers*, no reference is made to the actual ambience of the space described, despite the mention of 'many platforms, offices, waiting rooms and shops'. Hence what we are presented with is an idealised version of a public transport environment that might be alien to anyone used to commuting in London.[17] Notable, too, is the total absence of any non-Caucasian figures. In the next picture (p.11), we are introduced to the white male station manager, standing in front of what looks like a miniature version of Euston (or perhaps a generic modern station). As in *The Policeman*, the figure's uniform, posture and gaze, combine with the architecture to create an image of unquestionable authority. The third image based on Euston is that of a white mother and son buying a ticket from the, again male, white, ticket clerk, featuring large expanses of glazing between ticket office and customer (p.18). All three images portray a space or building well lit and characterised by modern methods of construction, sparse modernist detailing and building elements such as escalators, free-standing columns without base or capital, large amounts of curtain wall glazing, but above all free of the one thing that characterises modern means of transport most of all, namely speed and its associated noise. The words are likewise silent on the matter.[18]

The world of work as presented in the 'People of Work' Ladybird series is thus, as we have seen and to quote Nodelman once again, 'not necessarily the world all viewers would agree to seeing' (Nodelman, p. 131), certainly not now in the 21st century, but also not then in the second half of the 1900s – post-war and post-Windrush.

Ladybird and modern architecture

The modern architecture portrayed in the Ladybird books discussed here is reminiscent of what Kimberley Reynolds observed in her book *Left out: the forgotten tradition of radical publishing for children in Britain 1910–1949*, where she discusses a number of books published during the war and shortly after, which encouraged children to actively imagine a different – modern – built environment (Reynolds, 2016). For example, Reynolds refers to Maxwell Fry and Jane Drew's *Architecture for Children* (1944), S R Badmin's *Village and Town* (1944) and Oliver Hill's *Balbus: A Picture Book of Buildings* (1944), all of which contain didactic advice to the young reader that a better society also requires better or rather different and in this case modern architecture. The difference between the books discussed by Reynolds and the Ladybird books analysed here is a short but significant time span. In the 1940s, radical modernism was a valid vessel for hopes in a better society; by the mid-1960s, it had become apparent that, particularly with regards to high-rise housing, things weren't quite what they had promised to be and that problems were outweighing the benefits in the tower block schemes realised. The ideals of interwar modernism had, partly due to economic constraints and partly because Britain perhaps wasn't ready or willing to go all the way to a more balanced and just model of society, been only very partially implemented. Thus the path laid out by the socially progressive interwar modernism in architecture got somewhat caught in the middle and apart from notable exceptions of course, never materialised on a large scale.

The reality of the only partially realised dream for a better society was, however, not part of the Ladybird universe, in which a clever combination of format, text and illustration kept alive the idea of a Britain as a progressive society, driven by and realised through modern technology – albeit without ensuring that gender and racial equality were also part of the agenda.

Notes

1 There are a variety of ways the relation of words and pictures in books may be read: Nodleman in both 'Words and Pictures' and 'Decoding the images' assumes the pictures take priority, both in the act of reading and in interpretation, and so may endorse the words and enhance their meaning or act as 'shadow text' offering an alternative to them. Philip Pullman, Sonia Sandes, William Moebius and Uri Shulevitz suggest the words and pictures may be distinct narratives, acting in counterpoint rather than simple harmony with each other. For Shulevitz books where the pictures serve to depict only what the words say and no more are more correctly regarded as illustrated books, not picturebooks.

2 This garage is depicted as a room, possibly a kitchen, in the full colour illustration on p. 51; on the end papers, it appears as a garage but with its up-and-over door closed. Only on the title page is the garage door raised and the car visible.

3 *Ladybird by Design: 100 years of words and pictures*, Lawrence Zeegen (Penguin Random House, 2015), p. 67. As its title indicates, this richly illustrated book focuses on the evolution of the distinctive look associated with the Ladybird books, including the logo and fonts. *The Ladybird Story: Children's Books for Everyone* by Lorraine Johnson and Brian Alderson (The British Library, 2014) offers a detailed and also heavily illustrated history of the Wills & Hepworth press. Together, these two books provide a comprehensive and fascinating history of the imprint, to which this chapter is much indebted.

4 Peter Hunt usefully summarises the various different positions taken on the relation between words and pictures in his chapter, 'Criticism and the Picture Book' in *Criticism, Theory, & Children's Literature* (Oxford: Blackwell, 1991), pp. 175–188. See also William Moebius, 'Introduction to picturebook codes' (1986) and Uri Shulevitz, 'What is a picture book?' from *Writing with Pictures* reprinted in *Only Connect: Reading on Children's Literature* 3rd edition, Sheila Egoff, Gordon Stubbs, Ralph Ashley and Wendy Sutton (eds) (Oxford: OUP, 1996), pp. 238–241 (240).

5 Nodelman refers to storybooks and in books that are not telling stories – like our Ladybird sample here – one might expect that irony to be absent. In a way it is, but there is perhaps a different irony in some cases, present more often in the pictures than in the words, which is to simply omit such contrasts.

6 For an interesting selection of images referring to modernism also, see John Grindrod's blog: https://dirtymodernscoundrel.blogspot.com/search/label/Ladybird.

7 Twenty-two Ladybird Books displayed in the 2019 RIBA North exhibition 'Building Children's Worlds' in Liverpool, curated by Schmiedeknecht, formed the initial sample, as they all contained images of modern architecture and modernity. The titles were chosen as to their suitability following a research visit to the Seven Stories Archive in Newcastle in the autumn of 2018. The following 11 books from the initial selection are discussed here: (authors and illustrators in reference list). *GOING TO SCHOOL* (M.E. Gagg, 1959); 'People at Work' Ladybird 'Easy-Reading' Books: *THE POLICEMAN* (I. & J. Havenhand, 1962), *THE NURSE* (V. Southgate & J. Havenhand, 1963), *THE BUILDER* (I. & J. Havenhand, 1965), *THE ROAD MAKERS* (I. & J. Havenhand, 1967), *THE CAR MAKERS* (I. & J. Havenhand, 1968), *IN A HOTEL* (I. & J. Havenhand, 1972) and *ON THE RAILWAYS* (J. Forbes, 1972); Ladybird 'Achievements' Books: *THE STORY OF OUR Churches and Cathedrals* (R. Bowood, 1964), *THE STORY OF HOUSES and HOMES* (R. Bowood and R. Anton, 1963); Ladybird Leader books (titles in this series were presented without capital letters): *roads* (J. Webster, 1974b); *man and his car* (J. Webster, 1974a); *homes* (J. Webster, 1975); Series 999 *THE HANGOVER* (J.A. Hazeley and J.P. Morris, 2015).

8 Bettina Kümmerling-Meibauer and Jörg Meibauer demonstrate that non-fiction, information books rely on narration, alongside description and explanation, to engage their readers. They refer to three dominant frameworks and two main scripts which are used by both words and illustrations to convey each book's information. See 'How descriptive picturebooks engaged children in knowledge about coal, oil, and gas' in *Verbal and visual strategies in nonfiction picturebooks* N. Goga, S. H. Iversen, and A.-S. Teigland (eds) (Oslo: Scandinavian University Press. 2021), pp. 196–197.

9 For accounts on relevant post-war debates on housing in this context, see *Tower Block* by M. Glendinning and S. Muthesius (1994), N. Bullock's *Building The Post-War World* (2002), J. R. Gold's *The Practice of Modernism* (2007) and *Municipal Dreams* by J.Boughton (2018).

10 Although never employed full-time as a poster or advertising artist (as Robert Ayton and Harry Wingfield were), John Berry was recruited to be a war artist on the strength of a poster he

produced for a national day of prayer in the Middle East. Post-war, he undertook freelance advertising work alongside illustrating children's books and painting portraits (see Zeegen, p. 158).

11 Pages 32–33 carry the headings 'An empty house is not a home' and 'People make a house into a home' respectively. These sit above pages showing on the left, a room in an empty house, which is specifically not a home, and facing the same room redecorated and now inhabited and thus now a home.

12 The series also features the titles such as *The Whitey; The Acid Trip; The 12-Step Programme; Bouncing Back*; and *The Halfway House*.

13 For the debate of empiricism versus brutalism surrounding post-war school building, see the chapters 'A Touch of Genius' (Grindrod, 2013) and 'The Architecture of Educare' (Kozlovsky, 2013), and Andrew Saint's *Towards a Social Architecture* (1987).

14 The authors commissioned for the original series were Vera Southgate (four books), Ina and John Havenhand (13 books), Max Dunstone (1) and John Forbes (1).

15 https://www.youtube.com/watch?v=SsHHu520cEk.

16 Zeegen's book credits an image of a female traffic officer as being from *The Policeman* (Zeegen, 2015, p. 153); however, the 1962 version of the book we examined did not contain this image.

17 Interestingly and considering that *On The Railways* was published in 1972, the effects of The Beeching Report and the resulting closures of stations and lines are not part of the equation here either.

18 While it might be thought that it is impossible to represent noise in pictures, *The Story of Railways* (a book on an obviously similar topic published in the same year, 1961, as part of the 'Achievements' series) managed to convey both the sound and chaos of George Stephenson's Locomotion terrifying people and animals as it steams past a horse-drawn carriage, belching smoke and sparks (p. 13). In contrast, it is the horse-drawn mail coach, complete with man sounding the coach horn, which is depicted creating the noise as it gallops over a bridge under which the (implied) comparatively quiet Royal Mail train is seen running (p. 25). In each case, the words on the facing page make no mention of noise; the pictures communicate it all.

References

Primary sources

Bowood, R. and Ayton, R. (illustrator) (1961). *The Story of Railways*. A Ladybird 'Achievements' Book. Loughborough: Wills & Hepworth Ltd.
——— (1963). *The Story of Houses and Homes*. A Ladybird 'Achievements' Book. Loughborough: Wills & Hepworth Ltd.
——— (1964). *The Story of Our Churches and Cathedrals*. A Ladybird 'Achievements' Book. Loughborough: Wills & Hepworth Ltd.
Forbes, J. and Berry, J. (illustrator) (1961). *On the Railways*. 'People at Work'. A Ladybird 'Easy-Reading' Book. Loughborough: Wills & Hepworth Ltd., 1972.
Gagg, M. E. and Wingfield, J. H. (illustrator) (1959). *Going to School*. A Ladybird Learning To Read Book. Loughborough: Wills & Hepworth Ltd.
Havenhand, I. & J. and Berry, J. (illustrator) (1962). *The Policeman*. 'People at Work'. A Ladybird 'Easy-Reading' Book. Loughborough: Wills & Hepworth Ltd.
——— (1965). *The Builder*. 'People at Work'. A Ladybird 'Easy-Reading' Book. Loughborough: Wills & Hepworth Ltd.
——— (1967). *The Road Makers*. 'People at Work'. A Ladybird 'Easy-Reading' Book. Loughborough: Wills & Hepworth Ltd.
——— (1968). *The Car Makers*. 'People at Work'. A Ladybird 'Easy-Reading' Book. Loughborough: Ladybird Books Ltd.
——— (1972). *In a Hotel*. 'People at Work'. A Ladybird 'Easy-Reading' Book. Loughborough: Wills & Hepworth Ltd.
Hazeley, J. A. and Morris, J. P. (various illustrators) (2015) *The Ladybird Book of the Hangover* (Ladybirds for Grown-Ups). London: Penguin Random House.

Southgate, V., Havenhand, J. and Berry, J. (illustrator) (1963). *The Nurse.* 'People at Work'. A Ladybird 'Easy-Reading' Book. Loughborough: Wills & Hepworth Ltd.
Webster, J., Witcomb, G. and Aitchison, M. (illustrators) (1974a). *man and his car.* A Ladybird Leader. Loughborough: Wills & Hepworth Ltd.
Webster, J., Witcomb, G., Aitchison, M. and Hall, R. (illustrators) (1974b). *roads.* A Ladybird Leader. Loughborough: Wills & Hepworth Ltd.
Webster, J., Robinson, B., Aitchison, M. and Thomas, B. P. (illustrators) (1975). *homes.* A Ladybird Leader. Loughborough: Wills & Hepworth Ltd.

Secondary sources

Bader, B. (1976). *American Picturebooks: From Noah's Ark to the Beast Within.* New York: Macmillan.
Boughton, J. (2018). *Municipal Dreams. The Rise and Fall of Council Housing.* London/Brooklyn: Verso.
Buchanan, C. (1963). *Traffic in Towns.* London: H.M. Stationary Office.
Bullock, N. (2002). *Building The Post-War World.* Abingdon: Routledge.
Burchardt, J. (2020). Ladybird landscapes: Or, what to look for in the What to Look For books. *Rural History*, 31, pp. 79–95.
Glendinning, M. and Muthesius, S. (1994). *Tower Block. Modern Public Housing in England, Scotland, Wales and Northern Ireland.* New Haven and London: Yale University Press.
Gold, J. R. (2007). *The Practice of Modernism.* Abingdon: Routledge.
Grindrod, J. (2013). *Concretopia. A Journey Around The Rebuilding Of Postwar Britain.* Brecon: Old Street Publishing.
———.(2015) 'Ladybird Modernism Live' https://dirtymodernscoundrel.blogspot.com/2015/07/ladybird-modernism-live.html
Johnson, L. and Alderson, B. (2014). *The Ladybird Story*, London: The British Library.
Hunt, P. (1991). *Criticism, Theory, & Children's Literature.* Oxford: Blackwell.
Kozlovsky, R. (2013). *The Architectures of Childhood: Children, Modern Architecture and Reconstruction in Postwar England.* Farnham: Ashgate.
Kümmerling-Meibauer, B. and Meibauer, J. (2021). How descriptive picturebooks engaged children in knowledge about coal, oil, and gas. In N. Goga, S. H. Iversen, and A.-S. Teigland (eds), *Verbal and Visual Strategies in Nonfiction Picturebooks.* Oslo: Scandinavian University Press, pp. 189–200.
Moebius, W. (1986). Introduction to picturebook codes. *Word and Image*, 2.2, pp. 141–158.
Nodelman, P. (1990). *Words about Pictures: Narrative Art of Children's Picture Books.* Athens and London: University of Georgia Press.
——— (1999). Decoding the images: How picture books work. In P. Hunt (ed), *Understanding Children's Literature.* Abingdon: Routledge, pp. 128–139.
——— (2004). Picture books and illustrations. In P. Hunt (ed), *International Companion Encyclopedia of Children's Literature.* Abingdon: Routledge, p. 157.
Reynolds, K. (2016). *Left Out: The Forgotten Tradition of Radical Publishing for Children in Britain 1910–1949.* Oxford: Oxford University Press.
Saint, A. (1987). *Towards A Social Architecture. The Role of School Building in Post-War England.* New Haven and London: Yale University Press.
Shulevitz, U. (1996). What is a picture book? Reprinted in S. Egoff, G. Stubbs, R. Ashley and W. Sutton (eds), *Only Connect: Readings on Children's Literature.* Toronto and Oxford: Oxford University Press, pp. 238–241.
Wall, C. (2019). 'It was a totally different approach to building!': Constructing architectural concrete in 1960s London. In J. Gosseye, N. Stead, and D. van der Plaat (eds), *Speaking of Buildings. Oral History in Architectural Research.* Princeton, NJ: Princeton Architectural Press, pp. 50–75.
Zeegen, L. (2015). *Ladybird by Design.* London: Penguin Random House.

3

READING AS BUILDING

Modernist architecture and book space in picturebooks

Honglan Huang

In books about buildings, professional knowledge of architecture is transmitted, far away landmarks are brought near, ephemeral structures are preserved, and future constructions are imagined and discussed. In addition to serving as 'a storehouse of ideas' (Hvattum, 2018, p. 16), books, like buildings, interact with living bodies, leading them through sequences and paths and curate their experience of physical space. Since the early 20th century, architectural books have experimented with the spatial organisation of visual and textual information on the page so as to effectively convey Modernist ideas about built space and transform the turning of pages into virtual movement through the site.[1] Like architectural books, picturebooks for children pay particular attention to generating meaning through non-verbal means. This chapter offers a close reading of three picturebooks: El Lissitzky's *About Two Squares* (1922), David Macaulay's *Unbuilding* (1980), and Fanny Millard's *Upside Down* (2019). Spanning almost a century, they all move beyond using the book simply as a container for architectural representations. The carefully constructed pages not only train the child readers to learn to perceive spatial forms or expand their architectural imagination beyond the conventional, but also turn reading into an exercise of building, whether metaphorically or literally.

In *About Two Squares*, geometric shapes float in space, and their inherently unstable configurations introduce the possibility of movement, showing how architecture can expand beyond the immovable and the monumental. The dynamism of space is not only depicted but also enacted as the reader animates the forms into different views of the same space or consecutive phases of a transformation. In *Unbuilding*, the reader gains a comprehensive understanding of the structure of the modern skyscraper by not only following the narrative of its dismantlement, but also actively connecting text and image, diagrams and perspectival views, design and logistics, throughout the pages of the book. In *Upside Down*, reading becomes building in the literal sense. By embodying two opposing spatial logics within the same book, Fanny Millard invites the reader to experience the Modernist idea of architecture as a set of interrelationships rather than a single object (Croset, 1988, p. 207), therefore opening up new ways of imagining space. While each of these works approach the relationship between book space and architectural space in a different way, together, they

DOI: 10.4324/9781003131755-5

show us how picturebooks can promote ideas about Modernist architecture through the material structure of the book itself.

El Lissitzky's *About Two Squares*: tectonics of the book

El Lissitzky's *About Two Squares* (1922) is one of the earliest avant-garde picturebooks created for children. Conceived during the time when Lissitzky taught at the People's Art School in Vitebsk (1919–1920), *About Two Squares* challenges both the stasis of conventional books and the unity of classical perspective. The book curates a sequence, allowing geometric shapes to 'revolv[e], swi[m], fl[y]' and transform in time (Lissitzky-Küppers, 1980, p. 330), and the page, like the surface of a canvas, becomes a virtual 'building site' for architectural imagination (Lissitzky-Küppers, 1980, p. 329). Lissitzky, who originally trained as an architect, graduated from the Technische Hochschule Darmstadt before the First World War. In 1922, he returned to Germany and published *About Two Squares* with the Scythian Press. In the following years, Lissitzky went on experimenting with typography and page layout in his contribution to two avant-garde architectural magazines, *G* and *ABC* (Tavares, 2016, p. 144) and the printed page continued to offer Lissitzky a means of practicing architecture beyond physical building.[2]

The images of *About Two Squares* are filled with abstract architectural forms, bearing immediate relation to one of his largest bodies of works referred to as the Proun (acronym for 'project for the affirmation of the new' in Russian), a series of paper architecture rendered through painting, drawing, and print. Using axonometric drawing and isometric projection alongside other spatial structures, Lissitzky transformed the plane of the plan from a unified diagrammatic surface into a system of forces where forms interact and transform to generate motion and rhythm. In the first in the series of Proun, *P1*, various rectangular cuboids interlock and intersect at different angles, creating an overall impression of instability and tension. The cluster at the bottom begins with an elongated cuboid. The tilted angle at both of its ends induce one to read the surrounding space as one that recedes backward, but the depth of the field is made ambiguous by a grey plane resting on top whose edges refuse to be in parallel with those of the cuboid underneath. The possibility of any perspectival space is completely shattered as another elongated cuboid rendered in axonometric projection meets the grey plane. The second cluster above seems a repetition of the first one but with variation: the width of the bottom cuboid extends deeper into space, yet the continuity of its three-dimensional extension becomes disturbed by the insert of a thin black rectangle in between the cuboid and the flat plane. It is as if the cuboid has rotated somewhere in the middle and its volume becomes concealed behind a frontal view on the left. The black rectangle initially leads us to read it as a sunken shadowy space between the white plane and the discontinued cuboid, but once we perceive its slightly protruding edge on the right side, the black rectangle becomes a surface floating before the entire structure. In the third cluster, the intersection between surfaces and volumes continue to generate tension and dynamic movement. This time, the thin elongated cuboid cuts through the rectangular prism in the middle to create another ambiguous space. The triangular protrusion created by the intersection therefore oscillates between a continuous surface projecting forward in space and a concave volume. The repetition of the configuration of two cuboids and a plane invites the viewer to see the composition as representing different phases of a continuous movement.

Lissitzky was interested not only in the virtual movement evoked by the arrangement of shapes and forms on paper—in other words, movement produced by means of symbols—but also in the literal production of movement through movement. As Samuel Johnson notices, the printed sheet of *P1* 'is titled on all four sides of its frame', inviting 'the viewer to lay the image flat and circle around it, or to rotate the sheet itself' (Johnson, 2015, p. 52). So the physical book itself also has the capacity to produce movement on multiple levels. The book, according to Lissitzky, is at first a mobile structure, 'a carriage, locomotive and aeroplane for thought' that 'goes to the people and does not stand like a cathedral in one place', directly echoing his own vision for the future of architecture where everything approaches 'the state of floating in air and swinging like a pendulum' (cited in Lissitzky-Küppers, 1980, pp. 365–366).

About Two Squares opens with a cover that presents, at first glance, a clean, diagrammatic surface (Figure 3.1.a). The title is enclosed within a square frame, consisting of letters spelling the word 'Про' (about), an Arabic numeral 2, and a geometric shape of a red square. Upon closer look, we discover that the surface is in fact imbued with two contrasting energies. The numeral 2 and the red square face us frontally, whose differences in colour seem to stretch the space inside the framing square both forward and backward, whereas the two lines of text, one within the frame and one outside the frame, unfold along two oblique axes that are going to 'intersect at a point…which is off the page', evoking virtual movement occurring on a different plane (Bois, 1979, p. 127). As the narrative begins, the red square shrinks in size and tilts towards the right and a black square appears at a spot diagonally opposite to where the red square was on the cover, facing us frontally (Figure 3.1.c).

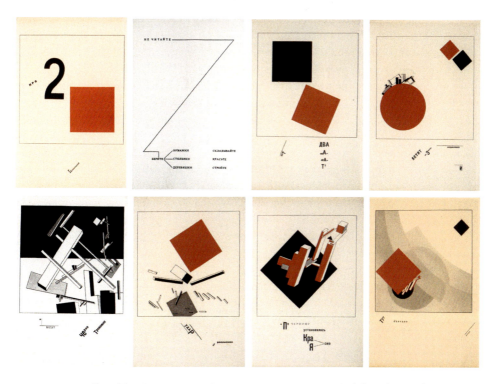

FIGURE 3.1 *About Two Squares: In 6 Constructions, a Suprematist Tale* by El Lissitzky, 1922, Berlin. Public Domain. Image: Courtesy of Fine Arts Library, Harvard University. (Top row, from left to right: 3.1.a, 3.1.b, 3.1.c, 3.1.d; bottom row, from left to right: 3.1.e, 3.1.f, 3.1.g, 3.1.h)

One of the recurrent motifs throughout *About Two Squares* is the diagonal,[3] which in 1920 Lissitzky called 'the most significant expression of the age' (cited in Johnson, 2015, p. 55). In 1924, the diagonal reappeared in Lissitzky's design for the *Lenin Tribune*, a reworking of Chashnik's earlier drawing: compared to its precedent, the diagonal is shortened to function as a structural spine rather than being dramatically displayed as a graphic statement (Johnson, 2017, p. 158). In *About Two Squares*, the diagonal appears in compositions of various kinds. In the second spread (Figure 3.1.d), the horizonless space becomes that of the universe and the two squares are in the midst of their interstellar journey 'to the Earth' (Lissitzky, 1922).[4] Picking up the forward thrust of energy coming from the diagonal axis of the framing square, the two squares charge towards the red circle on the opposite end of the diagonal. Upon the red circle, a cluster of rectangular volumes overlap and interlock, challenging the flatness of the page. To the right, a cuboid is slightly lifted up from the edge of the red circle by two interconnected shapes, and the weight is counterbalanced by a series of rectangular prisms stacked on top. The alternation between black and white allows the forms to be read either two- or three-dimensionally. The malleability of the diagrammatic surface is further put to test when the final rectangular shape stretches out to match the curve of the circle, and a cross-like shape firmly binds it to the floating foundation, translating the curve into a tangent line. This sets the angle at which all the tilted shapes in the cluster are inclined and none of them is in parallel with the diagonal of the framing square. An intersection between the two oblique axes, the diagonal of the square and the tangent line of the circle, within the frame of the page, is therefore inevitable, prefiguring the clashing between the world of the squares and that of the circle.

As the squares continue to fly in our head, we land at the third spread (Figure 3.1.e). The world of the red circle is now so close to us that the curved horizon becomes a straight line and we are seeing it from the perspective of the squares. The tranquillity brought forth by the horizon line stands in contrast with the world of chaos and unrest evoked by clusters of interconnected shapes. The dominant diagonal axis now runs in the opposite direction, suggested by the three parallel bars, each of a different length and width, intersecting a rectangular volume at various depths—one at the front, one right through the middle, and the other behind. One triangular prism connects two of the cuboids as it intersects them perpendicularly at the bottom. The rhythm of the parallels and the stability of the perpendicular, however, are soon disturbed. One of the two shapes that are about to meet the other ends of the cuboids is sloped on one side, skewing the parallel between the two as well as with the nearby rectangular volume. At the bottom-right corner, the perpendicular edges of the framing square intersect with lines that are all slightly tilted, echoing the other subtly slanted shapes shooting upward from the horizon. According to Lissitzky, the horizontal, the perpendicular, the diagonal, and the curve are the 'basic line-directions on the plain surface': when a form is placed 'in alignment with the [perpendicular] edges of the surface, then it has a static effect (rest)' and when it is placed 'diagonally, then it has a dynamic effect (agitation)' (cited in Lissitzky-Küppers, 1980, pp. 355–356). Here, each of the forms is considered not only in relation to the edges of the frame, but also in relation to one another: the parallel is always on the verge of converging and the perpendicular is always on its way to rotate into an oblique angle. The dynamic effect of the diagonal becomes multi-layered, fitting a scene that is all about agitation and restlessness.

At the next turn of the page, in the fourth spread, everything disentangles (Figure 3.1.f). The forms no longer attract each other but scatter across the space. The triangular prism that we recognise from the previous spread is now free-floating, unattached to any other shape.

The contact between the two produces a large white circle that opens up the black plane and a number of geometric shapes and volumes burst through and intersperse. It is worth noticing that Lissitzky here decides to omit any mark that would indicate the plane where the force of impact would be received. Not only does the disappearance of the horizon add momentum to the vertical force of the red square, but it also shifts our attention from space to time. The rectangular form closest to the red square is also spatially the most ambiguous, as if on the verge of transforming into a similarly solid colour shape. As we move downward, time thickens, and the strike of the red square becomes no longer an instant event as its impact reverberates outward. At the bottom–right corner, the repetition of a small rectangular volume introduces a temporal element: with each appearance, the rectangular volume tilts at a different angle, inducing us to read it as a sequence of rotational movements across space.

As we step into the fifth spread (Figure 3.1.g), the once free–floating volumes reconnect with one another to form a new structure. The red square is cut up into different shapes to replace the shaded portions previously in black, creating the impression that assembling and disassembling take place simultaneously. Everything is drawn in axonometric perspective, leading the eye from looking down at the black square ground below, to slowly climbing up the vertical shapes, and then finally following the horizontal forms to arrive at the small cube on the edge, looking out into the distant space beyond. Parallels dominate the new structure at every plane, except at the very top where the two sets of bars create two oblique axes that intersect at the vertex of the square frame. The diagonal axis is again activated: not only are the viewer's eyes invited to move through the structure, but the building itself is now on the verge of moving. The small black triangle helps further to thrust the entire structure forward, by aligning one of its sides in parallel with the slanting bars and pointing one of its vertices in the direction of the cube. The dynamism of this new structure embodies Lissitzky's original interpretation of Gottfried Semper's theory of tectonics (Johnson, 2015, p26). While Semper expands the realm of architecture beyond the stone and the monumental, seeing the weaving of elastic and mobile material as the origin and essence of architectural structure (Semper, 2004, p. 247), Lissitzky pushes the notion of tectonics one step further. Here, the building is not only made of mobile elements but is made moveable by its own dynamic structure. The geometric forms bend and interweave not simply to trick us into a seemingly impossible space, but to create a kinetic force that can power the potential movement of the structure.

In the final spread (Figure 3.1.h), the red square reappears. The mobile structure undergoes a similar kind of rotation as the reader's turning of the page. The volumes are now connected in a new way and shaded in a different direction except for the small cube. This final spread echoes the second spread in its composition around a diagonal axis. The red circle has transformed into a red square. The structure that previously stacks on top of the circle now supports the floating square from underneath. Depth is evoked by the black circle that pulls the structure backward in space. The black square remains roughly at the same place, except it is now floating away into space rather than flying in towards the Earth. The impression of movement is conveyed through the various shades of grey that create the effect of multiple exposures, transforming the paper into a sheet of film transparency. They capture two motions that occur simultaneously. Waves of light ripple across the picture plane, rushing in from the direction of the top right corner where the black square is headed. At the same time, rings of energy radiate from the black circle, creating additional wrinkles on the surface of the picture plane and propelling the black square into another horizonless world beyond the page of the book. The narrative is left beautifully open-ended, as the final word 'further' (дальше) offers multiple ways to make sense of the ending as well as what it might mean to read. First, it can suggest that the narrative goes on and it is now the reader's turn to imagine what may happen. Second, 'further' is an echo of the book's prologue (Figure 3.1.b) which begins with an explicit command 'Do not read'. Instead of simply consuming what is printed on each page, the reader is asked to 'take paper/columns/blocks' and to 'fold/color/ build'. Reading is not the opposite of building, but a rehearsal for production in real space. *About Two Squares* therefore inherits not only the architectural thinking that underlies Lissitzky's Proun works but also the dream of the creative act as a collective activity: the book ends so that the readers can 'ste[p] out into life itself and build its forms' (Johnson, 2015, p. 36). As Yve-Alain Bois observes, while the book is printed only on one side, evoking the filmic genre of flip book in which pages are rapidly leafed through for images to come alive, it exposes the discontinuity between the images rather than drawing the readers into 'the optical illusion of cinematic continuity' (Bois, 1979, p. 119), which flip books invoke. Instead, pages are transformed by their encounter with one another, and reading becomes an active process, like building, in which pieces are assembled and connected to form a dynamic whole.

David Macaulay's *Unbuilding*: constructing the double-page spread

Printed as a standard codex, *Unbuilding* is one of many picturebooks that David Macaulay has written on architecture and design. In it, the Empire State Building, a landmark piece of modern architecture, becomes fictionally disassembled in order to be re-erected in the Arabian desert, a dramatic process that recalls Domenico Fontana's narration of the magical move of the Vatican obelisk, documented with both text and illustrated plates in the 1590 book *Della transportatione dell'obelisco Vaticano*. The focus of *Unbuilding*, however, lies not in the transportation of the skyscraper but in its dismantlement. The fictional process of taking the building apart not only sheds light onto the internal structures of a skyscraper, but also helps the reader understand how the building was put together in the first place. To document the process of 'unbuilding' in full detail, the picturebook presents itself as a montage of black and white illustrations of various types, ranging from annotated diagrams, informational sketches, composite images, to drawings resembling photographic shots. These different images offer the reader various lenses to examine architectural form, turning reading into an exercise of seeing and architectural thinking.

The single-sided pages in Lissitzky's *About Two Squares*, as we have seen, create tension between continuity and discontinuity. Each turn of the page allows the images to overlap in our mind to accumulate into a sequence, yet it also draws our attention to the gaps in between, as the images are literally separate sheets of paper. David Macaulay's *Unbuilding* (1980), like Lissitzky's *About Two Squares*, focuses its effort on embodying architectural thinking through the manipulation of the page layout, generating sequences and juxtapositions that activate the reader's perception of space, but it does so through expanding the unit of the narrative from the single page to the entire double spread. In this sense, *Unbuilding* follows the lineage of architecture photo books produced by Modernist artists in the early 20th century where every double spread was conceived as a design unit.

The double-page spread has long been a vehicle for conveying architectural ideas. It offers the possibility of a continuous space within the discontinuous structure of the codex and presents a mirroring symmetrical space which lends itself well to the visual language of montage and juxtaposition.[5] The contrasting power of the double-page spread reached its height in Le Corbusier's unfinished book *France ou Allemagne* (*France or Germany*, 1915–1916), which compares the two countries 'page against page, object against object, date against date' (Tavares, 2016, pp. 164–165) to demonstrate the superiority of one over the other (Brooks, 1997, p. 410). He went on to take the form further in the famous book *Vers une architecture* (*Towards a New Architecture*, 1923), which shows photographs of ancient Greek temples paired with images of contemporary automobiles. As one moves from the left to the right side, one can trace how standardised structures in both temples and cars undergo the process of further selection and perfection. At the same time, the images of the automobiles themselves evoke speed and movement, echoing the text which describes the race between different designs towards perfection and imbuing the Greek temples above them with a sense of immediacy and urgency.

Inspired by *Vers un architecture*, Sigfried Giedion pushed the double-page spread composition to greater complexity in his second book on modern architecture, *Befreites Wohnen* (*Liberated Dwelling*, 1929). In the initial pages of text, aspects of contemporary life described on the left-hand pages are juxtaposed against those same aspects in the past on the right-hand pages (Tavares, 2016, p. 81). The following 86 images take the double-page spread composition to a new level: the position of the images on the page and the order in which they are placed connect the spreads into 'a complex web of materials and meanings' (Tavares 2016, p. 87). The images on the left-hand side pick up the subject or the theme developed on the right-hand side of the previous page, while spinning it into related but different topics. In other words, not only are the even and odd sides of the spread in dialogue with one another, but the spreads also work together to flow as a series, moving the readers' eyes up and down, left and right, in and out of the architectural spaces presented on the pages.

Macaulay's *Unbuilding* shares many similarities with architectural books like *Befreites Wohnen*, from the details in the layout to the vision of reading as a visceral experience of moving through space. In both cases, the spreads connect with one another to string interrelated spaces into a series of views, leading the reader's eyes from page to page as if from one space to another. All of the full-page illustrations in *Unbuilding* bleed to the edges without blank margins surrounding them, a layout option that now commonly appears in magazines and on book covers, but was first extensively used in *Befreites Wohnen* to gain page area and to dramatise the tension in diagonal compositions (Tavares, 2016, p. 85). Like *Befreites Wohnen*, the picturebook also places technical drawings and photograph-like illustrations side by side to generate meaningful comparisons, showing the building in different stages of its construction and from multiple angles, activating the reader's perception of structure and form. Moreover, in both *Befreites Wohnen* and *Unbuilding*, the orientation of the page shifts between the horizontal and the vertical from time to time, guiding the reader to rotate the book physically to enact movement in space, showing that even bound pages can work together to generate motion (not unlike the loose leaf print of Lissitzky's Proun 1). The dynamic layout allows the book to not only generate its own narrative but also to direct its own physical performance.

In Macaulay's *Unbuilding*, the double-page spread often not only divides itself into two juxtaposing units but also operates as a continuous visual space, allowing one single image to occupy both facing sides. The book begins with a prologue (pp. 2–3), showing a bird's eye view of the building from above the clouds, followed by a worm's eye view of the skyscraper from the level of the street (pp. 6–7), and sandwiched in between, a double-page spread of two parallel diagrams (pp. 4–5), one highlighting the exterior shape of the building and the

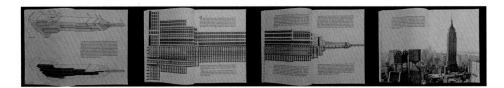

FIGURE 3.2 *Unbuilding* by David Macaulay, p. 4–5, 10–11, 12–13, 14–15, reproduced by permission of the author from *Unbuilding* published by Houghton Mifflin Harcourt, 1980.

other mapping the position of elevators inside. The text, placed in between, binds the two diagrams together, revealing the shape and the height of the building as interrelated: both are determined as much by the external regulation of the zoning laws as by the building's internal structural needs. It is as if the text invites us to stitch together the two diagrams in our mind's eye, searching for interconnections between the two aspects of the building and thinking through the architectural process that involves balancing between form and function.

After the title page, the visual narrative resumes with two continuous double-page spreads (pp. 10–13), offering a simultaneous view of both the section and the elevation of the Empire State Building. The two previously parallel diagrams now seem to converge into one composite image: the building becomes flattened and the scale is enlarged to include more details. To emphasise the verticality of the structure, Macaulay rotates the skyscraper sideways so that the entire building extends horizontally across the space of two double spreads. The fact that the skyscraper cannot be grasped within a single spread turns the reader into a pedestrian looking upwards at a structure exceeding human scale. The need to turn the page in order to scroll through the entire building reproduces the experience of such discontinuous perception. The book thus calls attention to itself as an architectural space like the building it describes. At another turn of the page, we land at the end of our first visual sequence (pp. 14–15): two-dimensional diagram gives way to perspectival drawing in light and shade, the building resumes its usual vertical position, gravity returns, and the surrounding urban landscape suddenly emerges out of the empty white spaces. The horizontality of the composition contrasts with the earlier emphasis on verticality. The vanishing point is placed at the very centre of the spread, creating a moment of stillness and the shifts in perspectives and forms come to a halt. This is our final chance to see the Empire State Building in its entirety.

The second visual sequence is about the planning of the procedures for 'unbuilding.' At the next opening of the page (pp. 16–17), we switch from the building's outer appearance to its structural inner workings. The composition of the page too undergoes transformation. The two sides of the spread, no longer treated as a continuous visual whole, become divided into two separate units. The left side is about height, focusing on the foundation of the building below the largest columns that hold the whole building up. The right side is about shape, showing the structural frame that consists of interconnected spandrels and beams and two other main parts of the building, the concrete floors, and the exterior walls. Yet the dotted lines that bleed into the top edge on the left-hand side suggest the possibility of continuity beyond the page. As we turn from left to right, our eyes move up and down across the spread, mentally connecting the underground to the above ground, the foundation to the steel frame of columns and beams.

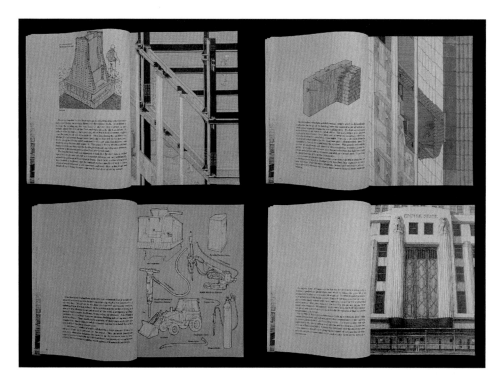

FIGURE 3.3 *Unbuilding* by David Macaulay, p. 16–23, reproduced by permission of the author from *Unbuilding* published by Houghton Mifflin Harcourt, 1980.

As we move onto the next spread (pp. 18–19), we are introduced to the final most 'distinguishing feature' of the building apart from its height and shape: the outer skin (Macaulay, 1980, p. 16). The layout remains more or less the same, yet the energy of the spread transforms from a vertical stretch into a horizontal pull. On the right, the cast aluminium panel now covers almost the entire façade; the steel skeleton is no longer exposed but is dressed with plaster, masonry wall, limestone, and glass. A wired telephone lies on the concrete floor, hinting at the presence of the underfloor ducts that were visible in the previous spread. Both the telephone and the unfolded newspaper nearby echo the standing technician by the window, turning the diagrammatic drawing into an active scenario. On the right, a removed part of the exterior limestone layer replaces the foundation underground to hover above the text. In stillness, the two sides of the page seem to offer two contrasting views on the composition of the exterior wall: one seamless and smooth, the other rough in texture and exposing the position of joints and the means of attachment. But if we remind ourselves that the double spread is a moveable structure, one that reveals itself through the movement of the reader's hand turning the page from right to left, we are then able to see the removed block on the left and the partially dismantled section of the building on the right as two sides of the same action. In this case, the act of turning the page not only pulls the upcoming spread into our view but also enacts the process of peeling away the outer skin from the building. By inviting the readers to virtually participate in the planning process of 'unbuilding' and to discover the building as composed of interconnected units and layers through their very own hands, the book draws our attention to the relationship between surface and structure, parts and whole.

In the third visual sequence, we move from conceptual plans to the logistics of 'unbuilding' at the site. Tools and materials are brought in and different groups of technicians arrive to take part in different procedures of the 'unbuilding' process (pp. 20–21), from breaking up the interior, smashing the concrete and masonry, cutting and removing all the steel, to setting up scaffoldings to enclose the entire building, and scheduling the visits of trucks to haul the rubble and steel away from the site (Macaulay, 1980, p. 20). While the text on the left lists the various activities that go on simultaneously, the illustration on the right offers an isolated view of some of the 'smaller equipment' that 'had to be gathered for the project' (Macaulay, 1980, p. 20). The composition is a shift from the previous two spreads where the anatomy of the building was displayed alongside interacting human bodies and set in a unified perspective. Here, the scale is in constant fluctuation, the operators of the machines are absent, and the instruments are lifted out of their immediate context to be displayed against the abstract grey background. Yet the page is still active.[6] The instruments, though isolated, are not completely deprived of life: the hoses and the tubes are lifted against gravity, ready to be assembled in the reader's mind.

The diagrammatic drawing of equipment and tools is followed by a perspectival view (pp. 22–23) showing the front door of the Empire State building surrounded by 'a sidewalk shed' that protects the 'passers-by from possible falling debris' (Macaulay, 1980, p. 22). In the next spread (pp. 24–25), our view zooms out and moves upwards to follow the assembly of scaffolding above the shed which 'make[s] it possible to work from the outside of the building' (Macaulay, 1980, p. 24).

FIGURE 3.4 *Unbuilding* by David Macaulay, pp. 24–31, reproduced by permission of the author from *Unbuilding* published by Houghton Mifflin Harcourt, 1980.

The composition shifts from the juxtaposition between text and image to that between close-up and long shot. The drawing on the left zooms in on what constitutes the dense crisscrossing lines on the right. The contrast in scale between the two sides of the spread encourages the reader to seek connections between the two and to think of structure as possibly an extensive repetition of a single small unit rather than the opposite of detail.

The following spread surprises us (pp. 26–27); our field of vision expands as we are invited to look down at the scaffolding structure from an oblique angle. The once parallel lines suddenly converge towards the centre of the spread, collapsing the previously monumental and vertically extending structure into a radiating pattern of rhythmic alternation between light and shade. As an individual image, this spread recalls architectural photographs captured by Alexander Rodchenko, in which the artist explores the building from non-conventional points of view and makes 'use of light to intensify relationships between forms' (Lodder, 2014, p. 2). As one unit within a visual sequence, the spread brings to mind the photograph of the Eiffel Tower in *Befreites Wohnen*, where the light iron structure was captured from 'a diagonal angle that stresses the dynamism of its spiral staircase plunging over Haussmann's Paris' in contrast with the frontal view of 'a monumental façade' on the preceding page (Tavares, 2016, p. 87). Here, the plunging view creates a similar turning point in the narrative, mediating the transition from visible exterior to hidden internal structures and shifting the direction of our gaze from rising upward to looking down.

The next spread (pp. 28–29) reverts to the earlier composition of division into two juxtaposing units. This time, however, the weight of the full-page illustration is shifted to the left. The displacement offers a visceral experience of crossing from the exterior to the interior, as the text turns our attention from 'the scaffolding rising around the building' to the construction of the wooden chute taking place inside the building for the transportation of the rubble (Macaulay, 1980, p. 29). On the left is a cross-section of the internal structure of the building represented through a grid-like surface. The diagram invites the reader to trace the downward travel of the rubble along the path of the chute marked by a single white line. On the right, a three-dimensional sketch presents the structure of the transfer box, a wooden container that serves to connect different sections of the chute. Several of its wooden panels are removed to give us an inside view of the sloped floor installed between the two openings of the box, exhibiting the mechanism through which the flow of the rubble down the chute is directed and regulated. The light grey strips extending from the two openings of the transfer box help the readers to map the three-dimensional detail back onto the flattened overview of the chute on the other side of the spread. By providing just enough information for the readers to imagine the entire path of the chute in three dimensions and to animate every movement of the rubble falling down the chute, the spread exploits the expressive possibilities of the surface to create spatiality and motion.

The diagrammatic and the perspectival again switch place in the next spread (pp. 30–31). On the left page, a scene of live action shows the installation of pipelines to carry oxygen and other air supply from the outside to the inside of the building. The vertically oriented image is met by a drawing of the mooring mast 'completely enclosed in scaffolding' (Macaulay 1980, p. 31) that splits the right-side page horizontally in the middle. The dark enclosed interior stands in contrast with the tip of the building in open air. The block of text in the upper half concludes the second visual sequence which documents the various preliminary preparations happening both inside and outside the building. At the same time, the piercing mast functions almost like a page divider, marking the beginning of a new visual sequence that will focus on its disassembly. By no longer uniting the ending of a sequence with the turning of the page, Macaulay draws our attention to the tension between the structure of the book and the structure of the visual narrative it carries.

We have now come to the end of our first 'architectural promenade' that begins at the bottom of the building and concludes with a glimpse of the skyscraper's highest tip. This lengthy description of these opening sequences shows how the double-page spread structures our experience of the book, as it spins a web of meaning that continuously shifts and transforms at every page turn. Like in *Befreites Wohnen*, the full impact of the narrative cannot be grasped by focusing on the images, text, or page layout alone (Tavares, 2016, p. 87). The rest of the book goes on with the removal of the mast, the dismantling of the outer skin, the disassembly of the structural skeleton, the clearing of the site, and the final development of a new park, where the mooring mast is re-erected as a memorial for the building. While the Empire State is not a modernist building in the strict sense, the story of its deconstruction unfolds through gesturing towards various ideas central to modernist thinking about architecture. The inclusion of detailed technical drawings of air compressors and oxypropane torches remind us that architecture is more than a conceptual arrangement of form and space: technologies equally have the power to determine how buildings are 'unmade' and made. Moreover, the book opens up multiple ways for the readers to think about the concept of structure: the part of a building that allows it to stand up, systems of interconnection, the composition and arrangement of parts that give cause for the perception of structure, and finally, the means by which things become intelligible (Forty, 2000, p. 283). This last idea about structure is embodied by the book itself. The rhythmic rotation, expansion, and contraction of the picture plane generate meaningful sequences, and the juxtaposition between different kinds of images encourages the reader to draw immaterial links that activate the pages, connecting parts to whole, light to dark, interior to exterior, conception to construction, diagrammatic to perspectival, space to time.

Fanny Millard's *Basic Space* and *Upside Down*: the art of the fold

In *The Anatomy of the Architectural Book*, André Tavares describes the book as 'a fixed sequence of bound pages', which, unlike 'the leaves of a portfolio', cannot be easily disassembled and reassembled (Tavares, 2016, p. 237). This presents both limitations and possibilities to the translation of built forms onto the surface of printed pages. While binding eliminates the flexibility in the ordering of pages, making it difficult to perceive different spatial locations simultaneously, the sequential structure is perfectly adapted to showcase the transformation of architectural forms in time. This includes leading the reader 'step by step' through an architectural space, documenting the construction of a building 'brick upon brick' or bringing a spatial structure 'closer-and-closer still' into view (Tavares, 2016, p. 239). In Lissitzky's *About Two Square*, the page-by-page sequence not only leads us 'step by step' through the infinite space of the universe, but also shows us 'brick upon brick' the construction of a new world upon Earth. In *Unbuilding*, the 'brick upon brick' logic turns into a narrative of 'floor by floor' disassembly, and not only does the scale shift, but the picture plane becomes constantly flattened and inflated, divided and reunited, rotated and reoriented. Curating a fixed sequence is, however, only one of the organisational structures that the book offers, even though it is the one most frequently chosen. The book can also be a mutable form as Fanny Millard's picturebooks remind us, blurring the boundary between surface and volume, interior and exterior, beginning and ending, and containing within its preconceived structure multiple possibilities for variations and transformations.

In all of Fanny Millard's picturebooks, space is not only imagined but also physically constructed. Pages do not unfold only in one direction, but both forward and backward, forming provisional structures and bringing opposing spatial logics into conversation with one another. Rather than thinking about reproducing architecture in books or how to recreate the spatial experience of three-dimensional forms through the orchestration of the page, Fanny Millard's picturebooks focus on a different set of questions: How does our physical interaction with the book form open up new ways of architectural thinking? How does spatial knowledge transmit through both tactile and visual perception? What is the relationship between embodied experience of space and its virtual perception or imagination? In this sense, the book becomes a built form in its own right and reading becomes, as Lissitzky envisons, a literal form of building.

Working at the intersection between architecture and bookmaking, Fanny Millard explores the notion of space and especially how it is embodied through both built forms and printed pages. She founded the association of EXTRA éditeur d'espace with a group of architects in 2014. The aim was to raise public interest in the questions of space and architecture through publications and workshops. In 2015, their first book *Basic Space* was published. While both *About Two Squares* and *Unbuilding* choose the conventional codex as means to explore the transformation of spatial forms through sequential progressions, *Basic Space* makes use of the flexibility of the accordion format to transform the book itself into an ever-changing structure. *Basic Space* is made of an 'L' shaped strip of cardstock paper and comes in both illustrated and blank versions.

The art of building condenses into the art of folding. Each leg of the 'L' shape can be folded into a cube or a triangular prism. Combinations multiply when the entire strip shifts and reconfigures as a whole. Each time a new book is added to the mixture, more possibilities open up for creating even more complex forms.

According to Fanny Millard, the book originated from the observation that space emerges not only from the configuration of solid volumes but also the void between them (Millard, 2015 b). The folding of the accordion strip therefore always involves both enclosing and opening up space at the same time and building becomes a dialectic process that draws our attention to both what is present and what is absent. In the illustrated version, the strip is printed in red and white on both sides: one predominantly in red and the other predominantly in white. Each page of the strip contains a geometric pattern.

When some of the pages are flipped, not only do the negative and positive spaces switch place, the red becomes the white and the white becomes the red, but the composition also flips horizontally or vertically, the back mirrors the front and the front mirrors the back. The square page at the centre of the 'L' strip, for example, has on the red side, one white square aligned with the bottom corner, and on the other white side, one red square positioned at

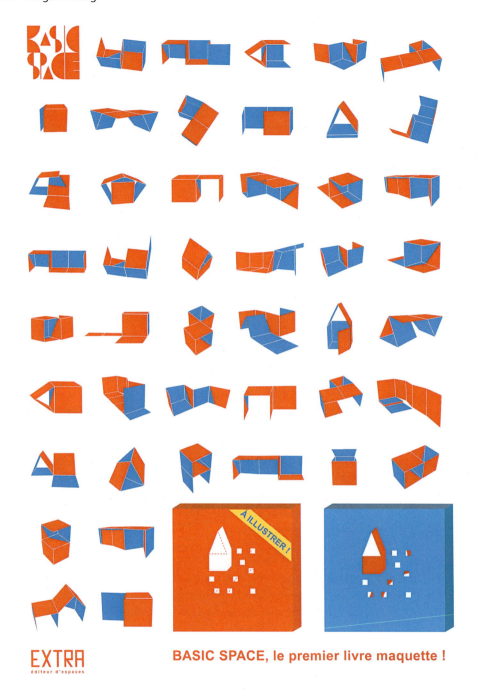

FIGURE 3.5 Poster for *Basic Space* by Fanny Millard © EXTRA Fanny Millard 2021.

FIGURE 3.6 *Basic Space* by Fanny Millard © EXTRA Fanny Millard 2021. (Multiple illustrated and blank versions are assembled here together to create a spatial form.)

the top corner. This choice of printing creates an interplay between the front and the back of the page: the two sides of the page are not simply image bearing units but interrelated parts of the same structure. The reversibility between the positive and the negative on the page echoes the interchangeability between the solid and the void in the dimensional space as well as the invertibility between the inside and the outside, up and down.

Each geometric pattern, in fact, evokes a primary architectural component: windows, stairs, doors, roofs. As the strip of paper changes shape, the roof becomes the floor and the windows become doors, the rows of semi-circles in the geometric pattern transform from tiles on the roof to decoration of the façade, and the diagonal line of squares switches from a flight of stairs to the surface of the floor. Sometimes, the geometric pattern spills from one page into another: what appears to be a single elongated window on one side multiplies into a sequence on the next side to evoke a fence-like structure and what seems like an extra bit of the floor pattern continues onto the neighbouring vertical surface as stairs. The book is therefore not only aware of the double-sidedness of its surfaces but also the continuity of its structure. The squares, the lines, and the semi-circles invite us to experience them as both visual shapes in space and dynamic forms in time. Every turn of the corner presents a possibility for transformation and every transformation is effected by our movement through space in time.

In 2017, Fanny Millard was invited by the association Les Trois Ourses for an artist residency, during which she continued to research ways to embody spatial notions through the physical structure of the book and focused specifically on the relationship between language and space. The result is a series of six books titled *Upside Down* published by EXTRA in 2019, each of which explores an elementary spatial notion like inside and outside, front and back, horizontal and vertical, small and big, up and down, around and in the centre.

FIGURE 3.7 *Upside Down* by Fanny Millard © EXTRA Fanny Millard 2021.

In *Basic Space*, the colour reversal between the opposite sides of the page generates two contrasting spatial logics that stretch the solid surface of the page into a dynamic three-dimensional space. *Upside Down* takes this a step further by expanding the field of tension from the opposite sides of the same page to the entire structure of the book. The book *petit small grand big*, for example, is on one side a large blue square sheet with the word 'grand big' (big) in yellow. On the other side, a small blue square is nested at the centre of a large yellow square sheet. The sheet is cut halfway across the square on one side, allowing it to be folded either inwardly or outwardly to form a three-dimensional shape. The 'big' blue square therefore can either sink inward or push outward (Millard, 2019, video 0:20). Similarly, the 'small' blue square can form either the inside or the outside of half of a cube (Millard, 2019, video 0:19). The moveable structure of this single-sheet book thus allows the expansion and contraction in size to take place in tandem with the flattening and the inflation of space. More than stretching the picture plane simultaneously forward and backward, the reversal of colour also dramatises the tension between real and implied space.

Similarly, in the book about 'en haut' (up) and 'en bas' (down), a triangular flap is added to a simple folded sheet to hold the two opposing spatial logics in one space. This allows the turning of the flap to physically enact a change in direction. The colour reversal further adds to the momentum of the action. The blue, darker in tone, sinks downward and the yellow, lighter and brighter, rises upward. At the same time, the book can be folded into a 'Y' shaped structure, yellow on one side and blue on the other. The triangular page is no longer the only moveable part of the book. It becomes the head of the structure and the two squares its flapping wings, propelling the shape to move up and down freely in the reader's space (Millard, 2019, video 0:36) following the direction pointed by the triangle. As Pierre-Alain Croset puts it, an architect's work is 'incomplete in the sense that it is not a simple object, but rather a structure of relationships connecting to the world of the inhabitant' (Croset, 1988, p. 207). Here, the book makes use of the versatility of the fold to show us that the 'up' and the 'down' exist in relationship to one another: these seemingly contrary forces can not only inhabit the same page, but also give rise to each other to generate movement in space. The book embodies their interconnectedness, scripting the turning of the page as the revelatory moment of their mutual embeddedness. At the same time, the book leaves it open for the readers to create their own relationship with the page and the space around them.

The series of *Upside Down* also contains one book in the codex format which focuses on the relationship between what is around ('autour') and what is at the centre ('au centre'). Rather than using the codex form to curate a sequence, Millard draws our attention to the spatial energy released by the act of unfolding and the potential of the codex to evoke a virtual cylindrical volume out of its joined but disparate surfaces. Millard is not the first one to notice the possibility of opening up a book 360 degrees to create a spatial structure. In the late 19th century, a specific form of panorama books known as the star book, the carousel book, or the circular peep show, became popular. The book is true to its name as it looks like a star from the top, and reading it involves turning the circular shape around which resembles the experience of watching an ever-revolving carousel. Initially conceived as a variation in the tradition of toy theatre publication, the book usually consists of multiple layers of paper engineering so that each section becomes a pop-up scene when fully opened. The book can therefore either be used as a revolving stage to accompany the reading out loud of the story or 'left tied open as a nursery decoration' (McGrath, 2002, p. 35). The idea of the book as an expandable circular structure undergoes further transformation in Yusuke Oono's series of '360°BOOK', first launched in 2015 in co-operation with the publisher Seigensha. Each 360°BOOK is structurally no different from a standard codex, except that each of the pages is cut out to create shapes in silhouette. Rather than thinking of each opening as a separate scene, the Japanese designer and architect lets the negative spaces run through the entire 360-degree circle, connecting each two-dimensional slice to form one three-dimensional world. Thus, as the reader rotates the fully opened book, each page oscillates between evoking an illusion of spatial depth and representing a passing moment in time. In Fanny Millard's version, the structure of the book is further simplified to focus on the tensions and relationships within its form rather than its representational possibilities. No page is cut out, and the visual contrast between the complementary colours of blue and yellow replaces the literal interplay between the negative and the positive spaces. Volume is no longer created by physically piercing through multiple layers but by virtually connecting surfaces of the same colour. The unfolding of the book is more than a single leap from the two-dimensional into the three-dimensional world, but a double event where the enclosure and expansion of space take place simultaneously.

At the surface of the pages, Millard's *Upside Down* brings to mind the Suprematist space created by Lissitzky, where solid colours and basic geometric shapes generate tension and invite multiple ways of realising them in space. At the level of structure, Millard's books echo *Unbuilding*, as each turn of the page shifts the angle of perception and effects movement in imagined space. Millard's books, however, also differ from the previous two, as the idea of dynamic space is not only imagined but also enacted. Each of the books originates from a careful reading and understanding of the book as an architectural structure in itself. Rather than reproducing or recreating the spatial experience of another building, the book draws our attention to its own structural possibilities and limitations. A careful reading of how pages connect and interact leads to creative ways of manipulating the book to form mobile, moveable structures. The book's invitation to build and to create highlights the lived experience of space, a topic essential to modernist thinking of architecture (Croset, 1988, p.

202). By sensing how spatial relationships form and transform through both the eyes and the fingers, the child readers learn not only to think of space as a network of changing, interdependent forces, a skill transferable to future perception and conception of real buildings, but more importantly that architecture itself is about the transformation of an embodied experience. For El Lissitzky, David Macaulay, and Fanny Millard, architectural space is both represented and embodied through books. Reading, therefore, involves actively animating the surfaces of the page and the book structure to construct virtual and physical spaces and to experience them as transformations in time.

Notes

1 Some of the notable designers of architectural books in the early 20th century include El Lissitzky (1890–1941), who contributed to the graphic design of seminal international architecture magazines like *G* and *ABC* and expressed architectural thoughts through these typographical projects. László Moholy-Nagy (1895–1946), like Lissitzky, explored the spatial configuration of the page in his design of the *Bauhausbücher*, using bold lines, asymmetrical compositions and mixing text, image and graphic signs to break up the surface for visual impact. Le Corbusier's (1887–1965) *Vers une architecture* (1923) was an influential book not only for the polemic nature of its contents but also for the effectiveness of its form. Though the book was conceived for large print runs, the page layout was still carefully planned so that text and image work together to draw readers into the arguments about architectural theory. For more on this topic, see André Tavares, *The Anatomy of the Architectural Book*.
2 Lissitzky's sole built construction is the printing plant of Ogonyok magazine, co-designed with Barshch Mikhail Osipovich; the building was completed in 1932. Earlier in 1924, Lissitzky also submitted his entry in the tradition of paper architecture with the design of Wolkenbügel.
3 The diagonal appeared in several architectural designs produced later in the same year: in Vladimir Tatlin's *Monument to the Third International*, the functional diagonal core of the girder is concealed underneath a spiral facade, but in Ilya Chashnik's *Project for a Tribune for a Smolensk Square*, the diagonal is visible, freestanding, dramatically unaided, and exposed (Johnson, 2017, p. 159).
4 The text in Russian (Летят на земля издалека) can be translated into English as '[They] fly to the earth from far away'.
5 Heinrich Wölfflin popularised the practice of placing contrasting images on the facing pages through his influential book *Kunstgeschichtliche Grundbegriffe* (1915) whose double-page spread was a translation of the double projection of lantern slides through which two images can be viewed simultaneously, side by side. Spinning a historicist argument using pictorial comparison emerged as early as in Augustus Pugin's book *Contrasts* (1836). The English architect paired the images to present an elementary opposition between 'good' and 'bad', contrasting 'the noble edifices of the middle ages' (Pugin, 1836, p. 1) with the 'degeneracy' of the pagan styles of his time (Pugin, 1836, p. 53). The book established 'a mode of argument' for later authors; for more information, see Stierli (2018, p. 83).
6 In this way, the spread calls to mind the two complementary forms of visual representation in Diderot's *Encyclopédie*, best exemplified by the plates dedicated to the tiles at the end of the section on architecture in the first volume (Tavares, 2016, p. 294), where the object is shown both in its frozen, paradigmatic state and as a metamorphic substance that undergoes a series of actions and processes of making.

References

Primary sources

Corbusier, Le. (1923). *Vers une Architecture*. Paris: Éditions Crès.
Fontana, Domenico. (1590). *Della Trasportatione Dell'obelisco Vaticano et Delle Fabriche di Nostro Signore Papa Sisto V.* Rome: Appresso Domenico Basa.
Giedion, Sigfried. (1929). *Befreites Wohnen*. Zürich: Orell Füssli Verlag.

Lissitzky, El. (1922). *Pro dva Kvadrata: Suprematicheskii Skaz v 6-ti Postroikakh*. Berlin: Skify.

———— (2014). *About Two Squares*. London: Tate Publishing.

Macaulay, David. (1980). *Unbuilding*. New York: Houghton Mifflin Harcourt.

Millard, Fanny. (2015a). *Basic Space*. Bordeaux: EXTRA éditeur d'espace. (Link to the video showing the possible ways of reading the book. https://youtu.be/4_0au-4Jb_M)

———— (2015b). *Basic Space: The First Book Marquette to Explore Architecture!*. Ululue. Accessed August 31, 2021. https://www.ulule.com/basic-space/

———— (2019). *Upside Down*. Bordeaux: EXTRA éditeur d'espace. (Link to the video. https://associationextra.fr/?p=1559)

Pugin, Augustus. (1836). *Contrasts: Or, a Parallel between the Noble Edifices of the Middle Ages, and Similar Buildings of the Present Day*. London: Charles Dolman.

Wölfflin, Heinrich. (1915). *Kunstgeschichtliche Grundbegriffe: Das Problem der Stilentwickelung in der neueren Kunst*. München: F. Bruckmann A.-G.

Secondary sources

Bois, Yve-Alain. (1979). 'El Lissitzky: Reading Lessons.' *October: Essays in Honor of Jay Leyda*, 11(Winter), pp. 113–128.

Brooks, Harold Allen. (1997). *Le Corbusier's Formative Years: Charles-Edouard Jeanneret at La Chaux-de-Fonds*. Chicago: University of Chicago Press.

Croset, Pierre-Alain. (1988). 'The Narration of Architecture.' In J. Ockman and B. Colomina (eds), *Architectureproduction*. New York: Princeton Architectural Press, pp. 201–211.

Forty, Adrian. (2000). *Words and Buildings*. New York: Thames & Hudson.

Hvattum, Mari, and Anne Hultzsch. (2018). *The Printed and the Built: Architecture, Print Culture, and Public Debate in the Nineteenth Century*. New York: Bloomsbury Visual Arts.

Johnson, Samuel. (2015). *"The Architecture of the Book": El Lissitzky's Works on Paper, 1919–1937*. PhD diss., Harvard University.

———— (2017). 'El Lissitzky's Other Wolkenbügel: Reconstructing an Abandoned Architectural Project.' *The Art Bulletin*, 99(3), pp. 147–169.

Kinchin, Juliet, Aidan O'Connor, and Tanya Harrod. (2012). *Century of the Child: Growing by Design 1900–2000*. New York: Museum of Modern Art.

Lissitzky-Küppers, Sophie, and Herbert Read. (1980). *El Lissitzky: Life, Letters, Texts*. London: Thames and Hudson.

Lodder, Christina. (2014). 'Revolutionary Photography.' In M. Abbaspour, L.A. Daffner, and M.M. Hambourg (eds), *Object: Photo. Modern Photographs: The Thomas Walther Collection 1909–1949. An Online Project of The Museum of Modern Art*. New York: The Museum of Modern Art. https://www.moma.org/interactives/objectphoto/assets/essays/Lodder.pdf

McGrath, Leslie A. (2002). *This Magical Book: Movable Books for Children, 1771–2001*. Toronto: Toronto Public Library.

Semper, Gottfried. (2004). *Style in the Technical and Tectonic Arts; or, Practical Aesthetics*. Los Angeles: Getty Research Institute.

Stierli, Martino. (2018). *Montage and the Metropolis*. New Haven: Yale University Press.

Tavares, André. (2016). *The Anatomy of the Architectural Book*. Zurich: Lars Müller Publishers.

4

REPRESENTATIONS OF MODERN ARCHITECTURE AND URBANISM IN COLOMBIAN CHILDREN'S LITERATURE FROM THE MID-20TH CENTURY ONWARDS

Carolina Rodríguez, Roberto Londoño and Antonio Manrique

Introduction

Social and political transformation processes during the 20th century in Colombia were accompanied by imaginaries of the modern city and its ideal architecture, which were formed against a backdrop of external influences and co-existing quests for national identity. This chapter studies the representations of these imaginaries in children's illustrated books across four distinctive periods and reviews the events, narratives, and adaptations that affected their emergence, development, demise, and legacy. It inquires when and how modernist ideals appeared in children's literature from the perspective of local authors, illustrators, and editors. Using principles of semiotics, a representative sample of seven illustrations is analysed, considering the signs used by their authors to convey their intended messages and how the illustrations and signs are interpreted by children. The results show that illustrations not only communicate or suggest imaginaries but also help to sculpt them, mingling fiction with reality. Their suggestive power can extend to the construction of utopias and dystopias regarding our connection with the built environment.

The history of illustrated children's books in Colombia is connected to various events and technological advancements that triggered the development of local printing and introduced modern ideology. Modernity is here assumed to be an historical period of profound change in Western society, instilled in this country through progressive transformations in the arts, science, politics, and ways of life. This history has been little studied, especially regarding the imaginaries represented within children's book illustrations. This chapter focuses on the effect of modernity on the construction of cities and architecture's imaginaries and their translations into children's literature. Particular attention is paid to representations of the modern movement, which cover a wide spectrum of production linked to the so-called international style, and vernacular constructions influenced by its language and techniques.

Imaginaries generally correspond to symbolic fabrications of what we observe, what frightens us, or what we wish existed (Lindón, 2007). Therefore, they refer to idealised images that may diverge from those empirically observed. The imaginaries linked to modernity were influenced by universal paradigms of efficiency, transparency, mechanisation,

DOI: 10.4324/9781003131755-6

and automation. In Colombia, they were framed within nationalist models fuelled by the pursuit of local identity, social justice, and the consolidation of democracy by the middle and working classes, in response to accelerated processes of urbanisation.

The introduction of modernity, which began in the late 19th century, was not linear or homogeneous, but marked by contrasting ideas. It followed long periods of civil and political confrontation, inherited from the independence efforts that emerged as a response to the Spanish hegemony. In this era, two political parties co-existed, maintaining the *status quo* in terms of structure, social, and economic order. However, their policies and actions strongly diverged, especially regarding education, which was used as an agent to transmit their ideology. The transformation of children's literature is a perfect example of the fluctuations experienced during the modernisation process in Colombia, which directly affected how cities and architecture were represented in children's books.

Methodological approach

This study was carried out with an exploratory literature review, semi-structured interviews with authors, illustrators, and specialised editors, and an online questionnaire answered by 13 professionals registered in the catalogue of Colombian authors and illustrators of children's and youth literature (Fundalectura, 2017). The interviews and questionnaire comprised questions such as: When and how did the ideals of modern architecture and urbanism appear in the text and graphics of children's books in Colombia? What influence did books imported from abroad have on the way modernity was represented in Colombian children's literature? And how were these books different from those produced in the country regarding modernity narratives?

Following this initial review, the authors searched for representative examples of these imaginaries in a list of 35 books recommended by the professionals interviewed as well as 604 books from 47 publishers produced between 2015 and 2020, available in the *Catalog of Children's and Youth Literature in Colombian* (Cámara Colombiana del Libro y de la Asociación Colombiana de Literatura Infantil y Juvenil, 2020). A sample of seven illustrations was chosen with a selection criterion based on relevance (illustrations showing urban or architectural elements of the modern movement), context (related to Colombia), and recognition (award-winning or recommended illustrations). Principles of semiotics were used for a deeper reading of these illustrations. Their authors were interviewed to inquire about the intended messages and a survey conducted with a group of 12 children between 5 and 13 years of age was used to collect information on their perception and interpretation of these messages.

Transformation of the imaginaries of modernity

Four periods were identified to study illustrated children's books, following categories frequently found in art history (Panzarowsky, 2010), architecture history (Arango, 1989), and children's literature (Paz, 2012). These explore the emergence of modern imaginaries and its subsequent development, demise, and legacy. Three genres are considered here within the universe of illustrated books: books used in schools mainly for teaching purposes, albums associated with reading as a leisure activity, and the comic book structured through comic strips.

Roots of modern imaginaries (1930–1945)

The year 1930 marked the end of a long period of conservative hegemony, which started in 1886, and gave rise to the Liberal Republic that lasted until 1946. The country entered a phase of economic recovery and the hasty growth of urban centres as a product of incremental migrations from rural environments forced by constant territorial conflicts (Caballero, 2018). Colombia rapidly became a country of cities, with new citizens who were originally from the countryside and had little urban tradition. This radical phenomenon was locally referred to as 'changing a mule for a jet'. As a result, many of the cultural and literary productions that emerged during this time reminisced about rural life. However, the construction of major infrastructures, electrification, and public transport gave a clearer signal for the changes to come with the social and cultural modernisation of the country. This encouraged the emergence of alternative literature portraying urban environments as symbols of change and modernity.

The First World War, the 1929 world economic crisis, the 1936–1939 Spanish Civil War, and the Second World War hinder the growth of modern imaginaries. However, as imports of books from Europe were restricted, the printing industry expanded to meet local demands (Naranjo, 2012). National and regional libraries, literary fairs, and cultural missions appeared, strengthening this new industry and placing books at the centre of the educational programme (Silva, 2008). This environment prompted experimentation with novel ideas which slowly diverted from traditional religious schemes. For example, active schooling and education through the senses began, where illustrations and images aided the visualisation and understanding of abstract concepts. *Las Cartillas Charry* (1917–1982) and *La Alegría de Leer* (1930–1980) were the first schoolbooks in Colombia to explore these principles. Their iconography progressively began to incorporate archetypes of modernism, mainly focusing on Euro-centrist and colonial perspectives (Venegas, 2012). However, the common thread was still the idealised discourse of Christian citizenship committed to the progress and well-being of the nation, excluding other indigenous, Afro-descendant, or secular views:

> [In this period], the child begins to be recognised as an individual subject, who requires or has different needs, who deserves to go to school and who has rights. Before, the concept of childhood did not exist, then there was no children's literature.
>
> *(Interview with Zully Pardo 12.04.2021)*

With the introduction of feature films, the radio, and the establishment of newspapers, comics and children's magazines also appeared (Villadiego, Bernal and Urbanczyk, 2007; Osses, 2015). Their function was less educational and more focused on entertainment and leisure. Adolfo Samper was amongst the first to introduce comic strips as a means of communication imported from abroad. One of his characters was *Mojicón* (1924–1930), an adapted version of the strip *Smitty* by cartoonist Walter Berndt from the *Chicago Tribune* and in the *New York News* (González, 1989). *Mojicón* showed the imaginary of Bogotá as a progressive hub and a symbol of development in the country. Between 1943 and 1952, Samper focused on satirical comics such as *Godofredo Cascarrabias, Don Amacise*, and *Misia Escopeta y Polín, which presented a* more critical view of modernity.

Popular children's magazines such as *Chanchito* (1933–1934) and *Rin Rin* (1936–1938) and a variety of album-books offered alternative entertainment for the new generation and identified them as potential consumers in a developing publishing market. The commercial spirit of these types of publication allowed greater freedom for editorial and graphic exploration. Unlike in schoolbooks, the images dominated the visual space by conversing directly with the text (Diaz, 2007). The image was used to tell, underline, characterise, exaggerate, contradict, portray, create an atmosphere, or insert a new point of view (Colomer, 2002). Authors such as Eco Nelly and Oswaldo Díaz laid the foundations of novel urban and domestic narratives in these books, where children were the protagonists. Additionally, Sergio Trujillo Magnenat, a precursor of modern art and the first illustrator of children's books in the country, was actively involved in the development of the graphic component (Robledo, 2010). His illustrations, for *Rin Rin* and many album books, recreated different aspects of modernity through a distinct representation of the human figure, the characters' expressions and attire, and the use of modern typographic styles:

> Trujillo understood that illustration was not only a matter of technique, style and line, but that it was necessary to build an aesthetic communicative component of allegorical value, using its own code of signs, images, situations and characters.
>
> *(Venegas, 2012, p. 102)*

By the mid-20th century, children's books in Colombia already had a recognisable modernist language in their content and aesthetics, a product of the different influences in their timeline (Figure 4.1). However, their representations of domestic and urban environments still did not correspond to the developments of architecture and urbanism that were happening simultaneously in Colombian cities. For example, the *Bogotá futuro* plan (1923–1925) presented new proposals for health, transport, urban development, organisation, and legislation in the capital, inspired by international parameters of *city planning* (Alba, 2013). *La Ciudad Universitaria* (the university campus), one of the leading modern initiatives of Alfonso López Pumarejo's liberal government, began construction in 1935. This project

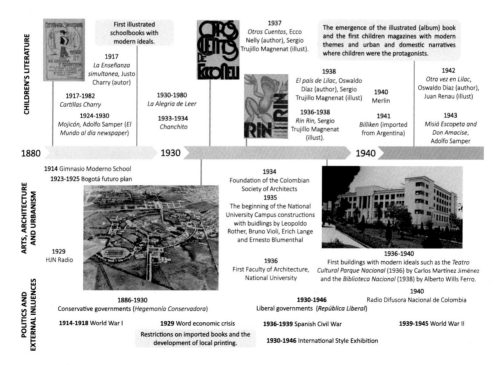

FIGURE 4.1 Central aspects influencing the development of children's books between 1880 and 1945.

La historia del viento de agosto

FIGURE 4.2 Illustration by Juan Renau Berenguer in Oswaldo Diaz, *Otra vez en Lilac*
(Editorial Ferrini, 1942).

(designed by the German architect Leopoldo Rother following Fritz Karsen's pedagogical ideas) aimed to represent secular and scientific thought. It comprised great symmetrical gestures, proportions, and rhythms, and a series of mainly white and rectilinear buildings scattered over green fields, built in concrete, and with a large amount of glazing.

An illustration from this period by Juan Renau Berenguer, in the book *Otra vez en Lilac* (1942) written by Oswaldo Díaz, portrays the imaginary of modern architecture created by projects such as the university campus (Figure 4.2). It shows a child with a kite in the middle of an open field surrounded by white buildings. It idealises a harmonious interaction between architecture and natural elements, represented by mountains, vegetation, the wind raising the kite, and a clear sunny sky to the left of the image and rain from dark clouds to the right. The buildings show typical characteristics of the modern movement architecture, such as regular volumes, modular windows, the absence of decoration, stilt constructions, and permeable ground floors.

Materialisation of the international style principles (1945–1970)

When the Conservative Party returned to power in 1946, repressed social problems exploded at national level. This marked the beginning of a period locally known as

La Violencia (the violence), exacerbated in 1948 by the assassination of the political leader Jorge Eliécer Gaitán in Bogotá. This episode unleashed weeks of social uprisings throughout the country, during which important parts of Bogotá's historic centre were reduced to rubble. The violence continued for many years despite failed attempts to achieve conciliation with the period known as the National Front (1958–1974). This was a very unfertile period for aesthetic creation and literary thinking. Children's books were limited to school instruction, bringing back 19th-century imaginaries from imported books. The so-called *useful art* characterised extracurricular activities as being useless, suspicious, or rebellious (Venegas, 2012). Local literature moved away from modern principles by returning to traditionalist narratives, mainly from myths and legends in rural and colonial contexts. It also reinstated iconographic motifs and stereotypes, which have been labelled by contemporary authors as patriarchal, classist, sexist, and racist (Cantillo Barrios, 2016):

> What children and young people read was 90% foreign books [...] That promoted moralistic literature, with a great emphasis on good and bad characters with European characteristics [...] I would like to emphasise on the characterisation of the protagonists as Europeans, while the Colombian ethnic diversity is not considered. Likewise, the animal characters are represented by foreign animals, and the diversity of the country's ecosystems is not shown.
>
> *(Questionnaire response by Gloria Beatriz Salazar de la Cuesta)*

> We grew up with these books; we were a colonised country, and we are multicultural. So, our approach is never going to be unique because we don't have a single identity. Culturally, people in the city have idealised 'The First World' [...] in the illustrations, there is a certain stylisation of foreign architectural patterns.
>
> *(Questionnaire response by Sandra Marcela Restrepo)*

In the early 1960s, comics such as *Copetín* by Ernesto Franco and *Policía en Acción* were popular. These introduced some urban scenarios with characters who lived on the streets. During this period, many children grew up in developing urban centres and were exposed daily to ideals and examples of modern architecture and urbanism, clearly different from colonial or republican architecture. However, these imaginaries had very little representation in illustrated books and comics and were still not widespread until decades later. Instead, books continued to reconstruct stories of heroes and chronological sequences of political and military events to be memorised according to the objectives and competencies of the official school programmes. This could be linked to the lack of local publishers and illustrators and the small market for independent publishers at the time, as explained by the architect, editor, and children's books specialist Maria Osorio:

> The editor did not exist, there was only the publisher... the texts were infantilised [...] and [illustrators] did not have aesthetic training. There was no graphic designer [...] you [can] see that in the production. The world of culture was in the hands of educational [institutions]. There were companies that made the reading plans

(teachers did not do it, editors did) [...] The book was no longer literature, it became a tool... their value was on the number of books sold to captive audiences [...] there was no social control.

(Interview with María Osorio 21.04.2021)

In contrast, the architecture scene in the main Colombian cities flourished during this period (Figure 4.3). The Second World War caused the immigration of European and North American architects and urban planners to Colombia, who were remarkably influential (Pérgolis and Rodríguez, 2017). Their contribution was evident not only in their architectural production but also in their work as teachers at the National University. The first generations of Colombian architects were inspired by these and other foreign professionals, such as Josep Lluís Sert and Paul Lester Wiener from *Town Planning Associates*, who were invited to implement modern development plans for Tumaco and Medellin. Le Corbusier was also invited to work with local professionals in a Master Plan and a Regulatory Plan for Bogotá (1947–1953), which at that time had around 600,000 people and was beginning to show disorderly growth (O'Byrne, 2010). The urban landscape of the major cities in Colombia combined formality with informality and spontaneous growth and a mixture of imported ideas and local reinterpretations. In this process, the so-called *architecture of the place* emerged seeking to relate architecture, topography, climate, history, memory, and idiosyncrasies. It combined elements of the rationalist movement with suggestive organic forms, sensitive to the culture, heritage, and geography

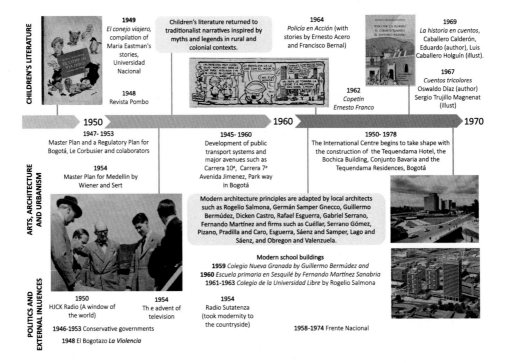

FIGURE 4.3 Central aspects influencing the development of children's books between 1945 and 1970.

of the Andean tropics, with brick as a material and technique related to local traditions. Renowned architects such as Fernando Martínez Sanabria, Guillermo Bermúdez, Rogelio Salmona, and Enrrique Triana were pioneers of this type of modern architecture (Ramírez Potes, 2009).

Dystopias of modernism (1970–1990)

In the 1970s and 1980s, historians and other education professionals began writing school texts that critically discussed issues such as slavery and the diversity of social structures (Navarro, 2019). Families with greater purchasing power and a higher educational level were progressively more conscious of the importance of the illustrated book in children's learning. Therefore, the market for graphic books and publishing companies was boosted and supported by a more favourable legal framework. This resulted in creating institutions to promote reading, the improvement of public libraries and bookstores networks, the development of new mass sales channels, and initiatives such as the Enka Prize for Colombian Children's Literature and the First Seminar of Children's and Youth Books Editing (Pardo, 2010):

> At that time [1970s and 80s], the first writers of this genre began to describe their own environments and show the city or town in which their characters lived [...] there were not really many authors, and the rural environment exerted a great influence.
>
> *(Questionnaire response by Gerardo Meneses Claros)*

Artists such as Antonio Caballero, Lorenzo Jaramillo, Ivar Da Coll, Diana Castellanos, Alekos, Olga Cuéllar, Esperanza Vallejo, Yezid Vergara, Daniel Rabanal, Irene Vasco, Yolanda Reyes, and Edgar Ródez led a generation of professional children's book illustrators (Osorio, 2012). Local publishers that specialised in this genre also emerged, such as Silvia Castrillón, María Osorio, Margarita Valencia, María Candelaria Posada, and Alberto Ramírez. Their work was supported by the National Law 98 (1993) which exempted books from the value added tax (VAT). However, comic books were left out until 2003, because they were not initially considered to be works of cultural value. Many authors, illustrators, and publishers began to capture urban life and landscapes in books such as *La Casa que Juan Construyó,* illustrated by Diana Castellanos. This is an adaptation of the popular British children's rhyme *This Is the House That Jack Built,* showing *La Perseverancia,* a popular and traditional neighbourhood in Bogota (Figure 4.4).

La Perseverancia is next to an area known as the International Centre, where, since the 1950s, the most canonical guidelines of international architecture were being explored. It comprised megaprojects of very tall buildings with innovative structural systems, promoting a mixture of uses and generous public spaces to articulate urban life. Figure 4.4 illustrates a traditional domestic environment from which the city can be observed through the window. The frontline houses (with traditional clay tile roofs and colourful items of daily life) contrast against the image at the back of the iconic Hilton Towers (1970–1983) by Fernando Martínez Sanabria:

> The urban landscape that is presented in the foreground and on the horizon is in line with what was observed in 1986 from the east of the city [...] In the process, some

FIGURE 4.4 Cover illustration by Diana Castellanos in the book *La Casa que Juan Construyó* (Editorial Norma S.A 1987). © Diana Castellanos Aranguren.

characters were changed, since the original story takes place in the English country-side, so it was necessary to adapt the narrative to the context I proposed. My intention as an illustrator and my discourse as a graphic artist, was channelled to show what children and young people would observe in their environment…in contrast to the images that were usually offered, which exhibited characters and urban landscapes product of foreign cultures.

(Description of the illustration provided to the authors by Diana Castellanos)

The comic genre was reactivated during this period in newspapers such as *El Tiempo*, *El Espectador*, *El Colombiano*, and *La Prensa* and magazines such as *Soldados Zona Bananera*, *Click*, *Los Monos*, and *Montecristo*, which addressed with satirical humour the inequality, hardness, and insecurity of the country's capitals. Unlike the illustrated album, these showed a more critical and less idealised urban reality. They emphasised the tragic relationship between overwhelming technology, dehumanised development, the impositions of the system, and the built environment. The country's conflict and violence were a constant in comic book narratives and became an essential component to shape *dystopias* of modernism (Roncallo, Aguilar and Uribe, 2019). In this collective imaginary, negative visions emerged, usually carrying moral messages associating the city and its constructions with the artificial and harmful and against the natural and healthy. Many of these ideas permeated into children's books.

This period was instrumental in outlining subsequent conceptual and expressive representations of modern architecture and urbanism in Colombian children's literature. Studying the narrative created at this time helps to explain why the earlier progressive, ambitious, and utopian imaginaries never had a significant place or development. The economic, political, ideological, and normative conditions of the second half of the 20th century prevented these ideals from being transmitted to a generation that grew up with formal architectural references to the international style, but that did not idealise or identify them as iconic because they conflicted with a latent informal reality:

> Modernity in each community is quite different and obeys very particular dynamics [...] to speak of 'modernity' within the country already simplifies it, because in a territory like Colombia there are many narratives of the modern.
>
> *(Questionnaire response by Santiago Guevara)*

The legacy of the modern movement (1990–2020)

Representations of modern architecture have a significant role in children's book illustration only from the end of the 20th century and the beginning of the 21st century. However, by then, they were already influenced by dystopian imaginaries inherited from the different views of modernity that had been adapted to Colombian reality. The boundaries between pre-modernity, modernity, and postmodernity are often blurred in Colombian historiography because contrasting conditions tend to overlap for long periods. This is reflected in children's literature, where prosperity and poverty, hope and violence, reality and illusion, and innovation and tradition co-exist. Some elements of modern architecture quickly transpired into the illustrations, such as the search for new material expressions. One of the main legacies that remains is the constant exploration of different artistic techniques (e.g. photomontage) to represent the city. These techniques changed rapidly with the use of new digital media and the advent of the internet. Other elements took longer, such as the representations of new formal languages for the buildings. Modern architecture is still rarely celebrated or glorified in the illustrations, as its aesthetic opulence often conflicts with the hardships faced by the book characters in modern cities.

Efforts to stimulate reading and activities around children's books continued, led by organisations such as Fundalectura and Biblored. Likewise, professional children's illustration courses began to be offered at university level, encouraged by awards to acknowledge, and appreciate this trade:

> The illustration is not an embellishment. The illustrator is an interpreter of the text, who must enrich it and offer second readings [...] the illustration is for oneself, when one was a child.
>
> *(Interview with Daniel Rabanal 15.04.2021)*

Publishers such as Babel Libros, Gato Malo, Tragaluz, Loqueleo, and Cataplum specialised in the production of books of this type and gave rise to a new generation of authors and illustrators, including Jairo Buitrago, Diego Francisco Sanchez, Rafael Yockteng, David Consuegra, Gerardo Meneses, Santiago Guevara, Daniel Fajardo, Sandra Marcela Restrepo, Roberto Sánchez, Francisco Montaña, Gloria Salazar, Rocio Parra, and Victoria Peters, among others. Many comic magazines also became available, such as *ACME, Agente Naranja, TNT, Hixtorieta, Shock*, and *ComicBuk*. However, in the case of many large-scale productions, quantity and commercial interests have often taken precedence over quality and graphic value, which has created debate amongst illustrators:

The illustration allows [the book] to bring complex and difficult topics of gender issues or violence to children, [compared to] literary language. Now thousands of children's books are produced, and the relevance of the image is only incidental. It has missed the opportunity that it had to narrate and participate [...] now the image is exaggeratedly everywhere [...] this has to do with the [advent of] media, advertising, television and the internet.

(Interview with María Osorio for CERLALC, 2017)

As illustrations do not necessarily convey reality but representations in the consciousness of their authors (which are influenced by their vision of Colombian history, society, and culture), a deeper analysis was needed to understand the components that intervene in their production and reading. For that purpose, seven illustrations were selected from this period. Figure 4.5 shows their timeline, political and external influences, and connections to iconic buildings of the modern movement in Colombia. Most of these buildings were featured in children's books over 20 years after they were built. Therefore, their immediate context and appearance changed as well as the imaginaries that they originally embodied.

The analysis of these illustrations was addressed here through the lens of semiotics, observing the signs and artistic expression used. Three points of view were considered: the view of the authors of this chapter who concentrate on the image's *representation,* the view of the illustrator who designed the *message,* and the perception of the children who do the *interpretation.* Table 4.1 lists the characteristics that were examined in each image and the guideline questions used for the collection of information.

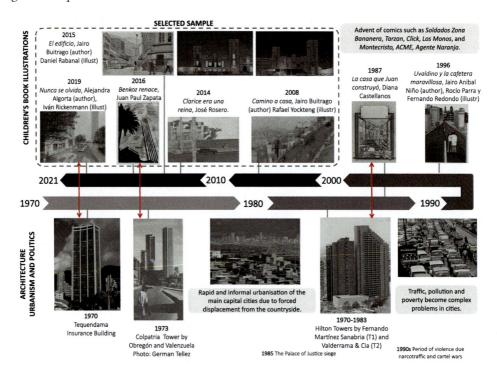

FIGURE 4.5 Timeline of selected illustrations linked to representative buildings from 1970 to date.

TABLE 4.1 Structure used for the analysis of the selected sample of illustrations

Characteristics			Guideline Question		
			Researcher *Representation*	Illustrator *Message*	Children *Interpretation*
Signs	Type	• Icon • Index • Symbol	• What signs, related to the architecture or urbanism of the international modern style, are used in illustration to convey the message?	• What message did this illustration intend to convey?	• What do you think is happening in the illustration? • What feeling can you associate with the illustration?
	Context	• Urban/rural • Indoors, outdoors • Day, night • Climatic conditions	• What context is being represented?		
Artistic Expression	Technique	• Methods • Type of line • Colour palette • Textures	• What characterises the artistic representation used?	• What was the reason behind the choice of artistic expression used?	• Why do you think the artist chose the colours, textures, and shapes in this illustration?
	Composition	• Proportion, scale • Contrast, énfasis • Movement	• How is the image composed?		
	Style	• Figurative • Abstract	• What style is used?		

Three concepts suggested by Charles Sanders Peirce were used to identify the signs in the images: icons, indexes, and symbols (Merrell, 1997). Icons directly represent an object through a relationship of similarity. For example, a building could be depicted with an icon of a recognisable construction that a child could clearly identify as a building. Indexes establish a causal ratio of reason to result where the sign or image indicates a consequence. Thus, the illustration of a street where there is rubbish and deteriorated buildings could be an index related to feelings, such as abandonment or neglect. Symbols convey a consensual meaning represented by a convention. In this case, the image of a factory chimney throwing out smoke is a symbol of air pollution. Peirce points out that this classification is not exclusive since the sign can belong to more than one category at a time or mutate from one to another.

Analysis of the selected illustrations

Camino a casa

This book tells the story of a girl who lost her father during a very violent episode in Colombia's history, where members of a guerrilla group took over the Palace of Justice in Bogotá in 1985. Many civilians died or disappeared when military forces stormed to retake the building. This event is commonly used as a symbol of suffering and abandonment of the victims of violence in Colombia. The book addresses this complex subject through the eyes of a child seeking protection and company from an imaginary lion as she navigates the city.

FIGURE 4.6 Illustration by Rafael Yockteng for Jairo Buitrago, *Camino a casa* (Fondo de Cultura Económica, 2008) © Rafael Yockteng.

Representation: Figure 4.6 shows a densely populated urban environment with icons of grey, monolithic, and repetitive buildings. These serve as a backdrop to contrast with a more domestic, colourful, and active neighbourhood scene, where the protagonist walks energetically with the lion down the middle of the road. Symbols such as smoke from factory chimneys, overflowing rubbish bins, mice, and homeless are used to represent negative aspects of modernity, such as chaos, pollution, and poverty. Positive aspects could be read on indexes showing active citizens riding bikes or selling street food and the presence of some elements of nature and urban animals. The building icons show austerity in their geometry and level of detailing with assorted colours and materials.

Message

> In this image, I am placing the characters in a city, which could be Bogota or another city, to show how the journey of these children is every day. When I draw these images, I was looking for my way to tell a story. I decided to use the computer and I found a sea of possibilities [...] I had to contain myself not to fall into the tricks and effects that digital illustration can have. So, I tried to emulate watercolour to have textures and mid-tones. That is why the images have that shade of brown that I needed to show a city (description of the illustration provided to the authors by.
>
> *(Rafael Yockteng)*

Interpretation

A bus is going through a world that is upside down. There are lions in the city, there are separated neighbourhoods, there is a lot of smoke, the neighbourhood in the background looks more neglected. I like how the colours fit and show a story and I dislike that the colour is lost when you go further back.

(Example of a description given by a child)

Clarice era una reina

Clarice, the main character of the book, was inspired by a real person who lived on the street and dressed in rags and scraps she found. The book seeks a contrast between the aesthetic of a fairy tale and the rawness of a hard and real story. According to the author, the eclectic use of these fragments represents the passage of time, abandonment, and a way of relating to the environment. This is also the case in the modern city, which is built like a patchwork quilt.

Representation: Figure 4.7 shows an urban environment with icons of streetlights and wide concrete paths, including indexes of stains and patches, which indicate amendments to the infrastructure done over time. One side of the pedestrian path is bound by a high, continuous, and closed brick and concrete wall that drastically separates public and private space. It is used as a surface to paint graffiti, which could be a symbol of rebellious expression. Behind the wall, there is the icon of an abandoned building with nature already taking over. The building features elements of the modern movements, such as a symmetrical facade with little ornament and rectangular windows subdivided into modular panels. A human face is painted on the derelict facade, with its baggy eyes looking over the fence wall. Emphasis is placed on the use of the car, with icons such as pavement, traffic signs, and a car positioned at the centre of the image. The car is a Renault 4, which was a symbol of modernity in the country and recognised in the 1970s as the *Colombian car* for being locally assembled. The image of Clarice walking alone on the path and looking down could be an index of loneliness and sadness.

FIGURE 4.7 Illustration by José Rosero for the book *Clarice era una reina* (Loguez, 2014)
© José Rosero.

Message

The intention of the image, through the architecture and urban space, was to build a *"kingdom"* for Clarice, corresponding to her mental universe, solitary and introspective [...] with the purpose of creating a poetic mixture between abandonment, memory, creation, and fantasy... It was an illustration, mixed with painting [...] which allowed me to create a whole aesthetic... a poetics of abandonment, of oblivion, of silence [...] With painting I have many possibilities of texture and volume. The finishes correspond to the rustic nature of the character, and her situation of introspection and madness [...] Both Clarice and her environment are a consequence of time, and not an immediate construction.

(Description of the illustration provided to the authors by José Rosero)

Interpretation

There is a transition between what we associate with a dangerous neighbourhood and a neighbourhood considered safe. I like the colour palette; I dislike that we judge a neighbourhood on how it looks with respect to safety.

(Example of a description given by a child)

El edificio

The book *El edificio* (*The building*) tells the story of Mr. Levin, a watchmaker, who arrived in Bogotá in the early 1930s and settled in a building in the city centre. Using the analogy to the clocks that he fixes, the illustrations show how time passed in his life and the neighbourhood around him. The arrival of a little child (Ivan) to the building brings fresh energy and hope.

FIGURE 4.8 Illustration by Daniel Rabanal for Jairo Buitrago, *El edificio* (Babel Libros, 2015) © Daniel Rabanal.

Representation: Figure 4.8 uses icons of architecture and urbanism present in the main modern avenues of Bogotá, showing a type of modernity full of contrasts. For example, high-rise and monolithic buildings with large windows, built with exposed materials (brick, concrete, metal, and glass). There are positive indexes that indicate a direct connection between the built and the natural environment (e.g. tree-lined avenues and backdrop mountains) as well as a strong emphasis on active urban life and movement. Likewise, negative symbols evidence the chaos that is characteristic of Latin American cities, such as rubbish in the street, disorderly networks of electrical cables, walls with propaganda and torn banners, illegal windows on side walls, street vendors, and old buses. The grey and brown palette used in this urban scene helps to resemble the sadness of many people who migrated to cities in the early 20th century and experienced the deterioration of their central areas. In contrast, the brighter colours used for Ivan's clothes represent optimism for the future.

Message

The idea with this work was to tell, graphically, the urban development—deterioration, in this case—of a sector of the city over time. It was modelled on a particular neighbourhood in Bogotá, La Favorita, and specifically on a road with historic buildings. The passage of time, melancholy and a criticism of the socio-political 'disorder' that allowed this urban degradation were the issues that drove the proposal.

(Description of the illustration provided to the authors by Daniel Rabanal)

Interpretation

It is a busy city, like Bogotá, in which people have eagerness. I like that it expresses eagerness and tranquillity at the same time. I dislike the dull colour palette.

(Example of a description given by a child)

FIGURE 4.9 Illustration 1 of San Jorge theatre by Daniel Rabanal for Jairo Buitrago, *El edificio* (Babel Libros, 2015) © Daniel Rabanal.

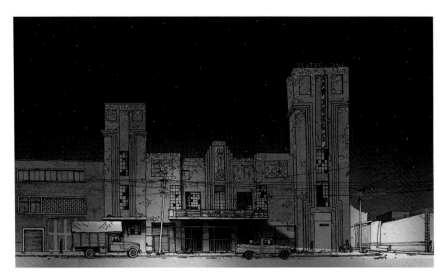

FIGURE 4.10 Illustration 2 of San Jorge theatre by Daniel Rabanal for Jairo Buitrago, *El edificio* (Babel Libros, 2015) © Daniel Rabanal.

Representation: Figures 4.9 and 4.10 from the same book illustrate the icon of a building (the San Jorge theatre in Bogotá) viewed from the same angle, but under very different conditions. This building, designed in 1938 by Alberto Manrique Martín, followed principles of the European art deco style, which substantially influenced the later international style in the country. The building is not part of the story told in the book. However, it is used as a representation of the flourishing of modernity and its subsequent decadency. This relates to the feeling of nostalgia experience by Mr. Levin as he reminisced about his prosperous youth.

In Figure 4.9, the theatre is illuminated, full of activity and movement, standing out within its context. A group of people arrive in luxury cars and gather at the entrance as a prelude to the event. The icons, indexes, and symbols of this scene represent success, vigour, and wealth. In contrast, in Figure 4.10, the building has a deteriorated facade, broken windows, and disorganised electric cables which are symbols of obsolescence and abandonment. There is a new building on the left and the building on the right was replaced by a fenced-off street. The entrance of the theatre is boarded up to avoid any unwanted access. The cars parked are no longer luxurious and the pedestrians passing by do not seem to be interested in the building. The icons, indexes, and symbols of this scene represent failure, lethargy, and death.

Message

The illustration had to be realistic enough to achieve an efficient description of the environment. It had to be able to clearly express the passage of time and the change of fashions and design, both architectural and industrial (cars, for example). On the other hand, the use of colour aimed to achieve that melancholic feeling that we proposed for the book. The technique used was pen and watery ink on paper and then digital colouring.

(Description of the illustrations provided to the authors by Daniel Rabanal)

Interpretation

I see first a modern building and then a broken building. It is the story of the building in two images. It's like before and after.

The first image shows the past of this place, when it was in use. There was an audience, and it was used, it conveys achievement. The second image shows the same place but abandoned and conveys disappointment.

(Example of descriptions given by children)

Benkoz renace

Benkoz is a character inspired by Benkos Biohó, a leader who commanded a rebellion of maroon slaves in the 17th century, becoming the first emancipator of black people in Latin America. The book provides a contemporary and urban version of the story, where the villain is a society that discriminates, ignores, and marginalises. It deals with themes of freedom, tradition, and reinvention of cultural relationships with ancestors.

FIGURE 4.11 Illustration by Jean Paul Zapata for the book *Benkoz Renace* (N.N. GRAPHICS 2016) © Jean Paul Zapata.

Representation: Figure 4.11 shows two modern building icons. The 50-storey Colpatria Tower on the right was constructed by Obregón-Valenzuela & Co following the main architectural ideals of the international style (grand-scale concrete buildings, tube-in-tube structure, rectilinear forms, plain surfaces with no applied ornament, and open interior spaces). The ten-storey office building on the left was designed by Enrrique Triana adopting some of these principles (a permeable ground floor, modular facades, and minimum ornamentation) but adapting them to traditional materials and construction techniques with brickwork. These illustrate the different architectural interpretations and adaptations of the modern movement in Colombia.

In this image, however, the architectural differences between the buildings are secondary as they are both compared to the palm tree and criticised for trying to surpass it and outshine it. The annotations on the top of the image say: 'Grey November', 'Today is Tuesday, a good day to return to the capital', 'This sleepless place where the stone tries to be taller than the palm tree'. The contrasting built and natural elements are used as an index to stress the anthropocentric design of cities, where humans believe they are separate and superior to nature. These are emphasised by the artistic expression of the black ink drawing against the pink and yellow watercolour background. At the same time, the perspective looking up from a pedestrian point of view stresses the oppression created by these buildings (which represent society) on the common citizens destined to live in them as their prison. This is accentuated by the annotations 'Everyone in their concrete cells, with their machines, their screens, [...]', 'I am sleeping [...]', 'I am in the streets' (highlighted in red), 'Condemned to freedom'.

Message

> This is the view that the character [Benkoz] has as a pedestrian, walking on seventh avenue by 24th street. As he looks up, he sees a palm tree that reminds him of his land, which contrasts with the height of the Colpatria building. I wanted to show the paradoxes of civilisation produced by architecture in cities, which makes the natural element an ornament, and how nature in the city is stone.
>
> *(Description of the illustration provided to the authors by Jean Paul Zapata)*

Interpretation

> It is the Colpatria building at an angle where you can see the palm trees and a building next door.
> I think people are expressing their feelings and ideas are caught in the air, as the whole of society.
>
> *(Example of descriptions given by children)*

Nunca se olvida

The book tells the story of Fabio, an eight-year-old boy who forgot how to ride a bicycle, which is for him the most important thing in his life. This makes him feel insecure and fearful, since being able to move is a principle of life. All the images in the book are pencil drawings from distinct urban scenes in Bogotá.

FIGURE 4.12 Illustration by Iván Rickenmann for Alejandra Algorta, *Nunca se olvida* (Babel Libros, 2019) © Iván Rickenmann.

Representation: The scene in Figure 4.12 takes place in the middle of the International Centre, showing two of its most symbolic buildings, the Tequendama Insurance Building and the Colpatria Tower, which epitomise the formal and functional principles of the modern movement. Most of the icons used represent movement as a central urban characteristic. For example, roads, pathways, active pedestrians, and different forms of transport, including public buses, cars, bicycles, and street vendor trolleys. The pencil strokes aligned with the perspective highlight movement along the city's arteries. Icons of modern, tall, slender, and monolithic buildings with permeable first floors are the vertical elements of the composition. The balanced combination of buildings and trees could be an index of an ideal ratio for the built/natural environment, which humanised urban spaces and allows the development of social life between buildings. Likewise, the proportioned widths of the path, road, and bicycle lanes could also be an index linked to the ideal relationship between pedestrians, cars, and bikes. This replaces the common imaginaries from cities of the modern movement that placed the car as the protagonist, although the illustrator may have a different view.

Message

The illustration responds to a tour of Bogotá, in which the bus is the protagonist. It is a look at the different universes of a city, and the personal identity that these spaces suggest. Charcoal is more expressive in nature, since it is a medium that allows great contrasts, and given its rough character, it is very beautiful to work in detail, thanks to the handling of tones, lights, and shadows. It is a medium that allows [the artist] to recreate the space, giving it character and strength, thus moving away from the simple description.

(Description of the illustration by its author Ivan Rickenmann)

Interpretation

> It is a very modern city. The buildings are very tall and there are also people waiting for the bus.
>
> *(Example of a description given by a child)*

All the children's responses to the questionnaire were analysed further using coding for the most frequently used words. These were grouped into five categories (built environment, neglect/contamination/poverty, natural environment, people, and transport) to identify central aspects perceived across all the illustrations (Figure 4.13). The results showed that elements of the built environment were the most commented upon, followed by natural elements and people. Word clouds were also examined to identify the components that drew more attention in each illustration. It was found that in *Camino a Casa*, the lion was the most mentioned element associated with happiness and tranquillity, whilst the city and the pollution were linked to sadness, anger, and discomfort. In *Clarice era una reina*, the car was frequently cited as well as the woman or girl looking down, which was related to sorrow and worry. The city was again the central element in *El edificio*, linked to people actively moving and using transport, while the images of the theatre incited sadness and anger associated with the neglect and abandonment of the building. In *Benkoz renace*, most children recognised the Colpatria building and noticed the palm tree. Despite the written messages on this illustration, all the responses connected it with happiness, hope, and tranquillity due to the colourful background. In contrast, the scene from *Nunca se olvida*, which also includes trees and the Colpatria building, was associated with both happiness and sadness because of the grey palette.

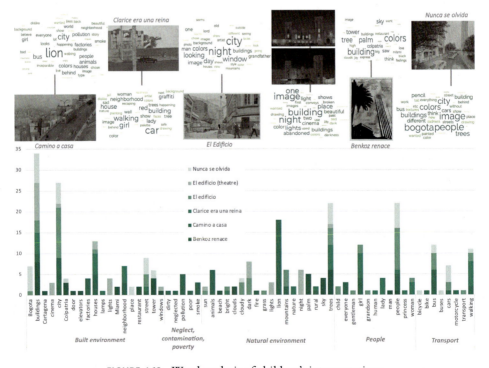

FIGURE 4.13 Word analysis of children's interpretations.

Discussion and conclusion

The emergence of modernity as a concept linked to the built environment had, in Colombia, its own characterisation that in cultural terms referred to the transition from a rural society to an urban society. The emergence of the modern was gradual and accompanied by imaginaries forged in parallel but always in tension between the longed for and the real. In this process, a local system of representations, based on what is perceived as national and Catholic, sought identification from international models using languages proposed by avant-garde movements. However, the fluctuations in government guidelines and pedagogical models coupled with political instability and internal conflict had lasting effects on the imaginaries of the modern city and its architecture, represented belatedly in children's books. Only until the 1980s did these ideals start to emerge visually, combined or contrasted with traditional and colonial archetypes. It took two more decades for these to establish and become regular components in children's literature.

Imported books had a significant influence on defining the aesthetics and content of locally produced images. However, they also encouraged the search for a distinct identity within a new generation of professional illustrators. The comic strip had a central role in this process as a venue for satirical reflection. Most of the references to modernity found in the selected books were directed at urban and public space rather than domestic settings or indoor environments. At first glance, the imaginaries of the modern city are drawn from a place of dystopia, influenced by stereotypes of pollution, poverty, chaos, deterioration, neglect, and segregation. However, they co-exist with other principles that children can experience and verify in their urban landscape, which include movement, transformation, active lifestyles, transportation, community, public space, and the awareness of being a citizen.

The children's books studied for this project speak of universal, transversal, and vital themes. However, the authors, illustrators, and editors clearly state their intention to also promote a sense of belonging and identification with the surrounding built environment. As mentioned by Daniel Rabanal, there is a necessity for the 'affectionate recognition of the city'. In an analysis of the interview responses by the authors, *city* and *urban environment* were the most used words, often linked with the passing of time and the local narrative. This aligns with the most used words by children to describe the illustrations, which suggests an effective interpretation of the intended message. Thus, interesting questions are raised regarding the role of the authors, especially the illustrators, in the formation of imaginaries that may lengthen or shorten the distance between the presentation of architectural ideals and the representation of reality.

However, the children's responses showed that fiction and reality are not necessarily in conflict; both may be interpreted from multiple signs and elements within the artistry of the illustrators. A girl and her lion happily walking along in a chaotic neighbourhood can be considered by children as a plausible scene in their city. Likewise, a sense of belonging was evidenced by the children's reaction to dilapidated buildings, rubbish, and pollution, which provoked discomfort, sadness, and anger. Certain aspects of the artistry, such as the composition of the images and their colour palette, also impacted on the delivery of their message and the feelings they incited.

This chapter shows how the advance of illustration in children's literature is recognised nowadays as a significant contributor to the field of cultural production. In doing so, the art of illustration has helped to form and convey utopian and dystopian ideas about the relationship between humans and the built environment. Its definite communicative and suggestive power leaves open questions and new areas of research concerning its vocation and destiny in the production of urbanism and architecture, which can be both critical and poetic.

References

Alba, J. M. (2013). 'El plano bogotá futuro. Primer intento de modernización urbana', *Anuario Colombiano de Historia Social y de la Cultura*, 40(2), 179–208.

Algorta, A. (2019). *Nunca se olvida*. Bogotá: Editorial: Babel Libros.

Arango, S. (1989). *Historia de la arquitectura en Colombia*. Bogotá: Centro Editorial y Facultad de Artes, Universidad Nacional de Colombia.

Buitrago, J. and Rabanal, D. (2015). *El edificio*. Bogotá: Editorial Babel Libros.

Buitrago, J. and Yockteng, R. (2008). *Camino a casa*. Ciudad de México: Fondo de Cultura Económica.

Caballero, A. (2018). *Historia de Colombia y sus oligarquías*. Bogotá: Planeta.

Cámara Colombiana del Libro y de la Asociación Colombiana de Literatura Infantil y Juvenil (2020) *Catálogo de derechos LIJ Colombia*. Available at: http://www.lijcolombia.com.co/ (Accessed: 26 May 2021).

Cantillo Barrios, L. (2016). 'El currículum oculto en los textos de lectura escolar: La cartilla "Nacho", libro inicial de lecturas', *La Manzana de la Discordia*, 11(1), 95. doi: 10.25100/lmd.v11i1.1637.

Castellanos, D. (1987). *La casa que juan construyó*. Bogotá: Editorial Norma S.A.

CERLALC (2017). *Por qué se ilustran los libros infantiles?* Available at: https://cerlalc.org/por-que-se-ilustran-los-libros-infantiles/.

Colomer, T. (2002). *Siete llaves para valorar las historias infantiles*. Madrid: Fundación Germán Sánchez Ruipérez.

Diaz, F. (2007). *Leer y mirar el libro álbum: Un género en construcción?* Bogotá: Grupo Editorial Norma.

Diaz, O. (1942). *Otra vez en lilac*. Bogotá: Editorial Ferrini.

El Congreso de Colombia (1993) *Ley 98 de 1993*. Colombia.

Fundalectura (2017). *Catálogo de autores e ilustradores Colombianos de literatura infantil y juvenil*. Available at: https://catalogo.fundalectura.org/content/catalogo-de-autores-e-ilustradores-colombianos-de-lij (Accessed: 21 March 2020).

González, B. (1989). *Adolfo Samper 1900*. Bogotá: Biblioteca Luis Angel Arango, Banco and de la República.

Lindón, A. (2007). 'Diálogo con Néstor García Canclini ¿Qué son los imaginarios y cómo actúan en la ciudad?', *Revista Eure*, 33(99), 89–99. doi: 10.4067/s0250-71612007000200008.

Merrell, F. (1997). *Peirce, signs, and meaning*. Toronto: University of Toronto Press.

Naranjo, J. (2012). 'Dos décadas decisivas: 1920–1940', in Paz-Castillo, M. F. (ed) *Una historia del libro ilustrado para niño en Colombia*. Bogotá: Ministerio de Cultura, Biblioteca Nacional de Colombia, pp. 51–83.

Navarro, C. P. (2019). *Desarrollo del pensamiento histórico en la escuela*. Tunja: Editorial UPTC.

Rabanal, D. (2001). 'Panorama de la historieta en Colombia', *Tebeoesfera*. Available at: https://www.tebeosfera.com/documentos/panorama_de_la_historieta_en_colombia.html (Accessed: 15 December 2020).

Rosero, J. (2014). *Clarice era una reina*. Bogotá: Editorial Loguez.

O'Byrne, M. C. (2010). *Le corbusier en Bogotá: 1947–1951*. Bogotá: Uniandes.

Osorio, M. (2012). 'Para recuperar la memoria: Dieciocho imágenes del siglo XX', in Paz, M. F. (ed) *Una historia del libro ilustrado para niño en Colombia*. Bogotá: Ministerio de Cultura, Biblioteca Nacional de Colombia, pp. 246–267.

Osses, S. L. (2015). 'Cincuenta años de radio comunitaria en Colombia. Análisis sociohistórico (1945–1995)', *Revista Científica General José María Córdova*, 13(16), 263–283.

Panzarowsky, G. (2010). *Artes visuales en Colombia desde 1810. A propósito de la exposición curada por Eduardo Serrano en el museo de arte moderno de Bogotá*. Available at: http://esferapublica.org/nfblog/artes-visuales-en-colombia-desde-1810/ (Accessed: 22 March 2021).

Pardo, Z. (2010). 'El desarrollo del libro álbum en Colombia: 1970 – 2008', *Bellaterra Journal of Teaching & Learning Language & Literature*, 2(2), 138. doi: 10.5565/rev/jtl3.126.

Paz, M. F. (2012). *Una historia del libro ilustrado para niños en Colombia*. Bogotá: Ministerio de Cultura, Biblioteca Nacional de Colombia.

Pérgolis, J. C. and Rodríguez, C. I. (2017). *Imaginarios y representaciones, Bogotá: 1950–2000 forma urbana y vida cotidiana*. Bogotá: Universidad Católica de Colombia.

Ramírez Potes, F. (2009) 'La arquitectura escolar en la construcción de una arquitectura del lugar en Colombia.', *Revista Educación y Pedagogía*, 21(54), 81–101. Available at: http://dialnet.unirioja.es/servlet/extart?codigo=3291473.

Robledo, B. H. (2010). *Literatura infantil Colombiana: Hilos para una historia*. Available at: https://biblioteca.org.ar/libros/155763.pdf (Accessed: 22 April 2021).

Roncallo, S., Aguilar, D. and Uribe, E. (2019). 'La Bogotá distópica: Los cómics sobre una ciudad en caos', *Co-herencia*, 16(30), 27–56. doi: 10.17230/co-herencia.16.30.2.

Silva, R. (2008). 'El libro popular en Colombia, 1930–1948', *Revista de Estudios Sociales*, 30, 20–37.

Venegas, M. C. (2012). 'Pocos, pero excepcionales: Los libros ilustrados para niños en Colombia entre 1940 y 1970', in Paz-Castillo, M. F. (ed) *Una historia del libro ilustrado para niño en Colombia*. Bogota: Ministerio de Cultura, Biblioteca Nacional de Colombia, pp. 91–128.

Villadiego, M., Bernal, P. and Urbanczyk, M. (2007). *La modernidad Colombiana contada por el relato publicitario: 1900–1950*. Available at: http://www.javeriana.edu.co/redicom/documents/LamodernidadColombianacontadaporelrelatopublicitario1900-1950.pdf.

Zapata, J. (2016). *Benkoz renace*. Bogotá: Editorial N.N GRAPHICS.

PART TWO

Domestic space

5

DOMESTIC ARCHITECTURE AND ENVIRONMENTAL DESIGN IN AUSTRALIAN PICTUREBOOKS

John Stephens

Representations of domestic architecture are remarkably elusive in Australian picturebooks, where exteriors appear mainly as settings or as background fragments. Domestic interiors are seldom elaborated except by means of metonymic images, especially a kitchen table, a couch, or a window frame. Significance stems more from elements of design: a collection of artefacts, especially items of furniture which evoke a particular period, simply indicate the house is pre-contemporary or suggest the family is more concerned with affective warmth than tidiness or fashionable style. A discussion of architecture in Australian picturebooks thus needs to include more than the fabric of buildings, but also embrace design and contents, and then extend outside to take in suburban landscape architecture, which further shapes and is shaped by suburban houses. Underpinning these elements are notions of well-being in Australian communities.

Because picturebooks deal with living things rather than material objects, buildings are seldom represented as the central theme of a book, but nevertheless often play an important, albeit implicit, role in dominant narratives of Australian childhood. Domestic architecture appears in three main forms: inner city terraced houses and free-standing cottages, often referred to as workers' cottages, built in the second half of the 19th century; rural cottages, which in the 1970s and 1980s were the predominant housing style to appear in picturebooks; and detached (or semi-detached) dwellings which became the preferred housing style in the early 20th century and thence in modern picturebooks. A simple example of how architecture functions metonymically is found in *Night Noises* (1989), set in 'an old cottage in the hills', where Lillie Laceby, an elderly woman, sits dozing and dreaming about her life but is woken by her descendants for a surprise 90th birthday party. The first opening depicts a small rural Australian village, consisting of a couple of shops, a church, a hotel, and a few houses. The scene is reminiscent of, for example, Tilba Tilba, a National Trust-classified heritage town in Southern New South Wales, where many buildings date from the 1890s and have survived modern development. The houses in *Night Noises*, like the heritage houses in Tilba Tilba, are built of timber (weatherboard) and have red, corrugated iron roofs with one or two chimneys. Most have panelled sash

DOI: 10.4324/9781003131755-8

windows and panelled front doors. That Lillie Laceby's house is not specifically identified in the text may suggest it could be any of those shown, as the township epitomises a shared way of life. More practically, however, a child is likely to identify it as the house closest to the foreground and the only one reproducing a common schema for a child drawing of a symmetrical house: it is a two-dimensional rectangle topped by a triangle forming a gable roof perpendicular to a central door, a panelled window on either side of the door, and a front wicket gate with a path to the door.[1] This simple architectural conception usually indicates that its maker sustains a positive view of their household and family and it may thus perform a scene-setting cognitive-affective function. In other words, the familiar symmetrical house schema presupposes a positive viewer orientation, but it also has a capacity to imply a broader social significance in a desired relationship between an individual and an imagined community. My contention is that the child-imagined house schema functions in Australian picturebooks to ground notions of well-being in a relationship between the Australian present and a part-historical, part-fictionalised past. Variants of the symmetrical house schema appear in a wide spectrum of books: see, for example, *Dog In, Cat Out* (1991) by Gillian Rubinstein and Ann James (Figure 5.1). The persistence of the schema and its resonance is apparent in *Paperboy* (2019) by Danny Parker and Bethany Macdonald: a young boy engages with the trauma of moving house and a sense that all around is disintegrating by making collages out of scraps of paper he collects, and his endeavours culminate in a somewhat cubist collage of the symmetrical house. The accompanying text invokes a feeling of well-being inherent in the affective impact of the schema: 'It all fits so well together'.

FIGURE 5.1 The symmetrical house schema as the establishment image in *Dog In, Cat Out* (1991), illustrated by Ann James. Reproduced with kind permission of Ann James.

Localities such as the village in *Night Noises* have become rare in modern Australia, but were documented during the second half of the 20th century in the watercolour paintings of Kenneth Jack (1924–2006), which include images of many Australian small towns. Of particular interest here is 'Sunlight Breaking Through – Tilba' (1982), which was quite well known as a limited edition, signed collotype print. Jack travelled throughout Australia and specialised in painting images of 'an Australia that has all but vanished from the public consciousness' (Stark, 2005, n.p.). Of an exhibition of a collection of his prints in 2005, most of which portrayed urban buildings, the curator observed that strong interest was shown by people from an architectural and historical background (quoted in Stark 2005), precisely because they portray a world that has disappeared. The painting of Tilba depicts the town from afar and as generally dilapidated (its iron roofs are not painted red but are rusting) and there are few people seen: a man walks with a horse and dog and three men talk in a group outside the General Store. A War Memorial stands in the centre of a crossroad in the lower left of the picture. It is not a strong focal point but is one end of a vector of light that falls across the scene as the sun emerges from the clouds. The theme of this realist painting is a symbiosis of memory and loss and has important implications for picturebooks because a myth about a universal Australian experience, forged from rural settler life, the heroism of ANZAC soldiers during World War I, and a notion of decent, small town, family values, was still strong in the 1980s and endures as a palimpsest in values implied in picturebooks.

Night Noises is a sketch of Lillie Laceby's life story, told as six dream vignettes. For most of the book, she is depicted dozing in an armchair beside a gas fire, which has replaced the log-burning fireplace usual in such houses (the other houses in opening 1 have smoke rising from the chimneys). A mantelpiece above the fire holds an assortment of objects, painted in low definition, which may be understood as mementos of a long life: they include, among other things, a wedding photograph, a pot plant, and an elephant figurine. The dreams begin with the death of Lillie Laceby's husband and step back in time through the birth of her first child, her wedding, horse-riding as a young adult, leaving for school by train, and sitting on a swing as a pre-teen. As Heather Goodall remarks about life stories she collected from rural people in the 1990s, 'memories are never transparent glimpses of the past but are always created in a narrative process that is shaped by questions and concerns of the narrator's present' (Goodall, 2014, p. 91). Tinged with an element of rural nostalgia, the dream memories articulate a particular conception of womanhood persisting in the late 20th-century Australian society, expressed not only in rural cottage architecture but more generally in the symmetrical house schema. In combination with the arrival of the old woman's 55 descendants to celebrate her birthday, the dreams represent the idea of a full, traditional life.

Night Noises is unusual because it is set mostly in one room of the house, whereas characters in other books more usually move amongst several spaces. Such movement is horizontal, because most houses depicted in Australian picturebooks, reflecting most suburban houses, are built on a single level. An illuminating example, which explores design features of a cottage built in South Melbourne *circa* 1869, is *Finding Jack* (Ann James, 1992). The author describes the book as a portrait of her 'own little cottage', which preserves its original features, inside and outside (personal communication). Readers are taken on a search for one of the narrator's cats and thus visit most rooms in the house and go out into the garden. The tour starts at the open front door, a panelled door featuring a brass knocker and a large, amber glass knob at its centre. A design feature of such cottages is that the door opens directly into the lounge, with a view through to the rear of the house, where the search begins. After viewers have visited the kitchen, laundry, bathroom, garden, and lounge room, encountering five cats and a dog in the search, Jack is finally discovered asleep in an open drawer in a bedroom. For young readers, the pleasure will lie in meeting each of the animals, some of whom are up to mischief, but the book is also a picture of an older world. Each of the images consists of two glimpses: first, a view into a room through a doorway, which thus shows only a part of the room and, second, a close-up of the cat in the room. Older viewers may appreciate the heritage features that are part of these glimpses, such as half-panelled walls and tongue and groove cupboard doors with strap hinges. The bathroom, for example, has an old claw foot bath standing in front of a wooden wall panelled with horizontal strips, a technique sometimes referred to as 'rustic chic' when employed in contemporary houses. The blending of heritage architectural details and the universal behaviour of cats – stealing food, fishing in the goldfish pond, sleeping in cosy places – is another strategy for bringing the past into the present.

A tour of a house expressing traditional domestic architecture is also a feature of *Dog In, Cat Out* (see Figure 5.1). Working on Gillian Rubinstein's text that simply navigates all possible variations of four words, 'dog in cat out', Ann James brilliantly portrays a day in the life of an Australian family as it is obliquely reflected by the movements of their dog and cat in and out of the house. The family consists of a couple, two school-age children, and a toddler, although the mother's late stage pregnancy indicates that the family is still growing: that the mother reads a picturebook about twin kittens to the youngest child hints that she is herself carrying twins.[2] Of the book's 16 openings, the first and last are framing images of the house, at dawn and night, five are set in the kitchen, a large space where principal family activity happens, four depict the outside yard, two the boundary area between inside and outside, two the parents' bedroom, and one the lounge room. The images reveal little about the architecture, but key features have a metonymic function: the house is weatherboard with a corrugated galvanised iron roof (seen in opening 13), that is, it incorporates two of the most iconic picturebook features of Australian domestic architecture. The weatherboard house with iron roof represents the essence of Australian family life, even though such dwellings are now rapidly disappearing – unprecedented low interest rates in response to the COVID-19 pandemic of 2020–2021 have accelerated a 'knock down and rebuild' frenzy that has seen such houses replaced by 'McMansions', duplexes, and townhouses. To date, picturebooks have not reflected this architectural shift. Rory Hyde, editor of *Architecture Australia*, laments that architect-designed buildings in the suburbs 'are but tiny jewels within a boundless sea, with limited impact on the larger whole' (Hyde, 2021, p. 14). He argues that the practice of the architecture discipline of 'making good buildings one at a time' needs to change if it is to have an impact upon the 'growth machines driven by the powerful forces of housebuilders, investors and the real-estate industry, with little concern for what architects may think'.

As Marnie Campagnaro concludes from her research into representations of domestic life in Italian picturebooks, the quality of a domestic landscape is determined not only by the dynamic of a family but also by objects and accessories (Campagnaro, 2019, p. 38). Campagnaro draws particular attention to the refrigerator and the dining table, both of which have prominent places in Australian picturebooks, which also focus on the lounge suite, the parents' bed, and the yard. Any image in a picturebook narrative has a potential to be metonymic because everyday metonymies are cultural rather than created and don't require interpretation. Pictorial metonymies signify on the basis of part for whole, concrete for abstract, object for function, or all of these. A kitchen table can thus be a metonym for the food eaten while sitting there, for the companionship of a family, for a whole kitchen, for a preferred style in furniture, and so on. Just as children develop a schema for a table (what it looks like, how many legs, how it is used), so they develop a range of metonymic meanings from the range of contexts in which tables appear. The traditional architecture of the house interior in *Dog In, Cat Out* is glimpsed only in the wood panelled walls, both fully panelled or half-panelled, and the sash windows. However, the large wooden table in the kitchen and its accompanying set of bentwood chairs is another icon of traditional family life in picture-books, often as a background feature, as in opening 1 of *John Brown, Rose and the Midnight Cat* (1977) and in *Tilly* (2019), or it may have a more narrative function, as in *Running Away from Home* (1996) and *The Trouble with Dogs* (2007). In *Running Away from Home*, a solid wooden table with ladder back wooden chairs is a focal point, always associated with the parents, and instrumental in the reintegration of the would-be runaway child when he leans on it to eat a piece of cake. Opening 3 of *Dog In, Cat Out* concurs with Campagnaro's observation that the table 'registers the emotional and affective temperature of family life' as it depicts the family at breakfast (at 8:00 am), each quietly absorbed in her or his own thoughts or activities (Campagnaro, 2019, p. 38). The dog lies under the table, where it is being patted by the toddler, and the cat looks into the room from the window ledge. At 8:30 am, the older children leave for school on bicycles and then the dog, who had followed them to the gate, bounds back into the house leaving a trail of muddy footprints. An aspect of the equanimity of this family is that any small elements of mayhem, such as this one, are caused by the animals. The mother's attempt to have an afternoon nap is disrupted when the dog jumps onto the bed and wakens the toddler, and in the penultimate opening, when the family is asleep, the cat leaps in through the kitchen window and knocks a vase to the floor, thus creating another mess. The lounge suite is another marker of equanimity. At 10:00 pm, the older children have gone to bed, the dog sleeps in an armchair, and mother and father are on the couch, he watching television with the wakeful toddler, she leaning against him asleep.

The function of the television set here is significant but not surprising, as television sets (and technology in general) are not core objects of picturebook domestic landscapes. They often appear as items of furniture but are rarely turned on. When characters watch television in Shaun Tan's *The Lost Thing* (2000) and *Rules of Summer* (2013), it connotes banality and lack of imagination. In *Running Away from Home*, a partly occluded TV set appears as the background to a close-up of a teapot as a cup of tea is poured. A vector runs from the teapot through the TV to a portrait of the parents of Sam, the would-be runaway. The juxtaposition is of social inclusiveness and social alienation. On top of the TV is a small pile of VHS tapes (this is 1995) and a larger heap of books, in an affirmation of reading culture over watching culture. The story ends with Sam's Dad reading him the chapter from *Winnie-the-Pooh* in which 'Eeyore lost his tail, but then found it again', which becomes a metaphor for Sam's tantrum and reconciliation with his parents. A rare example of television watching appears in Tohby Riddle's whimsical *My Uncle's Donkey* (2010), in which the donkey is depicted as absorbed by his favourite film on television, Charlie Chaplin's *The Kid* (1921). However, this activity is quality watching, as *The Kid* is recognised as perhaps the greatest film of the silent era. The donkey does not only watch television, however, but is also an avid reader.

Spaces where a child can sit and read or be read to are an important component of domestic architecture, as also are spaces of interchange between interiors and landscape architecture. The children in *Dog In, Cat Out* are physically active, whether this involves kicking a football or feeding the pets, activities that are aspects of physical and empathetic development. Interactions and disjunctions between domestic and landscape architecture are both influenced by the horizontal direction of childhood activities. After World War II, an urgent need for increased housing was matched by Government policies (and ideology) which promoted the desirability of single-storey detached houses with ample yard space on 'a quarter-acre block', although the size was more commonly around 650m². This development nurtured a desire for distance and privacy, but also coincided with an era of stay-at-home mothers and changing cultural beliefs about the family and the role of the child. A consequence of these changes was an increasing restriction upon the activities of pre-teen children and the emergence of detached house designs which facilitated a mother's surveillance of children by allowing her to observe play areas within open-plan living spaces or in a backyard through a window (Collins, 2009). Kitchens are normally at the back of the house overlooking the yard, and the principle of surveillance presupposed that a mother would spend much of her time there. The layout of the house shown in Figure 5.2 captures both *desiderata*: a room has been added which doubles as a play space and dining area and its three large windows enable a view of the whole back garden.

This practice is hinted at in *Dog In, Cat Out*, when the housework sharing father is seen looking from the window while the children are outside feeding the cat and the dog. It is most overt in *Drac and the Gremlin* (Allan Baillie and Jane Tanner, 1988). This book about cooperative fantasy play works by sustaining a constant discrepancy between sign and thing – that is, everything represented visually is renamed to accord with the language of a highly conventional fantasy quest script. Examples include the renaming of the family cat, Minnie, and her kittens as 'General Min and her Hissing Horde' and of a car tyre suspended by a rope as an 'Anti-Gravity Solar-Powered Planet Hopper'. A swing made from a used car tyre is the most iconic and constant play object in the gardens of Australian picturebooks. It also connotes, if only implicitly, Australian pride in creative improvisation as an element

FIGURE 5.2 The kitchen as site of surveillance. Photograph by author.

of mythic Australian identity. In *Andrew Jessup* (Nette Hilton and Cathy Wilcox, 1992), the tyre swing in a deserted garden functions as a visual and verbal metonymy expressing physical and social desolation: 'The weeds got longer. The windows got dustier. And the rope on the swing broke'. The creative improvisation in the renaming of things in *Drac and the Gremlin* is a sustained reminder that the game requires continuous negotiation of its components and rules and thus situates readers at a linguistic remove from represented events. This distancing develops further significance in opening 13 when an additional frame of reference is introduced: most of the image is framed within a wide window through which the game is being observed by a woman seen from behind, standing to one side. This is her only appearance in the book, but it suggests that the children's play has always been observed from the house. However, the central surveillance position is occupied by the reader, positioned further back. In the next opening, the mother, now renamed as 'the White Wizard', presents the children with ice cream cones as a reward for 'saving the planet', which readers can re-signify as a reward for negotiated co-operative play between a girl and her younger brother. Reader outside the text and mother within it here share the same viewing position, and presumably the same judgement.

As the possibilities of street play diminished for pre-teen children, picturebook representations of 'the street' as a community of children now seemed optimistic or nostalgic (although cul-de-sacs do still function as outdoor play spaces where children gather). A compromise situation is depicted in *Mr Plunkett's Pool* (1992). Set in an Adelaide inner-city street of somewhat dilapidated workers' cottages, the book depicts children sharing domestic backyards, but not wandering the streets: 'In the street there were two swing sets, one trampoline, five good climbing trees, a cubby house and a storm water drain'. The children lack access to a swimming pool and become excited when one is built in the garden of an old mansion renovated by a wealthy yuppie who works in advertising. When their plan to invade the pool inspires a successful TV commercial, in which they star, the children earn enough money to build their own pool and 'Everyone in the street swam in it'. The children thus preserve community, and even enhance it, by entering the capitalist economy.

Another element that has disappeared from Australian childhood mobility is an unaccompanied walk to a corner shop to 'do the messages'. This was for a long time a normal part of life and was still common when Duncan Ball and Craig Smith used it as the frame for *My Dog's a Scaredy-Cat* (1988), but it has disappeared for two reasons. First, adults now deem that it is no longer possible for children to negotiate public space safely and, second, the corner shop itself is a vanishing amenity. In an interview about his pictorial record of Australian corner stores, *The Milk Bars Book* (2018), Eamon Donnelly said that:

> For himself and millions of others, a trip to the corner store was a part of growing up in Australia. … It was that first taste of independence, it was the first place many people bought something of their own.
>
> *(Quoted in De Poloni, 2019)*

But as Donnelly and others have shown, this cultural institution has been steadily disappearing since the early 1980s, unable to compete with convenience stores located within service stations and local shops set up by major supermarkets. Thus, restrictions on unaccompanied excursions outside home space combine with the disappearance of local shops to eliminate this activity. In 1987, however, it could be used as the basis of a humorous narrative about a boy's walk with his dog, and Craig Smith's cartoon illustrations can freely employ exaggeration and distortion to depict setting, encounters, and elements of the boy's imagination.

Using a setting of an inner-city suburb consisting of workers' cottages, Smith makes intriguing use of an architectural detail as a metaphor within a thematic configuration. Figure 5.3 is a version of a cottage schema that appears in Australian picturebooks, at least, as often as the symmetrical house schema discussed above: it also has a symmetrical façade, but now topped with a bullnose veranda and a roof parallel with the façade. The cottage has end gables and there is commonly an external chimney at one or both gables, as in Figure 5.3.[3]

A playful visual metaphor in this illustration is the appearance of three false dormers on the roof. They are not only excessive but out of place on a Victorian era cottage, and I assume the addition exemplifies the kind of sly satirical touch often to be discerned in Smith's illustrations. The inclusion of a man at work renovating the cottage suggests an urge to 'improve', which destroys the original character of the structure.[4] Perhaps a further part of the joke here is that such dormers are also known as 'doghouse dormers', which reinforces a metaphorical connection between adding embellishments that detract from the character of a building and the narrator's wish that his dog, Stanley, could be different.

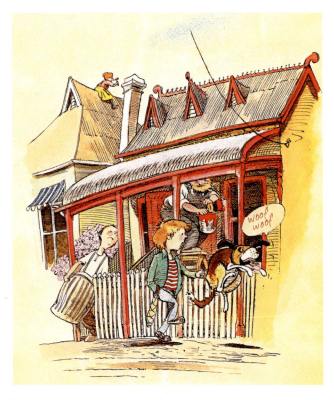

FIGURE 5.3 Walking to the corner store. *My Dog's a Scaredy-Cat* (opening 1, recto) by Duncan Ball, illustrated by Craig Smith, reproduced with kind permission of HarperCollins Publishers Australia Pty Limited.

At its conclusion, the book becomes a story about sharing love, accepting another as he/she is, and not demanding 'improvement'. The theme is affirmed when the narrator's affirmation of his love for his imperfect dog – 'most of all I'm glad he's Stanley' – is illustrated by his mother's unfussy observation that he completed the shopping task imperfectly, bringing home only half the quantity of milk she requested. In its first opening, the picturebook juxtaposes a shopping task assigned to the narrator and an architectural folly which detracts from a heritage building. The story then triangulates these elements with the narrator's overcoming of his embarrassment at Stanley's timidity. The theme does not depend on a reader understanding the point of the dormers, but it does give substance to the idea of building an authentic self.

Building children's lives has evolved a further new dimension with the decrease in the size of yard space surrounding a detached house that began in the late 20th century as house sizes increased and renovation meant the demolition of post-war detached houses and their replacement by larger houses or townhouse complexes (Hall, 2010). As a consequence, private play space is also disappearing and there is less distance between houses. Tony Hall argues that:

> There are significant consequences for children as there is little space for them to run around and make a noise without disturbing others while, at the same time, remaining in a secure environment with a responsible adult keeping watch from inside the house. This is especially important for very young children.
>
> *(Hall, 2010, p. 427)*

Hall also points out that in more recent subdivisions, reduced private space has not been compensated by public open space and playgrounds. Two further aspects of the built environment impact on childhood in a somewhat contradictory way. The knock-down-and-rebuild mentality is part of a 21st-century trend towards bigger houses: Australia vies with the USA to build the world's biggest houses, in floor area and number of bedrooms. Curiously, though, there are fewer people in them: according to the first census of 1911, the average number of people per household was 4.5, but by the 2016 census that number had fallen to 2.6. Proliferation of smaller households has meant proliferation of dwellings and a demand for high-rise apartments and townhouses, which now account for about half of all new homes built (James and Felsman, 2020, p. 4). Where will children go to play?

A response to diminished private play space has been the renovation of public space playgrounds and emergence of a landscape architecture focused on themed 'adventure playgrounds' which incorporate the usual swings, slides, roundabouts, and so on. Figure 5.4 (Lynelle Park, Eastwood, NSW), for example, is a modest attempt to offer a 'pirate ship' theme. Thus, there is a cabin, entered via a stepladder and exited via a slide (sometimes the notorious plank), and a crow's nest attached to a mast, accessed by a rope ladder. Children who recognise the theme may play out a familiar story on their own terms and climb up and down talking like pirates. Pirate stories are a predominantly Anglo conception, however, and most of the small children from this multicultural suburb will not recognise the theme unless they have encountered a picturebook at day care or school, but they do use the space to create their own adventures, often in collaboration with a parent.[5] Landscape architect

FIGURE 5.4 Simple themed playground in a small suburban reserve: Lynelle Park, Eastwood, NSW. Photograph by author.

Mary Jeavons, who specialises in playground design, contends that play spaces should not be over-designed but leave scope for:

> The exceptionally detailed perception that children have of their world. A puddle or a little thicket of vegetation can be way more significant to children than we, as adults, could imagine. Unless we observe their behaviour closely and talk to children, we miss a lot.
>
> *(Cited by Salt, 2020 p. 53)*

Lynelle Park includes an uncultivated area which enables an adventure to be extended into 'wild' space.

Families living in apartments or townhouses have made increasing use of such spaces or may appropriate other spaces. When Macquarie University was established in the 1960s, 19 km from Sydney's CBD, it was built on small farm land in a semi-rural area. Half a century later, it is densely surrounded by a rapidly increasing population living in apartments and townhouses with minimal outdoor play space. An unfolding high-rise development adjacent to the university will accommodate 5,000 people when completed. In 2020, the University landscaped a large open space around a creek and a small lake as part of a rebuilding programme. Although there are no facilities for children, the space was quickly appropriated by families within walking distance, and at any time on a fine Saturday or Sunday, there will be upwards of 50–60 people with children running about patting dogs, feeding wild ducks, tossing stones into the creek, or building little tepee frames with sticks. Children thus experience an interaction with nature, albeit a constructed nature, as they are too little to stray far from their parents or enter a bushland wilderness that marks the northern perimeter of the landscaped area.

Such an adventure outside the home is captured in *Puddle Hunters* (2018) by Kirsty Murray and Karen Blair (illustrator). The book's premise is simple: after it has been raining, two pre-school children, Ruby and Banjo, wish to go outside and splash in puddles. The underlying script is familiar: departure from home, journey to a site of adventure, and return to the security of home. In opening 1, the children kneel or stand on a couch and look out through a bay window, excited that the rain has stopped and they can go in search of puddles. On the other side of the street, three workers' cottages have been hazily sketched: all have bullnose verandas, two are based on the symmetrical house schema, and the third, a cottage schema less often represented in picturebooks, has a hip roof and asymmetrical façade. While it might seem like an over-interpretation of a simple story, it is hard to overlook that the establishing image brings together two iconic cultural metonymies of Australian picturebook discourse – the couch and the workers' cottage schema – as departure points for an adventure. In other words, the culture (also) writes the story. Just as childhood is a movement out from the proximal contexts of the home to more distal and more risky contexts starting with the neighbourhood and beyond, so children's literature maps a widening of experiential contexts. As the children go in search of puddles, with 'Mama' as sidekick, they travel through built environments to a kind of wilderness: first into the garden of their house, then to the street, to the park, and finally across a wooden pedestrian bridge to the river flats, where they finally find puddles. Visually, this is a journey from a 1930s Tudor Revival house in an English cottage garden to a bare street, then to a cultivated park devoid of native Australian trees, and so to the naturally drained river flats and Australian eucalyptus, here used to represent the unbuilt environment of the bush. The bridge thus functions as a threshold to the less civilised location, with a hint of danger in Ruby's injunction to Banjo, 'Hold hands'![6] However, the children aren't alone in moving from civilisation to wilderness: their 40-something, stay-at-home (single?) mother, neat in a Messy High Bun hairstyle, granny glasses, and overalls, also gets to jump up and down with the children in their last puddle. The book closes with a return home to civilisation. The children are bathed and, as falling rain presages more adventures, the trio settle down on the couch to read a picturebook. Recurrent schemas associated with built environments can be seen to bring resonant signification to a story about and for pre-school children.

In its progression from proximal to distal space and back again, the spatiality of *Puddle Hunters* is horizontal. As noted earlier, this feature is shared with other books, such as *My Dog's a Scaredy-Cat*, and also applies to books in which movement is limited to a domestic house and garden. Horizontality may not be a unique feature of Australian picturebooks, but it is a distinctive feature of their visual narrative. In contrast, in a study of British domestic architecture in picturebooks, Emma Hayward and Torsten Schmiedeknecht explore verticality. To do this, they draw on a contention advanced by Gaston Bachelard that verticality expresses emotional/psychological responses to imagined forms, and without it, the home, specifically the spaces within it, become nondescript and lose their distinctive character (Hayward and Schmiedeknecht, 2019, p. 491). As I have suggested, domestic architecture in Australian picturebooks seeks distinctiveness through its orientation towards heritage cottages, and there is no comparable tradition for representing multi-storey houses. A two-storey house is found in *Tilly* (Jane Godwin and Anna Walker, 2019), but here domestic space is only sketched and lacks definition. The only visual information necessary for the narrative is that there are internal stairs leading to a second level (partly visible in opening 1) and then up to a small dormer room which is Tilly's. The top step has a secret cavity where Tilly, youngest of four children, hides her treasures. When a newly laid carpet prevents access to the cavity, Tilly is plunged into grief, but rises above it through the operation of memory and imagination. Verticality has a double function here: it initially renders Tilly vulnerable, but then enriches her. The setting of *Tilly* is unusual as verticality is rare in Australian picturebooks. Where it does occur, its significance is best approached as a realisation of vertical conceptual metaphors that depend on the contrast UP-DOWN.[7]

To conclude this chapter, I will discuss two examples in which the physical structure of a high-set house introduces a vertical metaphor expressed primarily in visual images. In their foundational study *Metaphors We Live By* (1980), Lakoff and Johnson argue that conceptual metaphors are based on our interaction with the physical, social, and cultural dimensions of the world around us. They are thus presupposed cultural models which play a significant role in how we make sense of the world, especially of abstract concepts. They are not innate, however, but learned as language is learned, and picturebooks are a source of such knowledge. Metaphors listed by Lakoff and Johnson as examples of the vertical UP-DOWN contrast, and which may be discerned in the focused examples, include: HAPPY IS UP, SAD IS DOWN; HAVING CONTROL IS UP, BEING SUBJECT TO CONTROL IS DOWN; HIGH STATUS IS UP, LOW STATUS IS DOWN; GOOD IS UP, BAD IS DOWN; and RATIONAL/REASONABLE IS UP, EMOTIONAL/UNREASONABLE IS DOWN.

A good site on which to create a vertical metaphor visually is an Australian house type known as a 'Queenslander'. As the name suggests, they are unique to the State of Queensland, where they evolved during the 19th century. While there are many regional variations around the State, the typical Queenslander is a single-storey detached house made of timber with a corrugated iron roof. One of its most distinctive characteristics is its elevation: it is built on poles, frequently about three metres in height, and thus has a large open space beneath it. Various explanations have been offered for the elevation: flooding, hillslope sites, defence against mosquitoes or termites, or the avoidance of malaria, which in the 19th century was then attributed to miasma arising from damp ground (Bell, 2002, pp. 22–23). Other features are wide verandas, usually on two or three sides, with lattice-work sometimes added for privacy screening. Gregory Rogers's illustration of a heritage Queenslander for *Running Away from Home* (Figure 5.5) is a variation of the type which

FIGURE 5.5 Visualisation of a vertical metaphor. Illustration, 1995, by Gregory Rogers; from *Running Away from Home* by Nigel Gray. Used by permission of Andersen Press and of Alfred A. Knopf, an imprint of Random House Children's Books, a division of Penguin Random House LLC. All rights reserved.

incorporates stylistic features from the California Bungalow, popular in Australia in the early 20th century. These involve the construction of a main and secondary gable and the prominent staircase at the front of the house.

Vertical metaphors appear in opening 5. In the darkness beneath the house, directly below the main window, stands Sam, the would-be runaway, who has come down the stairs from the veranda. The rain 'poured down in a torrent', Sam doesn't want to get his toy gorilla or pillow wet, and his backpack, over-filled with inappropriate items, is already feeling too heavy. As his unhappiness increases, two instantiations of the vertical UP-DOWN metaphor are suggested by the visual scene: first, GOOD IS UP, BAD IS DOWN – Sam has descended from his beautiful heritage house, his family, and 'the room that he'd lived in all his life' to a dark place of loneliness and alienation. Second, Sam's movement down and up the stairs is prompted by a temper tantrum and the resolution of the temporary rift thus caused invites interpretation as a contrast between REASONABLE IS UP, UNREASONABLE IS DOWN. In other words, narrative and images are embodying without stating some abstract concepts as part of the book's significance. Sam becomes angry and decides to leave home in the opening paragraph because, '[His] dad was being even more bossy and obstreperous than usual'. The story is narrated from Sam's perspective, so 'obstreperous' – not a child's word but a word an adult might use of a child – offers a ready hint that it has been used in reference to Sam, who has appropriated it to counter his father's attempt to correct him (a visual image indicates he has been riding his skateboard inside the house).

When the rain eases and Sam prepares to leave, he remembers something he has forgotten, a gift from his brother, and returns up the stairs and into the house. Here, he encounters the love and simple *reasonableness* of his parents:

'Would you like a piece of cake before you go?' Dad asked.
'No!' said Sam.
'You don't have to leave home if you don't want to,' Mum said.
'I want to,' said Sam.

And Sam changes his mind about the cake and accepts his father's offer to read him a chapter from *Winnie-the-Pooh*, which Sam had found too difficult to read himself when huddled outside the house. By giving him (apparent) options for co-operation and space to find himself, Sam's parents enable him to choose his only option – to ascend and rejoin the family – without humiliation and with a retained illusion of agency: 'I'll give you one last chance', he tells his father, in a final quotation of adult talk.

The REASONABLE IS UP metaphor affirms that Sam has ample space, both physically and emotionally. The desirability of one's own space is also a theme in another picturebook set in a Queenslander, *In My Father's Room* (2000) by Gary Crew and Annmarie Scott. Although the illustrations do not evoke a clearly identifiable architectural style within which to locate the vertical UP-DOWN metaphor, the structure does so effectively. Only interior views of the house are offered, and these are mostly restricted to four places: the narrator's room, the father's storeroom positioned directly beneath, a veranda, and a wooden stair leading outside and close to the door of the storeroom, which is accessed from outside the house. A window in the narrator's room is placed diagonally above this door. The narrator's room has two doors, one opening onto the veranda and the other leading into the rest of the house. This limited information indicates that the house is also a Queenslander type, with a storeroom added underneath, as was frequently done.

The Up-Down vertical metaphor is portrayed visually in terms of the rooms as metonymies for their occupants and the prominence of the stairs in opening 2 foregrounds the up-down movement. The primary metaphorical contrast is RATIONAL/REASONABLE IS UP, EMOTIONAL/UNREASONABLE IS DOWN. The narrator embraces reason and is bemused and a little scornful of her father's dilettantism and lists numerous, diverse hobbies he has briefly taken up on a whim and then abandoned in his room below hers. He thus falls into the EMOTIONAL/UNREASONABLE category, as does the narrator's mother, who maintains repeatedly, 'Your father's a dabbler … That's why I love him'. The narrator herself is highly focused and an avid reader, and throughout the story adds layers to a papier mâché bust of her father, working sometimes on the veranda but mostly in her room. Her devotion to the task, and so to her subject, moderates the REASONABLE/EMOTIONAL dichotomy, which is dismantled at the story's close when she creeps downstairs at night and into the storeroom to investigate a secret project. Her descent is drawn from a high angle and from behind her, defamiliarising her destination. By entering her father's mental space, she embraces EMOTION/UNREASON and also discovers he is moving towards her mental space by writing a story for her upcoming tenth birthday. The interchange between reason and emotion in *In My Father's Room* reaches out to include an offer of trust, understanding, and respect for an other's space.

Domestic and landscape architecture in Australian picturebooks are notable in two main aspects, heritage and horizontality, and these shape the values which the books largely embrace. Heritage affirms the persistence of the material past in the present and its status as a bearer of values that continue from the past, albeit selectively. *Puddle Hunters*, for example, conveys a strong sense of childhood well-being underpinning its adventure script.

The transparent, almost ghostly 19th-century cottages opposite the children's house are a reminder that even as we shape aspects of our present, we continue to be shaped by the past, even if that past is a tradition in picturebook illustration. Horizontality is also metonymic in its own way, as it is conducive to journeys and adventures imagined in domestic space which flows easily between inside and outside. The lives of children may have become more circumscribed by the end of the 20th century, but picturebook representations of movement across domestic spaces and out into distal built environments (with a guardian, of course) present realms of possibility to the imagination.

Notes

1 In children's drawings, the triangle is commonly equilateral, but adult versions of the schema favour an isosceles triangle. Terry Denton's version has some embellishments: veranda posts; a finial at the front of the gable; a letterbox on the gatepost; some furniture on the veranda. Denton evokes the schema elsewhere, as in *Mr Plunkett's Pool* (1992), text by Gillian Rubinstein.

2 There are numerous books about twins, but the allusion here is probably to the 1960 classic picturebook *The Kitten Twins* by Helen Wing and Elizabeth Webbe (Rand McNally).

3 Pamela Allen, *Who Sank the Boat* (1983); Alison Lester, *The Journey Home* (1989); Ian Edwards and Rachel Tonkin, *Papa and the Olden Days* (1989); Ann James, *Finding Jack* (1992).

4 For further discussion of such 'improvements', see the blog by architect Heidi Bowman: 'Adelaide Villa. Renovating a Heritage House – Where to Start'. http://adelaidevilla.blogspot.com/2017/12/renovating-heritage-house-where-to-start.html.

5 There is a plethora of picturebooks about pirates, from John Burningham's classic *Come Away from the Water, Shirley* (1977) to more recent examples: Claire Freedman and Ben Cort, *Pirates Love Underpants* (2013); Eve Bunting and Julie Fortenberry, *Pirate Boy* (2011); Kim Kennedy and Doug Kennedy, *Pirate Pete's Talk Like a Pirate* (2007); Peter Harris and Deborah Allwright, *The Night Pirates* (2006); Melinda Long and David Shannon, *How I became a Pirate* (2003); and, from Australia, Mem Fox and Kathryn Brown, *Tough Boris* (1994).

6 Tudor Revival Architecture was popular in Australia between World War I and World War II, although some features, such as gable fronts with white plastering between black-painted timber strips, were incorporated into other styles.

7 I follow the usual convention of placing conceptual metaphors in small capitals.

References

Picturebooks

Baillie, A. and J. Tanner (1988). *Drac and the Gremlin.* Ringwood: Viking Kestrel.

Ball, D. and C. Smith (1988). *My Dog's a Scaredy-Cat.* London: J M Dent & Sons Ltd.

Crew, G. and A. Scott (2000). *In My Father's Room.* Sydney: Hodder Children's Books.

Fox, M. and T. Denton (1989). *Night Noises.* Norwood: Omnibus Books.

Godwin, J. and A. Walker (2019). *Tilly.* Gosford, NSW: Scholastic.

Graham, B. (2007). *The Trouble with Dogs!* London: Walker Book Ltd.

Gray, N. and G. Rogers (1995). *Running Away from Home.* Sydney: Random House Australia.

Hilton, N. and Wilcox C. (1992). *Andrew Jessup.* Montville, Queensland: Walter McVitty Books; (1993) Boston, MA: Houghton Mifflin.

James, A. (1992). *Finding Jack.* South. Melbourne: Oxford University Press.

Murray, K. and K. Blair (2018). *Puddle Hunters.* Crows Nest: Allen & Unwin.

Riddle, T. (2010). *My Uncle's Donkey* Camberwell: Viking.

Rubinstein, G. and T. Denton (1992). *Mr Plunkett's Pool.* Milson's Point: Random House.

Rubinstein, G. and A. James (1991). *Dog In, Cat Out.* Norwood: Omnibus Books.

Tan, S. (2000). *The Lost Thing.* Port Melbourne: Thomas C. Lothian Pty Ltd.

Tan, S. (2013). *Rules of Summer.* Sydney: Lothian Children's Books.

Wagner, J. and R. Brooks (1977). *John Brown, Rose and the Midnight Cat.* Harmondsworth: Kestrel Books.

Works cited

Bell, P. (2002). A History of the Queensland House, Adelaide: Historical Research Pty Ltd, 2002. A Paper Based On Extracts from an Unpublished Report to the Queensland Heritage Council. *Guidelines for Entering Houses in the Queensland Heritage Register.* https://www.academia.edu/20465274/A_History_of_the_Queensland_House

Campagnaro, M. (2019). 'Narrating' Homes and Objects: Images of Domestic Life in Italian Picturebooks since the Mid-20th Century. *Ricerche di Pedagogia e Didattica – Journal of Theories and Research in Education*, 14 (2), pp. 9–48.

Collins, J. (2009). 'Small Children Dictate Home Plan': Uncovering the Influence of Childrearing Ideals on the Design of the Modern Post-war House. *Australian Historical Studies*, 40(2), pp. 197–214.

De Poloni, G. (2019). The Slow Death of the Australian Icon That Is the Corner Store (or milk bar, or deli), *ABC News,* 21 July. https://www.abc.net.au/news/2019-07-21/the-death-of-the-milk-bar-deli-corner-store-an-australian-icon/11279638

Donnelly, E. (2018). *The Milk Bars Book.* Melbourne: Ellikon Fine Printers.

Goodall, H. (2014). 'Fixing' the Past: Modernity, Tradition and Memory in Rural Australia.In Timothy Neale, Crystal McKinnon and Eve Vincent (eds), *History, Power, Text: Cultural Studies and Indigenous Studies.* Sydney: CSR Books, pp. 91–111.

Hall, T. (2010). Goodbye to the Backyard? –The Minimisation of Private Open Space in the Australian Outer-Suburban Estate. *Urban Policy and Research*, 28(4), pp. 411–433.

Hayward, E. and T. Schmiedeknecht (2019). Absent Architectures: Post-War Housing in British Children's Picturebooks (1960–Present). *Journal of Architecture*, 24(4), pp. 487–511.

Hyde, R. (2021). The Suburbs on their Own Terms. *Architecture Australia*, 110(4), pp. 12–14.

James, C. and R. Felsman (2020). Australian Houses Are Again the World's Biggest: CommSec Home Size Trends Report. *Economic Insights*, Commonwealth Bank. https://www.commbank.com.au/content/dam/caas/newsroom/docs/CommSec%20Homes%20Size%20Trends%20Report_201106.pdf

Lakoff, G. & M. Johnson (1980). *Metaphors We Live By*. Chicago: The University of Chicago Press.

Salt, L. (2020). Dedicated to Play: Mary Jeavons. *Landscape Architecture Australia*, 166, pp. 52–57.

Stark, J. (2005). An Artist's Prints Are a Bold Recollection of a Time Long Past. *The Age*, June 22, 2005. https://www.theage.com.au/entertainment/art-and-design/melbourne-in-a-past-light-20050622-ge0dwp.html

6

THE HOUSE, WHERE EVERYTHING BEGINS

Christophe Meunier

It is unsurprising that in many children's picturebooks, the house appears as an important place. Dedicated to children, their primary function is to make the world intelligible for young readers and future citizens. Picturebooks can be the reflection of the common assumptions of society. They express the spatial ideology of a society, both verbally and visually. This chapter shows that picturebooks about architecture and houses provide children with a social ecology, a habitus, a spatial and cultural capital.

According to French psychoanalyst Alberto Eiguer, the house reveals our own deep being and a personal *modus habitandi* that we carry inside us, which allows us to move in new places (Eiguer, 2013, pp. 24–25). I suggest naming this specific skill 'inside dwelling'. It allows us to overcome the pain of moving on or the loss of a residence. This 'inside dwelling' is a social construction insofar as it is built, thanks to the relationships that we weave, at first with relatives, and later with people we meet. It is also a temporal construction insofar as it is built across time, and so it relates to Passeron and Bourdieu's concept of 'cultural capital', that is to say, 'the cultural possessions that are transmitted by the different pedagogical family actions' (Bourdieu, 1977, p. 488). In the same way, we could consider that this 'inside dwelling' is a part of 'spatial capital' (Lussault, 2003), constituted by the addition of all the spatial competences acquired by a person all along his life.

Gaston Bachelard suggests that 'all really inhabited space bears the essence of the notion of home' (Bachelard, 1964, p. 5), and thus the house, for Bachelard, is the human being's first world:

> In the life of a man, the house thrusts aside contingencies, its councils of continuity are unceasing. Without it, man would be a dispersed being. It maintains him through the storms of the heavens and through those of life. It is body and soul. It is the human being's first world. Before he is 'cast into the world', as claimed by certain hasty metaphysics, man is laid in the cradle of the house. And always, in our daydreams, the house is a large cradle.
>
> *(Bachelard, 1964, p. 7)*

DOI: 10.4324/9781003131755-9

With this in mind, it is unsurprising that in many children's picturebooks, the house appears as an important place, a fundamental step, and often marks the beginning of adventures. Everyone remembers the Three Little Pigs' houses or the Three Bears' cabin. These houses contribute to building our imagination and our representations of home and from them, we create our dream houses. So, we must consider, with John Stephens, that picturebooks are 'ideological artifacts' (2018, p. 137). Dedicated to children, their primary function is to make the world intelligible for young readers and future citizens. Picturebooks can be the reflection of the common assumptions of society, but they are also an implicitly or overtly propagandistic medium. 'Picturebooks express the ideology of a society both verbally and visually', Stephens wrote. 'The interaction of the dual semiotic codes can work to produce an ideological conjunction' (2018, p. 138). Picturebooks about architecture and houses provide children with a social ecology, a *habitus*, a spatial and cultural capital.

This chapter will show how, at first, children's picturebooks used simple constructions of the house, granting it only elementary functions that were designed to reassure young readers. Then they seized on the house as a way to transmit important values, sometimes new ones, sometimes just different ways of dwelling. Finally, I will demonstrate that the house is very often the starting point to dwell and to live in the world. The several examples that will be used to illustrate my argument are extracted from a selection of almost 330 picturebooks printed in France that constituted my corpus of research about space and spatiality in children's picturebooks. They have been chosen because of their relevance and their engagement with the spatial ideologies that run throughout children's literature.

Hut, cabins and other houses: the marks of primitive habitation

Numerous picturebooks, and especially those which were published before 1960, represent the house using the language of primitive architecture. Picturebooks overflow with huts, cabins, shacks and shelters that host different characters, very often animals. The Three Bears' house in *Goldilocks and the Three Bears* by Rose Celli and Gerda Muller, published in 1956 in the collection *Les Albums du Père Castor*, overseen by Paul Faucher, is a very good example of a primitive hut. This is a small house in the middle of the forest. Its walls, made of stone and wood, are thick and small. Its roof, in wood and straw, is slightly sloping, increasing the impression that the house is firmly anchored in the ground. This chtonian seat reminds us that the house is a burrow, a refuge. Near the hut, a well, three beehives and a fireplace provide the nourishing function of the house. The Three Bears' house, with its opened windows, reassures Goldilocks, the poor girl lost in the forest. The text says: 'À la fin de la journée, bien fatiguée, bien triste, elle allait se mettre à pleurer quand, soudain, elle aperçut à travers les arbres une très jolie maison' [At the end of the day, tired and sad, and about to cry, suddenly, she saw through the trees a very pretty house] (p. 6).

In a recent Anne Herbauts picturebook, *Monday*, published in 2004 by Casterman and again in 2006 by Enchanted Lion Books, we also find these symbolic functions of the primitive house. Monday's house is summed up as a symbolic shape that appears cut into the cover: one horizontal line for the ground, two vertical for the walls, two segments at right angles for the roof and a chimney. In her house, in the middle of vacant land, Monday receives friends for hot tea and music. The seasons pass, bringing wind, rain, cold and snow, but Monday's house always resists and stands solidly on the ground, providing security and warmth to its dwellers.

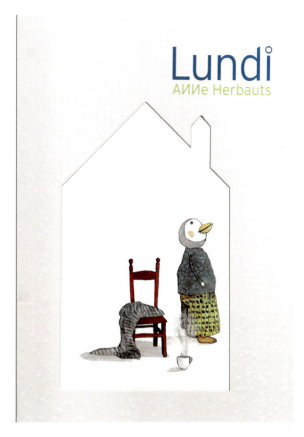

FIGURE 6.1 Cover of Anne Herbaut's *Lundi* (2006).
Source: © Casterman

These symbolic functions of the house—shelter, refuge and hearth—can be read in the etymology of 'house' and 'build'. The two words came from the Old English 'hus' and 'byldan', meaning, for the first one, 'roof, shelter', and for the second, 'enclosed by walls'. Building a house is etymologically raising walls above one's head to avoid danger. In *The Poetics of Space*, Bachelard defines the ideal house by referring to an extract from Victor Hugo's *Notre-Dame of Paris/The Hunchback of Notre Dame* (book IV). For Quasimodo, he writes, 'the cathedral had been successively egg, nest, country and universe. [...] One might almost say that he had espoused its form the way the snail does the form of its shell. It was his home, his hole, his envelope…' (Bachelard, 1964, p. 90).

The first illustrated version of *The Story of the Three Little Pigs* by Joseph Jacobs and Leonard Leslie Brooke in 1904 makes construction an art. Indeed, the neglect and fun of the two first pigs, who have chosen to build in wood and straw, lead them to death. The third pig takes his time. He makes a blueprint, constructs scaffolding, makes thick brick walls. He behaves like a true architect. Etymologically, he is the one who oversees the carpenters' work. In the Walt Disney version (1933), the fate of the first two pigs is less cruel; owing to his wisdom the third pig becomes a saviour and protector of his brothers. So, the houses that we see in the picturebooks we are engaging with in this chapter and published before the 1960s are very often traditional and western. There is no room for any originality.

FIGURE 6.2 Claude Ponti, *My valley* (2017, p. 7).

Source: © Ecole des Loisirs

The young reader meets primitive houses or houses that he/she is familiar with even when the form of the book itself is novel. One of the very first of the French collection 'Les Albums du Père Castor' is quite innovative. For example, a certain R. Citroën published in 1938 a very unusual folding picturebook, *Ma Maison* (*My House*). It is composed of four pages that the child reader can fold and link to create a house with four walls. Each page is a room of a kind of dollhouse: the kitchen, the bedroom, the dining room and the entrance. We recognise the symbolic functions of the house: eating, sleeping, being safe and protected. Two other pages offer characters that can be cut out by young readers to play with in the picturebook and thus create their own stories.

At the beginning of the 1950s, philosophers and psychologists began to question the representations children have of the house. Françoise Minkowska (1949) and Sylvia Markham (1954), who studied children's drawings, conclude that these drawings reveal a 'state of mind'. The house is the image of intimacy, the natural place of the dwelling function. Slowly, by entering the privacy of the house, children's picturebook authors are going to be able to show their characters' inner selves as well as theirs too, in a way.

The functions of the primitive house are completed by another function which seems more modern: the function of identification. These functions can be found in oneiric houses like the ones which appear in Claude Ponti's picturebooks. Claude Ponti's houses occupy a special place in this artist's work. In *My Valley* (1998), for instance, we discover a house-tree, with solid roots deeply buried in the ground, rising to the sky. The sectional plan Ponti provides shows a deep cellar, which seems rather like a cave, and an attic turned towards the stars and the 'elsewhere'. So, to the cellar, kingdom of the irrational, Ponti, inspired by Bachelard, opposes the attic, kingdom of the rational. But also, in the Twim's house-tree, the attic contains books and telescopes to encourage the reader/inhabitant to project outward, whereas in the cellar there are a lot of dark galleries and an abundance of food to encourage them to sink into dreams. Between these two polarities, the different floors are linked by stairs which give access to different worlds. Each room responds to the quest of identity of each dweller of the house-tree. Bachelard speaks of the 'heroism of the staircase' (Bachelard, 1964, p. 27) that we need in order to climb and reach the sky. Poutchy Blue's bedroom is at the highest, most inaccessible and most protected place. According to Ponti, if the house is the image of the world, the world is also the image of the house. Each part of the world is closed: we go from one room to another, crossing initiation thresholds. The French philosopher, Gilbert Durand, follower of Gaston Bachelard, describes with precision to what the image of the tree refers. He writes:

> Through its verticality, the cosmic tree is humanised. It becomes the symbol of man as a vertical microcosm […]. […] the tree is really the psycho-physiological totality of human individuality: its trunk is intelligence, its inner cavities sensitive nerves, its branches sense-impressions, its fruits and flowers good and bad actions.
>
> *(Durand, 1999, p. 330)*

Tell me what house you live in and I'll tell you who you are

In *Don Quixote*, Miguel Cervantes, the Spanish author, in a very long soliloquy, lets Sancho say what could define him. Don Quixote's faithful servant refers to an old proverb: 'Tell me what company thou keepest and I'll tell thee what thou art' (Cervantes, Part 2, chapter X, 2003, p. 540). He specifies, 'Not with whom thou art bred, but with whom thou art fed'. In our turn, we could add that identity is both a social and spatial construction. Following Cervantes, we could say, 'Show me where you live and I will tell you who you are'. Let's take the example of a picturebook by Annette Tison and Talus Taylor in 1972, *La maison de Barbapapa* (*Barbapapa's house*). Each alveolar room has been conceived in the image of its occupant. One of the rooms has even been moulded around each member of Barbapapa's family: 'They cover Barbapapa with plastic. When the plastic is dry, the house is finished' (p. 21). Barbapapa's house reminds us of the cocoon house or the chrysalis developed by Bachelard (1964, p. 65), but it also brings to mind the bubble house imagined by the architect Antti Lovag in 1955. Besides, this picturebook can be inscribed in the anti-conformist ideology that followed the Second World War, which wanted to oppose the rigidity of administrative rules. The bubble house, with its organic and sculptural shapes in concrete, is based upon modularity and the free expression of the individual. It was another way to dwell for Lovag and his follower Pascal Haüsermann.

Several picturebooks aim to show the *modus vivendi* or *habitandi* of other societies. The purpose is not to lean on an archetype of habitation but to stereotype a dwelling which could correspond to the entire depicted society, as in the Korean artist Kwon Yoon-Duck's *Man-hee's House* (1995). In this publication, the young hero and his family must leave a small apartment in the city to move into his grandparents' house in a small town. The new house he is going to live in is a two-storey house with a garden. Man-hee shows his new house to the readers. The route proposed by the child is relevant to the values given to the domestic space in Korea.

The visit begins with a view of the house from the street (pp. 5–6). The house is surrounded by tall walls surmounted by barbed wire. Multicoloured climbing flowers try to hide the fence that could make the house look like a bunker. Korean domestic space seems to be very protected from the street. On the following double-page spread, we come inside the grandparents' bedroom, a kind of sanctuary dedicated to the story of the family, the glory of the ancestors and traditions; here, we find very old pictures, some lacquered furniture and some porcelains. Then, the child has us go through the kitchen and the different stories: the cellar for fruits, cereals and alcohol, the courtyard for the jars of salt, soya and dried fish. When Man-hee has us come into the house again, he leads us into his bedroom, the bathroom and his father's office. The plan of the house, which we discover at the end of the picturebook, suggests that the space is very open inside and that modularity is a characteristic of Korean houses. Man-hee says, 'At the right, when we come in, is my bedroom. Even if it is not very big, when I invite all my friends, we play all the way to the corridor' (Kwon Yoon-Duck, 1995, p. 21). As occidental observers, we may be surprised by the extreme porosity that exists between the outside and the inside spaces. Man-hee goes from one to the other easily. As a stereotype, Man-hee's house is a representation of a kind of Korean domestic spatiality whose principles of habitation form a triple function: protective (significance of the fence), identity (importance of the family and the ancestors) and nutritive (importance of storage and cooking spaces).

The illustrators for children often choose to depict builder animals which transform their natural environment into a living environment. Through building, each living being succeeds in organising his/her own territory, his/her own living place. To build is thus characteristic of every living being. Each one is gifted with subjectivity, as Jakob von Uexküll

FIGURE 6.3 K. Aoyama, *Qu'est-ce que vous faites monsieur l'architecte?* (2016, pp. 24–25).
Source: © AOYAMA Kunihiko 2003 *Dwarf Jiisan No Iezukuri* by Froebel-kan co.ltd.

showed in his different works at the beginning of the 20th century: Every living being arranges the natural data (*Umgebung*) to make its own environment (*Umwelt*), especially adapted to its species (von Uexküll, 1934). In *Need A House? Call Ms Mouse* (1981) by George Mendoza and Doris Susan Smith, the animals of the forest ask Henrietta, a little mouse, to conceive for each one of them their own habitation: 'Henrietta is a world famous home decorator, which means she is an artist, a designer, a dreamer, a builder, a creator, all that and more too' (p. 6). For Lizard, Henrietta designs 'a splendid beach house––a place to enjoy the sun coming up and the sun going down' (p. 31). The reference to Franck Lloyd Wright's organic architecture is obvious. Lizard's house recalls the Waterfall House designed in 1935 by Wright for Edgar Kauffman and built just on the rocks where Kauffman and his wife used to picnic. Mendoza and Smith's picturebook is a real catalogue of architectural objects. Another example is Cat's House: 'Cat, lazy Cat, purrs for lots of beds and wrap-around terraces for the sole purpose of being what cats like to be best, lazy' (p. 18). So, Henrietta chooses a Japanese minka: a squared one-floor house opening onto a closed garden. All the floors of the house are covered by tatami mats and the rooms are all composed of sliding partitions. This habitation is perfectly suited to the way of life of a cat.

Kunihiko Aoyama, a Japanese author who first studied architecture at Waseda University in Tokyo, expresses the merits of an architecture close to individuals. In his picturebooks, *Qu'est-ce que vous faites, M. l'architecte?* [*What Are You Doing, Mr. Architect?*] (2003), he tells the story of an old dwarf who lives in the depths of a forest. He is designing blueprints and a model of a house he wants to build for himself with 'a big belvedere to admire the landscape'

FIGURE 6.4 A. Brière-Haquet, Barroux, *On déménage!* (2018, pp. 2–3).
Source: © Little Urban

(2003, p. 2). As the construction progresses, he receives help from different animals of the forest who ask him in return for a room especially conceived for them. Bear wants a large room according to his dimensions; monkey wants a room near the branches. Finally, the dwarf's house becomes a kind of Noah's Ark where each animal of the forest has his own habitation. The ideology that appears through these books translates the extreme interdependence between two words that Heidegger wants to relay: building and dwelling. We build because we dwell, but we also dwell because we build.

Numerous picturebooks have moving for a main theme. Leaving one's house is always a very difficult ordeal. A human being has to face what Deleuze names a 'phase of deterritorialization' (1980, p. 230), which relates to a phase of disappropriation of the domestic space. The French picturebook *On déménage!* [*We Are Moving!*] by Alice Brière-Haquet and Baroux gives a good example of deterritorialization. Reviewing every room of the house he must leave, a young boy describes what he must leave behind in the style of a classified advertisement: 'À vendre/Ma maison/Mon chez moi/À moi' ('For Sale/My house/My home/Of mine') (2018, p. 2). These first sentences suggest how difficult it is to leave a place the boy appropriated. Separated by the folding of the book, the double-page sets side by side the house and a tree whose foliage looks like an egg. The Bachelardian association between the house and the egg is still carried out. After the inventory of what the boy leaves physically but keeps in his mind, a last sentence lets us think about a possible reterritorialization: 'Il faut partir…vers une autre vie dans une maison à acheter où tout sera à inventer' ['I have to go…to another life in another house where everything is yet to be invented'] (p. 27).

The French psychoanalyst Alberto Eiguer created the concept of 'inside dwelling', similar to the idea of a plan of immanence developed by Deleuze and Guattarri. The human being carries his house in his head. His 'inside dwelling' allows him to reterritorialize each time he moves out and he moves in. The 'inside dwelling' has been built from the first house of childhood. Referring to a Francis Ponge poem, 'The Snails', we could talk about a 'snail syndrome' that would be part of us:

> Unlike the ashes that make their home with hot coals, snails prefer moist earth. Go on: they advance while gluing themselves to it with their entire bodies. They carry it, they eat it, they shit it. They go through it, it goes through them. [...] He sticks to Nature, he enjoys his perfect nearness, he is the friend of the soil which he kisses with his whole body. And he befriends the leaves, and the heavens toward which he proudly stretches his head, with eyes sensitive enough to signify nobility, slowness, wisdom, pride, vanity, fire.
>
> *(Ponge, 2016, pp. 316–317)*

Anne Lemonnier and Claire Gastold's picturebook *La Souris de Paris* [*The Mouse of Paris*] (2011) seems to be a good example of the 'Snail Syndrome' felt by a young girl who is moving in. Like a little mouse in the city, she knows every corner, every street of her district. But she must face the problem of moving out, of uprooting. The picturebook peels away the process of deterritorialization and reterritorialization. In this process, the house plays an essential role. In the first phase, the young girl introduces the reader to her district, her living place that she is going to leave. She goes from a general view of the area to the Bachelardian 'corner', the bottom of a moving box. This 'corner' is like a refuge against the stress of moving out. On pages 11–12, she entirely fills the box where she sits in a foetal position. The second phase is completely constructed in opposition to the first one. The reader goes from the house (personal space) to the close environment (public space). This is from the new reterritorialized house, reappropriated, that the young girl begins the conquest of her new living space. The space, in which the entire walk takes place, belongs to what French geographers call 'close space', a blurred notion that is always very difficult to define because it includes a random and subjective distance around the person. Anglo–Saxon geographers refer mostly to the frequency of attendance and name these spaces 'everyday spaces' (Holloway & Valentin, 2000, p. 11).

In *The Poetics of Space*, Bachelard evokes too the behaviour of the snail. He writes: 'the mollusk's motto would be: one must live to build one's house, and not build one's house to live in' (Bachelard, 1964, p. 106). What the hero of a picturebook 'does' in his domestic space allows him to project this 'doing' into the outside space, the public and social one. The house is not only a 'machine for living in', as Le Corbusier believed (1923/2014, p. 4), but also a 'machine for dwelling the world'.

Living in a house for dwelling the world

When Martin Heidegger tried to define what to dwell is, in 1951 in Darmstadt, he linked three words without any comas: building dwelling thinking. According to him, these three words are interdependent. And if building is really dwelling, 'dwelling is the manner in which mortals are on Earth' (Heidegger, 2011, p. 350). The house seems to be the place where everything starts. As in a chrysalis, characters of the picturebooks prepare themselves inside to face the 'Great World'. And, finally, able to appropriate it, they dwell in it. Such is the case of the little girl drawn by Max Ducos in *Jeu de piste à Volubilis* [*Treasure Hunt in Volubilis*]. In this French picturebook of 2006, the protagonist remembers how she succeeded in unlocking the secret of her parents' modern house: 'Each house is unique and owns its secret', said her father, 'when you discover those of your house, you'll finally love it as your best friend' (p. 2). The house which appears on the cover seems to be designed by Robert Mallet-Stevens. It presents a lot of similarities to the Villa Cavrois, built in the North of France in 1932. Max Ducos suggests that the reader follow the young girl through the treasure hunt inside and outside the house. The itinerary allows the young reader to appreciate different great designers' creations, like Eerio Aarnio's ball chair, the Mondrian table by Bernard Vuarnesson and the LC2 sofa by Le Corbusier.

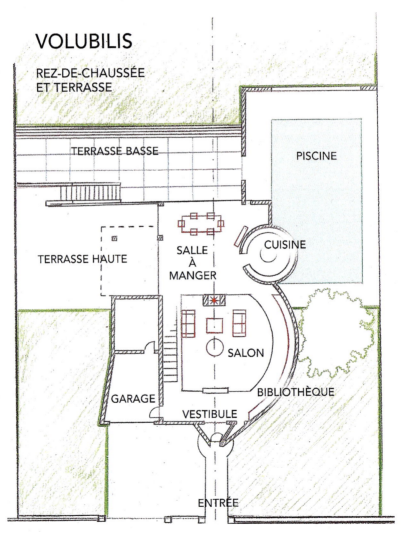

FIGURE 6.5 Max Ducos, *Jeu de piste à Volubilis* (2006, p. 27).
Source: © Sarbacane

The little girl must discover ten clues that lead her from the vestibule to an open window, to the end of a tunnel, to dig at the back of the garden. The trip taken by the young hero is the symbolic route of her childhood, from her birth to her departure from the family home. The secret message may be: finding her way to dwell the world. The reader can follow the little girl on a blueprint of the house (p. 27) where they may clearly distinguish the silhouettes of the mother and the father, back to back. The first clue is in the vestibule at the beginning of the trip. This triangle room (p. 8), with red walls, symbolises the uterus. From inside the house, the little girl must pass through a round door and a red curtain. All these elements make us think about the expulsion of the baby and childbirth. The nine other clues force the young girl to circumscribe the house, going from right to left and up and down. Along a route that looks like a circle, the young girl undertakes a territorialization, an appropriation of this house which seemed to her so strange.

The last step drives the young girl to a second birth. In a double spread, she crosses a dark tunnel opening onto an orifice, still barred by a red curtain. Once past the membrane that separates her from the big world, she discovers an enlightening, heavenly space bringing together all the characteristics of a *locus amoenus*: green vegetation, shadow and a refreshing water point. So, the house prepares us to live in the world. More precisely, Max Ducos seems to show us that living in our childhood house conditions our way of dwelling in new spaces, all the houses of our lives, throughout the entire world. The better you live in your first house, the better you build your 'inside dwelling', the better you dwell in the world. The message expressed by Gerda Muller's *Devine qui fait quoi… Une promenade invisible* [*Guess Who Does What… An Invisible Walk*] is very similar (2000).

In Muller's picturebook, published in 1999 at L'Ecole des Loisirs in France, the hero, a little boy whom we glimpse asleep beneath his covers on the illustration of the first page, is waking up. After he gets washed, he plays in his bedroom with a wooden box that he decides to turn into a boat. When he realises that he is missing a mast, he goes out, facing the snow that covers all the nearby countryside. It is across the stream, a few strides away from the house, near the pony's enclosure, that he finds a branch ripped from a tree. With this branch, he can complete his boat as soon as he comes back to his bedroom. The adventure told by this picturebook could be divided into three phases. The first one corresponds to the preparation of the adventure and takes place in the meso-space of the house (pp. 2–7). The second phase is the proper adventure which takes place in macro-space and throws the hero into 'public space' (pp. 8–29). The third and last phase is devoted to the conclusion of the adventure and to the realisation of what initiated it. We are back then in the meso-space of the house (pp. 30–33).

Gerda Muller's young hero lives a real adventure by going far and away from the family nest to pick a branch from the other side of a stream, which he needs to build his boat. Muller's hero realises himself in the movement: it is in his progression through his lived-in space that the little boy builds himself. We could even add that it is through the 'elasticity of limits' (Moles, 1972, p. 35) that he grows up, crossing one by one the boundaries that get him further and further away from his bed and his nest. According to Bachelard (1964), it is inside the corner-shelter, which 'rejects and restrains, even hides, life' (p. 136), that the child, motionless, goes to imagine, to invent, to dream before embarking in the realisation by action. Bachelard continues, 'And all who live in corners will come to confer life upon this image, multiplying the shades of being that characterise the corner dweller' (1964,

p. 140), making the corner the starting point of inhabiting. The itinerary realised by the child is a crossing of successive boundaries, at first authorised and regulated, then new and unexpected.

According to Abraham Moles, 'only marginal freedom is interesting for the individual' (1966, p. 230). Could we consider that the child's construction would be finally only a succession of topographic limits that the child is invited to cross? Would not the book have the ambition to show the child the importance of projects, ideas or feelings born into the intimate space of the house and their realisation by facing the other spaces? The house represents the place where you dream your life before you realise it in the big world.

The 11 picturebooks that follow Kazuo Iwamura's *The Family of Fourteen on the Move* are 11 explorations of the everyday space around the 14 forest mice's house-tree. This series is an interlocking of different spaces around the house-tree, the witnessing of a proxemic as Edward T. Hall defined it:

> In old Japan, space and social organization were interrelated. The Tokugawa shoguns arranged the daimyo, or nobles, in concentric zones around the capital, Ado (Tokyo). Proximity to the core reflected closeness of relationship and loyalty to the shogun; the most loyal formed an inner protective ring. [...] The concept of the center that can be approached from any direction is a well-developed theme in Japanese culture.
>
> *(Hall, 1966, p. 149)*

The 'centre that can be approached from any direction' that Hall speaks about is the house-tree. All the forest mice's expeditions start from this place and finish in this place. It is inside this place that the members of the family develop their relationships. *The Family of Fourteen on the Move*, the first book of the series published in Japan in 1983, describes the process of territorialization. Included at the end of this first book and also at the beginning of the second (*The Family of Fourteen Fix Breakfast*) is a sectional view of the house-tree. All the living functions of the house are situated on the first floor, at the same level as the adults' bedroom: storage room, kitchen, dining room. Only the children's bedrooms are placed on two stacked mezzanines. We find in this description the main principles of the traditional Japanese minka. The first Japanese treatise on architecture, written by Doami in 1523 entitled *Okazashiro* or *The Book of Ornamentations*, provides some specifications about the organisation of the minka. The interior of this popular house is usually divided into two parts: the first floor is covered with rammed earth called *doma* where most of family life takes place (cooking, dining, housing); the second floor, named *irori*, is covered with tatamis and is used as a bedroom. All the rooms converge on the *doma*, the heart of the house.

The 14 mice's house-tree is inspired by organic architecture: relations with the environment are privileged; the limits of the different rooms are blurred thanks to movable partitions. From this intimate centre, we can draw a series of concentric areas that emerge through the map of the 14 mice's explorations related in the 11 books of the series. After the first one, which describes the arrival in the forest glade and the settlement in the minka-tree, the second one leads the family to the other side of the nearby stream. In *The 14 Forest Mice and the Winter Sledding Day* (1991), the family seems to move away from the house-tree, looking for a slope for sledding. In *The 14 Forest Mice and the Spring Outing* (1986), the exploration takes them to the edge of the forest. *The 14 Forest Mice and the Autumn March*

(1992), the tenth issue of the series, takes place in an unexplored part of the forest where a deforestation human operation seems to have begun. The *14 Forest Mice and the Dragonfly Pond* (2002) transports us to the edge of the mice's territory.

The space suggested by Iwamura could be classified as psychological, as Moles conceived it. Indeed, we can observe the different 'shells' that man builds around himself. One of the fundamental laws of the proxemic, stated by Moles, is: 'the importance of every thing decreases with the distance from the central point'. Thus, the mice's itinerary, through the series, is the expression of what Moles names 'the elasticity of the limits' in a field of freedom that human beings maintain with the topological space. The route browsed by the mice family is a successive crossing of limits, at first very well known, then new and unforeseen. According to Moles, only the marginal freedom is interesting for the individual. The narrative takes birth in the crossing of limits, in the mice's movements. It seems that, for Iwamura, the story begins as soon as characters decide to leave and move out of the house-tree and the circular glade. Thus, from the house, the narrative is the result of the crossings of limits, trajectories and phases of deterritorialization/territorialization.

From the domestic space to the public space, the child is invited to cross limits, always farther and farther from their private space, always more and more stimulating for their development. Children's picturebooks are thus 'machines to pass through', they are about border crossings, they are *vade-mecums* or also transpatial guides, referring to the concept of transpatiality defended by the French geographer Michel Lussault as 'a specific spatiality of the main experimentation which consists for the individual to cross a limit, a border, a threshold' (Lussault, 2013, p. 1025).

Most prominently, picturebooks suggest an accommodation of the crossing. In quite a structural way, they very often ignore the real obstacles to moving and widening out to the world. Characters pass from one space to another, from one story to another, without any major trouble. The house in picturebooks is a 'machine to live in'. In the house, the first rudiments of dwelling are made. It is the personal protective shell in which the projects of adventure are imagined and elaborated. Undeniably, picturebooks contain spatiality, transfer ways of dwelling, suggest a refrain, this little music of the territories as it is described by Deleuze and Guattarri (Deleuze, Guattarri, 1987).

References

Primary sources

Brière-Hacquet, A., & Barroux (2018). *On Déménage!* Paris: Little Urban.

Celli, R., & Muller, G. (1956). *Boucle-d'or et les Trois ours.* Paris: Flammarion/Père Castor.

Cervantes, M. (2003). *Don Quixote. A New Translation by Edith Grossman.* London: Harper Collins Publishers.

Ducos, M. (2006). *Jeu de Piste à Volubilis.* Paris: Sarbacane.

Herbauts, A. (2004). *Lundi.* Paris: Casterman.

Herbauts, A. (2006). *Monday.* New York: Enchanted Lion Books.

Iwamura, K. (1982). *The Family of Fourteen On the Move.* New York: Gareth Stevens Pub.

Iwamura, K. (1983). *The Family of Fourteen Fix Breakfast.* New York: Gareth Stevens Pub.

Iwamura, K. (1986). *The 14 Forest Mice and the Spring Outing.* New York: Gareth Stevens Pub.

Iwamura, K. (1991). *The 14 Forest Mice and the Winter Sledding Day.* New York: Gareth Stevens Pub.

Iwamura, K. (1992). *The 14 Forest Mice and the Autumn March.* New York: Gareth Stevens Pub.

Iwamura, K. (2002). The *14 Forest Mice and the Dragonfly Pond.* New York: Gareth Stevens Pub.

Jacobs, J., & Brooke, L. L. (1904). *The Story of the Three Little Pigs.* London/New York: Frederick Wame & Co.

Mendoza, G., & Smith, D. S. (1981). *Need A House? Call Ms Mouse.* New York: Grosset & Dunlap.

Muller, G. (2000). *Devine Qui Fait Quoi… Une Promenade Invisible.* Paris: L'École des Loisirs.

Tison, A., & Taylor, T. (1972). *La Maison des Barbapapas.* Paris: L'École des Loisirs.

Yoon-Duck, K. (1995). *Man-hee's House.* Seoul: Gilbut Children's Book Publishers.

Secondary sources

Bachelard, G. (1964). *The Poetics of Space.* New York: Penguin Books.

Bourdieu, P. (1977). Cultural Reproduction and Social Reproduction. In Karabel, J. & Halsey, A.H. (eds), *Power and Ideology in Education.* New York: Oxford University Press, pp. 487–511.

Deleuze, G., & Guattari, F. (1987). *A Thousand Plateaus: Capitalism and Schizophrenia.* Minneapolis: University of Minnesota Press.

Durand, G. (1999). *The Anthropological Structures of the Imaginary.* Brisbane: Boombana Publications.

Eiguer, A. (2013). *L'inconscient de la Maison.* Paris: Dunod.

Hall, E. T. (1966). *The Hidden Dimension.* New York: Anchor Books.

Heidegger, M. (2011). *Basic Writings: Martin Heidegger.* London: Routledge.

Holloway, S. L., & Valentine, G. (2000). Spatiality and the New Social Studies of Childhood. *Sociology* 34(4), pp. 763–783. doi: 10.1177/S0038038500000468.

Le Corbusier. (2014). *Towards a New Architecture.* New York: Brewer, Warren & Putnam.

Lévy, J., & Lussault, M. (2013). *Dictionnaire de la Géographie.* Paris: Belin.

Markham, S. (1954). An Item Analysis of Children's Drawings of a House. *Journal of Clinical Psychology* 10(2), pp. 185–187.

Minkowska, F. (1949). *Guide-catalogue de L'exposition: de Van Gogh et Seurat aux Dessins d'enfants. À la Recherche du Monde des Formes.* Paris: Musée pédagogique.

Moles, A., & Rohmer, E. (1972). *Psychologie de L'espace.* 2. éd. augm. et modifiée. Paris: Casterman.

Ponge, F., Corey, J., & Garneau, J.-L. (2016). Snails. *Poetry,* 208 (4), pp. 316–319. http://www.jstor.org/stable/44016178

Stephens, J. (2018). Picture Books and Ideology. *The Routledge Companion to Picturebooks, Routledge Companions to Literature Series,* édité par B. Kümmerling-Meibauer. London, New York: Routledge, pp. 137–145

Uexküll, J von. (1934). *A Foray into the Worlds of Animals and Humans: With A Theory of Meaning.* Minneapolis: University of Minnesota Press, 2010.

7

ARCHITECTURE AND INTERIOR DESIGN IN ITALIAN PICTUREBOOKS

A case study of Bruno Munari

Marnie Campagnaro

Introduction

The home and its architecture represent a setting in children's literature where identities are shaped, connections are established and boundaries are defined in one's daily interactions with the world. The home includes both centripetal forces (when the home is intended as a protected and intimate nest) and centrifugal forces (when the home is intended as the starting point of new adventures and as the point of departure from a violent and oppressive family).

The idea of the home as a *domestic hearth* was first conceptualised and codified in the 19th century. However, it was only in the 20th century that the home assumed its central role in reflecting the evolution of certain social identities and new lifestyles, which continue to develop up to the present day. These developments inevitably had impacts on children's books.

The imposing and often inhospitable dwellings described in some classical novels of the 19th century, such as the stories by Charles Dickens, Edgar Allan Poe, Lewis Carroll and Carlo Collodi, were followed—in the early 20th century and in the aftermath of World War II—by a mushrooming of little fictional homes that seemed to fit perfectly the lives of their inhabitants. Some international examples include the home in *Little House on the Prairie* (1935), a reminiscence of a family's stay in US Indian Territory; the naïve Pippi Longstocking's house, Villa Villekulla (1945); the arboreal retreat of *The Baron in the Trees* (1957); the hostile Dakota's 'White Flats' (1988); and the threatening parallel house in the novel *Coraline* (2003). This same literary richness is also present in picturebooks, which often portray homes through their intimate, lively rooms and their soft beds, warm dishes, steaming mugs, crackling fireplaces, snug sofas and bursting bookshelves. The characters are *at home* in a regenerating space that reflects their identities, behaviours, inclinations and values (Campagnaro, 2019a; Goga, 2019; Kümmerling-Meibauer, 2019; Narančić-Kovač, 2019; Ramos, 2019). However, not only positive representations of the home are depicted in picturebooks but also negative ones, as walls, windows, doors and ceilings can convey the protagonist's feelings of disempowerment or imprisonment, as, for instance, in Armin Greder's *The City* (2010).

DOI: 10.4324/9781003131755-10

Inside their houses, characters not only eat, sleep, play with friends and interact with their parents but also internalise identity bonds and the cultural and social bonds of their communities. Architectural layout, furniture arrangements and interior design elements may reveal the balanced or imbalanced gap that separates children's own needs, inclinations and wishes from those imposed by adults. Hence, domestic landscapes in children's books can portray the ideas, values, feelings, habits and customs of contemporary societies. Architecture and interior design in picturebooks may also be conceived as catalysts to inspire social reflections on children's culture and education. The creation of special architectural perspectives and interior design settings may therefore transform visual fictitious spaces into *living matter*.

After some preliminary reflections on the historical development of architecture and interior design in Italian children's culture in the 20th century, this paper will investigate how Bruno Munari, a major international designer and artist, was able to entangle his children's books with architecture, exploiting the representations of buildings and interior design elements to convey family, social and cultural values.

Insights into the history of architecture and interior design in children's culture and literature

The concept of a private space or domestic environment, as we consider it today, is the culmination of a long period of change. In the series *A History of Private Life*, Philippe Ariés and Georges Duby demonstrate how, although a process of progressive transformation of housing architecture had begun as early as the 15th century driven by the formation of numerous new spaces in different sectors of public life, it was not until the 19th century that a full and conscious privatisation of domestic space was developed and the house became the private domain par excellence, the concrete foundation of the family and pillar of the social order (Ariés & Duby, 1988). Hence, the house became an element of stability based on the segmentation of private spaces, adequately protected by walls, curtains and other elements to ensure the privacy of family members.

This transformation is highlighted by the creation of separate domestic spaces which are necessary to guarantee a certain family intimacy. A growing interest is given to cleanliness and order, and these two domestic practices are used to reveal the good and bad habits (and inclinations) of the individual and of the family. Between the end of the 19th and the beginning of the 20th centuries, this renewed architectural attention is gradually supported by the creation of innovative furnishing components. A new dynamic industrial branch specialising in domestic interiors began to produce child-friendly decorated furniture, soft and pleasantly adorned fabrics for curtains and eye-catching wallpapers, to name a few. The repertoire of wallpapers for children's rooms, for example, evolved so rapidly that, in a few decades, numerous characters from the history of children's literature, such as the protagonists of the fairy tales by Perrault, Grimm and Andersen or the characters of British and American children's literature such as Peter Rabbit, Winnie the Pooh, Félix the Cat and, later, Mickey Mouse, were used by furnishing firms to decorate wallpapers or design objects (Perrot, 2011).

Italian children's interior design in the first half of the 20th century

In Italy, attention to domestic architecture and interior design especially created for children have also become increasingly common. During the beginning of the 20th century, importing of foreign furniture for children was replaced by an increasing production in

Italy by small manufacturers dedicated to furniture. They showed a growing interest in the needs of the new bourgeois family and offered innovative furniture solutions to respond to the desire to create a special space for children where they could build their own small universe. Beds, wardrobes, tables and dressers became more and more appealing. Furniture artisans and manufacturers started using extraordinary wooden decorations or illustrations depicting famous characters out of children's imaginary worlds (Maino, 2003).

The attraction to the child's room captivated famous Italian artists and illustrators of the early 20th century. In 1918, the futurist painter Giacomo Balla developed an avant-garde project devoted to the futurist reconstruction of the universe. Connected to this all-round cultural project, which involved both public life (cinema and theatre) and private life (including the furnishings of houses, everyday objects and fashion), Balla designed a memorable child-sized bedroom for his daughter. He creatively collaborated with some fine craftsmen and gave birth to a beautiful domestic space while anticipating the role that the playful-aesthetic dimension would play in the second half of the 20th century in the creation of children's spaces.

Four years later (1922–1924), another remarkable creation left a mark in the history of Italian architecture and interior design. I am referring to the *Camera dei bambini* [Child's Room] designed by Antonio Rubino, one of the most popular children's book illustrators and comic artists in Italy during the first half of the 20th century. He stunningly designed the headboards, doors of night tables, dressers, drawers and anthropomorphic chairs of an enchanting child's bedroom, in which his colourful and dreamlike drawings seemed to re-spond perfectly to the needs (and anxieties) of the infantile imagination when falling asleep during the night. Influenced by the Italian Art Nouveau, the Liberty style, the drawings of his decorated furniture seemed to echo the uncanny Freudian atmosphere of that time. Rubino was able to represent the child's interior world in his images in a very innovative and contemporary way. The correlation he created between pictures, objects, spaces and children's mental life was characterised by a rich and sophisticated emotional landscape.

FIGURE 7.1 Anthropomorphic children's chairs, a table and a wallpaper of a charming child's bedroom designed by the Italian illustrator Antonio Rubino in the 1920s. Licensed under CC BY-SA 4.0 https://creativecommons.org/licenses/by-sa/4.0

His drawings were conceived to intercept children's wishes and fears to accompany them into their night dreams. For instance, in the two big wall pictures, Rubino visually counterpointed the moral imagination of 'Il bambino buono' [the good boy] and 'Il bambino cattivo' [the bad boy] (Figure 7.1). The intertextual and interpictorial references to children's literature, such as *The Adventures of Pinocchio* by Carlo Collodi (a smiling Pinocchio with his long nose or a bizarre dialogue between a boy with a distorted face and donkey ears and a real donkey), *The Wonderful Wizard of Oz* by L. Frank Baum (the representation of the Scarecrow close to a shrivelled tree) and the characters and objects of well-known Grimms's and Andersen's fairy tales (Snow White, the dwarfs, the apple or the magic mirror), were quite explicit. He emphasised the controversial nature of children's emotions by putting surrealistic characters and human feelings in dialogue with each other through visual counterpointing compositions, which marked the inseparable relation of the rational and the irrational, order and disorder. In his drawings, Rubino attempted to problematise the idyllic (and not real) representation of children's feelings and interior lives.

Rubino's artistic approach to building visual children's worlds both in books and furniture, emphasising a more multifaced depiction of childhood and children's imagination, was also pursued by other relevant Italian children's illustrators, such as Yambo, Attilio Mussino and Sergio Tofano, in the 1920s and 1930s. Their works contributed to improving the children's publishing market and ways of communicating with children, and also appealed to some new manufacturing companies. In fact, new furniture companies started producing a special niche of furniture for children's needs and wishes. The company Lenci, located in Torino and the Industria veneziana mobili laccati, developed original fine furniture decorated with the drawings of Antonio Rubino or Attilio Mussino (Maino, 2003).

During World War II, a transitory setback stopped this experimental diffusion focused on children, architecture and interior design. However, the social challenges that emerged in the post-war period would breathe new life into it.

Italian children's interior design in the second half of the 20th century

Starting in the 1950s, the design of new domestic interior design and the attention of architects to the worlds of children became increasingly significant. I would like to focus my attention on two major challenges that emerged. The first is related to the social transformation of domestic habits and the second is related to an international consensus on some fundamental principles of children's rights.

First, after World War II, huge economic and political efforts were made to rebuild the European countries completely devastated by war. This miraculous reconstruction marked extraordinary economic growth and social transformation, which transformed human society more profoundly than any other historical period of analogous brevity. This reconstruction led Italian society to develop new social and cultural needs. At the same time, housing became a major political problem because of the migration of thousands of farmers from the south to the urban and industrial areas of the north of Italy. Houses played a new central role. They slowly became new spaces for the catalysation of consumerist behaviour. It was also inside the house that the representation of new life habits and the rapid emergence of cultural and ideological elements occurred. Different from the past, houses also became crucial spaces for children. Unlike the countryside, the city was no longer considered a safe place for childhood by parents. From being assiduous and wandering flaneurs of open spaces and outdoors, children were forced to spend much more time at home and become more permanent inhabitants of domestic spaces. One of the main architectural challenges of building domestic spaces at that time was offering architectural solutions to respond to this transformation. This challenge was linked to the creation of spaces not only devoted to children (a room of their own) but also capable of responding to their other needs, such as creating a space for family love and fun even in the absence of parents, who both spend most of their day outside at work.

Second, in 1959, the United Nations General Assembly adopted the Declaration of the Rights of the Child. This document, which represented the first primary international consensus on the fundamental principles of children's rights, stated that children had the right to full and harmonious physical, mental, moral, spiritual and social development. Together with adequate nutrition, housing and medical services, love, understanding and education in conditions of freedom and dignity are needed by children. Furthermore, the creative and wild side of childhood, which mostly includes play and recreation, should be promoted and guaranteed. In the 1960s, testing and developing children's critical thinking, individual judgement and sense of moral and social responsibility received growing attention from figures and institutions that should take care of children. For children, experimenting and exploring their own creativity and imagination were amongst the main features at the centre of many pedagogical, cultural and social reflections of that time. Hence, it was inevitable that architecture and interior design were influenced by these dynamics. In the second half of the 20th century, the design of Italian houses began to change. They were not organised any longer around a clear distinction between the living area, the sleeping area and the service rooms, with many corridors and anterooms. The living room was not used only as a representative space to welcome other family members or guests, but it became a new intimate space for the family like the kitchen. The needs of childhood inside a house started to be considered. In those years—1970s— under the pressure of the contesting instances of 1968 and of new lifestyles, changes in family and social ties resulted in a reinterpretation of domestic spaces, also affecting children's domestic spaces and interior design. New, original architectural solutions were developed. Famous brands of Italian design, such as Kartell and Danese Milano, developed innovative projects tailored to respond to children's needs for play, recreation and personalised spaces. In 1964, Kartell produced the K1340 (later K 4999) child's chair, a very inspiring piece of Italian design. This chair, which is part of the permanent collection at the Museum of Modern Art in New York, was designed by Marco Zanuso (who was also involved with Bruno Munari and other famous artists in the Italian Concrete Art movement) and Richard Sapper and was made of a highly innovative plastic material for that time. It was conceived to be used as both a chair and a toy or an original domestic entertainment park (Figure 7.2). It was a notable example of how interior design was able to interpret the cultural and educational instances of that time, translating them into a concrete manufacturing product that embodied children's primary needs within the limited space of a house.

FIGURE 7.2 A chair, a toy or an entertainment park at home? The innovative Kartell K1340 child's chair produced in 1964. © Kartell. All rights reserved to Kartell.

Bruno Munari was a pioneering Italian designer, artist and writer; a polyhedric figure who actively interacted with children's needs and experimented with ludic architectonic projects. In his long career, Munari had many other opportunities to develop fruitful connections between architecture and childhood. From his pedagogical perspective—he was strongly influenced by Piaget's theories on discovery learning and children's intrinsic motivation to learn—the interaction of children with the environment and its architecture could be fostered in different ways, and even specific elements of furniture could support their curiosity and need for exploration and experimentation. *Abitacolo*, his project created in 1971 for a company called Robots (Figure 7.3) and which is still produced today, embodies one such experience. It is a multifunctional modular habitable structure in multipurpose plasticised steel for children's bedroom spaces (Munari, 1981/2009). This space can be personalised and equipped with shelves, steel wire storage baskets, hooks and a reclining table connected to the structure; children can organise it according to their personal needs—a place to sleep, play, invite friends, study, read, listen to music, relax and think. For this reason, *Abitacolo* could be used as a bed, a sofa, a bookshelf or 'a big toy' (Munari, 1981/2009, p. 188). Like the child's chair of Kartell, *Abitacolo* is a domestic playground capable of transforming the quotidian reality of childhood into a creative, constructive and educational 'container of microcosmos' (Munari, 1981/2009, p. 197).

As an interpreter of the children's culture of the 20th century, Munari was able to translate the needs of childhood (play, exploration and intimacy) into active projects. These, in turn, helped children to become aware of the transforming role of architecture in their lives, to understand and interact with it and to design their own spaces by engaging with architectural and interior design elements according to their preferences and interests.

FIGURE 7.3 *Abitacolo*, the multifunctional, modular, habitable structure for children's bedrooms by Bruno Munari, 1971. © Bruno Munari. All rights reserved to Maurizio Corraini s.r.l.

The historical and cultural transformations of architecture and its relationships with city planning, houses and representations in children's books have been investigated by several scholars (Campagnaro, 2021; Hayward & Schmiedeknecht, 2019; Meunier, 2016; Swope, 2014). However, research on children's literature has paid little attention to the role that interior design, furniture and objects may play in forging children's ideas about the environment they live in and the impact that these have on building and shaping their identities, their family relationships and their entanglements with others and the world. Social, design and educational historians and scholars (Brandow–Faller, 2018; Calvert, 1992; Lange, 2018) have demonstrated how investigations on 'artefact constellations' (Calvert, 1992, p. 4), such as children's playground, furniture, toys and clothes, played a fundamental role in defining cultural beliefs and assumptions on children's culture. I would like, therefore, to present two examples of 'artefact constellations', a unique concept book and a picturebook, both by Bruno Munari, that may shed some light on this issue.

Representations and values in Italian picturebooks: a case study of Bruno Munari

Matching the above historical and cultural frameworks with picturebook theory, I aim to explore to what extent the representations of houses and interior design in Italian picturebooks may convey educational assumptions about children's culture and how these depictions have been purposely used by children's authors to portray social and cultural transformations in picturebooks.

I will focus my investigation on the Italian designer Bruno Munari for different reasons. First, he played an important role in the history of children's literature and in contemporary picturebook research, both in Italy and internationally. Second, the settings of Munari's major picturebooks are located in urban architectonic contexts and the adventures of his characters are often entangled with the representations of domestic landscapes and interior design elements. Finally, although the analysis is limited to two examples, the concept book of the *Architecture Box LC N 1* (1945) and the picturebook *Little Yellow Riding Hood* (1972), they show how a children's author, like Bruno Munari, could interact with the representations of architecture and interior design in rather different ways. In these two works, Munari considered architecture as a community-based democratic instance and as a tool for representations and depictions of emerging values in Italian children's culture after the post-war period.

Architecture as a community-based democratic instance

Often described as an artist crossing disciplinary borders, Bruno Munari (1907–1998) is an influential figure in the history of Italian and international design. Influenced by Modernism, Futurism and Concrete Art (an artistic movement free of any basis in observed reality and without any symbolic meanings), Munari conceived his innovative projects, spanning across ages, genres and goals (Meneguzzo, 1993). Trained as a painter, sculptor and experimenter of different artistic disciplines (Antonello et al., 2017), Munari was also a praised children's author (Campagnaro, 2019b). He experimented in the graphic arts, advertising and became the art director for several magazines and publications. Amongst them, his collaboration with the monthly magazine of architecture and design *Domus* is worth mentioning. From autumn 1943 to the end of 1944, Munari was the creative director of this influential magazine, founded in 1928 by Gio Ponti to spread new ideas in the architectural and interior design field. Through this professional collaboration, Munari was able to promote an in-depth reflection of the role of architecture and visual communication through his unconventional and eclectic graphics, while also writing some articles addressing issues related to the aesthetic problems of reconstruction or issues projected beyond the end of war (Colizzi, 2012).

Thanks to this experience and his research on movement, forms and materials, Munari created the *Architecture Box LC N 1* for the Officina Meccanica Luciano Castelletti in 1945, a year after his collaboration with *Domus* ended (Figure 7.4). The box consisted of an architecture construction toy containing a series of small wooden bricks of seven different shapes which could be used in various ways to build both houses (houses on stilts, mansions with porticos, balconies, verandas, etc.) and other buildings, such as hotels, towers, stations, churches, castles or multi-storey car parks.

A tiny black-and-white instruction concept book with 32 pages (format: 6 × 4 ¼ in.; 15 cm × 11 cm) containing 65 examples of buildings was included in the box. The book was conceived as an illustrated compendium, showing children various ways to use the wooden bricks to construct different buildings. As a matter of fact, an in-depth analysis revealed that Munari's little book offered not only a rich illustrated repertoire of Italian Rationalist architectural projects, echoing some technical and aesthetic experimentations of European avant-garde designs, such as those of Le Corbusier (Bosoni, 2015), but also a visual conceptualisation of how urban developments could be designed to meet citizens' needs and wishes extensively.

FIGURE 7.4   The *Scatola di Architettura LC N 1* [*LC N 1 Architecture Box*] with the instruction picturebook created by Bruno Munari in 1945 (Mantova: Corraini, 2018). © Bruno Munari. All rights reserved to Maurizio Corraini s.r.l.

In the book, Munari depicted buildings of great appeal for children, such as castles, towers, old city gates and fortresses. He also paid attention to buildings related to rural children's experiences, which were still very common at the time, such as mills, stables and farms. However, Munari mainly focused on modern buildings in urban contexts. Some of his buildings, mostly those connected to the political power, paid tribute to the historical periods during which the book was conceived. Probably, with the purpose of bypassing the intimidating logic of fascist censorship of that time (Fabre et al., 2000), Munari chose to include buildings that referred to the most established architectural movement during the regime. In the book, in fact, he portrayed the Italian Air Ministry's building in Rome (picture n. 10 Air Ministry) and the Palace of Justice in Milan (picture n. 31 Palace of Justice), two of the most representative examples of architecture under the fascist dictatorship. The first one, known as *il Palazzo dell'Aeronautica* [Palace of the Air Force], was commissioned by the Minister of the Royal Air Force (1926–1933) Italo Balbo, who, for its design, turned to an architect who was only 28 years old, Roberto Marino (Billiani & Pennacchietti, 2019). This structure represented the first Italian building entirely built of reinforced concrete. The second building, *Palazzo della Giustizia* (Palace of Justice) (Figure 7.5), was the largest to be built in Milan in the inter-war period and probably the most significant of several law courts built during the fascist era (Maulsby, 2014). It was designed by Marcello Piacentini, one of the most influential Italian architects of his time who was intimately associated with Benito Mussolini; his works aimed to modernise Italian architectural language by combining several elements of modern concrete buildings with classical monumentality. The *Palazzo della Giustizia*, whose construction began in 1932 and was completed in 1940, had profound architectural, artistic and cultural impact on the city of Milan. Munari, who was deeply attached to this city, could not remain indifferent about this building.

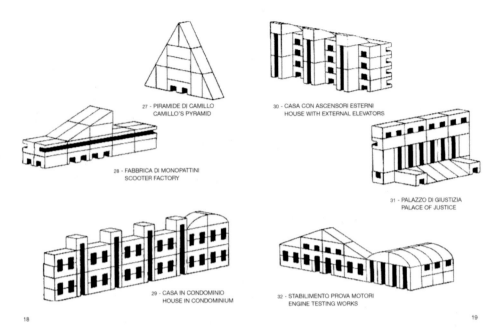

Nevertheless, what is interesting in this work is Munari's idea about how a new modern city should be planned according to a community-based democratic architectural perspective. During World War II, Milan, Munari's beloved city, was heavily bombed; one-third of the building heritage was destroyed and the main symbols of the city were damaged, including the Duomo in 1943. This was probably what inspired Munari to create a toy and a book about architecture and the endless possibilities of building new worlds. In his book, he portrayed a city built as a net-like system which should respond to some urgent social and democratic needs. It consisted of five architectural groupings: homes, factories, cultural buildings (schools, recreational or science centres) and socialising spaces. This forward-thinking choice allowed him to open an implicit dialogue with his readers about architecture, good urban design and their contribution to making cities both functional and aesthetically attractive to residents.

At the time, accommodation was a key issue because wartime devastation aggravated housing shortages. It is worth considering that by 1945, five million new habitable rooms were needed in Italy, and to respond to this pressing demand, the Italian government established the Ina-Casa plan (1949–1963) (Di Biagi, 2001). Probably aware of the difficult situation in 1945, Munari focused on the issue of housing, and he depicted 15 different typologies of houses in his book; some houses were marked by a strong sense of identity (houses depicted in pictures n. 11 Albertino's house, n. 13 Leo's house, n. 21 Giuseppe's house, n. 23 Ernesto's house, n. 36 Pino's house and n. 54 Ottavio's house) while others were given more general and less individualised references (n. 9 A house in Capri, n. 12 A house with steps, n. 17 A Nordic house, n. 18 A house in a condominium, n. 30 A house with external elevators, n. 44 A house with external stairs, n. 48 A house with balconies, n. 60 Low-cost housing and n. 62 A house in Nuremberg). Munari also concentrated on another essential aspect—the importance of factories in providing men and women with work and enabling economic sustainability (n. 3 A chocolate factory, n. 28 A scooter factory, n. 32 Engine testing works, n. 46 A clock/watch factory and n. 57 Stock exchange). However, education, recreation and cultural activities were also central issues, according to Munari's perspective. Going to school and using recreation centres offered children the possibility of training their cognitive, imaginative, physical and problem-solving skills. Building schools (n. 24 Elementary school) and sport, science and recreation areas were fundamental initiatives to protect and support citizens, even the smaller projects (n. 37 A swimming pool with triple trampoline, n. 39 Stadium stand and n. 55 Cycle-racing track stand). His democratic and anti-elitist ideas of art and science encouraged Munari to consider these disciplines as cultural output destined to foster the cultural and scientific development of open-minded citizens. This perspective may be traced in his choice to include different interdisciplinary places, such as a research laboratory (n. 19 A volcano observatory), an art gallery or museum (n. 25 A painter's house), a cinema and theatre (n. 34 An ideal cinema and n. 41 A modern theatre). Finally, Munari included in his imaginative modern city also many other different typologies of architectonical spaces for socialisation, such as markets (n. 20 A covered market), hotels (n. 4 A lakeside hotel, n. 7 A mountain hotel and n. 33 A seaside hotel), villas (n. 5 Villa Maria and n. 52 Villa Giuseppina), new and old palaces (n. 47 Skyscraper, n. 53 Congress Building, n. 8 Palazzo with porticoes and n. 16 Neoclassical palazzo), places of historical, cultural and religious identity, such as towers and bell towers (n. 6 Tower, n. 26 S. Giacomo's Bell Tower), churches (n. 18 A Gothic church and n. 22 A Romanesque church), monuments (n. 51 Nemo Monument), old ancient walls (n. 14 Old city gate) and spaces of mobility (n. 59 Electric train station).

This long list of buildings reveals Munari's conception of a modern city and the role that architecture played in forging a democratic, progressive and cohesive community. For him, architecture is a fundamental medium to collect and relaunch the many features and aspirations embedded in modern society. At first glance, Munari's book seemed to portray many isolated buildings. However, each of these buildings, in fact, represented the parts of an organic and lively architectonic net-like system, capable of capturing and satisfying the needs of a democratic and co-operative community rooted in the relationships between the buildings, the roads and spaces that they front and the people who make use of them. These building projects were visually stimulating, but also they were able to represent the features of a well-designed city which took into consideration the fundamental relationships between humans, buildings and the beauty of the city as a whole.

Architecture and interior design as tools to interpret new cultural and social aspirations

Munari's reflections on the role of architecture can be further investigated by focusing on the analysis of the picturebook *Cappuccetto Giallo* (*Little Yellow Riding Hood*) published in 1972. Drawing inspiration from everyday life, Munari created a new adaptation of the popular fairy tale *Little Red Riding Hood* by setting the story in a contemporary

To get to her grandma's Little Yellow Riding Hood has to cross the town traffic, which is very dangerous, like going through the wood.

There are dangers in the traffic too but Little Riding Hood has thought up a secret plan with her canary friends.

FIGURE 7.6 The new and modern architectural skyline of Little Yellow Riding Hood's city. *Cappucetto Giallo* by Bruno Munari (Mantova: Corraini, 2017). *© Bruno Munari. All rights reserved to Maurizio Corraini s.r.l.*

urban context and taking into consideration also the demands and expectations of Italian cultural and civil society at a time when social and cultural requests were quite vigorous.

The heated debates and innovative experimentations that followed the 1968 social protests severely affected Italy's cultural and political institutions, school and academic systems, mass media and the publishing industry, including children's literature. New children's publishing houses and projects were launched, such as the Einaudi 'Tantibambini' collection, which was set up by Bruno Munari in 1972 to offer young readers new contemporary stories and tales (Campagnaro, 2020). The picturebook I am analysing is part of this series (*Cappuccetto Giallo* is number 12 in the series).

The setting in the picturebook is a real modern city—Milan. The adventures are set in everyday situations. It is the unexpected contemporary architectural context that makes these adventures unique. In *Cappuccetto Giallo*, the graphic collages and montages convey a rather chaotic setting. The city traffic frenzy and the skyscrapers characterising the skyline of the big city where the protagonist lives (Figure 7.6) depict Little Yellow Riding Hood as living in a far more hazardous place than a forest. The story focuses on the 'yellow' adventures of a little girl moving around her city.

The visual dialogue that the story setting establishes with the Italian architecture of that time is quite interesting. The story starts by saying, 'On the ground floor of the biggest skyscraper in town lives ….' (Munari, 1972, cover). A close reading of this passage reveals an intertextual connection with a famous Italian building that became a symbol of the reconstruction of Milan as a new modern post-war city and an important keystone of the economic boom in Italy at that time (Tafuri, 2002).

I am referring to Pirelli Tower, Italy's first modern skyscraper. It was built in an area near the main train station in Milan in 1956 and was completed in 1958 by architect Gio Ponti, an Italian master of modern architecture and design. This tower, affectionately called the Pirellone, would become 'a model for innovative Italian architecture' (Ziegler, 2009, p. 14). It was the tallest reinforced concrete building in Europe, and for a long time, 'its shapes served as an inspiration for other skyscrapers built in the 1960s, such as the former Pan Am building in New York, Centre Point in London, and the Alpha Tower in Birmingham' (Pergoli Campanelli, 2014, p. 215). This reference to the new and modern skyline of Milan is so vital for Munari's story that he reproduced it both on the cover and on almost all double spreads. In this way, by telling the story of *Cappuccetto Giallo*, Munari also portrays the nature of a modern Italian city with some spaces represented as contemporary forests. For the purpose of my analysis, focusing on two double spreads is useful.

The first refers to the place where Munari set the meeting of the little girl with her grandmother. This encounter occurs on the top floor of a modern building, which seems to be designed according to the architectural principles of Modernism, based upon the use of innovative technologies of construction, such as glass, steel and reinforced concrete. The image of another building in construction next to it appears to confirm this hypothesis. However, a glance at the other surrounding buildings reveals a more profound dialectic of Munari's urban architectural aesthetics. For Munari, the urban landscape is an architectural melting pot produced by the dynamic historical contamination of different architectural styles. Together with Gio Ponti's skyscraper, contemporary Modernist houses were positioned by the Milanese designer next to ancient churches, whose profiles seemed to recall the images of some well-known Romanesque and Renaissance basilicas and cathedrals in Milan. The intergenerational meeting between Little Yellow and her grandmother in this modern city is thus framed by the parallelism reproduced by the encounters between different historic architectural styles within the same urban context.

The analysis of the second selected double spread focuses on the modality chosen by Munari to address some emerging cultural instances and social aspirations that were also at the heart of his editorial project 'Tantibambini', such as children's agency, family relationships, urban development, consumerism, environmental degradation. In the picturebook, an indisputable role is played by the representation of relationships between children and adults in their everyday lives. Munari showed the importance of building relationships with children forged by the power of family dialogues and children's agency. It is valuable to emphasise that these positive relationships were corroborated not only by the presence of caring adults but also by using some interior design objects. In *Cappuccetto Giallo*, these features can be traced, for instance, by looking at the use of a specific piece of furniture—the armchair.

Armchairs played a special role in Munari's poetics and experimentations. While he was the art director of the architecture journal *Domus*, Munari wrote a hilarious photo reportage entitled 'Seeking Comfort in an Uncomfortable Chair' (1944) (Figure 7.7). In this photo article, Munari questioned the choice of some designers who preferred novelty and aesthetics over functionality, without considering that these two aspects were inseparable in interior design, as demonstrated by the 14 self-portraits of this reportage. He also reflected on the functional, artistic (and symbolic) role of seating on many other occasions, for instance, while creating his sophisticated carving 'Chair for Very Brief Visits' (manufactured by Zanotta in 1945), which has a diabolically sloping seat that would have threatened any

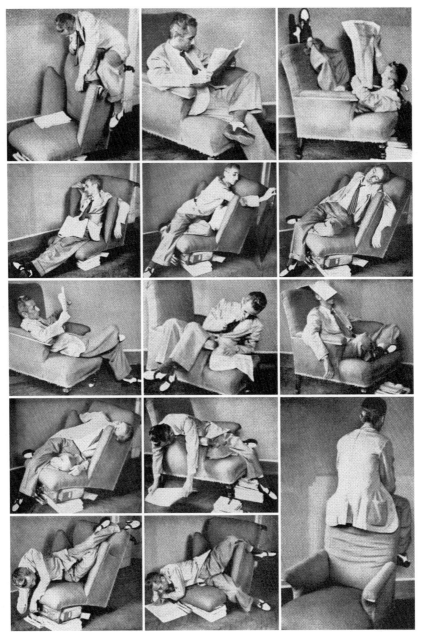

Ricerca della comodità in una poltrona scomoda   Bruno Munari   Seeking comfort in an uncomfortable chair

FIGURE 7.7 'One comes home tired from working all day and finds an uncomfortable chair'.
Domus 202/October 1944 page detail by Bruno Munari (Mantova: Corraini, 2017).

guest, or when he depicted 257 different detailed types of chairs and armchairs for a chapter in his essay 'Arte come mestiere' [Design as Art] (1966).

It is therefore significant that almost 30 years after his self-photo reportage, Munari decided to include in the last double spread of *Little Yellow Riding Hood* an illustration of

Little Yellow Riding Hood talking with her mother about her bad urban adventures with the wolf. The mother is sitting in an armchair with an unusual rich disposal of newspapers, magazines and books around her (Figure 7.8).

This illustration represents Munari's emblematic choice and embeds a relevant cultural change in children's literature. At that time, most Italian domestic stories about children's everyday life presented models of mothers in a rather conformist and stereotypical way. In many books, mothers were depicted cooking, serving food, cleaning or waving from the door. They were often in slippers and aprons, confirming that the women depicted in Italian picturebooks were affected by the so-called 'cult of the apron' (Pace Nilsen, 1971, p. 918). It was very difficult to come across women relaxing inside a house, and if it happened, it would turn out they were sitting in sofas or chairs sewing or knitting. There were almost no representations of women sitting in armchairs. The representation of this furniture was basically reserved for men. Both in reality and in fiction, the armchair was a privileged piece of furniture for fathers and more generally for men. As in Munari's photo reportage, they were usually represented sitting in it, relaxing, reading newspapers or watching TV. As a matter of fact, the armchair embodied the seat of family power and was also a symbol of patriarchal oppression in children's literature. Next to the cult of the apron, coined to emphasise the representational role of women as domestic servants, I suggest that another cult was emerging in Italian children's literature, the cult of the armchair for men.[1] These visual representations highlight a crucial issue: furniture and indoor objects can be used implicitly or explicitly to reinforce or fight social, cultural and gender stereotypes.

FIGURE 7.8 New cultural family models: dialoguing on an armchair. *Cappuccetto Giallo* by Bruno Munari (Mantova: Corraini, 2017). © Bruno Munari. All rights reserved to Maurizio Corraini s.r.l.

Munari chose to represent Little Yellow Riding Hood's mother in a rather different way with respect to the stereotypical representations of that time. He depicts her at home, wearing a fancy yellow dress and a pearl necklace, in dialogue with her daughter in a confident and relaxed way, sitting on an elegant and polished yellow armchair which seems to echo the well-known 'Modello 904' Poltrona Frau, which went into production in 1930. There are not only books but also newspapers and magazines all around her. This representation reveals the profile of a rather non-conformist, modern and independent woman, a mother, but also a thinker, who likes to be up to date on news and cultural and artistic facts, as the books and journals around her suggest. From this point of view, there is a strong difference between the modern and innovative representation of this mother and the traditional figure of mothers that emerged from research described in a very popular feminist book published the following year (1973) by the Italian writer Elena Gianini Belotti, *Dalla parte delle bambine* [What Are Little Girls Made Of?]. Belotti analysed family attitudes towards children, the behaviours of nursery, elementary and secondary school teachers, the use of toys and the depiction of males and females in traditional roles in children's literature. In her study, she found how social and family rituals, conventions and representations reinforced stereotypical sex attitudes both in family and social life. She denounced the unfair pay of female domestic labour and the exclusion of women from the world of culture, academia and employment, governed by asymmetrical roles and by an educational model which condemned women (and girls) to placid, passive and frustrating roles of wives and mothers. By contrast, Munari's use of domestic settings and interior design demonstrated the possibility (and the opportunity) of depicting alternative models in children's books capable of responding to new cultural and social aspirations.

Conclusion

Architecture and interior design elements in picturebooks can be relevant tools to portray the ideas, values, habits and customs of contemporary societies in children's culture. In some picturebooks, such as those by the Italian designer Munari, these elements are used not only as appealing settings but also as mediums or vehicles to inspire cultural and social reflections on children's aesthetics and to reflect on the importance of giving form, shape, and characters to groups of buildings in a city. For Munari, architecture makes connections between people and places, which portray specific identities and values.

Ahead of his time, Munari understood how representations in children's literature could influence children at a time when they are developing their own individual, social and cultural identity and the roles which are more appropriate for them as future citizens. His visual and graphical experimentations portrayed urban landscapes in which architectural settings could reflect liberal and progressive adult values and at the same time influence the formation of early childhood values.

My analysis shows that Munari considered architecture to be a significant narrative element. His careful selection of visually challenging settings generated new playful children's stories and actualised old tales, too. In his concept book included in the *Scatola di Architettura LC N 1*, Munari presented a rich corpus of buildings, which revealed his beliefs about the role of architecture in a modern city. In the book, he blended architecture and city planning together to make urban areas functional and attractive. For him, architecture is also essential to forge a democratic, cohesive human community in a modern society, and children should gain insight into buildings at a very early stage. By contrast, in his picture-book *Little Yellow Riding Hood*, the relationships he established between the characters and interior design elements are significant: the armchair was used as a symbolic object in the narrative which also emphasised new cultural family models in line with the 1968 spirit.

For Munari, architecture, houses and interior design function as a dynamic means through which to communicate with young readers about the possibility of building new worlds based on modern democratic ideas of community as well as based on original representations of new cultural and social aspirations, thus reinforcing positive models of citizenship, family, cultural and social behaviours.

Note

1 In several Italian picturebooks, the armchair often appeared as a symbol of patriarchal power. A very relevant example is represented by the picturebook *Una fortunata catastrofe* (*A fortunate disaster*) by Adela Turin and Nella Bosnia published in 1975. Adela Turin was the historical founder of the publishing house Dalla parte delle bambine, a publishing house created to combat gender stereotypes in children's books in the 1970s. The picturebook deals with family roles and the sharing of domestic duties between mother and father. In the story, the mother abandons her role of housewife and becomes an explorer. Meanwhile, the father, who no longer has an armchair in which to read his paper, decides to spend his time in the kitchen, preparing delicious dinners (Campagnaro, 2019a).

References

Antonello, P., Nardelli, M. and Zanoletti, M. (eds) (2017). *Bruno Munari: The Lightness of Art*. Oxford: Peter Lang.

Ariès, P. and Duby, G. (eds) (1988). *La vita privata. L'Ottocento*. Roma-Bari: Laterza.

Billiani, F. and Pennacchietti, L. (2019). *Architecture and the Novel under the Italian Fascist Regime*. London: Palgrave.

Brandow-Faller, M. (ed) (2018). *Childhood by Design: Toys and the Material Culture of Childhood, 1700–Present*. New York: Bloomsbury Visual Arts.

Calvert, K. (1992). *Children in the House: The Material Culture of Early Childhood, 1600–1900*. Boston: Northeastern University Press.

Campagnaro, M. (2019a). 'Narrating' homes and objects: Images of domestic life in Italian picturebooks since the mid-20th century. *Ricerche di Pedagogia e Didattica/Journal of Theories and Research in Education*, 14(2), pp. 9–48. DOI: 10.6092/issn.1970-2221/10030

———— (2019b). Do touch! How Bruno Munari's Picturebooks work. *Rivista di Storia Dell'educazione*, 6(1), pp. 81–96. DOI: doi.org/10.4454/rse.v6i1.194

———— (2020). Libri per liberare i bambini dalla banalità. Ullallà. Riflessioni intorno alla collana 'Tantibambini' (1972–1978). In Tiziana Pironi (ed), *Autorità in Crisi. Scuola, Famiglia, Società Prima e Dopo il '68* (pp. 227–234). Roma: Aracne. DOI: 10.4399/978882553255519

———— (2021). Stepping into the world of houses. Children's picturebooks on architecture. In Nina Goga, Sarah Hoem Iversen and Anne-Stefi Teigland (eds), *Verbal and Visual Strategies in Nonfiction Picturebooks: Theoretical and Analytical Approaches* (pp. 202–219). Oslo: Scandinavian University Press. DOI: 10.18261/9788215042459-2021-14

Colizzi, A. (2012). Bruno Munari: art director, 1943–1944. *Domus*. Retrieved from https://www.domusweb.it/en/from-the-archive/2012/03/24/bruno-munari-art-director-1943-1944.html

Di Biagi, P. (ed) (2001). *La Grande Ricostruzione. Il piano Ina-Casa e l'Italia degli Anni Cinquanta*. Roma: Donzelli.

Fabre, G., Pelini, F. and Schwarz, G. (2000). Censura fascista, editoria e autori ebrei. *Quaderni storici*, 104(2), pp. 521–539.

Gianini Belotti, E. (1973). *Dalla Parte delle Bambine. L'influenza dei Condizionamenti Sociali Nella Formazione del Ruolo Femminile nei Primi Anni di Vita.* Milano: Feltrinelli.

Goga, N. (2019).Home is outdoors. A study of award-winning Norwegian picturebooks. *Ricerchedi Pedagogia e Didattica/Journal of Theories and Research in Education*, 14(2), pp. 145–174. DOI: 10.6092/issn.1970-2221/10035

Hayward, E. and Schmiedeknecht, T. (2019). Absent architectures: Post-war housing in British children's picture books (1960–present). *The Journal of Architecture*, 24(4), pp. 487–511. DOI: 10.1080/13602365.2019.1641736

Kümmerling-Meibauer, B. (2019). Is there really no place like home? Changes in the perception of domestic spaces in German picturebooks from 1945 to the present. *Ricerche di Pedagogia e Didattica/ Journal of Theories and Research in Education*, 14(2), pp. 117–143. DOI: 10.6092/issn.1970-2221/10034

Lange, A. (2018). *The Design of Childhood. How the Material World Shapes Independent Kids.* London: Bloomsbury Publishing.

Maino, M. P. (2003). *A Misura di Bambino. Cent'anni di Mobili per L'infanzia in Italia (1870–1970).* Roma-Bari: Laterza.

Maulsby, M. L. (2014). Giustizia Fascista: The representation of fascist justice in marcello piacentini's palace of justice, Milan, 1932–1940. *Journal of the Society of Architectural Historians*, 73(3), pp. 312–327.

Meneguzzo, M. (1993). *Bruno Munari.* Roma-Bari: Laterza.

Meunier, C. (2016). *L'Espace dans les livres pour enfants.* Rennes: PUR.

Munari, B. (1945). *Scatola di Architettura LC N 1.* Milano: Officina Meccanica Luciano Castelletti.

——— (1966). *Arte Come Mestiere.* Bari: Laterza.

——— (1972). *Cappuccetto Giallo.* Torino: Einaudi.

——— (1981/2009). *Da Cosa Nasce Cosa.* Bari: Laterza.

Narančić Kovač, S. (2019). Lived spaces in Croatian picturebooks: Public and private places and the sense of belonging. *Ricerche di Pedagogia e Didattica/Journal of Theories and Research in Education*, 14(2), pp. 49–85. DOI: 10.6092/issn.1970-2221/10031

Pace Nilsen, A. (1971). Women in children's literature. *College English*, 32(8), pp. 918–926.

Pergoli Campanelli, A. (2014). Restoration of the façade of the Pirelli skyscraper in Milan and the repair of damage to reinforced concrete structures caused by a plane crash: An example of critic conservation. *Frontiers of Architectural Research*, 3, pp. 213–223. DOI: 10.1016/j.foar.2014.03.005

Perrot, M. (2011). *Storia Delle Camere.* Palermo: Sellerio.

Ramos, A. M. (2019). Depiction of home space in Portuguese picturebooks. *Ricerche di Pedagogia e Didattica/Journal of Theories and Research in Education*, 14(2), pp. 175–202. DOI: 10.6092/issn.1970-2221/10036

Swope, C. (2014). Modern architecture, national traditions, and ambivalent internationalism: An East German architectural text for young readers. In Heather Snell and Lorna Hutchison (eds), *Children and Cultural Memory in Texts of Childhood* (pp. 87–102). New York: Routledge.

Turin, A. and Bosnia, N. (1975). *Una fortunata catastrofe.* Milan: Dalla parte delle bambine/ Contact Studio.

Tafuri, M. (2002). *Storia Dell'architettura Italiana. 1944–1985.* Torino: Einaudi.

Ziegler, C. J. (2009). Out of ashes and rubble: The Pirelli tower. *Places*, 21(1). Retrieved from https://escholarship.org/uc/item/16v9d2pd

8

REPRESENTATIONS OF ARCHITECTURE IN CHILDREN'S PICTUREBOOKS IN AUSTRALIA, SINGAPORE AND CHINA

Sabine Tan, Xinchao Zhai, Lyndon Way and Kay L. O'Halloran

Introduction

This chapter examines representations of architecture in children's illustrated books to explore how they function to socialise children in different social and cultural contexts in a modern, globalised world. Specifically, we have chosen nations with diverse cultural backgrounds, physical geographies and histories in the Asia-Pacific region: (1) Australia, where the majority of people work and live in low-/medium-density environments, (2) Singapore, where the majority of the population work and live in high-density habitats and (3) China, where traditional, low-rise buildings co-exist with modern, high-density buildings. More specifically, we investigate the role of representations of architecture and how the social practices, depicted in various spaces defined through modern architectural design, function to instil core values in relation to the individual, family, community and society. Also, comparisons with traditional buildings are drawn in order to examine how the three nations have adjusted to the pressures of modernity. In this regard, representations of architecture are seen to play a key role in how a society views itself in a rapidly changing world.

In what follows, we provide a brief overview of how architecture and architectural representations function to construct meaning from a critical multimodal discourse analysis and social semiotic perspective. Following this, we present a multimodal social semiotic framework for analysing architectural representations in children's picturebooks from Australia, Singapore and China. Last, we discuss the analysis of the representations in the picturebooks and offer some concluding comments about the significance of architectural design in relation to instilling socio-cultural values today.

Background

Scholars agree that although architecture 'fulfils a primarily practical function' (O'Toole, 2011, p. 64), it is also inscribed with meanings. Architecture has been attributed with constructing knowledge, affecting how we think about how we should live (Kress & van Leeuwen, 2001; Ravelli & McMurtrie, 2016). Studies have demonstrated how architecture communicates a sense of identity, belonging, comfort and even security (Ravelli &

DOI: 10.4324/9781003131755-11

Stenglin, 2008; Dovey, 2010; Jones & Svejenova, 2017). Much of this communication is affective: buildings giving viewers the feeling of belonging or intruding; being inviting or intimidating; comfortable or uncomfortable (Ravelli & Stenglin, 2008; McMurtrie, 2012). These responses are a result of designers' 'conscious attempts … to create a sense of place', exclusivity and identity expressed in visual styles of buildings and whole cities (Dovey, 2010, p. 3) as well as how we interpret these (Grynsztejn, 2007; McMurtrie, 2012).

Representations of architecture, like architecture itself, are semiotic systems that articulate knowledge as well as feelings of identity and belonging, though like most other social semiotic approaches, this is dependent 'on the texts' resonance with audience's experiences and expectations' (Jones & Svejenova, 2017, p. 229). For the most part, representations of architecture in illustrated books are restricted to two-dimensional images and lexica where 'we cannot feel the represented three-dimensional spatial text in the same way as we might if we were immersed in the actual space' (McMurtrie, 2012, pp. 516–517). Regardless, closely aligned architectural experiences can be communicated through two-dimensional representations (McMurtrie, 2012; see also Kress & van Leeuwen, 2020).

We adopt a social semiotic perspective to examine representations of architecture in children's illustrated books, given the role these books play in educating and socialising children. In addition to promoting literacy, increasing vocabulary and building sensory awareness in children (Hughes-Hassell & Cox, 2010), illustrated books are powerful tools conveying values, essential concepts and attitudes in social and cultural learning (Wee, Park & Choi, 2015). In these books, representations of architecture, especially dwellings, are ever-present, with the house being the most common (Casonato, 2017). These spatial representations combine with a child's 'real experience of space' to 'play a significant role in the construction of the idea of space and dwelling […]' (Casonato, 2017, p. 1). This has cultural significance, as representations act as 'a basic source of education in architectural thought in childhood' (Casonato, 2017, p. 1). By allowing children to familiarise with spatial representations, they 'orient themselves in the spaces they live in and they imagine, thus preparing to act on real space' (Meunier, 2016, p. 1).

Children engage with picturebooks to help them construct a sense of identity in terms of their lived culture (Casonato, 2017). However, these architectural representations have been seen to articulate an ideology of culture that favours heritage and tradition at the expense of modern housing (Nodelman 1999; Taylor & Tison, 2003). This can be articulated through visual and lexical representations of well-known architecture (Luigini, 2019), nostalgic depictions of architecture in foreign cultures (Wee, Park & Choi, 2015) and negatively representing modern buildings while positively representing traditional homes, particularly in France (Taylor & Tison, 2003) and post-war Britain (Hayward & Schmiedeknecht, 2019). For example, 'architecture associated with post-war reconstruction is significantly underrepresented in children's picture books of the period', where nostalgic representations of 'the home, the street, and the high street are … associated with Georgian, Edwardian, and Victorian architectural ideals' (Hayward & Schmiedeknecht, 2019, p. 487). As we shall see, this trend may be compared to nations in the Asia-Pacific, which appear to celebrate the present and the future rather than look back to the past.

Theoretical framework

Our analysis of representations of architecture in children's picturebooks is inspired by critical multimodal discourse analysis and social semiotics. The approach is modelled on Michael Halliday's systemic functional theory, which posits that semiotic resources are structured

TABLE 8.1 Analytical framework for representations of architecture

Function/ Rank	Experiential	Interpersonal	Textual
Outdoor space	Practical function: Public, private, communal Purpose: Industrial, commercial, agricultural, governmental, educational, medical, cultural, religious, residential, recreation, play, unknown Type: Domestic, utility Specific functions: Access, entry, front yard, back yard, laundry, retreat Sub-functions: Access, working, selling, administration, storing, walking, sleeping, parking, family life, playing, bathing, relaxing, community life Orientation: Light, wind, earth, water, service	Orientation: Neighbours, road, entrance, city Spaciousness: Spacious, cramped Material: Grass, stone, brick, wood, marble Colour: Warm, cool Texture: Hard, soft Accessibility: Accessible/Inaccessible View: Neutral, good view, bad view, no view Sites of power: Grandparents, parents, children, family, guests, community Separation of groups/spheres: Public, private Foregrounding of function: Comfort, utility, play Welcome: Open, reserved	Relation to city, road, adjacent buildings Degree of separation: Separated, open Connectors: Doors, windows, gates
Building	Practical function: Public, private, industrial, commercial, agricultural, governmental, educational, medical, cultural, religious, residential, domestic, utility, orientation to light, wind, earth, service (water, sewage, power)	Size Verticality Chthonicity Facade Cladding Colour Modernity Exoticism Opacity Reflectivity Orientation to neighbours, road, entrant Intertextuality: Reference, mimicry, contrast	Relation to city, road, adjacent buildings Proportions Rhythms: Contrasting shapes, angles Textures: Rough, smooth Roof/wall relation Opacity Reflectivity

(Continued)

Function/ Rank	Experiential	Interpersonal	Textual
Floor	Sub-functions: Access, working, selling, administration, storing, waking, sleeping, parking	Height Spaciousness Accessibility Openness of vista View Hard/soft texture Colour Sites of power Separation of groups	Relation to other floors Relation to outer world Relation to connector: Stairs, lift, escalator (external cohesion) Relation of landing, corridor, foyer, room (internal cohesion) Degree of partition Permanence of partition
Room	Specific functions: Access, entry, living room, family room, kitchen, bathroom, bedroom, study, toilet, laundry, game's room, retreat, ensuite, servery, foyer, restaurant, kitchen, bar	Comfort Modernity Opulence Lighting Sound Welcome Style: Rustic, pioneer, colonial, suburban, 'Dallas', working class, tenement, slum Foregrounding of function	Scale Lighting Sound Relation to outside Relation to other rooms Connectors: Doors, windows, hatches, intercom Focus (e.g. hearth, dais, altar, desk)
Element	Light: Window, lamp, curtains, blinds Air: Window, fan, conditioner Heating: Central, fire, stove Sound: Carpet, rugs, partitions acoustic, treatment Seating function: Comfort Table: Dining, coffee, occasional desk, computer, drawing board	Relevance Functionality: Convention, surprise Texture: rough, smooth Newness Decorativeness 'Stance' Stylistic coherence Projection (e.g. TV)	Texture Positioning to light, heat, other elements Finish

Adapted from O'Toole (2004, 2011); see also O'Halloran and Tan (2015).

in terms of the functions they serve in society. These functions are conceptualised as *meta-functions*, namely: (a) *ideational*, for construing world happenings (i.e. experiential meaning) and the logical connections between events (i.e. logical meaning); (b) *interpersonal*, for enacting social relations and for expressing stances and attitudes; and (c) *textual*, for organising meanings into coherent wholes (e.g. Halliday 1978; Halliday & Matthiessen 2014). These meaning-making systems are often modelled as system networks, and in some cases, organised according to different ranks or strata (e.g. O'Toole, 2004, 2011; O'Halloran et al., 2019).

O'Toole (2004, 2011) proposes a stratified and metafunctionally organised system framework for the analysis of architecture. He argues first that:

> [o]ur experience of the built world is realised in systems of features and relationships at every rank of unit and, insofar as we engage with the entire building, a separate floor, a room, or the individual elements in a room, it is useful to distinguish the rank-scale of these systems.
>
> *(O'Toole, 2011, p. 64)*

Second, it can be reasoned that built structures have interpersonal meaning, for example, as realised through the way a building or room relates to its occupants. Last, it can be assumed that built spaces also have textual meaning, as they function as a coherent whole in relation to their immediate and the wider environment (O'Toole, 2011).

O'Toole's (2004, 2011) rank-based system framework provides the basis for our analysis of visual representations of architecture in children's picturebooks. In addition to analysing the illustrations of buildings, rooms and elements within, we have added ancillary systems for the rank of outdoor space to determine how these representations relate to the wider environment (e.g. neighbourhood and city) to explore cultural values associated with social groups, communities and society at large. The analytical framework is presented in Table 8.1.

Data and method

Our data for this study on representations of architecture in children's picturebooks consists of three publications each from Australia, Singapore and China. These books are: (a) Australia: *Bluey: At Home with the Heelers* (2021), *Max* (Graham, 2002) and *Wren* (Lehman & Beer, 2018); (b) Singapore: *Maddie's New Neighbours* (Ho & Yee, 2015), *Little Red in the Hood* (Goei & Tan, 2014) and *There was a Peranakan Woman who Lived in a Shoe* (Lee, 2014); and (c) China: *Xiao Ai's Dragon Boat Festival* (Wang & Zhang, 2005), *Tooth, Tooth, Throw it onto the Roof* (Liu, 2004) and *Blooming Season* (Wu & Xiao, 2018). These books were selected on the basis that the story was specifically located in each country, as evidenced by the illustrations, the publisher and the language.

Images from the books which featured representations of modern and/or traditional architecture were extracted and grouped into separate categories for Inside to be analysed at the ranks of Floor, Room and Element (although in most cases the rank of Floor was found not to be relevant, as only rooms or parts of rooms were depicted in the illustrations), and Outside, Neighbourhood and City to be analysed at the ranks of Building and Outdoor Space (see Table 8.1). We then selected one representative image from each book for each of these four categories (it must be noted however that not all books had images in all four categories), resulting in a total sample size of 31 images.

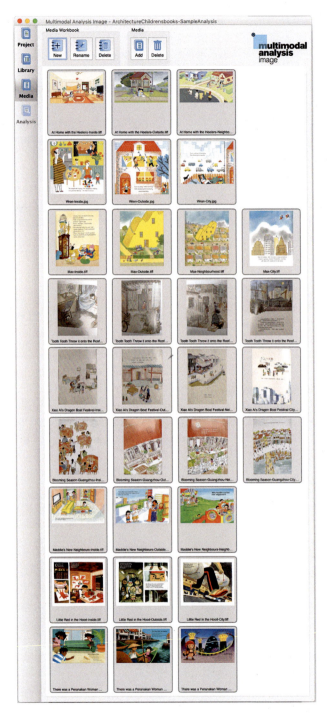

FIGURE 8.1 Sample media files used for analysis with *multimodal analysis image* (O'Halloran, K. L., Podlasov, A., Tan, S., E, M., et al., 2012).

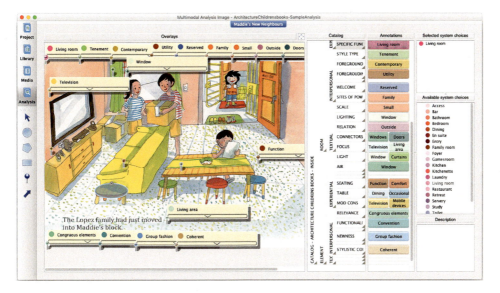

FIGURE 8.2 An annotated media file from *Maddie's New Neighbours* (Ho & Yee, 2015).

The analysis of the selected images was performed with *Multimodal Analysis Image*.[1] The purpose-built software has facilities for importing images as media files, creating catalogues of customised system networks, annotating the media files using overlays in the form of geometrical shapes and pins and attaching a system choice to each overlay based on the applicable system network, which in this case is an adaptation of O'Toole's (2011) systems for architecture (see Table 8.1). Figure 8.1 shows examples of the media files and Figure 8.2 is an example of an annotated media file, which in this case is a view of the interior of a Singaporean apartment (Ho & Yee, 2015). In what follows, we discuss the analysis of our data set.

Analysis

Australian picturebooks

Bluey: At Home with the Heelers. This board picturebook is based on the popular animated children's television show *Bluey*, which deals with the adventures of an anthropomorphised blue heeler[2] puppy and her family. The picturebook introduces the reader to the central character, Bluey, her family and, as suggested by the title, the Heeler family home. Modelled on the television series, the story is set in Brisbane, Queensland, Australia.

Experientially, the image selected from the category labelled Inside, featuring the interior of the Heeler home, depicts a modern-day living room (see Figure 8.3(a)). Its style is recognisably suburban and contemporary. Coloured in pastel hues, the foregrounded function of the room is focused on comfort, as suggested by the plush-looking, cushion-adorned, apricot-coloured three seater lounge, beige easy chair with matching footstool and lush area rug. As a site of welcome, the room seems to be reserved for use by its immediate occupants. Although several access points to the outside and other rooms are shown, the single

(a)
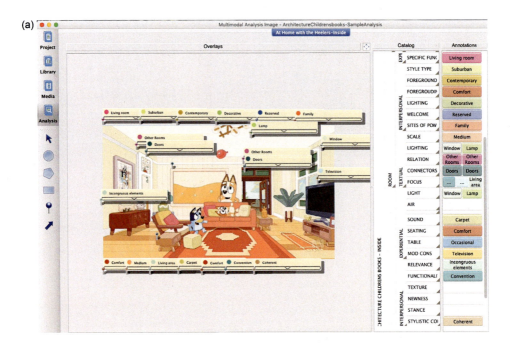

(b)

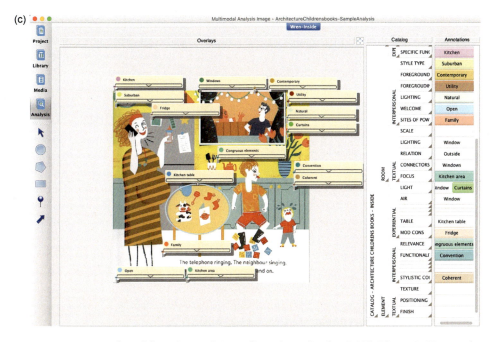

FIGURE 8.3 Examples of the annotated Australian picturebooks: 8.3(a) *Bluey: At Home with the Heelers* (Bluey, 2021) (Catergory: Inside); 8.3(b) *Max* (Graham, 2002) (Category: Outside); 8.3(c) *Wren* (Lehman & Beer, 2018) (Category: Inside).

stained glass window is shut, while an open door at the back of the room leads to an enclosed veranda. The chief source of light is provided by a decorative, contemporary-looking pendant light, suspended from the ceiling at the centre of the room. In terms of interpersonal relations, the room is orientated towards the family unit, showing Bluey and her little sister Bingo stretched out on the lounge and the Heeler mother as an authority figure presiding over them in a modern-day sitting room. The main function of the room appears to be geared towards supervised relaxation, not play, as suggested by the absence of any toys and the seemingly well-behaved Heeler pups. Textually, the focus of the room is the open space living area, which is surrounded by a large portrait of the Heeler family and a large flat-screen TV on either side and an abstract painting in the background. Fitted out with contemporary conveniences and decorative ornaments one would expect in a modern-day sitting room, the room does however contain some incongruous elements which are more in tune with the occupants' canine traits, such as the sculpture of a large T-bone displayed prominently on a low sideboard.

The Outside image depicts the Heeler family home, which is an iconic suburban 'Queenslander' style (Kennedy, 2005; Osborne, 2014). These homes are traditionally elevated, medium-sized, single-storey detached houses, located on a separate block of land. Other prototypical architectural features include timber cladding, steepled corrugated iron roofs and wrap-around verandas (Osborne, 2014). The Heeler house is no exception. Sitting on a single plot of land and surrounded on three sides by a white picket fence that separates it from its neighbours, the house is fronted by a spacious manicured lawn, complete with landscaped planters and a paved space for parking a car. While the closed doors and opaque windows of the house suggest an interpersonal orientation towards privacy, its immediate outdoor space is open and accessible to the public.

The image from the category Neighbourhood shows the Heeler home and a neighbouring property, which is also a typical Queenslander home. In the selected image, the Heeler family and their neighbours (comprising dogs of different breeds) can be seen gathering outdoors at the crescent end of a cul-de-sac. The function of this outdoor space is foremost communal. Well-tended, open and accessible, this communal space includes elements of play, indicted by hopscotch markings on the road. However, the image also contains hints of more mundane routine domestic utility, as suggested by a couple of wheelie bins strategically placed at the verge.

All in all, representations of architecture in *At Home with the Heelers*, although fictionalised and rendered in the form of a cartoon, can be considered to be of high visual modality, as the illustrations depict daily life, places and things as they might exist in reality in suburban Queensland. Moreover, the primacy and privacy of the family home for relaxation is demarcated spatially (i.e. through fences and access points such as the driveways and path), with neighbour gatherings taking place in public areas in the street.

Max. Authored and illustrated by Bob Graham, *Max* is a story about a superhero boy who has difficulties learning how to fly. Set in 'a street like any other street, in a town like any other town' (Graham, 2002), the story revolves around the domestic life of Max and his superhero parents and grandparents.

As in *At Home with the Heelers*, the image of Max's house from Inside depicts a living room. However, in this case, the style type is decidedly vintage, as suggested by the old-fashioned décor and items such as the tea set arranged on a low coffee table, the antique-looking glass display cabinet filled with plaques and trophies and other assorted bric-a-brac. The living room interior is reflective of the style one might expect to find in one's grandparents' abode. In terms of interpersonal relations, the room seems indeed orientated towards Max's grandparents, who, attired in blue and red superhero outfits, are shown resting on the slightly saggy sofa: napping (the grandmother) or reading the daily newspaper (the grandfather). As with *At Home with the Heelers*, the main function of the living room appears to be relaxation. Nonetheless, the superhero living room also seems to be designed to accommodate flying, as suggested by the high ceilings.

The idea of a home suitable for flying is also conveyed by the upward reaching but chthonic character of Max's house, as seen in the Outside image in Figure 8.3(b). According to O'Toole (2011), 'chthonicity' describes the degree to which a building is bound to the earth, 'an important aspect of the impact it has on both occupants and viewers' (p. 77). In this case, the image of Max's multi-level home virtually fills the vertically laid out page. Shaped like a lightning bolt with non-geometric angles and proportions, its architectural design is non-conforming and exotic, befitting a superhero family home. Interpersonally, however, its smooth, bright yellow surface, half-open curtained windows and open front door with the family dog curled up upon its step suggest a certain kind of openness and familial warmth.

The main functions of the outdoor space are oriented towards family life, which is divided into a front yard and garden and a laundry area at the back of the house. Separated by a low trimmed hedge and double gates from the public road and sidewalk, the front yard appears to cater to all kinds of recreational activities, such as Max's grandparents reclining in deckchairs and his father pottering in the garden. Max's front yard also includes elements of (vertically inclined) play, as intimated by a trampoline.

A high-angle image of Max's Neighbourhood shows that Max's non-traditional super-hero house stands out from the homes surrounding it. These are uniformly conventional, medium-sized, pastel-coloured, double-storey family homes of geometric proportions with an attached chimney, pitched roof, a small front yard and back yard for hanging laundry, all located on a single, uniformly spaced block of land. As the author himself suggests at the beginning of the book, the pictorial representation of Max's neighbourhood, with the shapes of grey high-rise buildings of the city looming in the distance, is synonymous with the generic architectural style of suburban estates which can be found in any large city in Australia (Graham, 2002). The image of the City itself shows Max and his parents soaring over the top of lofty, cool-coloured, modern high-rise buildings of unknown purpose, which provides a stark contrast and reflects a clear divide between the public and private spaces and spheres of urban, suburban and domestic life. Again, both the primacy and privacy of the family home is evident, but it is a fictional home purpose-built to meet the needs of the occupants.

Wren. Witten by Katarina Lehman and illustrated by Sophie Beer, *Wren* is a story about a little boy who does not like loud noise and, wanting to get away from his boisterous baby sister, moves to live with grandparents in the country, but soon discovers that he misses his rambunctious family and clamorous home environment.

In contrast to the two previously analysed picturebooks, the image showing the interior of Wren's home features part of a traditional kitchen (see Figure 8.3(c)). The absence of any modern conveniences, apart from a large refrigerator with pinned photographs and shopping lists, hints at a timeless suburban style. Above green-coloured kitchen cabinetry, a large open window provides light and access. Affording a view of the back yard and the father chatting over the fence with a neighbour, it also functions as a site of welcome. The focus of the kitchen area is a round kitchen table placed at the centre of the room. Too small to be intended for dining, it is strewn with an assortment of everyday items, including a steaming coffee cup, children's drawings, baby socks, a stuffed toy and a pram rattle. Nonetheless, the elements are congruous and synonymous with the objects one might find in a family kitchen with small children. Like most kitchens, the room's main function is utility, although it also appears to be regarded by its occupants as a site for play. In terms of interpersonal relations, the room – like the room in *At Home with the Heelers* – is arranged around the family unit. Only in this case, Wren's pregnant mother, who is talking on a mobile phone, appears to have relinquished her authority over her children, as suggested by the two siblings who are shown squabbling unimpeded over building blocks scattered on the floor.

The Outside image of Wren's home depicts a conventional, medium-sized, double-storey house with smooth, warm-coloured brick cladding, dormer window and terracotta roof. Bright open windows provide a welcoming environment, but little privacy, showing an adult figure showering in full view. The overriding function of the outdoor space is dedicated to all sorts of play, with children sitting on a swing, skipping rope and swinging from garlanded ropes from the upper-floor windows.

The functions of outdoor space in the image from the category City, featuring the front yard of the Wren family residence at the bottom of the image and a cityscape at the top, can be clearly divided into private and public. The purpose of the tiny front yard can again be segregated into relaxing for adults and playing for children. A wooden picket fence separates the apparently restful (and warm-coloured) private domain of the Wren family front yard from a busy and noisy public thoroughfare and the abstract (cool-coloured) sketches of high-rise buildings in the city beyond.

In summary, representations of architecture in these children's books from Australia are mostly concerned with domestic, residential spaces, with a strong focus on the characters' family life, and a clear separation between private and public domains. The dominant functions of indoor and outdoor spaces appear to be designed for relaxation and recreation, mostly enjoyed by adults or with adult supervision, with physical boundaries segregating the private (family) and public (community) spaces.

Singaporean picturebooks

Maddie's New Neighbours. Written by Ho Lee-Ling and illustrated by Patrick Yee, *Maddie's New Neighbours* is part of an initiative by the Singapore's Housing and Development Board (HDB), aimed at inspiring young children to be considerate and caring neighbours. The story follows the central character, Maddie, as she befriends her new neighbours, the Lopez family, who have just moved into a HDB flat, the most common type of public housing in Singapore. Mass-produced to house Singaporeans across all sections of society since the early 1960s, ranging from blue-collar to upper-middle-class families (Lee, 2015; Chee, 2017), today more than 80% of Singapore's population lives in HDB flats, with the majority owning their home.[3]

The image from the category Inside of *Maddie's New Neighbours* provides an authentic and realistic illustration of a prototypical modern-day HDB living room (see Figure 8.2). Compared to the living rooms depicted in Australian picturebooks, the proportions of the room are visibly more confined, with an emphasis on utility rather than comfort. The multipurpose nature of the living room is evidenced by the different sections that have been set aside for recreation (i.e. watching TV) and dining/studying. While the contemporary three seater sofa seems comfortable, it is markedly smaller in size and less plush than the lounge depicted in *At Home with Heelers*, for example, and its distance to the TV console is considerably shorter. The central focus of the Lopez's living area is a plain, flat-pack IKEA table and an assortment of low stools that are utilised as a site for studying or reading when not used for dining, highlighting the need for maximising space in Singapore's densely populated urban environment. Despite the room's simple, minimalist décor, its warm colouring and assortment of high-tech gadgets arranged atop a slim TV console suggest a comfortable middle-class lifestyle that caters to the needs of the small family unit.

Given the close proximity to the neighbouring flats sharing a 'common corridor'[4] (Chee, 2017; Kuah, 2018), points of access and sites of welcome to the flat (which commonly do not include a hallway) are naturally reserved and closed off to the neighbouring community. Window grills and metal gates, left open for the purpose of ventilation, assure privacy and security. Terrazzo or marble chip floor tiles provide for coolness and cleanliness in

(a)

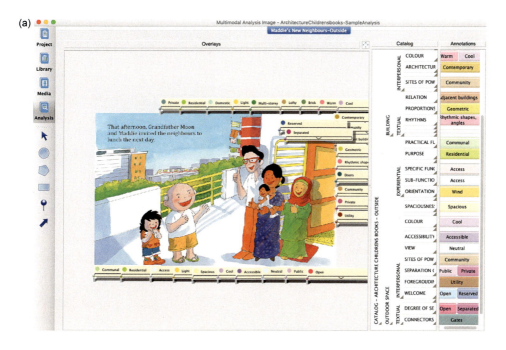

(b)

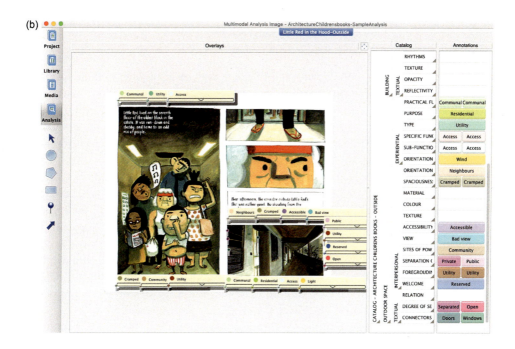

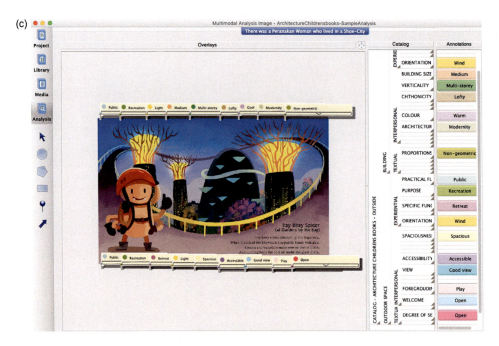

FIGURE 8.4 Examples of the annotated Singaporean picture books: 8.4(a) *Maddie's New Neighbours* (Ho & Yee, 2015) (Category: Outside); 8.4(b) *Little Red in the Hood* (Goei & Tan, 2014) (Category: Outside); 8.4(c) *There was a Peranakan Woman who Lived in a Shoe* (Lee, 2014) (Category: Neighbourhood).

Singapore's tropical and humid climate. The image of the Lopez's living room offers further insights into the minutiae of Singaporeans' cultural practices, such as outdoor shoes being habitually left on a mat outside the apartment.

The image from the category Outside (see Figure 8.4(a)) places Maddie and her grandfather in the common corridor, a communal space outside a neighbour's flat. The function of the common corridor, a key design feature of HDB apartment blocks (Lee, 2015; Chee, 2017; Kuah, 2018), is first and foremost to provide access to the flats. Whitewashed for coolness and open to the elements, it provides light and ventilation. On upper floors (as intimated in Figure 8.4(a)), it also affords a good view of the neighbouring HDB blocks and public amenities such as Singapore's Mass Rapid Transportation (MRT) system. The selected image conveys yet another detail of Singapore's idiosyncratic high-rise culture, where it is common practice to hang laundry on long bamboo poles out of kitchen windows for drying (Yuen et al., 2006).

The image from Maddie's Neighbourhood category features a stereotypical community park and children's playground. The image shows separate areas reserved for play – typically a concrete, often mosaicked, structure for climbing and sliding (Sini, 2020) – and adult recreation, represented by a sturdy, concrete pergola or pavilion. The representations closely resemble the architectural design features of community spaces commonly found in modern HDB estates (Foo, 2001).

Little Red in the Hood. This book is a modern-day adaptation of the popular children's fairy tale. Written by Singapore film and theatre director Glen Goei and illustrated by

Andrew Tan (aka Drewscape), the story of Little Red and her kickboxing grandmother is also set in a HDB estate in Singapore, although the overall theme is darker and less contemporary than *Maddie's New Neighbours*.

The image from Inside of Little Red's flat shows part of a child's bedroom at night. It features a narrow wooden bed occupied by Little Red and covered with 'fluffy red bags' that Little Red likes to sew (Goei, 2014), a wooden side table with a sewing machine, red desk lamp and a wooden slatted chair. Aside from sleeping, the foregrounded function of the room suggests industriousness, constructed around Little Red's favourite leisure activities: drawing and sewing things in red. Although the scale of room is small and cramped, the oppressiveness created by the dark brown ceiling and closed window grills is offset by the bright red décor, such as cheerful drawings of red wolves pinned to the wall, red accessories strewn on the bed and floor and red window coverings.

The image from Outside the flat depicts a common corridor (see Figure 8.4(b)). However, unlike the walkway in *Maddie's New Neighbours*, it is not airy and open, but dark and oppressive. Narrow and closed-off to the elements by an overhanging parapet, it is reminiscent of the dark and poorly ventilated common corridors of the 1960s and early 1970s, which were designed to provide access to the 'concrete pigeon holes' of former 'kampong' dwellers (Kuah, 2018, pp. 47–48). Indeed, Little Red lives in the Pek Kio estate, 'on the seventh floor of the oldest block' which was 'run-down and shabby, and home to an odd mix of people' (Goei, 2014). These people are shown crammed into an elevator, which is similarly suggestive of the cramped, enclosed HDB lifts of the past, where occupants often engaged in insalubrious, antisocial behaviour such as urinating, spitting and littering (Hee, 2009).

The image from the category City shows grandma, loaded with grocery bags, crossing the road at a busy intersection, against the backdrop of a FairPrice supermarket, Singapore's largest grocery retailer. Housed in a long, low, two-storeyed commercial building situated along the roadside, the image once again corresponds with an authentic setting of a past era where stand-alone retail outlets could still be found occupying small, self-contained commercial buildings in the city centre (Ooi, 1999).

Consequently, representations of architecture in *Little Red in the Hood* are instantly recognisable to Singapore's older generations. Overwhelmingly, the book serves to remind readers of the improvements made to public housing since the 1960s, where communal living in high-rise buildings involved some degree of physical threat from unsocial and potentially bellicose neighbours. Indeed, the title of the book is a play on the word 'hood' from Little Red Riding Hood to a slang abbreviation of the 'neighbourhood'.

There was a Peranakan Woman who Lived in a Shoe. Written by Gwen Lee and illustrated by Cheryl Kook, *There was a Peranakan Woman who Lived in a Shoe* is a nursery rhyme book set in a Singapore context, contrasting scenes and experiences of past and present lifestyles.

Like in *Maddie's New Neighbours*, the image from the Inside category of *There was a Peranakan Woman who Lived in a Shoe* offers a partial view of a contemporary HDB living room. The room is spartan but functionally furnished, containing only a slim IKEA sofa and a large potted plant, giving the impression of spaciousness. A large, open, curtained window provides light and ventilation and affords a view of the open sky and the flat roof tops of surrounding high-rise HDB blocks, suggesting an upper-floor unit as preferred by many Singaporeans (Yuen et al., 2006). The sites of interpersonal power relations in the room are, as in *Maddie's New Neighbours*, vested in the small family unit, comprising young parents and a single child. Amongst the elements depicted in this image are several geckos (a variety of small lizards), which are commonly found inside Singaporean apartments but not always tolerated by its inhabitants, as suggested by the accompanying nursery rhyme lyrics.

In contrast to the present-day scene provided by the interior of the HDB living room, the image from the category Neighbourhood depicts an outdoor scene of an area along the shores of the iconic Singapore River. However, as suggested by the sampans plying the river, the historic architectural style of the open-fronted, double-storeyed shophouses or 'go-downs' lining the riverfront as well as the traditional dress and hairstyle of the sampan's occupants, the image is reminiscent of an era long before the clean-up of the river in 1977 when it was still used for commercial, trade-related or industrial purposes (Tortajada, 2012).

This nostalgic Neighbourhood scene can again be contrasted against the image from the category City (see Figure 8.4(c)). Providing a backdrop to an adaptation of 'Itsy Bitsy Spider', the image shows a cute, anthropomorphised spider taking a night-time stroll in Singapore's Gardens by the Bay. A large, landscaped horticultural park sitting on 101 hectares (250 acres) of reclaimed land, the gardens are the result of the government's 'City in a Garden' concept which aimed to bring green spaces and biodiversity to the doorsteps of Singaporeans (Newman, 2014; Flannery & Smith, 2015). One of the park's key attractions is its man-made 'Supertrees' (see Figure 8.4(c)). The lofty tree canopies of the colour-co-ordinated 25–50-metre-tall structures which provide shade and cool air during day become spectacularly illuminated beacons of light by night (Flannery & Smith, 2015). The image and the nursery rhyme lyrics place Itsy Bitsy Spider on the 'Skyway' – a 128-metre-long aerial walkway suspended between two Supertrees at 22 metres above ground,[5] evidently enjoying the magical night-time atmosphere of the park. Although hugely abstracted and rendered in the form of a simplistic cartoon, Singapore's urban biophilic architectural design is clearly depicted in this picturebook.

In summary, representations of architecture in these children's books from Singapore are focused on both real and generic indoor and outdoor spaces which reflect Singapore's urban planning policy. The dominant functions of indoor spaces appear to be designed for space-saving utility, where sites of interpersonal relations are organised around the small family unit or a single child and friendly community relations in corridors and spaces beyond the front door of flats. These representations offer insights into past and present lifestyles of urban Singaporeans, and while they may include aspects of nostalgia (such as the sampans on the river), these are also reflections of the imperfections associated with high-rise life in HDB's early apartment blocks (Hee, 2009; Kuah, 2018) (as in *Little Red in the Hood*) and benefits of living in modern, technologically advanced Singapore today.

Chinese picturebooks

Xiao Ai's Dragon Boat Festival. Authored by Wang Yimei and illustrated by Zhang Xiaoyu, *Xiao Ai's Dragon Boat Festival* depicts city girl Xiao Ai's first visit to her grandmother in a small ancient town in southern China to celebrate the Dragon Boat Festival.[6] The illustrations in this book feature Dragon Boat Festival traditions and the local architectural and cultural landscape, providing a panoramic view of a traditional Chinese town in contrast to the uniformly constructed big cities.

Experientially, the image from the category Inside depicts the interior of the grandmother's house (see Figure 8.5(a)). Unlike western residential buildings, where space is divided into clearly defined functional units (e.g. bathroom, family room, living room), this image represents the interior space holistically without segregating walls or lines. In

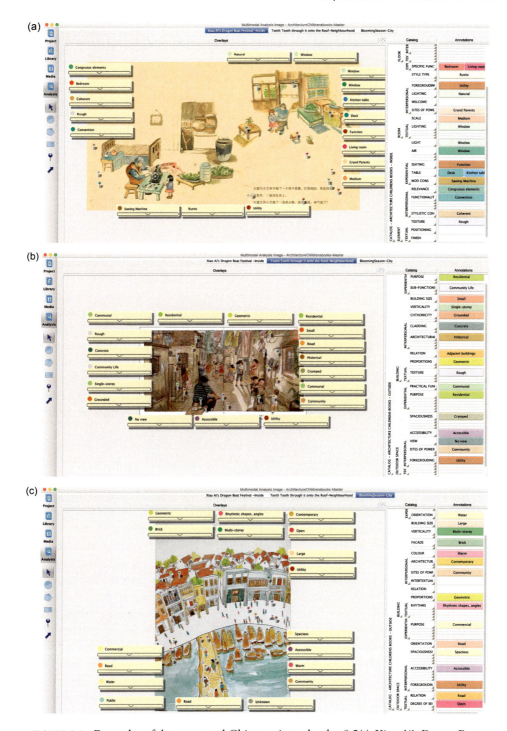

FIGURE 8.5 Examples of the annotated Chinese picturebooks: 8.5(a) *Xiao Ai's Dragon Boat Festival* (Wang & Zhang, 2005) (Category: Inside); 8.5(b) *Tooth, Tooth, throw it onto the Roof* (Liu, 2004) (Category: Neighbourhood); 8.5(c) *Blooming Season* (Wu & Xiao, 2018) (Category: Neighbourhood).

this case, the specific functional area can only be inferred from the spatial reference to the door and window as well as the distribution of furniture. The area can be divided into inner space (where the bed is placed) and outer space (equivalent to the living space). In terms of its interpersonal features, grandmother's room is characterised by a minimalist, rustic style, where only necessities are available (i.e. a bed, desks and benches). The furniture consists of home-made, heavy wooden artefacts, with an orientation towards utility, regardless of concerns about comfort. The space is free from modern conveniences and the chief source of light is a window. The representation of a big water tank suggests a lack of tap water in the town. The three huge kimchi jars in the corner of the inner space are indicative of the grandmother's diligent and thrifty life. All these visual cues point to the fact that this residential space satisfies only basic needs of living.

The Outside and Neighbourhood images depict the exterior space of the grandmother's house. It is a spacious, medium-sized, single-storey house made of brick and wood. The most striking feature is the textual organisation of the space. The residential buildings are detached houses. Because the houses do not have enclosed yards, the outside space is directly linked to the adjacent buildings without a fence or wall, orientated to other buildings and the road. The absence of a physical segregation makes this area an open space that is accessible to the public where anyone can walk in freely. It is also the grandmother's extended living space as she places her daily necessities in front of her door and uses it as a site of welcome. Crowds of people gather outside the house, waiting for her home-made rice dumplings which she sells to the public. As such, the public space and private space distinction is not defined by a physical segregation, but depends on the flexible use of space. These features, such as open access, no physical/permanent segregation, orientation towards other buildings and flexible and multiple uses of space, function to emphasise communal living.

Unlike images of the ancient town that is depicted with authentic local characteristics, the image from the City category resembles any big city in the world. From a bird's-eye view, the decontextualised skyscrapers resemble those in New York or Tokyo. The high-rise building takes up most of the page, except the upper left corner, which depicts a snapshot of busy transportation. These representations of high-density modern buildings symbolise China's economic achievements over the past half century.

From these representations, we can see two different types of Chinese buildings: traditional buildings in small towns and modern buildings in big cities. Images of ancient towns signify a traditional Chinese society, where life is frugal and members in the community work together. Accordingly, the architecture accommodates the socialising and work needs of the family and the community through open-plan living and community life with an absence of physical barriers allowing for flexible use of space. In contrast, the skyscrapers in modern urban China resemble those found in developed countries, resulting in the loss of traditional Chinese ways of life.

Tooth, Tooth, Throw it onto the Roof. Authored and illustrated by Liu Xun, this picture-book depicts life in the old alleys in Nanjing city in the late 20th century. The book centres on changes in the city landscape of Nanjing, when old buildings were demolished and residential buildings were upgraded throughout China. The story is concerned with the Chinese folk custom of throwing children's lower baby teeth onto the roof and burying their upper baby teeth into the earth in the hope that this can guide the adult teeth to grow in the right directions. In this case, NiuNiu loses her baby tooth and searches for her grandfather to let him know. The search takes place through old alleyways, depicting a series of lively and interesting life scenes, where people from all walks of life live in apparent harmony with each other (see Figure 8.5(b)). The illustrations in this book epitomise the disappearing alley culture in traditional Chinese society.[7]

Experientially, the image from the category labelled Inside depicts a corner of an old-fashioned bedroom furnished with a home-made wooden desk, a wooden bed with a dirty, worn-out mosquito net and a round dinner table. The furniture features an obsolete style that is typical of grandparents' abodes. This bedroom foregrounds a functional orientation without much concern for comfort. The image from the category of Outside depicts the immediate outside space (the front yard) of the house. The red-coloured, carved wooden door of the house is directed towards the main entrance of the front yard, which is a typical square yard fully enclosed by brick walls. Although the brick walls of the yard imply an interpersonal orientation towards privacy, the open gate makes the enclosed yard accessible to the public. Experientially, the small yard is cramped with many things that are typically found in China. A bicycle is placed against the left wall near the entrance gate. In the right-hand corner, there is a cement sink, equipped with tap water. Near the sink are three pots of flowers. The laundry hangs on clotheslines over the yard. Based on this visual evidence, it can be inferred that the yard is used as place for storage, laundry and washing up.

Representations of the neighbourhood provide snapshots of street scenes. It is a high-density residential area, and the walls link to each other without any segregation. The street is full of people of different ages, and the laundry that hangs overhead shades the street. People crowd in front of their doors, chatting with each other, and children play in groups on the street. Experientially, the street is both a public and a private space. The narrow street performs multiple functions, that is, it is a place for adult socialising, laundry, children having fun and a road for public transportation. Textually, the street connects buildings and organises them into a community, as all the houses (their doors and windows) are oriented towards the street. People living in this street are not only interpersonally close to each other (see the social interactions in Figure 8.5(b)), but also physically close to each other (absence of segregation between neighbouring houses). That is, the architecture represented depicts a busy street, where the space is used to its maximum.

The architecture represented in the image category City forms a striking contrast to the others. In these images, depictions of modern high-rise buildings occupy most of the space. These buildings feature smooth and shiny cladding and diverse shapes, where the low houses are dwarfed by these newly built modern buildings which tower over them. The contrast in size and prominence between modern buildings and old alleys indicate the destiny of these alleys to be replaced by high-rise buildings, which is also evidenced in the Chinese character '拆' (to demolish) on the walls of alleys in Figure 8.5(b).

In summary, this book contains details of community life in the old alleys. The illustrations are characterised by vivid, detailed depictions of buildings and life scenes, depicted in warm-coloured hues which function to convey an unfettered nostalgia about traditional life and times which have disappeared as the buildings and alleyways are demolished and replaced with modern high-rise buildings.

Blooming Season. Authored by Wu Heng and illustrated by Xiao Hai, *Blooming Season* depicts the famous New Year's Eve Flower Market in Guangzhou, which is a grand cultural event and is presented in a folk landscape with Lingnan characteristics. Different from the other two picturebooks (which take place in inland cities of China), *Blooming Season* depicts a typical middle-class family's urban life in Guangzhou, a coastal metropolis with a prosperous economy and lifestyle.

Different from the previous two picturebooks, where settings of different activities coincide without a clear division, *Blooming Season* presents a well-organised and well-developed urban space, where the functional areas (residential, commercial, entertainment and cultural) are clearly delineated as a result of city planning (Wu & Yeh, 1999; Chung & Zhou, 2011; Gong, Chen, Liu & Wang, 2014). Experientially, the representations zoom out from the immediate area outside the residential house to a broader view of the neighbourhood and adjacent precincts. The residential buildings, which are beautiful, large-sized, double-storey, western-style houses with verandas and half-enclosed front yards, stand in rows. Inside the yards, there are decorative flowers and electronic bicycles, and the verandas are equipped with drying racks. Obviously, the foregrounded function in this residential space is comfort. Textually, these uniformly constructed residential houses are characterised by a set of consistent features. They are of the same colour (red roof and white walls) and same decorations (casement windows and wrought iron gates). Each yard is enclosed by low walls, with the gate oriented towards a well-paved stone road leading to a park.

In the image of the Neighbourhood (see Figure 8.5(c)), the space is neatly divided into three colour strips that extend in parallel from left to right on the page. On top is the strip made up of the multi-storey buildings linked to each other with no space in-between. Their rhythmic shapes, continuous red roofs and consistent brown doors are coherent and uniform. The doors of these buildings are oriented towards the road, which is white, forming a colour contrast with the red roof buildings. Towards the bottom of the page is the light blue river, with wooden boats and a stone bridge. This well-ordered, spatial representation symbolises a developed and comfortable living environment. In the City image, the commercial area, vegetable market and public park are brought into view, confirming the impression of Guangzhou as a metropolis.

The architecture represented in the *Blooming Season* book is characterised by a modernist style, which foregrounds the aesthetics of the building and prioritises the comfort of its residents. As reflected in the images, different functional areas are well organised in space and the buildings are characterised by consistent colours, shapes and materials. This representation captures the typical scenes of Guangzhou as a modern city.

From the discussion above, the representation of architecture in the Chinese picturebooks discussed here display a clear division between traditional Chinese buildings (mostly residential houses) and community life in rural areas and modern buildings and life in big cities. These differences symbolise different levels of development and local lifestyles, with a nostalgic view of past times where people lived in close-knit communities. At the same time, the comfortable lifestyle of modern life in China is depicted, with a visual uniformity suggesting new forms of community identity.

Conclusion

Architecture and the accompanying use of space are fundamental to any culture. As Hall (1963) explains, the organisation of space in homes, buildings, neighbourhoods and cities determines how people interact with each other, as seen in the discussion above. In this case, there are similarities and differences in the representation of architecture in the picturebooks from Australia, Singapore and China. In each case, the family home is central and this private space is clearly demarcated from public spaces with physical barriers (e.g. fences, walls and doors). However, the nature of these spaces and the social activities which take place within them are different. In Australia and Singapore, the family home is depicted as a site for relaxation, while in traditional images from Singapore and China, these spaces are used for some form of industrious activity, for example, sewing or commercial cooking. In particular, images of traditional life in China depict a frugal lifestyle within one large room with basic amenities compared to the opulence of modern life in Australia and Singapore. In the images of traditional life in China, nostalgia is primarily directed towards community life in the alleyways and streets, although the depiction of items inside the family home adds to this nostalgia. However, the most obvious difference is the large space allocated to the family home in Australia (i.e. the house and yard), where socialising with neighbours takes place over the fence or in the street. In Singapore, community interactions take place in the public spaces such as walkways and open spaces in HDB estates.

The representations of architectural design, spaces and the accompanying social practices promote certain views of each nation. In essence, the Australian books celebrate an idealised version of modern life (with some fantasy in the case of *Max*) without explicitly looking to the past. However, the Singaporean books look to the past in order to celebrate the achievements of modern-day Singapore, where life is comfortable, communal and convivial. Indeed, Singaporean books also look to the future in terms of technological achievements of modern-day life (e.g. the 'Supertrees'). This stands in contrast with the nostalgia for traditional life and customs in the Chinese books, with evident concerns about the rapid move to modernity. Despite this, China looks to the past as a way to preserve traditional Chinese values and customs while at the same time celebrating the achievements and comforts of prosperous modern-day China (e.g. as depicted in the representations of Guangzhou).

These are observations rather than firm conclusions, given the limited size of the data set. However, what is clear is that unlike western European countries (e.g. United Kingdom, France) which look wistfully back at the past, nations in the Asia-Pacific, regardless of their differences, have their eyes firmly fixed on the present with aspirations for the future. These values and core themes of modernity are instilled in children and indeed society as a whole through representations found in the children's picturebooks.

Acknowledgement

We are grateful to Peter Wignell for suggesting the Australian children's picturebooks.

Notes

1 http://multimodal-analysis.com/products/multimodal-analysis-image/index.html.
2 Heelers are an Australian cattle dog breed.
3 https://www.hdb.gov.sg/cs/infoweb/about-us
4 A common corridor is a communal open walkway that is shared by the residents living in HDB flats in Singapore.
5 https://www.visitsingapore.com/en_au/see-do-singapore/nature-wildlife/parks-gardens/gardens-by-the-bay/.
6 The Dragon Boat Festival is a traditional Chinese festival in memory of the great patriotic poet Qu Yuan. People usually eat rice dumplings on this day.
7 The book was awarded the Feng Zikai Chinese Children's Picture Books Award. This is the first international Chinese children's picturebook award that is aimed at promoting original, quality Chinese children's books.

References

Bluey, (2021). *Bluey: At Home with the Heelers*. New York: Penguin Random House

Casonato, C. (2017). Images for Little Architects. Architecture and Architectural Drawing in Children's Books and Comics: An Interesting Case Study. *Proceedings, International and Interdisciplinary Conference IMMAGINI? Image and Imagination between Representation, Communication, Education and Psychology*, 1(9), pp. 1–12.

Chee, L. (2017). Keeping Cats, Hoarding Things: Domestic Situations in the Public Spaces of the Singaporean Housing Block. *The Journal of Architecture*, 22(6), pp. 1041–1065. DOI: 10.1080/13602365.2017.1362024

Chung, H. and Zhou, S. H. (2011). Planning for Plural Groups? Villages-in-the-City Redevelopment in Guangzhou City, China. *International Planning Studies*, 16(4), pp. 333–353. DOI: 10.1080/13563475.2011.615544

Dovey, K. (2010). *Becoming Places: Urbanism/Architecture/Identity/Power*. London; New York: Routledge.

Flannery, J. A. and Smith, K. M. (2015). Gardens by the Bay. In J. A. Flannery and K. M. Smith (eds), *Eco-Landscape Design* (pp. 88–103). Cham: Springer. DOI: 10.1007/978-3-319-07206-7_13

Foo, T. S. (2001). Planning and Design of Tampines, an Award-Winning High-Rise, High-Density Township in Singapore. *Cities*, 18(1), pp. 33–42. DOI: 10.1016/S0264-2751(00)00052-4

Goei, G. and Tan, A. (illustrator) (2014). *Little Red in the Hood*. Singapore: Epigram Books.

Gong, J., Chen, W., Liu, Y. and Wang, J. (2014). The Intensity Change of Urban Development Land: Implications for the City Master Plan of Guangzhou, China. *Land Use Policy*, 40, pp. 91–100.

Graham, B. (2002). *Max*. Cambridge, MA: Candlewick Press.

Grynsztejn, M. (2007). (Y)our Entanglements: Olafur Eliasson, the Museum, and Consumer Culture. In M. Grynsztejn (ed), *Take Your Time: Olafur Eliasson* (pp. 12–31). New York: Thames & Hudson.

Hall, E. T. (October 1963). A System for the Notation of Proxemic Behavior. *American Anthropologist*, 65(5), pp. 1003–1026.

Halliday, M. A. K. (1978). *Language as Social Semiotic: The Social Interpretation of Language and Meaning*. London: Edward Arnold.

Halliday, M. A. K., & Matthiessen, C. M. I. M. (2014). *Halliday's Introduction to Functional Grammar* (4th ed., revised by C. M. I. M. Matthiessen ed). London & New York: Routledge.

Hayward, E. and Schmiedeknecht, T. (2019). Absent Architectures: Postwar Housing in British Children's Picture Books (1960–present). *The Journal of Architecture*, 24(4), pp. 487–511.

Hee, L. (2009). Singapore's Public Housing Spaces: Alter–'Native' Spaces in Transition. In M. Butcher and S. Velayutham (eds), *Dissent and Cultural Resistance in Asia's Cities* (pp. 86–105). London and New York: Routledge.

Ho, L. L. and Yee, P. (illustrator) (2015). *Maddie's New Neighbours*. Singapore: Housing & Development Board.

Hughes-Hassell, S. and Cox, E. (2010). Inside Board Books: Representations of People of Color. *Library Quarterly*, 80(3), pp. 211–230.

Jones, C. and Svejenova, S. (2017), The Architecture of City Identities: A Multimodal Study of Barcelona and Boston. *Research in the Sociology of Organizations*, 54B, pp. 1–42.

Kennedy, R. J. (2005). *Principles of Subtropical Design for Detached Houses*. https://www.academia.edu/23594780/Principles_of_Subtropical_Design_for_Detached_Houses

Kress, G. and van Leeuwen, T. (2001). *Multimodal Discourse: The Modes and Media of Contemporary Communication*. London: Arnold.

Kress, G. and van Leeuwen, T. (2020). *Reading Images: The Grammar of Visual Design*, 3rd edn. London: Routledge.

Kuah, A. T. (2018). Tropical Urbanisation and the Life of Public Housing in Singapore. *ETropic: Electronic Journal of Studies in the Tropics*, 17(1), pp. 41–59. DOI: 10.25120/etropic.17.1.2018.3641

Lee, C. C. M. (2015). Type and the Developmental City: Housing Singapore. *The Journal of Architecture*, 20(6), pp. 988–1031. DOI: 10.1080/13602365.2015.1115419

Lee, G. and Kook, C. (illustrator) (2014). *There Was a Peranakan Woman who Lived in a Shoe*. Singapore: Epigram Books.

Lehman, K. and Beer, S. (illustrator) (2018). *Wren*. Brunswick, Victoria: Scribble.

Liu, X. (2014). *Tooth, Tooth, Throw it onto the Roof*. Shanghai: China Welfare Institute Publishing House.

Luigini, A. (2019) Houses, Objects and Architects. Architectural Drawing in Children's Literature. *Diségno*, 1(4), pp. 161–174.

McMurtrie, R. (2012). Feeling Space Dynamically: Variable Interpersonal Meanings in High-Rise Apartment Complexes. *Visual Communication*, 11(4), pp. 511–534.

Meunier, C. (2016). *L'espace dans les Livres Pour L'enfant*. Rennes: Presse Universitaires de Rennes.

Newman, P. (2014). Biophilic Urbanism: A Case Study on Singapore. *Australian Planner*, 51(1), pp. 47–65. DOI: 10.1080/07293682.2013.790832

Nodelman, P. (1999). Decoding the Images: Illustration and Picture Books. In P. Hunt (ed), *Understanding Children's Literature* (pp. 128–139). London: Routledge.

O'Halloran, K. L., Podlasov, A., Tan, S. and E, M., et al. (2012). *Multimodal Analysis Image*. Singapore: Multimodal Analysis Company.

O'Halloran, K. L., Tan, S. and E, M. K. L. (2015). Multimodal Semiosis and Semiotics. In J. Webster (ed), *The Bloomsbury Companion to M.A.K. Halliday* (pp. 386–411). London: Bloomsbury.

O'Halloran, K. L., Tan, S. and Wignell, P. (2019). SFL and Multimodal Discourse Analysis. In G. Thompson, W. L. Bowcher, L. Fontaine and D. Schönthal (eds), *The Cambridge Handbook of Systemic Functional Linguistics* (Cambridge Handbooks in Language and Linguistics, pp. 433–461). Cambridge: Cambridge University Press. DOI: 10.1017/9781316337936.019

Ooi, G. L. (1999). Urban Policy and Retailing Trends in Singapore. *Urban Studies*, 28(4), pp. 585–596. DOI: 10.1080/00420989120080671

Osborne, L. (2014, June 17). Sublime Design: The Queenslander. *The Conversation*. https://theconversation.com/sublime-design-the-queenslander-27225

O'Toole, M. (2004). Opera Ludentes: The Sydney Opera House at Work and Play. In K. L. O'Halloran (ed), *Multimodal Discourse Analysis: Systemic Functional Perspectives* (pp. 11–27). London: Continuum.

O'Toole, M. (2011). *The Language of Displayed Art*, 2nd edn. London: Routledge.

Ravelli, L. and McMurtrie, R. (2016). *Multimodality in the Built Environment: Spatial Discourse Analysis*. London: Routledge.

Ravelli, L. and Stenglin, M. (2008). Feeling Space: Interpersonal Communication and Spatial Semiotics. In G. Antos and E. Ventola (eds), *Handbook of Interpersonal Communication* (pp. 355–395). Berlin, New York: De Gruyter Mouton.

Sini, R. (2020). The Social, Cultural, and Political Value of Play: Singapore's Postcolonial Playground System. *Journal of Urban History*, 38(3), pp. 1–30. DOI: 10.1177/0096144220951149

Taylor, T. and Tison. A. (2003) *La Maison de Barbapapa*. Paris: Les Livres du Dragon d'Or.

Tortajada, C. (2012, April 5). Clean-up of the Singapore River: Before and after. *Global-Is-Asian*. https://lkyspp.nus.edu.sg/gia/article/clean-up-of-the-singapore-river-before-and-after

Wang, Y. and Zhang X. (illustrator) (2005). *Xiao Ai's Dragon Boat Festival*. Shanghai: China Welfare Institute Publishing House.

Wee, S. J., Park, S. and Choi, J. S. (2015). Korean Culture as Portrayed in Young Children's Picture Books: The Pursuit of Cultural Authenticity. *Children's Literature in Education*, 46(1), pp. 70–87.

Wu, F. and Yeh, A. G. O. (1999). Urban Spatial Structure in a Transitional Economy. *Journal of the American Planning Association*, 65(4), pp. 377–394. DOI: 10.1080/01944369908976069

Wu, X. and Xiao Hai (illustrator) (2018). *Blooming Season*. Shanghai: China Welfare Institute Publishing House.

Yuen, B., Yeh, A., Appold, S. J., Earl, G., Ting, J. and Kurnianingrum Kwee, L. (2006). High-Rise Living in Singapore Public Housing. *Urban Studies*, 43(3), pp. 583–600.

9

BUILDING DIVERSITY IN BRITISH AND AMERICAN CHILDREN'S PICTUREBOOKS (2000 TO PRESENT)

Emma Hayward

Introduction: The diversity problem

In recent years, the demand for diversity in children's picturebooks and literature has increased. A number of grassroots organisations and charities, such as We Need Diverse Books (WNDB) in the USA and No Outsiders in the UK, have been established and designed specifically to tackle the under-representation of marginalised social groups and their experiences. However, scholarly research examining the quality of diversity narratives in children's picturebooks has questioned the authenticity of these representations. Sexuality and racial identities, for example, are diluted when characters are simply assimilated into white, mainstream, middle-class, and heteronormative contexts (DePalma, 2016; Esposito, 2019; Rodriguez and Kim, 2018) or are undermined by the inclusion of demeaning stereotypes (Crisp et al., 2016, p. 33; Smith-D'Arezzo, 2003). Focusing on a selection of Anglo-American children's picturebooks published since 2000, this chapter asks what role architecture plays in both threatening and bolstering the authenticity of narratives that engage with diverse family configurations and socio-economic backgrounds.[1]

In a cartoon strip published weekly in the *Guardian* between 1977 and 1987, Posy Simmonds turns her satirical observations of contemporary middle-class life towards the publishing industry, specifically children's picturebooks.[2]

In the cartoon below, Wendy Weber has recently written a children's picturebook, which is heatedly discussed at the publishing house Walmer and Wilcox before being revised and returned to Weber and her illustrator. The original picturebook features an androgynous-looking young girl called Sal. Bored and hungry, Sal leans against a graffiti brick wall before deciding to play in the lifts of a high-rise residential block of flats while she waits for her mum to return from work. In the foreground, an older man walks across a desolate strip of open space carrying a bottle of alcohol; the ground is strewn with broken glass and litter. In the background, tower blocks rise upwards and factory chimneys pump heavy black smoke into the sky. Although two of the attendees draw attention to the book's socially diverse narrative, it is nevertheless decided by the notably non-diverse team that the book and its illustrations will be recast in a style more reflective of bourgeois values and experiences.[3]

DOI: 10.4324/9781003131755-12

FIGURE 9.1 Wendy Weber's picturebook is discussed at the publishing house Walmer and Wilcox. Her depiction of Sal and her inner-city, working-class childhood proves to be controversial. Artwork from *Mrs Weber's Omnibus* by Posy Simmonds, published by Jonathan Cape. Copyright © 2012 Posy Simmonds. Reprinted by permission of The Random House Group Limited.

Simmonds' strip concludes with Mrs Weber and her illustrator looking aghast at the new mock-up. Sal has transformed into Sally—a young girl in a polka dot dress, whose blonde hair is worn in pigtails. Sal's gender has been rendered unequivocal; her ambiguous androgyny has been replaced by conventional gender stereotypes. Where Sal spoke violently and colloquially—'mum', 'dead boring', 'starving', 'tea'—Sally speaks demurely and formally—'mummy', 'bored', 'hungry', 'supper'. Sal's vernacular style of expression evokes images of hardship and her use of 'mum' rather than the infantile 'mummy' makes her seem altogether more worldly and less innocent than Sally.

Sally's feelings of hunger, boredom, anger, and frustration are depicted in less extreme terms than Sal's, probably because Sally's mother is present within the home and shown standing at the kitchen sink preparing her family's supper. The physical presence of the mother figure and the domestic work which she is engaged in reassures both Sally and the imagined readers of the book that her hunger and boredom are temporary. By contrast, Sal's mother is physically absent from the home and visually missing from the strip; neither the reader nor Sal can anticipate for how long her state of boredom and hunger will last. For this reason, perhaps, Sal leans heavily against a blackened brick wall, frowning angrily. Sally, however, smiles as she skips carefree outside with her pet dog.

FIGURE 9.2 Wendy Weber's picturebook is returned with some significant alterations. Sal is transformed into Sally. Artwork from *Mrs Weber's Omnibus* by Posy Simmonds, published by Jonathan Cape. Copyright © 2012 Posy Simmonds. Reprinted by permission of The Random House Group Limited.

Simmonds' satirical critique of the publishing industry and the bourgeois attitudes that saturate it raise an important question about the absence of diverse cultural and social representation in children's picturebooks. In Simmonds' strip, the children's editor, who is one of only two women present at the meeting and who speaks up in favour of Mrs Webber's unorthodox depiction of childhood saying, 'the vast majority of children see no reflection of themselves or the world they live in, in the books they're given to read', is ignored. Moreover, when the strips were collected into the omnibus edition (2012), Simmonds embedded each cartoon into a diary entry. The entries include doodles, to-do lists, shopping lists, ideas for dinner, events, and sometimes function hypertextually by commenting either explicitly or implicitly on the content of the strip. The cartoon featuring Sal/Sally is framed with annotations about vegetable soup, the school run, getting the car fixed, etc. The annotations remind the reader that unlike Sal, Weber lives a comfortable middle-class life and is unlikely to go hungry or feel bored. Simmonds uses the diary form to align her protagonist with the very establishment she is satirising and in so doing, suggests that the absence of diversity is not just confined to the publishing houses but is also present within the creative community where there is also an absence of diverse writers and illustrators.

Simmonds' strip not only highlights the homogenous demographic that constitutes the publishing industry and the lack of social diversity depicted in children's picturebooks, but it also specifically invites readers to reflect on the role architectural representation plays in either sanitising childhood experiences or contributing to the development of genuinely diverse narratives. Sally's private garden, for example, signifies a certain level of affluence, suggesting that she lives in a single-occupancy household. The quaint cobble path and neo-Georgian windows conjure a particular kind of Englishness, rooted in tradition and conservative values. The relationship between internal and external domestic space is also represented in a way that narrates the security of the home. As Sally plays in her private garden, the door to her house is clearly visible, and on the other page the reader can see Sally's mother standing at the kitchen sink. The windows in the door and above the kitchen sink give the impression that Sally can be seen by her mother as she plays outside. The fact that the reader can see both Sally and her mother simultaneously creates a visual connection between the two, further amplifying the feeling of safety.

In contrast, the depiction of Sal's domestic environment affords her little in the way of protection: she does not have a mother who can (or wants to) stay at home and is therefore more likely to encounter strangers, she is surrounded by the material remnants of a disturbing adult world—smashed bottles, factories, choking pollution—and she does not have access to a private or communal garden, but instead appropriates a lift in a tower block, transforming it into a makeshift playground. The notion of makeshift playgrounds was a source of significant apprehension for urban planners in London during the Second World War. Even before the war had come to an end, urban planners, designers, and policy makers were already promoting a new cohesive social vision which was shaped by a desire to restore a sense of order and security. Abercrombie and Forshaw's *County of London Plan* (1943) attempted to manage every aspect of the individual's life through spatialisation, including commuting, weekend trips, play, shopping, work, and even the lunch hour. The London plans 'displayed a strong anxiety towards any urban spaces whose functional logic was unclear or unfocused' (Hornsey, 2010, p. 48). According to Abercrombie and Forshaw, the 1938 Street Playgrounds Act—an initiative which created makeshift playgrounds by enabling local authorities to ban non-residential vehicles from entering certain roads at certain times—was '"the worst recreation defect of the old London borough," [...] because it was "an attempt to use land for two incompatible purposes. Something properly designed for play in right relation to house and school should be provided"' (Abercrombie and Forshaw, 1943, in Hornsey, 2010, p. 48). As Richard Hornsey suggests, the 1938 Street Playgrounds Act was a concern for Abercrombie and Forshaw not merely because it reflected the spatial disarray their proposed plans were attempting to address, but also because it hinted at a kind of social disorder concerning the structure of the family: '[it] raised the spectre of an unstable and improper form of play, disordered, unmanaged, and away from the normative field of adult supervision' (2010, p. 48). The Street Playgrounds Act draws attention to absent parent figures and threatens the ideal vision of the nuclear family, the needs of whom were at the centre of this prescribed form of spatialisation because 'those future citizens – still in their infancy – [...] would grow up to perpetuate [a] stable social order' (Hornsey, 2010, p. 78). Designated play spaces for children, such as private or communal gardens and playgrounds, were seen as markers of 'wholesome' family life and more generally social stability.

Sal's subversion of the lift's designated function, then, creates precisely the kind of uncertainty and instability that the likes of Abercrombie and Forshaw saw as a threat to orderly and respectable family life. However, it also acknowledges the autonomy of the building's users. Although Sal's relationship with her home reflects the precarity of her childhood—dinner time is not fixed, leisure time is unstructured, both parent figures are absent—it also amplifies her independence and sense of ownership over her domestic environment: she determines how spaces within the building are used regardless of their intended purpose. Despite the ironic accusation made by the Editorial Director that Weber's picturebook is a condescending depiction of the 'less fortunate' class, Sal's engagement with the tower block highlights her agency and creative ability to make architecture and the spaces it produces her own.

No outsiders?

In 2014, WNDB was founded to put 'more books featuring diverse characters into the hands of all children'. Inspired by WNDB, the 2015 Children's Literature Assembly (CLA) conference held a workshop dedicated to exploring the 'perceived changes happening within the field of children's literature as related to diversity' (Johnson and Koss, 2016, p. 53). Reflecting on the discussions that took place, Denise Johnson and Melanie D. Koss point out that children's literature functions as a major socialising agent and therefore it is necessary for children to see their 'faces and situations reflected through the pages of books, to learn who they are, and to learn that they matter. All children have this right, regardless of their ability, race, ethnicity, gender, sexuality, or religion' (2016, p. 53). Children's author Sharon Draper adds to this sentiment, suggesting that effective representation relies on 'authenticity': 'having diverse characters or diverse issues is not enough; a book has to have that essence of truth' (cited in Johnson and Koss, 2016, p. 54).

The issue of authenticity has proven problematic both for picturebooks seeking to engage with diverse narratives and for organisations/projects whose aim it is to promote these narratives. The No Outsiders project initially began as a two-year collaboration (2006–2008) between primary school teachers from the UK and researchers from the University of Sunderland, the University of Exeter and Institute of Education, University of London. Its aim was to interrogate and disrupt the structures that support and maintain heteronormativity in primary school contexts in an attempt to address homophobic bullying in UK schools. Each teacher was provided with a 'resource pack that included 27 children's books exploring themes of gender and sexuality diversity' (Bryan, 2012) 'either directly or indirectly (i.e., by the presence of same-sex parents and/or gender non-normative characters)' (DePalma, 2016, p. 831). The participating teachers developed their own approaches for using the picturebooks to stimulate discussion around the themes of gender and sexuality diversity with their students in the classroom.

Reflecting on the project in 'Gay penguins, sissy ducklings … and beyond? Exploring gender and sexuality diversity through children's literature', Renée DePalma draws attention to concerns expressed by some of the participating teachers and scholars about the 'vanilla strategies' (Nixon, 2009, cited in DePalma, 2016, p. 830) deployed by authors and illustrators to dilute representations of sexual diversity as a means of creating texts that 'feel safe in primary school settings' (p. 830). Some of the participating teachers suggested that 'books like *And Tango Makes Three* (2005) might simply serve to replay heterosexual models of romantic monogamous partnering, only with gay characters' (p. 836).[4] DePalma goes on to suggest that the projection of homosexual characters into heteronormative contexts is to do with 'ease of representation': 'complexity and fluidity are difficult to represent, while it is much easier to present homosexuality in terms of clear-cut characters who behave in familiar and unthreatening ways' (p. 836). When homosexual characters are assimilated in this way, difference and diversity are ironically diminished.

Since 2008, the No Outsiders project has continued to grow. In 2015, Andrew Moffat (a teacher at Parkfield Community School in Birmingham) published *No Outsiders in Our School: Teaching the Equality Act in Primary School*—a resource designed to help teach children and young people about 'the benefits that exist in a society where diversity and difference are celebrated' (2015, p. 3). As with the initial project (2006–2008), the central resource is a catalogue of children's picturebooks included for their potential to encourage discussion and generate understanding around a range of topics, including sexuality and gender, as well as religion, race, different socio-economic contexts, and differently abled people. Using the resource, Moffat delivered the No Outsiders programme at Parkfield Community School. However, in 2019 Moffat received hostile criticism and resistance from parents of children who attended the primary school. As reported by the BBC at the time, parents protested outside the gates of the school and accused Moffat of 'promoting... personal beliefs and convictions about universal acceptability of homosexuality as being normal and morally correct' (2019).

While the programme's 'normalisation' of marginalised social groups is intended to promote inclusivity, the emphatically titled programme—No Outsiders—is potentially problematic: inclusion is achieved at the expense of difference. The title threatens to draw everyone in, ensuring everyone occupies the same 'space'. In her collection of essays *Architecture from the Outside*, Elizabeth Grosz explores the complex, symbiotic relationship between 'inside' and 'outside':

> One cannot be outside everything, always outside: to be outside something is always to be inside something else. To be outside (something) is to afford oneself the possibility of a perspective, to look upon this inside, which is made difficult, if not impossible, from the inside.
>
> *(2001, p. XIV)*

What Grosz draws attention to here is the power of the outside; she reimagines conventional narratives that associate the outside with negative feelings of alienation, disempowerment, and loneliness and instead considers the transformative power that derives from the interplay between inside and outside. First, by stating that to be outside something is still to be inside something else, Grosz suggests that the outside is still a space of belonging: it is a space in which communities and groups can form and develop. Second, the outside is a space from which to view the inside differently: it cultivates greater levels of critical awareness. The inside becomes different when viewed and engaged with from the outside. Not only can the outside empower individuals and groups who occupy it by providing a critical perspective, but this critical mode of engagement has the power to transform the inside by challenging the conception and understanding it has of itself. So, while the intention of No Outsiders may well be to promote diversity in schools, the title's implied denigration of the concept of the outside and the drive to ensure all children belong to the same conceptual space, so to speak, homogenises precisely the difference it seeks to celebrate. Put another way, the phrase No Outsiders undermines the very concept of difference, ignoring, as it does, the kinds of power, autonomy, perspectives, and experiences afforded to those who occupy 'the outside'.

The Family Book and *Heather Has Two Mummies*

Some of the picturebooks included on the No Outsiders reading list also struggle to represent complexity and uncertainty, and as such, struggle to deliver authentic and undiluted diversity narratives. Todd Parr's *The Family Book* (2003) sets out to detail different kinds of family formations. The book includes mixed-race families, lesbian and gay families, families with stepparents and stepsiblings, single-parent families, and families with adopted children as well as describing different preferences and ways of being: 'Some families like to be quiet. Some families like to be noisy. Some families like to be clean. Some families like to be messy'; 'Some families live near each other. Some families live far from each other'. Parr uses both animals and humans and their habitats/dwellings to represent the various strands of diversity explored in the book.

However, architectural representation (or lack thereof) threatens the authenticity of the diversity narrative. The illustrations accompanying the part of the narrative dealing with different kinds of homes can be seen to erase social difference rather than highlight or celebrate it. On the left-hand page, the text reads: 'Some families live in a house by themselves' (Parr, 2003). The accompanying illustration consists of a red house, with a pitched roof and chimney, a front door, and two windows. The house stands atop a hill by itself. It is nighttime and the windows glow yellow while the chimney pumps smoke into the sky. The family cannot be seen; presumably, they are safely hidden from the outside world within the walls of their home. The image communicates messages of security and privacy.

By contrast, on the right-hand side of the page the verbal narrative reads, 'Some families share a house with other families' (Parr, 2003). The house shared with other families could be taken to mean a tower block, or a large house that has been converted into smaller, private flats, or a single house shared by multiple families. Unlike the previous image, which depicted the single-occupancy house with a degree of verisimilitude, this architectural experience of the family home is visually depicted as a tree with a family of monkeys and raccoons living in the branches and another indiscernible animal family living in the trunk. Although on some level the verbal narrative acknowledges that not all families can afford or even desire to live in single-occupancy homes, by depicting the multi-occupancy home as a tree rather than in architectural terms in the form of a tower block or flat conversion, the pictorial narrative arguably dilutes the very experience it is trying to represent. The image that dominates the page is a solitary tree; the association with nature suggests space, cleanliness, tranquillity, suggestions which are amplified by the infinite stretch of clear blue sky and not at all reflective of the realities of living in multi-occupancy buildings or shared accommodation. Moreover, although the ultimate aim of *The Family Book* is to celebrate diversity, the visual absence of a multi-occupancy home might inadvertently replicate cultural prejudices about this type of housing: that it is ugly, for example, or uncomfortable and somehow inadequate.

Similarly, *Heather Has Two Mummies* (Newman and Cornell, 2015) has received widespread critical attention debating the extent to which its depiction of a lesbian family can be seen as 'reliable'. As the title suggests, the main character belongs to a lesbian family. Heather is a happy child who enjoys playing with her pets and her two mothers who bake with her when it rains and take her to the park when the sun shines. When Heather starts attending a playgroup, she is asked by another child called David what her dad does for work after their teacher Molly reads the class a book about a boy whose father is a veterinarian.

Heather explains that she doesn't have a dad and 'looks around the circle and wonders, *Am I the only one here who doesn't have a daddy?*' (2015). At this point the teacher suggests that all the children should draw a picture of their family. As Heather looks at the children's drawings, which depict a range of family types, including step-parents and extended family members, Molly tells her class, 'The most important thing about a family is that all the people in it love one another' (2015). After this, Heather leaves the playgroup with her two mums feeling content.

For Jennifer Esposito, the lesbian narrative at the heart of this story is ironically undermined both by the way in which it problematises not having a dad and by ignoring 'the social costs' of rejecting heteronormativity (2009, p. 69). In the first instance, Esposito suggests that the statement '"I don't have a daddy" illustrates the assumption that it is normal to have one' (p. 67). Heather's words here focus on absence rather than presence and in so doing, uphold the mother-father family dynamic as normal. Moreover, the textual narrative—'looks around the circle'—hints towards Heather's growing feelings of alienation and anxiety about not belonging: she is questioning her place within the circle. The fact that David questions Heather about her father in response to the comment she makes about her mother being a 'people doctor' reflects the prevalence of the assumption in society that everyone belongs to a heteronormative nuclear family. Heather's anxiety is triggered as she gradually becomes aware of this.

That said, Esposito's reading focuses heavily on the textual narrative and overlooks the way in which the distinctive verbal-visual properties of the picturebook form contribute to *Heather*'s diversity narrative. In a previous iteration of *Heather* (Newman and Souza, 2000), both the text and illustrations work together to emphasise the character's feelings of anxiety and alienation. For example, the verbal narrative includes two male characters—David and Juan—discussing their fathers' careers. Here, the verbal narrative lingers on Heather's negative response to David's question about her own father: 'I don't have a daddy', Heather says. She'd never thought about it before. 'Did everyone except Heather have a daddy? Heather's forehead crinkles up and she begins to cry' (Newman and Souza, 2000). The accompanying illustration depicts Heather alone on the page, no longer a part of the circle; she is staring out at the reader with a look of troubled confusion, searching for an explanation and seeking comfort. However, in the 2015 edition, there is an interesting discrepancy between the verbal and visual narratives which can be seen to articulate the complex relationship between inside and outside as understood by Grosz. On the left-hand side of the double-page spread, the illustration shows the children clustered together in a group on the floor, not a circle. Heather sits in the middle of the group; she is smiling with her hands in the air enjoying the book with the other children.

Derrit Mason argues 'the 2015 illustrations reinforce that queer adults are no longer a "problem" or source of sadness for Heather' (2020, p. 127). While the verbal narrative may still problematise lesbian families, the visual narrative tells a different story, one in which Heather is not at all troubled by the dynamics of her family. A formal complexity is thus created by the interplay between the verbal and visual narratives: Heather is simultaneously inside and outside the group, she is both content and anxious. The verbal narrative's positioning of Heather as an outsider need not be interpreted solely in terms of disempowerment. Using Grosz's understanding of the relationship between inside and outside, the reader can see that as Heather moves towards the outside, she simultaneously begins to develop an enhanced critical perspective of the inside. From the outside, she is able to 'look around' and reflect on the social dynamics of the group and her relation to the wider world. Intellectually she is empowered, and with this comes feelings of anxiety and perhaps alienation, but not necessarily disempowerment. Although Esposito criticises the sentimental conclusion to *Heather* (Newman and Cornell, 2015) for failing 'to communicate the message that in a homophobic world, it does matter what your family configuration looks like' (2009, p. 69), the text's formal complexity arguably enacts in places the difficulties and uncertainties of belonging to a lesbian family. In other words, the conflicting verbal and visual narratives reflect the 'social costs' of belonging to a non-heteronormative family—in this case, the anxiety of difference. Heather's position in the social group is not fixed or secure; she must negotiate and traverse both 'the inside' (represented by the illustration of the group) and 'the outside' (represented by the anxiety conveyed in the accompanying verbal narrative).

The verbal and visual engagement with American suburbia in both editions of *Heather* also plays an important role in the debate around authenticity and diversity. In both editions (2000, 2015), depictions of Heather's home contribute to the kind of processes of assimilation discussed by DePalma and Esposito, therefore threatening the authenticity of the diversity narrative. By contrast, the depiction of Heather's school in the tenth anniversary edition can be seen to support the book's message about diverse family structures through its functional versatility.

The 2015 edition opens with an illustration of Heather playing in her back garden in the long grass with her pet dog and cat. In the background, there is a detached wooden house with a pitched rooftop and chimney. The windows are gridded and a white fence divides Heather's house and garden from the house and garden next door. The verbal narrative at the top of the page reads: 'Heather lives in a little house with a big apple tree in the front garden and lots of tall grass in the back garden' (Newman and Cornell, 2015). The kind of suburban architecture depicted here suggests a comfortable middle-class life. In the foreground, Heather runs uninhibited with her pet dog and cat through overgrown grass that is as tall as she is. What is being emphasised here is freedom and space, which is amplified by Heather's interaction with nature. However, any sense of danger or uncertainty associated with nature and roaming freely is moderated by the white fence, which signals Heather's containment within a private, domestic setting. Like Sally in the revised version of Mrs Weber's picturebook, the private garden is used to communicate messages of safety. The fence is evocative of the white picket fence which has come to symbolise an idealised conservative version of middle-class family life in America. As Michael Dolan points out, the white picket fence came to represent 'an imaginary all-white realm' populated by the patriarchal nuclear family, as depicted in television programmes such as 'Father Knows Best' and 'Leave It to Beaver', where life is gentle and void of significant hardships (2019). With this in mind, the diversity suggested by the title—*Heather Has Two Mummies*— is, on the first page, abated by the visual depiction of Heather's home as the suburban setting situates Heather and her family within an architectural environment that is highly evocative of the all-white, middle-class, heteronormative family.

Moreover, although the verbal narrative describes Heather's home as 'little', subsequent illustrations reveal that there is enough room to have distinct spaces for a range of activities with her parents, including a large kitchen where they bake together, a tree big enough to build a tree house with Mama Jane, and a living area where Heather plays with Mama Kate as well as a spacious bedroom that easily fits a double bed, an armchair, a toy chest, and shelves where Heather is shown talking and reading with both her mums. The verbal and visual narratives work together here to depict Heather's home as spacious and simultaneously cosy, intimate, private, secure, and comfortably middle class.

However, the reality is that the suburbs have traditionally not been inclusive of gay and lesbian families and identities: 'With a long-established reputation for hostility towards any kind of deviation from its principal unit of organization, the heterosexual family home, suburbia is arguably the straightest place imaginable' (Dines, 2009, p. 1). For lesbians, access to the kind of middle-class suburban lifestyle evoked by the architectural illustrations in *Heather* (Newman and Cornell, 2015 and Newman and Souza, 2000) would have been further restricted by economic disadvantage: 'lesbians have been shown to be in a particularly disadvantaged position, since their economic status is often similarly marginalised. They are thus less likely than gay men to own their own homes' (Bell, 1991, p. 325). In addition, the architecture of the suburban house, particularly the organisation and division of space, can also be said to embody the power relations underpinning the nuclear family:

> The 'hegemony of heterosexuality' is seemingly enshrined in the very design of suburban architecture, from the organization of the interior of the family home, with its hierarchy of space encouraging normative familial relationships (with the master bedroom, or 'Bedroom 1', dominating a series of smaller compartmentalised spaces).
>
> *(Dines, 2009, p. 3)*

Hierarchy, domination, fixed structures—'normative familial relationships'—are characteristics shared with the nuclear family, in which a financially dependent mother/wife and children are organised around a patriarchal father who is positioned as head (or master) of the household. The interior depictions of Heather's home are evocative of this kind of suburban arrangement of space. After the initial double-page spread, which depicts Heather's house and garden, subsequent illustrations of the living room, kitchen, and garden are positioned in the centre of the page surrounded by thick white margins. The margins concentrate the reader's attention on the activity taking place within the room; the reader cannot see or begin to imagine how the rooms and garden might relate to each other, suggesting they are compartmentalised and reserved for specific activities.

The discrete organisation of domestic space gained popularity in America during the 17th century when the revival of Christian morality coincided with a rapidly expanding industrial economy (Urbach, 1996, p. 65). While the acquisition of wealth and material goods was encouraged, excess and decadence were also frowned upon by the Church. Domestic architectural design responded by developing a range of strategies to accommodate the conflicting economic and religious contexts of the period (Urbach, 1996, p. 65). For example, the introduction of the closet into the home meant that sartorial excess could be hidden. If a person's wardrobe represents the many facets of their personality, then the closet also ensures that 'only those garments worn at any particular moment would be visible. In this way, one's outfit could gain singular legitimacy, unchallenged by the other clothes tucked away' (Urbach, 1996, p.65). For Urbach, the closet eradicates uncertainty and plurality; it conceals the diversity of an individual's identity, ensuring only one persona can be visible at a given time. Similarly, spaces once joined were 'separated into discrete rooms with distinct degrees of privacy' (Urbach, 1996, p. 65). For Andrew Jackson Downing—an American landscape architect of the period—the ideal home is one in which each area of the house is 'complete' and intrudes 'little on the attention of the family or guests when not required to be visible' (cited in Urbach, 1996, p.65). The enhanced privacy of the rooms restricts spatial diversity by encouraging occupants to use and notice only one area at a time. The depiction of Heather's house, then, with its discrete rooms, expresses ideas of singularity and certainty, ideas which run counter to the text's diversity narrative.

The 2000 edition of *Heather* also portrays domestic architecture in a way that can be seen to temper ideas about sexuality diversity. In this edition, the house is still detached, with a pitched roof, small square windows, and a symmetrical front. The door is framed with neoclassical columns and the private garden extends in front of the house. In this edition, the illustration of the home is used to close the picturebook rather than open it. The image of the house occupies over half the page. Walking towards the house near the bottom of the page is Mama Kate and Mama Jane who stand either side of Heather holding her hand, with the cat and dog following closely behind. All of the figures take the form of silhouettes. The verbal narrative is printed at the bottom of the page and reads: 'Heather gives each of her mommies two kisses before she takes their hands and heads for home' (2000). The key signifiers of lesbian identity are diluted by the image. First, the sex of Mama Kate and Mama Jane is rendered ambiguous by the silhouette form. Second, the narrative which refers to the lesbian parents occupies a marginalised position on the page. The reader's eye is directed towards the suburban house which, as already mentioned, has strong associations with a particular kind of comfortable, middle-class, and heteronormative lifestyle. The suggested reading age for this picturebook ranges from three to seven. For those younger readers in particular, the illustrations play a vital role in conveying the narrative's diversity message. In this way, visual representation of architecture plays a key role in assimilating Heather's lesbian family into a middle-class heteronormative context and therefore contributes to the partial erasure of the family's lesbian identity.

Interestingly, the depiction of Heather's school in the tenth anniversary edition is more reflective of the kinds of 'non-traditional' family structures that the children explore through their drawings. The school Heather attends is in fact 'Molly's house'. Unlike the modern suburban architecture of Heather's home, this building has a dual purpose, functioning both as Molly's home and a school. The versatility of the building is amplified by the illustrations. The exterior is depicted using a minimalistic line drawing which gives the impression of steps leading up to a doorway. There is no gradation in shade or hue to give the illusion of depth. In this way, readers are invited to project their own ideas about the house/school onto the page. Inside Molly's house/school, the perspective is slightly distorted. A blank white background gives the impression that the table is floating (further suggested by the bird mobile hanging above) and, as she walks, Heather's foot also appears to be in line with the tabletop to her right. The subtly warped perspective generates a sense of fluidity and mobility, suggesting that the spatial arrangement inside is not fixed. The functional malleability of the building is also expressed in the verbal narrative: 'There's a big round table where Heather can eat her lunch and a quiet corner where Heather can take a nap'. The purpose is suggested rather than imposed. Heather can take a nap in the quiet corner, but that is not the only activity she might do in that space. The ambiguity of the building can be read as an architectural manifestation of the book's key message that families can take many forms. The versatility of the building is indicative of the ways in which homes can adapt to accommodate different kinds of family. In this case, the class itself can be seen as a kind of family. Given that children spend more time at school than at home, and that some of their teachers will see them more in a week than their own parents, this dynamic is not unusual or unexpected.

By contrast, in the 2015 edition, Molly's house is reimagined as a purpose-built school. There is no exterior illustration, but the image of the interior is detailed and in full colour. There is a giant map on the wall, pegs for children to hang their coats and bags, books in boxes on shelves divided into different categories, a place for children to display their collections of leaves and rocks, and large round tables where children sit and play with puzzles. Although the image is busy, there is a sense that everything has a designated place; its verisimilitude leaves little room for readers to 'disturb' the space by projecting their own image of the classroom onto the page. The ambiguity that characterised the school building in the tenth anniversary edition is significantly diminished and this newfound certainty is embedded within the verbal narrative: 'Heather also sees a big round table for snack time and a quiet cosy corner for nap time'. The modal verb 'can' is replaced with the preposition 'for'. Where the modal verb was suggestive, the preposition is more commanding in tone, implying that each space described has a specific purpose from which the children should not deviate. That said, the complexities of the verbal-visual form once again work to introduce an element of uncertainty. Although the verbal narrative explicitly states that there is a big round table for snack time, the children are shown playing with puzzles on the tables. The dialogism created by the interplay between the verbal and visual narratives contributes to the text's diversity message; the formal complexity draws attention both to the table's intended use and to the users' appropriation of the table, thereby suggesting the versatile nature of architecture and design. So, to some extent at least, the environment is depicted in such a way that it signals its potential to accommodate a range of different users with differing needs and desires.

Versatile homes

The Great Big Book of Families (2015) by Mary Hoffman and Ros Asquith is also included in the No Outsiders (2015) resource. The book opens with a double-page illustration of a young, white family, comprising '[o]ne daddy, one mummy, one little boy, one little girl, one dog and one cat'. All members of the family appear to conform to gender normative behaviours. The 'little girl' with blonde hair is dressed in pink and holds onto a doll whose appearance resembles that of its owner. The 'little boy', also blonde, wears blue socks, shorts, and a t-shirt, and holds onto a football. The children's toys reinforce a typical gender binary: the doll can be seen to prepare the 'little girl' for domesticity, associated, as it is, with motherhood, nurturing, and responsibility, whereas the football conjures images of freedom, play, athleticism, ambition, teamwork, etc. The parents in this illustration also function in a way that sustains gender stereotypes. The blonde-haired 'mummy' wears a pink jumper and skirt and holds onto a watering can while the 'daddy' holds onto a shovel immersed halfway into the earth. In a similar way to the doll, the watering can is associated with nourishment and care. The action of watering plants is also gentle; it requires little physical strength. By contrast, to dig up the ground demands strength and physical exertion; the action disturbs and displaces. Even the family's pets are depicted in a way that reinforces gender stereotypes. The dog (usually associated with boys) adopts an active posture, standing alert and ready to play. The cat (usually associated with girls) is sitting down. Given the way in which the two animals mirror the behaviour of the children, the reader can assume that the cat belongs to the girl and the dog belongs to the boy.

The family's arrangement on the page also supports a heteronormative vision of domesticity. The family stands in a line, posing for the reader. 'Daddy' comes first, then 'mummy', followed by the 'boy', and finally the 'girl'. 'Daddy' is presented as the patriarch, the head of the family who oversees his wife and small brood. The family's height further contributes to the gender power dynamics at play here: 'daddy' is the tallest, helping to bolster his position as head of the family. The line then descends in order of height with the 'little girl' being the shortest. The family's arrangement draws attention to the fact that the girl is the smallest and youngest member of the family, physically weaker than her older brother. Once again, the pets are used to reinforce these ideas: the boy's dog comes before the girl's cat in the family line up. The illustration is neat, the family tidy, with each member conforming to their 'correct' social role.

As well as their appearance, props, and arrangement on the page, the family's home also functions as a means through which to signal heteronormative domesticity. The family home resembles a detached cottage, with a pitched rooftop, a chimney, four small sash windows symmetrically placed on either side of the front door, and a private garden that is demarcated by a white picket fence. Like Sally's home in 'Mrs Weber's Diary' and Heather's home in *Heather Has Two Mummies* (2015), the garden, picket fence, and the detached house occupied by a single family all signal privacy and security and can be seen to reflect the structure of the nuclear family—a discrete, independently functioning social unit. The sense of privacy and security is amplified by the fact that the reader is positioned outside and is not invited to observe the family inside their home.

However, the verbal narrative—'Once upon a time most families in books looked like this'—undermines this portrait of family life. Not only does the adverbial phrase suggest that this vision of family life is outdated, but the conventional fairy tale opening also questions the veracity of the image, an idea which is reinforced by the fact that the family and their house are not drawn directly onto the double-page spread but framed within an old sepia-toned book with dog-eared pages. The visual framing device calls attention to the book's artifice and in so doing, functions as a reminder (to the adult reader at least) that the nuclear family is also a construct propagated by cultural production. In this way, the verbal narrative and visual framing device work together to undermine the authority of the all-white, middle-class nuclear family.

In the following double-page spread, the reader is confronted with a range of housing types: traditional terrace and town houses stand next to three imposing high-rise structures; in the distance, a cottage stands alone amidst rolling green fields; and bordering the page are individual housing types, including post-war suburban houses, fanciful castles and palaces as well as caravans and tents. Unlike the image of the house on the previous page, the reader is, to some extent, invited into these homes via the windows and doors (the illustrations only depict the buildings' exteriors). In one of the tower blocks, the main entrance to the building is open and in almost every window the reader is given a glimpse of life inside. The reader can therefore see the same room of each flat in relation to the whole building and in relation to the flats in the neighbouring tower blocks, simultaneously creating a sense of repetition and difference. Paradoxically, it is the uniform structure and design of the tower blocks that render diversity visible. The replication of the same room on each floor highlights contrast by bringing families into close proximity with one another. Where one couple watches television, another couple enjoy a glass of wine; one window is crowded with a family of eight, while another window reveals a solitary figure relaxing on the settee. What

Asquith's illustrations emphasise here is the way in which the autonomy of the occupants disrupts the uniformity and standardised design of post-war mass housing, much like Sal's appropriation of the lifts in *Mrs Weber's Diary*. By contrast, the kind of private and discrete suburban housing featured in both editions of *Heather* limit the extent to which difference can be seen and therefore experienced by its characters. The features of suburban architecture that are emphasised in these picturebooks—the white picket fence and private garden, the discrete rooms—create a strong impression of privacy and security. In this way, then, the home is shown to provide limited opportunities for Heather to notice difference because there are no other families, no other ways of living, which she can easily notice or observe from her home. It is unsurprising then that Heather's first encounter with different family structures is outside the home at school.

In Asquith's illustrations, the reader is situated both inside and outside, and the flats inside the high-rise buildings are simultaneously repetitive and varied. Moreover, the verbal and visual narratives also situate the buildings across time in relation to both the past and present. For example, the ground floor of the red-brick town house has been converted into a bakery and the verbal narrative tells us that 'some big families live in tiny flats' (2015). In a similar way to Molly's house in *Heather* (2010), which also functions as a school, both of these homes have adapted and changed over time: they fulfil a role beyond their original intended purpose. A house has become a hybrid of domesticity and business, a convergence of the private and public spheres, while a small flat metaphorically expands to accommodate a large family. The fact that these buildings bear the traces of their evolution also situates them in relation to the future by highlighting their potential for adaptation. The types of liminality created by Asquith's illustrations allow for uncertainty and ambiguity, and as such, invest the built environment with a sense of fluidity and open-endedness. In this way, the buildings are afforded qualities that make them amenable to change and difference.

The Invisible by Tom Percival (2021) also focuses on the versatile nature of architecture and design. The picturebook tells the story of Isabel, a young girl who is forced to move with her parents when the family can no longer afford to rent their home—a single occupancy, detached home with all the markers of traditional family life, including pitched rooftop, chimney, and a hearth with a roaring fire around which the family gather for tea and toast. Moreover, the surrounding area is characterised by historic period properties and large parks, giving the impression Isabel lives in an affluent part of London. The first illustration of the house's exterior suggests that Isabel, like Heather, has plenty of space and privacy. The house is positioned centrally and to each side of the house the reader has an unobstructed view of the background: a large flat park and beyond that, faint impressions of historic buildings. However, unlike Heather's house, the outside world intrudes upon the ostensibly private world of Isabel's home. In Isabel's bedroom, 'Ice curl[s] across the inside of the window and [creeps] up the corner of her bedpost' (Percival, 2021), and as the family gather around the hearth, a reminder about an overdue bill lies on the floor. The non-naturalistic, high-angle perspective Percival adopts for this image diminishes the sense of space and privacy suggested by the house's exterior depiction and surrounding area. The perspective is unsettling and creates a feeling of claustrophobia, enacting the way in which the family's debt encroaches more and more upon their happy domestic sphere.

And so the family relocate to a post-war council housing estate on the 'far side of the city' (Percival, 2021). The geographic position immediately signals the marginalised status of the family's new home, and the verbal narrative informs the reader that this part of the city looked 'cold, sad and lonely' and 'for the first time ever, Isabel couldn't find anything beautiful to cheer herself up' (Percival, 2021). The pictorial narrative adds to this sentiment: the estate is rendered in cool blues and greys, the courtyards and streets are eerily empty, windows and balconies are mostly unlit and void of any signs of life inside. In this way, Percival's illustrations might be seen to reiterate long-standing cultural prejudices about post-war council housing estates in Britain. Initially, council housing estates were built with the optimistic belief that the built environment could be designed in a way that would cultivate tight-knit communities amongst groups of strangers who had been relocated from urban slums. Features such as 'inward-facing courtyards, wide-access decks, and shared amenities were intended to enable the work of community formation' (Wetherell, 2020, p. 116). However, the 1980 Housing Act, which encouraged tenants to purchase their homes from the state, undermined 'the collective logic that guided council estates in the first place' (Wetherell, 2020, p. 107), as private residents resisted paying for services that they felt did not benefit them personally. Moreover, the emergence of a new kind of criminology in the 1970s and 1980s, which saw shared areas being fenced off or demolished all in the name of crime prevention, also threatened the communal ethos at the heart of council estates and contributed to its widespread denigration (Wetherell, 2020, p. 108). While Percival's verbal and visual narratives may well evoke the demise of post-war housing estates, there is, in fact, something beautiful about Percival's illustrations; the buildings are solemn and possess a stillness that lends them a certain gravitas. The interplay between the ugliness of the architecture communicated in the verbal narrative and the striking beauty of the illustrations creates a liminality which speaks to the protean nature of the built environment. The buildings are unpleasant, even hostile, but they are also stylised and therefore visually pleasing; the play of light and shadow, and the aestheticised emptiness call to mind the kind of melancholic loneliness conjured in Edward Hopper's paintings.

After moving to the estate, Isabel notices that she gradually becomes increasingly invisible to those around her. However, as Isabel grows more and more invisible, she becomes aware of other people who have also been rendered invisible by their socio-economic status. As she wanders around her new neighbourhood, Isabel observes people striving to make positive contributions to the area, including an old lady 'planting flowers in empty paint pots' and a man 'who slept on a bench feeding the birds in the park'. The disrupted teloi of the paint cans and park bench prime the reader for the larger transformation of Isabel's new home environment. Inspired by these acts of kindness, Isabel begins to make minor renovations to her neighbourhood, and before long, other residents join in too. Bare concrete walls become canvases for bold, colourful designs and blooming plants in old paint cans sit in windowsills and line stairways. These small acts lead to a significant change, which Percival reflects in his use of colour, shifting, as he does, from a palette of cold blues and greys to a warm and vibrant palette. There is also a stark contrast in the way in which space is used. Before the renovations, the streets and parks were mostly vacant and people passed each other without any form of interaction. After the renovations, the public spaces around the high-rise buildings are populated with people socialising and interacting with each other. Walkways are no longer empty and windows, occupied by residents, open on to the courtyard; they blur the boundary between the private domestic space of the home and the shared areas outside by inviting the reader (and the residents) part of the way inside. These images of architectural liminality and adaptability give material form to the complexities of diversity and difference. Percival also emphasises the agency of the residents and the power of community, and in so doing, draws attention to the potential of British post-war architecture to change and adapt to the needs and desires of its users. Ironically, by engaging creatively with the surfaces and spaces of the buildings in ways that go beyond their intended use, the residents succeed in recuperating something of the original idealistic vision for post-war, high-rise estates. In Percival's picturebook, then, post-war British architecture is deployed in a way that empowers socio-economically disadvantaged groups of people as they are shown to work in a kind of active collaboration with designers and planners.

Looming large on the front cover of Percival's story is Erno Goldfinger's Trellick Tower in West London—a 31-storey tower block constructed in the Brutalist style. The Tower was completed in 1972 for the Greater London Council. Although it was designed with the best intentions of replacing outdated and unsuitable housing—like many social housing projects of the period—it did not take long for the building to gain a notorious reputation. Demonised in the press, Trellick Tower embodied negative stereotypes of social housing in Britain at the time: rife with crime and badly maintained. However, in recent years, the Tower's public image changed for the better. In 1998, the building was awarded Grade II listing status by Historic England followed by a £17 million government-funded renovation. In addition to government support, social media also played a significant role in transforming the public image of the building. Alexandra Bullen's research on the role of social media in the popular reassessment of Brutalist architecture suggests that the active online documentation and celebration of the building's iconic brutalist features has contributed significantly to the building's current positive public profile (2014). Percival's inclusion of this highly recognisable post-war building embodies both of these narratives. On the one hand, dark blue and grey tones, the barren surrounding landscape, and unlit windows evoke feelings of loneliness, alienation, and threat. On the other hand, Percival's illustrations might be seen to function in a similar way to the kinds of images shared by the public via online social media platforms; they draw attention to the building's iconic brutalist features, expressing an interest in and even celebrating the building's style through detailed illustrations.[5] On one double-page spread, as Isabel begins to fade away, Trellick Tower features in the background in much the same way as it does on the front cover (Figure 9.3).

FIGURE 9.3 Trellick tower in *The Invisible*. Title Copyright © Tom Percival 2021. Published by arrangement with Simon & Schuster UK Ltd., 1st Floor, 222 Gray's Inn Road, London, WC1X 8HB. A CBS Company.

However, this time the building is rendered in softer grey tones and the sky is warmed by thick, cream-coloured clouds tinted in blush pink. Meanwhile, the foreground featuring mostly low-rise, traditional houses and buildings retains the cold blue palette used on the front cover. Although the verbal narrative expresses Isabel's feelings of alienation—'nobody saw her at all'—the illustration gives the impression that Trellick Tower itself and the high-rise building standing next to it are watching over Isabel. Moreover, the fact that Isabel is rendered in similar colours to the high-rise structures in the background create a homely sense of belonging and connection, challenging the prevailing negative stereotypes of post-war, high-rise housing estates. As in *Heather* (2015), the dialogism created by the interplay between the verbal and visual narratives articulates the complex relationship between inside and outside. From her new position on the outside—'the far side of the city'—Isabel's awareness of the unjust social inequalities that mark everyday life for many people and families in modern Britain grows, giving her a critical perspective that she previously lacked. For example, on one double-page spread, Isabel walks through her new housing estate. The scene is rendered in a palette of polluted greys and the buildings are half hidden in shadows. In the foreground, above a sad and lonely Isabel, is a golden-coloured billboard, illuminated further by a lamppost shining directly onto it. On the billboard, the word 'stuff' is capitalised and underlined and two women look out smiling confidently. In this way, Percival's narrative further challenges negative ideas about post-war, high-rise housing estates; Isabel's growing critical awareness ultimately leads her to recuperate the optimistic vision that originally informed the design of these estates in the first place.

Percival's decision to depict Trellick Tower on the pages of his picturebook in some ways validates his positive depiction of high-rise, post-war housing estates as amenable to all kinds of lives and as a power for positive living. The history of Trellick Tower—in particular, its transformation from tower of terror to the epitome of urban cool—mirrors the cheerful transformation of Isabel's housing estate, and in so doing, might suggest that such a response to non-traditional housing exists beyond the pages of children's picturebooks and the imaginations of optimistic urban designers. That said, as Trellick Tower and buildings like it grow evermore popular in the public imagination, so too does their value. With social housing significantly diminished, this leaves low-income families like Isabel's at risk of being squeezed out and becoming invisible once more.

Hoffman and Asquith, Newman, Cornell and Souza, and Percival, all in different ways emphasise the agency of the users of architecture. In so doing, they reject the notion that buildings are fixed for specific groups with designated purposes and highlight instead their potential to respond to the changing needs and desires of a range of family structures. In this way, diverse family configurations are given architectural expression and therefore a material form which goes some way to validating their identity and experience. Where the protean nature of architecture and the built environment historically signified a threat to wholesome family life in Britain and America, in contemporary children's picturebooks it is readily used to authenticate images and narratives of diversity.

Notes

1 The picturebook sample included in this chapter is small to allow for detailed analysis. To get a sense of what kinds of narratives are being promoted as diverse, the texts included in this chapter are mostly drawn from a teaching resource published in *No Outsiders in Our School: Teaching the Equality Act in Primary School* (2015). No Outsiders is a UK charity that specialises in promoting

inclusivity and diversity in primary schools. The books discussed in this chapter were selected because their detailed engagement with architecture demonstrates the significant role buildings play in both undermining and authenticating diversity narratives. https://no-outsiders.com/about-us.

2 Posy Simmonds' strip satirised contemporary life through the daily lives of three middle-class, middle-aged women—Wendy Weber, Jo Heep, and Trish Wright. The strips were later collected in *Mrs Weber's Omnibus* (2012).

3 Those attending the meeting are all white, middle class, middle aged, and mostly men. The two women in attendance are the Children's Editor and Secretary, neither of which tend to be roles that are fully respected or valorised. Through the job roles of these two women, Simmonds suggests that diversity at Walmer and Wilcox is merely tokenistic.

4 Written by Peter Parnell and Justin Richardson and illustrated by Henry Cole, *And Tango Makes Three* tells the story of two male penguins who create a family together. The two penguins are given an egg by a zookeeper which they both help hatch.

5 On the front cover of *The Invisible*, the low-rise buildings surrounding Trellick Tower lack definition and detail; they are indistinguishable smudges on the page. By contrast, Trellick Tower is minutely detailed and clearly defined against a dark winter sky. The low-angled perspective amplifies the building's dramatic scale, and only part of the main residential block features on the cover—it is cut off at the edge of the page—thereby emphasising the distinctive slender service tower and projecting boiler room.

References

BBC News [https://www.bbc.co.uk/news/uk-england-birmingham-47158357].

Bell, D. (1991). Insignificant Others: Lesbian and Gay Geographies. *The Royal Geographical Society*, 23(4), pp. 323–329.

Bullen, A. (2014). *The Twentieth Century Society*. https://c20society.org.uk/building-of-the-month/trellick-tower-london#:~:text=Commissioned%20in%201966%20by%20the, in%20Poplar%2C%20completed%20in%201967.

Crisp, T. et al. (2016). What's on Our Bookshelves? The Diversity of Children's Literature in Early Childhood Classroom Libraries. *Journal of Children's Literature*, 42(2), pp. 29–42.

Dines, M. (2009). *Gay Suburban Narratives in American and British Culture*. Basingstoke: Palgrave MacMillan.

DePalma, R. (2016). Gay Penguins, Sissy Ducklings... and Beyond? Exploring Gender and Sexuality Diversity through Children's Literature. *Discourse: Studies in the Cultural Politics of Education*, 37(6), pp. 828–845.

Dolan, M. (2019). How Did the White Picket Fence Become a Symbol of the Suburbs? *Smithsonian Magazine*. https://www.smithsonianmag.com/history/history-white-picket-fence-180971635/.

Esposito, J. (2019). We're Here, We're Queer, but We're Just Like Heterosexuals: A Cultural Studies Analysis of Lesbian Themed Children's Books. *Educational Foundations*, 23(3–4), pp. 61–78.

Grosz, E. (2001). *Architecture from the Outside*. Cambridge: MIT.

Hoffman, Mary and Asquith, R. (2015). *The Great Big Book of Families*. London: Frances Lincoln Children's Books.

Hornsey, R. (2010). *The Spiv and the Architect: Unruly Life in Postwar London*. Minneapolis: University of Minnesota Press.

Johnson, D. and Koss, M. (2016). Diversity in Children's Literature: 1 Year Later. *Journal of Children's Literature*, 42(1), pp. 53–56.

Mason, D. (2020). What Having Two Mommies Looks Like Now: Queer Picture Books in the Twenty-First Century. In Nathalie op de Beeck (ed), *Literary Cultures and Twenty-First-Century Childhoods* (pp. 109–137). Cham: Palgrave. DOI: 10.1007/978-3-030-32146-8_6.

Moffat, A. (2015). *No Outsiders in Our School: Teaching the Equality Act in Primary School*. London and New York: Routledge.

Newman, L. (2000). *Heather Has Two Mommies*. Los Angeles: Turnaround.

——— (2015). *Heather Has Two Mummies*. London: Walker Books.

Parr, T. (2003). *The Family Book*. New York: Little, Brown Books for Young Readers.

Percival, T. (2021). *The Invisible*. London: Simon & Schuster.

Rodriguez, N. and Kim, E. (2018). In Search of Mirrors: An Asian Critical Race Theory Content Analysis of Asian American Picturebooks from 2007 to 2017. *Journal of Children's Literature*, 44(2), pp. 17–30.

Simmonds, P. (2012). *Mrs Weber's Omnibus*. London: Jonathan Cape.

Smith-D'Arezzo, W. (2003). Diversity in Children's Literature: Not Just a Black and White Issue. *Children's Literature in Education: An International Quarterly*, 34(1), pp. 75–94.

Urbach, H. (1996). Closets, Clothes, Disclosure. *Assemblage*, 30, pp. 63–73. https://doi.org/10.2307/3171458.

Wetherell, S. (2020). *Foundations: How the Built Environment made Twentieth-Century Britain*. Princeton, New Jersey: Princeton University Press.

WNDB [https://diversebooks.org/about-wndb/].

PART THREE
Urban space

10

HIGHLY MODERN IDEAL HOMESTEAD

Lucie Glasheen

'The highly modern ideal homestead' in the 'Casey Court' cartoon, 1936–1939

On 15 February 1936, the cartoon 'Casey Court', published weekly in the children's comic *Illustrated Chips* (*Chips*, p. 8), featured the establishment of a house building company. The cartoon shows several 'modern up-to-date dwellings', including a 'villa wiv [sic] roof garden', a 'moovable [sic] villa' called 'Peacehaven' and an 'all glass house for sunshine!' (Figure 10.1). Subsequently, on the 28 March, 'Casey Court' held an 'Ideal Home Exibishun [sic]', complete with a number of gadgets (Figure 10.2). The real *Daily Mail* Ideal Home Exhibition had opened a few days earlier. Adverts emphasised modernity, innovation and spectacle (*Daily Mail*, 1936). A couple of years later, adverts promoted the Ideal Home Exhibition's own glass house (*Daily Mail*, 1938a). While the Ideal Home Exhibitions have become the subject of sustained academic work (e.g. Ryan, 2000, 2018; Cartwright, 2021), 'Casey Court' and other interwar cartoons have received little attention outside specialist catalogues, dictionaries and blogs (Gifford, 1971, Gifford, 1975, Gifford, 1985; Clark; 1998; Gray, 2021; Knudde, 2021; Stringer, 2021a, 2021b, 2021c; although see Glasheen, 2020). However, these cartoons brought together differing discourses about modernity, class and childhood, engaging children in debates about modern architecture and offering their own distinct yet complex construction of modernity.

'Casey Court' was a long-running cartoon series, starting in 1902 and continuing until the 1950s when *Chips* folded, but my research and this chapter is based on those issues published 1930–1939 (Clark, 1998).[1] Comics are not usually classed as children's picture books, yet were largely aimed at children during this period. They were made up of short and serialised illustrated stories and cartoon strips, usually drawn in a simplified style and designed to be humorous with abundant use of slapstick. Cheap prices (½–4d) and common practices of trading, swapping and sharing meant that comics were more likely to have been chosen by children than other children's literature and contributed to their popularity (Blacker, 1974; Gifford, 1985; Houghton, 2009; Chapman, 2011; Fairlie, 2014).[2] *Chips* was a popular title (see Jenkinson, 1940) priced towards the bottom end of the market (Gifford, 1985), reflected in its single-colour printing on coloured paper.

DOI: 10.4324/9781003131755-14

FIGURE 10.1 'Casey Court building ko. [sic]' in 'Casey Court', *Illustrated Chips* (1936a),
15 February, p. 8.
Source: ©The British Library, London.

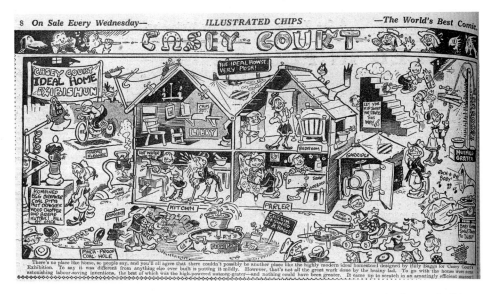

FIGURE 10.2 'Casey Court ideal home exhibishun [sic]' in 'Casey Court', *Illustrated Chips*
(1936b), 28 March, p. 8.
Source: ©The British Library, London.

'Casey Court' was unusual in taking the form of a large single frame cartoon with accompanying text. This allowed for a greater amount of environmental detail in the images and emphasised the event or spectacle over a linear narrative, making it of particular interest for research into representations of the built environment as well as creating ambiguous, multiple and open-ended meanings. The cartoon focused on a group of children creatively

playing in the 'court' or square between their housing.[3] Each week the children would create a different event and place such as an underground station, world tour, theatre or docks.
The children themselves were largely unidentified, and while there were some recurring
characters, in particular the unofficial leader Billy Baggs, in the main they were portrayed
as a group rather than as distinctive individuals. Roy Kozlovsky (2013) argues that the
child became central to modern architecture in post-war Britain, and other historians have
emphasised the interest in and valuing of children's play in this period, relating it to post-
war construction (e.g. Campkin, 2013; Highmore, 2013; Thomson, 2013; Glasheen, 2019).
Through analysis of 'Casey Court', this chapter will contribute to understanding the importance of the relationship between children and interwar modernity and, along with the
rest of this book, consider children as an audience for as well as subject of narratives about
modern architecture (see also Glasheen 2020).

At the beginning of the decade, the backgrounds of 'Casey Court' were fairly detailed,
representing a built-up urban area with rows of terraced housing, occasionally identified as located in East London (Figure 10.3; *Chips* 1931c, p. 8). The housing is marked as
poor-working class by the presence of signs advertising 'boots mended' and as disordered,
by the universal presence of broken windows. There aren't many architectural features, but
tall buildings with pitched roofs, sash windows and lamp posts give a Victorian air. By the
middle of the 1930s, the background had been simplified with seemingly detached houses
portrayed in silhouette. Despite this, the text continued to suggest that the houses were
small and cramped; so small that Micky Smiff's 'dog wagged its tail up and down instead of
from side to side' (*Chips*, 1939a, pp. 4–5).

As I have argued elsewhere, this can be characterised as 'slum' housing (Glasheen, 2020).
During the 1930s, a series of Housing Acts aimed to define and replace housing unfit for

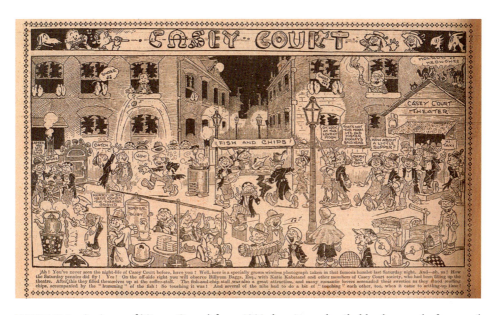

FIGURE 10.3 An issue of 'Casey Court' from 1931 showing a detailed background of terraced
housing with broken windows, *Illustrated Chips* (1931a), 26 September, p. 8.

Source: ©The British Library, London.

living in. The 1935 Housing Act in particular made provisions for the removal of housing deemed unsanitary or overcrowded, and the redevelopment of urban areas with new council housing aimed at the working classes (Yelling, 1992).[4] While the designation and construction of the slum in this period was on a seemingly methodical, scientific and universal basis (based on medical officer reports), it also continued to hold moral connotations and be linked to (particular) urban spaces (e.g. Campkin, 2013). Importantly, slums were also largely associated with old, outdated housing, so slum clearance and its increasing connection to town planning can be understood as a modernising project (Yelling, 1992).

Recent reconsiderations of British interwar architecture and design, as in literature, have expanded beyond a focus on 'high' modernism to looking at plural modernisms, how modernism interacted with other cultures of the modern and modernity more broadly (Darling, 2007; Bluemel, 2009; Yusaf, 2014; Ryan, 2018). Elizabeth Darling (2007, p. 4) argues that 'architectural modernism emerged as part of a wider project to modernise Britain' while Deborah Sugg Ryan (2018, p. 7) suggests that in the interwar period, 'popular conceptions of the "modern"... accommodated past and present, nostalgia and modernity'. The creations of the Casey Court were certainly not modernist: roofs are pitched, windows relatively small, tall and narrow and rooms are separate rather than open plan (Figures 10.1 and 10.2). Indeed, in form they bore a resemblance to the background housing. If in early iterations the urban environment was marked as disordered through the presence of broken windows, the windows of a house built by the children on 22 March 1930 are similarly jagged, and the uneven roof lines and crooked chimney pots of the children's 'modern' flats and villas are echoed in the silhouettes of the background houses (*Chips*, 1930a, p. 8; *Chips*, 1937, p. 8). At first glance, this may seem to have suggested either that children and modern architecture were antithetical or that children were inescapably shaped by their immediate environment and would imitate what they see. Such readings, however, simplify understandings of modernity and children in this period.

As this chapter will demonstrate, 'Casey Court' used key markers of modernity to engage with important ideas about modern architecture. The cartoon, in particular in its representations of Ideal Home exhibitions and house building, reveals a complex tension within different strands of thinking about modern architecture: spectacle, function and innovation. In the next section, I will outline the connections between 'Casey Court' and the Ideal Home Exhibition in their use of innovation and spectacle before moving on to consider how it responded to wider narratives surrounding modern architecture. The cartoon's satire of Ideal Home connected child audiences with a collective knowing experience of modernity.

Ideal home exhibishun: innovation and spectacle

The 1936 depiction of an Ideal Home exhibition was followed by two more portrayals in 'Casey Court' in 1937 and 1939 (*Chips*, 1937, p. 8; *Chips*, 1939a, pp. 4–5). It was in some ways an obvious choice of subject. The *Daily Mail* Ideal Home Exhibition first started in 1908 and by 1936 was well established (Ryan, 2000). Occupying 12 acres at Olympia in London, the exhibition was made up of a wide range of demonstrations and displays such as 'the village of to-morrow', fashion pageants, domestic labour-saving displays, 'television explained', 'the temple of fitness' and 'gardens of history and romance' (*Daily Mail*, 1933; *Daily Mail*, 1934; *Daily Mail*, 1936; A Special Correspondent, 1938; *Daily Mail*, 1938a; *Daily Mail*, 1938b). As these quotes show newness, modern architecture and design and consumerism were central to the Exhibition mixed with elements of nostalgia. The single larger frame of 'Casey Court' allowed cartoonists to show several things going on at once. Unusually for cartoons, the format encouraged an emphasis on the collective rather than individual characters and on a moment in time rather than a linear story. An exhibition was thus a perfect topic, and the connection with a real event gave a seasonal relevance. Moreover, the *Daily Mail* newspaper and *Chips* were both founded by the Harmsworth brothers at the end of the 19th century, although by the 1930s, *Chips* along with the rest of Amalgamated Press had been sold off.

The Ideal Home Exhibition's particular construction of modernity and modern architecture connected it to thematic concerns of 'Casey Court': innovation and spectacle. Adverts suggested the Exhibition would be a 'sparkling spectacle', providing 'thrilling and pleasurable revelations' (*Daily Mail*, 1938a). Issues of 'Casey Court' often featured subjects connected with display and occasion, such as pantomime, cinema, the Grand National and football Cup Final. Furthermore, the cartoon drew attention to viewing and being viewed. It nearly always incorporated some form of audience within the frame, with spectators peering over the fence in the background, looking down from windows at the side or appearing as the backs of heads in the foreground. This positioning created an alliance between the fictional viewer and real child reader/viewer, suggesting that they were part of a collective viewing public rather than gaining privileged access to a private space.

Ryan (2000, p. 19, p. 20) argues that labour-saving devices and inventions were a key feature of the interwar Ideal Home Exhibitions and crucial to their particular and criticised combination of 'tradition and modernity' or construction of 'suburban modernity' in which modernity 'entered through the back door'. Invention was emphasised by adverts which promised 'Brilliant up-to-the-minute wonders...a whole host of labour-saving inventions' (*Daily Mail*, 1938b). Similar to the building company and 'Ideal Home Exibishun [sic]' of 1936 (Figures 10.1 and 10.2), later Ideal Home exhibitions in 'Casey Court' displayed a variety of ingenious houses and gadgets: electric stoves and floor sweepers, roof gardens and sunshine roofs that lifted up or slid across and means of removing or escaping from landlords and rent collectors (*Chips*, 1937, p.8; *Chips*, 1939a, pp. 4–5). This was in-line with other issues of 'Casey Court', which similarly showed the inventiveness of the child characters.

However, while the real Ideal Home exhibition was described as 'Spectacular, yes...Yet... amazingly *practical*' (*Daily Mail*, 1938b; original emphasis), in 'Casey Court' labour-saving devices were clearly shown to be useless and new styles of house building were mocked. The 'landlord remover' and 'portable mansion' spoke to broader constructions of class and modernity, as will be explored below, while seeming to point out the inadequacies of modern architecture and technology in relation to the day-to-day lives of residents of somewhere like 'Casey Court'. The 'kombined egg breaker coal ditto nut cracker wood chopper and bread kutter [sic]' appears to have been inspired by the saying 'use a sledgehammer to crack a nut', the 'elektik stove [sic]' apparently 'takes three weeks to boil an egg' and the 'mansion fitted wiv never leak roof' simply has an umbrella on top of it (*Chips*, 1936b, p. 8; *Chips*, 1937, p. 8; *Chips*, 1939a, pp. 4–5). Objects of modernity or objects of modernity reimagined by 'Casey Court' children (an ambiguity that runs throughout the cartoon) were presented as ridiculous.

'Casey Court's' parody should not necessarily be understood as antithetical to the real Ideal Home Exhibition though. In 1934, the Exhibition featured a display created by cartoonist William Heath Robinson which 'affectionately lampooned' technological modernity and labour-saving devices (Ryan, 2000, p. 20). An advert from 1934 calls this model house, filled with mock-ups of the sort of improvised contraptions for which he became famous, 'The merriest jest of the year' (*Daily Mail*). Information about the multiple artists and authors of children's cartoons (which were unsigned) and their influences is notoriously lacking, although Alan Clark (1998) identifies Julian Stafford Baker as the creator and Albert Pease and Arthur Martin as contributors during the 1930s to 'Casey Court'. Nonetheless, it is likely that they were influenced, if not by 'Heath Robinson's Ideal Home', then by his illustrations which appeared in journals such as *The Sketch*, the children's Professor Branestawm books during the 1930s and in *How To Live in A Flat* in 1936, which celebrated and satirised modern architecture and design (Hamilton, 1992; Heath Robinson Museum, 2021). Ryan (2000, p. 20) argues that the audience of the Heath Robinson display were participating 'in a collective, knowing and joyful experience of consumer culture and modernity'. Through its representation of the Ideal Home Exhibitions and its focus on innovation and spectacle, 'Casey Court' involved child readers in this collective experience.

The cartoons should not be understood as simply a response to Ideal Home, however, nor as translating its culture of modernity for children (some of whom are also likely to have been part of the Exhibition audience). Turning to other contemporaneous portrayals of modern architecture, as I will now do, helps to reveal the ways 'Casey Court' intervened into wider 'narratives of modernity' (Darling, 2007) and childhood.

Modern architecture: light, air and vision

'We know the sort of homes we want,' said one of the housewives speaking in 1945 in *Homes for the People*, 'they must have light and space…and clean fresh air to breathe'. 'Casey Court's' references to sunshine roofs that lift up or slide off and glass houses did not simply satirise the inventions of the *Daily Mail* Ideal Home Exhibition but also linked to a wider understanding of modern architecture. *Homes for the People* (1945) was one of a number of documentaries made about new housing during the 1930s and 1940s (e.g. *Paradox City*, 1934; *Housing Problems*, 1935; *Housing Progress*, 1937; *The Proud City*, 1946). These were sponsored by housing associations and charities, private companies and increasingly by local and national government made to inform about and garner support (and sometimes donations) for slum clearances and the building of new working-class homes. The subject of these films was thus far closer to the imagined world of 'Casey Court' than the Ideal Home Exhibitions, which were largely aimed at a lower middle-class aspirational audience and constructed a suburban consumerist form of modernity (Ryan, 2000). That being said, housing campaigners and the government also exhibited examples of 'slum' housing and new flats at Ideal Home Exhibitions and at Building Trades exhibitions throughout the decade and beyond (Darling, 2007; Campkin, 2013; Cartwright, 2021). The homes shown in these documentaries were in a range of different architectural styles, encompassing modernist estates such as Kensal House, Dutch and neo-Georgian influenced flats such as the St Pancras Improvement Society's Block in Somers Town and Princess Alice House in Kensington, and garden cities and suburban estates. Nonetheless, they became 'narratives of modernity' (Darling 2007) despite the lack of a unifying form.

Modernity was instead figured in the repeated images of windows, signifying light and air. The camera pans across lines of open windows in exterior shots of flats in the films

FIGURE 10.4 Still from *housing progress*' portrayal of modern architecture, showing a row of windows, *housing progress* (1937). Directed by M. Nathan. London: Housing Centre. British Film Institute.

Paradox City (1934), *Housing Problems* (1935) and *Housing Progress* (1937) (Figure10.4). In the first interior shots of two different blocks of flats built by the St Pancras House Improvement Society, in *Paradox City* (1934), the window takes up the full screen. The more famous *Housing Problems* (1935) also featured several interior shots of new housing focusing solely on open windows, and a resident spoke to camera about being able to open the windows and 'let all the nice fresh air in' in front of a large window taking up the frame.

The difference in light between the old slum housing and new development is accentuated in *Housing Problems* (1935) by its cinematography. Sections in which slum residents talk about the conditions they are living in are artificially front lit from below, creating a dark shadowy background. Interiors of new housing as above are back lit with natural light, supplemented by front lighting to give the impression of a naturally light space. Use of windows and light and dark in this way can be seen as, in part, a distinctly filmic response to the problems of communicating modernity. However documentary films also discursively constructed air and light as crucial in modern development. For instance, planner Patrick Abercrombie likened city planning to gardening in the 1946 film *The Proud City: A Plan for London*, emphasising that you have to 'give the plants air and sunshine…and they've got to have room to grow'. *Housing Progress* (1937) similarly evoked light and air through wide-angled exterior shots of children playing in bright sunshine and of plants blowing in the wind.

The repeated presence of 'sunshine' roofs in 'Casey Court' helped to link the children's creations to other forms of modern architecture. As with the documentaries, it was the supposed function of the buildings rather than the architectural style that marked them out as modern. Health was a key concern, as the quote from Abercrombie suggests, and light and air was understood as necessary for healthy living (Zweiniger-Bargielowska, 2010; Kozlovsky, 2013). Yet, at the same time, the visual or verbal/textual evocation of that function became itself symbolic of modernity. In 'Casey Court', this is pointed out through the use of signs that describe creations as sunshine roofs whose function is questionable and that appear to be absurd or impractical.

Indeed, despite their names, the glass house and lifting and sliding roofs as well as the window openings appear to be used for seeing in and out rather than for letting in sunlight and air. This alternative function was hinted at in some of the documentary films. In *Paradox City* (1934), the windows allow observation and interaction between adult and child (unlike the windows of slum properties which had been used for throwing out waste). Adults are shown watching and waving to children outside, one of whom waves back as they run to see a small carousel in the street. Earlier images had shown both children and adults seemingly passive within 'slum' streets, so the implication is that new housing has provided both the separation and observation necessary for active children's play.

Roy Kozlovsky (2013, p. 33, p. 42) argues that in addition to allowing in sunlight and air, glass was used in the Peckham Pioneer Health Centre (opened in 1935) as a means 'for studying families' and 'constituting subjects as active agents who desire to be healthy' through observation and 'double observation'. The relationship between adult and child was, he suggests, central to this, with children encouraged to see and naturally choose healthy active behaviour and adults encouraged to watch and monitor their children and themselves. It is less clear that the windows in *Paradox City* (1934) serve a regulatory purpose, particularly as the children seem to be running out of sight. Instead, their function appears to communicate enjoyment and to create a relationship between inside and outside or public and private space. The transformation of private domestic space (itself made public through film) has allowed the proper use and enjoyment of public spaces by children. Children's play in the semi-public spaces surrounding housing estates is a feature of other documentaries too, but none involve viewing in this way. In contrast, 'Casey Court' makes the function of viewing through such architectural features explicit. An exploration of its glass house exemplifies this.

As mentioned in the opening paragraph, in February 1936, 'Casey Court' included an 'all glass house for sunshine!' in the modern dwellings created by its building company (*Chips*, 1936a). Two years later, the Ideal Home Exhibition promoted its own 'glass house' in an advert on its opening day: 'Building's latest and most sensational achievement…yet a really practical home you can live in!' (*Daily Mail*, 1938a). The illustration accompanying this advert emphasises light and energy. The picture is set at an angle against a sunburst background and lines suggest light streaming down onto and being reflected off what is presumably a glass building. The building's form appears to reference modernism and art deco, with a square cantilevered top section over a stepped entrance reminiscent of a cinema. This advert promoted the spectacular nature of looking at the glass house. An article in the *Daily Telegraph* similarly emphasised the visual qualities of looking at the glass house but also the light that the glass house allowed in. 'This house of the future is built of moulded glass bricks which cannot be seen through, yet permit a softly diffused light to penetrate', a Special Correspondent (1938) stated, while 'An exceptional amount of window space also helps to make it the ideal home for the sun worshipper'. The portrayal of the Ideal Home Exhibition's glass house was far more showy than the evocation of modern homes in the documentaries. Nevertheless, both representations combined looking at the outside of glass and windows with the penetration of light and air through them.

In form, 'Casey Court's' glass house closely resembles a greenhouse, although the sign accompanying the building similarly described it as a house 'for sunshine!'. However, this is undermined by the image (Figure 10.1). While the glass house in 'Casey Court' is to be looked at, it is the viewer rather than sunshine which penetrates inside. The couple in the centre of the image are clearly actively viewing life going on inside the different houses, and one of the two inhabitants of the glass house appears uncomfortably aware of being seen. In 'Casey Court', then, modern architecture exposes the inhabitant to public view rather than to light and air. In some ways, though, this connection between modern housing and public space or public view is simply an extension of the exhibition and the documentary film, both of which made modern architecture (interiors and exteriors) public. Darling (2007) even argues that they can be seen as tools of propaganda for modernist architecture at a time when actual buildings were rare and that they made viewers into a modern public.

As I've suggested, the presence of viewers, in particular in the foreground of images, aligned the real reader/viewer with the represented public, turning them into voyeurs. At the same time, the mutuality of viewing suggests that the real reader/viewer may themselves be seen, becoming part of a viewed and viewing public. Gillian Rose (1997, p. 285) argues that within the documentary movement, of which these films were part, 'all citizens could be subject to observation and through that observation become part of the public'. While the Ideal Home Exhibition adverts presented modernity as something to be seen, as a pleasurable spectacle, in 'Casey Court' it was possible to become part of this pleasurable spectacle, to embody modernity.

The portrayal of Ideal Home and Building Company exhibitions in 'Casey Court' did not just connect with the wider 'narratives of modernity' constructed around planned housing that replaced urban 'slums', however. The cartoon also made reference to very different forms of modern architecture and the contested visions of innovation and modernity they represented. In doing so, they responded to and revealed complex understandings of class and urban childhood.

Invention, class and childhood in the modern countryside/city

One of the buildings of the 'Casey Court Building Ko [sic]' in the cartoon of February 1936 is on wheels, and text announces: 'get away from the landlord wiv this moovable villa [sic]' (Figure 10.1). The sign on the front bears the name 'Peacehaven'. As I have mentioned, this was one of a number of inventions to escape from or repel landlords, rent collectors and 'tally[men]' (*Chips*, 1936a, p. 8). Movable buildings spoke to the practice of 'flitting': leaving accommodation in the middle of the night because rent couldn't be paid. I've argued elsewhere (Glasheen, 2020) that these creations humorously pointed out the failure of plans for working-class housing to address the real concerns of working-class life. In particular, they should be understood in light of a general antipathy to landlords and rent collectors in *Chips* and comics in general, including in the depiction of a rent strike in 'Casey Court'. Nonetheless, they can simultaneously be understood as representing the poor working class as semi-criminal and evaders of responsibility.[5] Other issues similarly showed the children involved in petty theft (for instance, using potatoes 'nicked from Mr O'Dooley's allotment', *Chips*, 1931b, p. 8) or suggested that they played truant. Indeed, 'Casey Court' maintained an uncertain balance between laughing at and laughing with its working-class child characters throughout the 1930s.

This complex portrayal of class is further evident in the use of the name 'Peacehaven'. While the name is clearly a simple joke about the usefulness of being able to escape from the landlord (making the dwelling a peaceful haven), it also significantly refers to the infamous interwar 'plotland' development on the Sussex coast near Brighton. Peacehaven was established in 1916 by Charles Neville, who bought 600 acres of land and sold it off (initially through a newspaper competition) as individual plots for development (Bernard, 2021). As with other plotlands, they were increasingly bought by urban working-class families who gradually built weekend and holiday homes, often reusing old railway carriages, omnibuses and army huts (Hardy and Ward, 1985).

Peacehaven was widely criticised by planners and preservationists who saw plotlands as destroying the countryside. David Matless (2016, p. 68) argues that Peacehaven 'became a national symbol' of bad development and it was described as 'the saddest monument of the Great Peace that was ever built' by the Royal Institute of British Architects in 1943 (RIBA in Matless, 2016, p. 263). The unplanned, self-built and piecemeal nature of plotlands, 'their inherent disorder and makeshift character' (Hardy and Ward 1985, p. 143), was antithetical to the orderly modernity that Matless (2016) identifies as key in conservationist and town-planning movements. Richard Bower (2017) argues that such informal housing continues to be seen as backward or anti-modern, while planned development is associated with progress and modernity. However, critics of plotlands and other unplanned development, including the aforementioned Abercrombie, emphasised their newness (e.g. Matless, 2016, pp. 68–69), allowing Peacehaven to represent an alternative modernity: American-influenced, based on mass consumerism and 'essentially democratic in its cheapness', termed a 'Third England' by author J.B. Priestley (in Matless 2016, p. 59). A.J.P. Taylor's 1965 (p. 301) history of wartime and interwar England similarly suggested that 'A new England was coming into existence which owed nothing to the planners, which indeed created itself in defiance of their efforts'. Moreover, while Taylor and Priestley's comments applied to a whole range of suburban speculative building, plotland developments exemplified ingenuity and can be seen as a corollary to the innovation celebrated in the Ideal Home Exhibition.

Peacehaven also particularly embodied the movement into and occupation of the countryside and coast by the urban working class, a source of anxiety for many middle-class commentators. Plotlands were thus problematic due to both their visibility, whereby their architecture and inhabitants were marked out as destructive and Other, and their invisibility, as their marginal status allowed them to evade governance. Matless (2016, p. 102) demonstrates that there were a number of discourses that presented the urban working class as out of place in the countryside, suggesting that 'Cockneys in the country denote cultural transgression'. The noisy, chaotic and anarchic inhabitants of 'Casey Court', with their interests in advertising, commerce and popular culture, match exactly the kind of 'anti-citizen' that these critics had in mind. As scholars have shown, a number of institutions such as the Scouts and Guides aimed to teach children how to behave well in the countryside, and books such as those by Arthur Ransome reinforced the idea that children should police their own and others behaviour (Matless, 2016; Edwards, 2018). As child characters, the inhabitants of 'Casey Court' appear to be resistant to such training, showing a disregard for any authority.

Of course, in 'Casey Court' the dwellings are placed in the city rather than the countryside or coast. The fact that some of them are on wheels, though, does hint at the instability and permeability of geographical categories and boundaries. 'Casey Court' had a number of issues that focused on transport, some of them explicitly referencing new and growing habits of working-class holidaymaking such as the 'Casey Court caravan club' (*Chips*, 1938a, p. 5; Hardy and Ward, 1985; Matless, 2016). Nonetheless, issues actually showing 'Casey Court' somewhere other than in their urban environment are relatively rare. Instead, these forms of mobility are trapped within the confines of the court, the name itself implying a limited and enclosed space. Furthermore, the children appear to be limited by their own constructions, with wheels constantly on the verge of falling off and boats, cars, buses, planes and trains always about to fall over or apart. This instability then helps to mitigate the sense that the 'Casey Court' children pose a threat to rural and coastal landscapes or the risk that they appear out of place.

However, children's presence in cities could also be seen as problematic. The countryside has often been imagined as the natural place for child development, with the children in the city seen as either at risk or posing a risk (or both) (Steedman, 1990; Jones, 2002; Hörschelmann and Van Blerk, 2012). During the 1930s, as Tom Hulme (2019) points out, anti-urbanism was less pronounced and interventions focused on making good citizens of the city as well as providing affordable rural holidays. Again, the children of 'Casey Court' do not obviously meet ideas of the good urban citizen. I would suggest however that the cartoon offers an alternative, positive view of children's place in the city based on play, creativity and change.

It is not at all clear that child readers were supposed to judge the children's behaviour unfavourably. The comic was after all itself part of the consumerist, American-influenced mass culture that preservationist and youth movements criticised. Children's cartoons in general had a strong anti-authoritarian streak. The cartoon includes knowing self-reference: a number of issues show *Chips* and other comics by the same publishers being advertised, sold and read (e.g. *Chips*, 1938b, pp. 4–5). As with the use of in-frame viewing subjects discussed above, this helped to implicate the viewer and destabilise hierarchical judgement.

Moreover, while the children's creations are portrayed as temporary and unstable, their imagination and resourcefulness is celebrated. The ingenuity and reuse (or 'upcycling') involved in plotland developments can be found throughout 'Casey Court', as everyday and waste objects are creatively transformed. As viewers we enjoy seeing what has been invented each week and are likely to be reading the cartoon for this very reason. The instability itself allows for this continuous reinvention. I suggested in the introduction that the inventions of 'Casey Court' are placed in the context of play, and the cartoon can be seen as a forerunner of a post-war valuing of constructive but anarchic children's urban play in the context of reconstruction (e.g. Campkin, 2013; Highmore, 2013; Kozlovsky, 2013; Thomson, 2013; Glasheen, 2019). While interwar planning and housing was on a smaller scale, programmes of slum clearance still involved themes of destruction (with demolition shots a feature of the above-mentioned films) and rebuilding. 'Casey Court's' capacity to constantly reinvent can be seen as a modernising impulse, but also one that recognises the city as a place of constant change.

Conclusion: homes and vision

'Casey Court' brought together the anarchic creative architecture of plotlands, the unifying symbolic functionalism of new planned housing and the commercialised spectacular innovation of the Ideal Home exhibition to create its own distinctive vision of modern architecture that placed working-class children at its centre. The cartoon's use of satire and play was both critical and celebratory of the inventions of architects, manufacturers and the working class. The format of the cartoon allowed it to maintain an ambivalent attitude to class, urbanism and modernity as multiple interpretations were kept open. However, I have suggested that, ultimately, creativity and play were portrayed positively and the city was represented as a space of change.

Perhaps the most significant feature of the 'Casey Court' cartoons' representation of modern architecture and modernity is the way that they engaged children in a whole range of issues concerning class, function, housing and urbanism. Rather than simply presenting modern architecture or the Ideal Home Exhibition for a child audience, they used the foregrounding of active viewing practices to include children in a modern collective public who could respond to it with enjoyment, scepticism, playfulness and optimism. The act of viewing in 'Casey Court' was not a regulatory one, but rather a practice of modernity. While children's views were not elicited or published by comics and they could not hope to reach or influence planners, architects or government officials (allowing them as Kimberley Reynolds, 2007, p. 15, says to '[fly] under the cultural radar'), 'Casey Court' did encourage children to observe and form their own opinions about architecture and to see themselves as involved in questions relating to housing.

It is worth noting the absence of the portrayal of day-to-day life in modern housing in the cartoons discussed in this chapter. Other portrayals of child-created housing in 'Casey Court' similarly focused on its construction, display and sale, although an issue in 1939 showed a rent strike (*Chips*, 1939b, pp. 4–5). The cartoon thus focused on the politics of the 'highly modern ideal homestead' that Billy Baggs wished to create (*Chips*, 1936b, p.8). Reynolds (2016) has pointed out that contrary to received wisdom, a rich corpus of children's literature engaged with politics in Britain during the interwar years. Nonetheless, overt politics was usually absent from mass popular literature, such as the comics discussed here. However, housing and play were arenas in which politics could emerge, or rather topics which were seen as suitable for children through which contested public issues of modern life, citizenship, community and class were raised.

Notes

1 My research is based on analysis of every issue of *Illustrated Chips*, focusing on 'Casey Court', published between 1930 and 1939. In addition, I looked at three issues of *Chips* from the previous decade.
2 Children's literature is often chosen by adults for children, although the prevalence of libraries (with open shelves) during this period also gave literate children (children were required to be able to read to join) choice, as memoirs reveal, for example, see Rayner (2003).
3 The fact that the figures were children and were playing rather than really doing these activities was never explicitly stated. However, adult characters semi-regularly appeared, usually in the background (identified through their height difference and their occasional interactions). For example, in 'The Guy-Makers of Casey Court' (*Chips*, 1930b, p. 8), one of the characters is caught by his collar by a taller woman who says, 'I'll teach you to run off with your dad's best boots'. The title image for much of the decade shows a boy using a pea shooter, and the children's creations never appear to be taken seriously or have any consequences, suggesting they should be understood as playing. This reading is somewhat complicated by the fact that arguably other cartoons incorporate similar features of play (i.e. consequences are short term and in the end do not matter).
4 Councils were required to provide a replacement number of dwellings for those displaced through slum clearances, either directly, meaning that they would receive the rental income, or by working with a local housing association or charity. As the prices charged were usually higher than those of the properties they replaced, this did not equate to rehousing those who had been living in clearance areas.
5 The perception that the poorest were semi-criminal was perpetuated by social researchers. The New Survey of London Life and Labour (Smith, 1930), an updating of Booth's Survey conducted by London School of Economics between 1928and 1934, still defined the 'lowest class' as 'degraded or semi criminal' in its updated 'poverty' maps.

References

A Special Correspondent (1938). Ideal Home of Glass. *Daily Telegraph*, 6 April, p. 9.
Bernard, S. (2021). *Peacehaven History*. Available at: https://www.peacehaventowncouncil.gov.uk/history-of-the-town/. (Accessed: 12 December 2021).

Blacker, H. (1974). *Just Like It Was: Memoirs of the Mittel East*. London: Vallentine, Mitchell.

Bluemel, K. (2009). Introduction: 'What Is Intermodernism?'. In K. Bluemel (ed), *Intermodernism: Literary Culture in Mid-Twentieth-Century Britain*. Edinburgh: Edinburgh University Press, pp. 1–18.

Bower, R. (2017). Forgotten Plotlanders: Learning from the Survival of Lost Informal Housing in the UK. *Housing, Theory and Society*, 34(1), pp. 79–105.

Campkin, B. (2013). *Remaking London: Decline and Regeneration in Urban Culture*. London: I.B. Tauris.

Cartwright, A. (2021). The Un-Ideal Home: Fire Safety, Visual Culture and the LCC (1958–1963). *The London Journal*, 46(1), pp. 66–91.

Chapman, J. (2011). *British Comics: A Cultural History*. London: Reaktion.

Clark, A. (1998). *Dictionary of British Comic Artists, Writers and Editors*. London: British Library.

Daily Mail (1933). Spend A Happy Day at the Foot of the Rainbow! Daily Mail Ideal Home Exhibition Now Open. *The Times*, 17 April, p. 9.

———— (1934). Daily Mail Ideal Home Exhibition Opens To-Day! *The Times,* 3 April, p. 15.

———— (1936). Daily Mail Ideal Homes Open To-Day! *The Times,* 24 March, p. 21.

———— (1938a). Daily Mail Ideal Home Exhibition. *The Times*, 5 April, p. 11.

———— (1938b). 'The House Is Imaginative...' Says The Times: Daily Mail Exhibition. *The Times*, 20 April, p. 15.

Darling, E. (2007). *Re-Forming Britain: Narratives of Modernity Before Reconstruction*. London: Routledge.

Edwards, S. (2018). *Youth Movements, Citizenship and the English Countryside: Creating Good Citizens, 1930–1960*. Cham: Palgrave Macmillan.

Fairlie, H. A. (2014). *Revaluing British Boys' Story Papers, 1918–1939*. Basingstoke: Macmillan.

Gifford, D. (1971). *Discovering Comics*. Tring: Shire Publications.

———— (1975). *Happy Days: A Century of Comics*. London: Jupiter Books.

———— (1985). *The Complete Catalogue of British Comics: Including Price Guide*. Exeter: Webb & Bower.

Glasheen, L. (2019). Bombsites, Adventure Playgrounds and the Reconstruction of London: Playing with Urban Space in Hue and Cry. *The London Journal*, 44(1), pp. 54–74.

———— (2020). 'The Casey Court House Builders': Nineteen-Thirties Children's Comics and the Material Transformation of East London. In L. Ameel, J. Finch, S. Laine, and R. Dennis (eds), *The Materiality of Literary Narratives in Urban History*. New York; London: Routledge, pp. 115–139.

Gray, P. (2021). 'Casey Court' for Chips by Julius Stafford Baker 1914–1915 examples. *Peter Gray's Comics and Art*, 28 December 2009. Available at: https://petergraycartoonsandcomics.blogspot.com/. (Accessed: 12 October 2021).

Hamilton, J. (1992). *William Heath Robinson*. London: Pavilion.

Hardy, D. and Ward, C. (1985). Landscapes of Arcadia. *Area*, 17(2), pp.141–145.

Heath Robinson Museum (2021). *William Heath Robinson*. Available at: https://www.heathrobinson-museum.org/william-heath-robinson/. (Accessed: 12 September 2021).

Highmore, B. (2013). Playgrounds and Bombsites: Postwar Britain's Ruined Landscapes. *Cultural Politics*, 9(3), pp. 323–336.

Homes for the People (1945). Directed by K. Mander. Daily Herald and Labour Party: Basic Films.

Hörschelmann, K. and Van Blerk, L. (2012). *Children, Youth and the City*. Abingdon, Oxon: Routledge.

Houghton, D. (2009). *A Bethnal Green Memoir: Recollections of Life in the 1930s–1950s*. Stroud: History.

Housing Problems (1935). Directed by E. H. Anstey and A. Elton. London: British Commercial Gas Association. British Film Institute.

Housing Progress (1937). Directed by M. Nathan. London: Housing Centre. British Film Institute.

Hulme, T. (2019). *After the Shock City: Urban Culture and the Making of the Modern Citizen*. Woodbridge, Suffolk; Rochester, NY: The Boydell Press.

Illustrated Chips (1930a). 22 March.

———— (1930b). 3 November.

———— (1931a). 26th September.

———— (1931b). 17th October.

———— (1931c). 19 December.

———— (1936a). 15 February.

———— (1936b). 28 March.

———— (1937). 3 April.

———— (1938a). 6 August.

———— (1938b). 15 October.

———— (1939a). 4 March.

———— (1939b). 26 August.

Jenkinson, A. J. (1940). *What Do Boys and Girls Read?: An Investigation into Reading Habits with Some Suggestions About the Teaching of Literature in Secondary and Senior Schools.* London: Methuen & Co.

Jones, O. (2002). Naturally Not! Childhood, the Urban and Romanticism. *Human Ecology Review*, 9(2), pp. 17–30.

Knudde, K. (2021). Charlie Pease. *Lambiek Comiclopedia.* Available at: https://www.lambiek.net/comiclopedia.html. (Accessed: 12 October 2021).

Kozlovsky, R. (2013). *The Architectures of Childhood: Children, Modern Architecture and Reconstruction in Postwar England.* Farnham: Ashgate.

Matless, D. (2016). *Landscape and Englishness.* Rev. edn. London: Reaktion.

Paradox City (1934). Directed by G. E. Belmont and L. A. Day. London: St Pancras House Improvement Society. British Film Institute.

Rayner, C. (2003). *How Did I Get Here from There?* London: Virago.

Reynolds, K. (2007). *Radical Children's Literature: Future Visions and Aesthetic Transformations in Juvenile Fiction.* Basingstoke: Palgrave Macmillan.

———— (2016). *Left Out: The Forgotten Tradition of Radical Publishing for Children in Britain 1910–1949.* Oxford; New York: Oxford University Press.

Rose, G. (1997). Engendering the Slum: Photography in East London in the 1930s'. *Gender, Place & Culture*, 4(3), pp. 277–300.

Ryan, D. S. (2000). 'All the World and Her Husband': The Daily Mail Ideal Home Exhibition, 1908–1939. In M. Andrews, and M. M. Talbot (eds), *All the World and Her Husband: Women in Twentieth-Century Consumer Culture.* London; New York: Cassell, pp. 10–20.

———— (2018). *Ideal Homes, 1918–39: Domestic Design and Suburban Modernism.* Manchester: Manchester University Press.

Smith, H. L. (1930). *The New Survey of London Life and Labour* (IV). London: P. S. King & Son.

Steedman, C. (1990). *Childhood, Culture, and Class in Britain: Margaret McMillan, 1860–1931.* London: Virago.

Stringer, Lew (2021a). Casey Court Broadcasting Stashun (1932) [sic]. *Lew.Stringer.Comics.Blogspot.com*, 1st December 2018. Available at: https://lewstringercomics.blogspot.com/. (Accessed: 12 October 2021).

———— (2021b). Happy New Year 1947 – Chips style. *Lew.Stringer.Comics.Blogspot.com*, 3 January 2009. Available at: https://lewstringercomics.blogspot.com/. (Accessed: 12 October 2021).

———— (2021c). The New Year CHIPS (1941). *Lew.Stringer.Comics.Blogspot.com*, 31 December 2018. Available at: https://lewstringercomics.blogspot.com/. (Accessed: 12 October 2021).

Taylor, A. J. P. (1965). *English History, 1914–1945.* Oxford: Clarendon Press.

The Proud City: A Plan for London (1946). Directed by R. Keene. Ministry of Information. London: British Film Institute.

Thomson, M. (2013). *Lost Freedom: The Landscape of the Child and the British Post-War Settlement.* Oxford: Oxford University Press.

Yelling, J. A. (1992). *Slums and Redevelopment: Policy and Practice in England, 1918–1945, with particular reference to London.* London: UCL Press.

Yusaf, S. (2014). *Broadcasting Buildings: Architecture on the Wireless, 1927–1945.* Cambridge MA: The MIT Press.

Zweiniger-Bargielowska, I. (2010). *Managing the Body: Beauty, Health and Fitness in Britain, 1880–1939.* Oxford: Oxford University Press.

11

ARCHITECTURE AND MAGIC – MAPPING THE LONDON OF CHILDREN'S FANTASY FICTION

Madison McLeod

Introduction

More than one childhood memory has revolved around the fascination of fantastical worlds, be it cloud-covered castles, gemstone-coloured dragons or a child's discovery of their own magical powers. Hours have been spent pouring over fantasy novels, either alone or in the company of family or friends. Love of certain fantasy worlds like those of Harry Potter, Narnia or the Lord of the Rings have been passed down from one generation to another. A few readers have even plotted their favourite fantasy worlds and constructed maps to better understand the movement of characters. Others have poured over maps made by the authors themselves. J. R. R. Tolkien hand drew the maps we find in the Lord of the Rings novels, painstakingly incorporating every detail of his fantastical world in a pictorial form for both himself and his readers (Fonstad, 1991). One may wonder why this link between fantasy and maps is so tight when the fantastical world and the cartographic one can seem at odds with each other. After all, isn't cartography an exact science and fantasy wholly imaginary? Stefan Ekman may offer an explanation. In *Here Be Dragons: Exploring Fantasy Maps and Settings* (Ekman, 2013), Ekman makes an important distinction, noting that the difference:

> Between the map that graphically represents the milieu and a map of an imaginary place is one of priority: a map *re*-presents what is already there; a fictional map is often primary—to create the map means, largely to create the world of the map.
>
> *(p. 20)*

The various works of fantasy literature set in London, in effect, create a map between them. This draws on the way all maps offer the user a way to understand the place mapped. Imagined maps ground fantasy locations and give them veracity. In front of them, a reader is able to place the protagonists and themselves within the fantastical world of the novel they are reading.

It is no wonder then that the world of children's fantasy literature is packed with books that contain maps depicting where the story takes place. Pictorial maps, which depict landmarks,

DOI: 10.4324/9781003131755-15

conquests, landscapes and countries are often placed at the beginning of the book to pre-pare the reader for the ensuing story. Verbal maps may also be included, which exist at the textual level only where they are described in full detail and propel the story forward and are connected with the narrative (Goga and Kümmerling-Meibauer, 2017). The distinction between the two sets of maps is that the first involves a collaboration between author and cartographer/illustrator to visually represent the map and the second is one described by the author through the text. There are also a range of novels which do not include maps at all, but that provide a large amount of 'geographic investment', a term Matthew Wilkens coined to refer to the number of words within a novel which name particular places (Wilkens, 2013, p. 804). A calculation of geographic investment is made possible by the ability of new tech-nologies to identify and count place names, instances of geographic specificity, within a large literary corpus (Heuser et al., 2016, p. 25). In contrast, I offer my own concept, which I've dubbed 'geographic specificity', which is the way an author accurately depicts the locations which they describe in their novels. For example, an author could write 'to the left of my house' if they were writing with little geographic specificity or 'on Regent Street, I walked three blocks and turned left' if they were writing with a lot of geographic specificity.

Novels which include more geographic specificity and geographic investment allow for a more accurate cognitive map. Roger Downs and David Stea in their seminal work *Maps in Mind* (1977) define cognitive mapping as 'an abstraction covering those cognitive or mental abilities that enable us to collect, organize, store, recall and manipulate information about the spatial environment' (p. 6). Downs and Stea stress that cognitive mapping is based on the individual's cognitive abilities where the outcome is determined by an active process. Similarly, Blaut et al. argue that cognitive mapping is the way in which children learn to navigate their surroundings (Blaut et al., 2003). Marie-Laure Ryan adds that a cognitive map is 'a mental model of *spatial* relations' (Ryan, 2014) which can represent both factual and imaginary landscapes, be they urban or rural. Furthermore, Ryan maintains that cog-nitive mapping is critical for the representation of space in narratives. This spatial mapping is one particularly researched in children's literature scholarship. However, such scholarship often does not incorporate digital humanities research methods to further explore the role of space within fantastical children's novels.

As lovers of children's literature know, many everyday places have been transformed and altered because they are the setting of a memorable work of children's fiction. P.L. Travers's colourful descriptions of St. Paul's Cathedral, for instance, will forever connect the world of Mary Poppins with the city of London (Travers, 2008). The works of Cassandra Clare, for her part, have enriched young people's appreciation of Blackfriars Bridge (Clare, 2010). Similarly, for many readers, the cityscape of London remains imaginatively and inexorably tied to fantastical stories of their childhoods from Paddington Bear to Harry Potter. Jenny Bavidge explains that books set within London fit into a 'nostalgic category', which can be seen throughout the city as children's fantasy literature is integrated into the material geography of London (Bavidge, 2006, pp. 324–325). Bavidge argues that 'the statues of Paddington Bear and Peter Pan [among other monuments of children's literature] all es-tablish a geographical correlative to the children's canon' (Bavidge, 2006, pp. 324–325). A comprehensive list of instances of fantastical layering of fiction over the actual space of London would easily fill its own atlas. The point is that in enumerating specific examples, one becomes aware that the physical geography of London is enveloped and enhanced by works of fantasy children's literature.

Scholars interested in such a geography of fiction have been investigating the relationship between literary spaces and actual places (see Piatti and Hurni, 2009). With the recent emphasis on and interest in digital literary cartography, however, efforts to map and analyse this relationship have greatly increased. The role of architecture and, more specifically, landmarks in literature also deserve attention. Oxford's *A Dictionary of Human Geography* (Rogers et al. 2013) defines a landmark as '[a] distinctive geographic feature that can be seen clearly from a distance and by which the viewer can establish their location. It may be natural or human-made, and is often of interest to tourists'. This is a particularly relevant definition when exploring the role of landmarks within the city of London and exemplifies the many ways in which landmarks can be interpreted.

My methodology consists of close reading over 60 fantasy children's and young adult novels set in London. By combining Geographic Information Systems (GIS), binary coding, literary mapping software and children's literature scholarship, I have developed a system of annotation that allows me to extract the relevant geographic information from my corpus. It also allows for a comparative analysis of the maps themselves. After coding each geographic instance in all of those novels, I use ARCGIS software—a digital mapping software—to map each novel. These maps allow me to investigate how gender, age and socio-economic status impact or alter protagonist trajectories in novels set in London. In this chapter, I will use the initial findings of my research to describe the architectural spaces within London that prompt magic while describing and explaining how a digital humanities methodology works and why it is essential to this kind of research. This chapter will explore the palimpsest of London and allow readers to pinpoint the locations within London where the veil between reality and literary fantasy are thinnest.

Literary geography versus literary cartography

Before describing London's landmarks, it is important first to explain the field in which this work is situated. Literary geography and literary cartography constitute two discrete yet interrelated areas of study (Piatti and Hurni, 2011), so it is useful to begin by drawing distinctions between the two. Literary geography is more generally the geographical analysis of literary works. Stemming from work of the late 19th and 20th centuries (see Sharp, 1904), literary geography examines the ways in which works of fiction engage with knowable places. The efficiency of this research, of course, depends on the frame of reference that a novel assumes in negotiating the relationship between the real world it inhabits and the fictional, and in this case fantastical, world it creates. Some works, such as those of Travers, Clare and Rowling, are strongly tied to actual locations, whereas others, such as the novels of J.R.R. Tolkien or C.S. Lewis, oscillate more liberally between the real and the imaginary. Regardless, the aim of literary geography is both to investigate how works of literature negotiate their relationship to the space of the 'real' world and to examine how this negotiation influences the way these novels are read and received. In contrast, literary cartography—the mapping of works of literature—can be seen as a subcategory of literary geography (Piatti, 2016). Whether in mapping a single novel and its geographically specific elements or in mapping several novels and their geographic elements, literary cartography uses abstract cartographic symbology and quantitative methodologies to condense the spatial information comprised in works of literature and to make those geographies visible on a map. Literary geography and literary cartography can therefore be linked in a hierarchy:

literary geography is the greater field of study, whereas literary cartography is one of the interpretations and practices within that field.

When considering the usefulness of literary cartography for fantasy children's literature scholarship, it becomes clear that certain novels are more amenable to geographical analysis and mapping than others. For instance, whereas the mapping of 19th century London-based novels provides, as seen in the research undertaken by the Stanford Literary Lab, convincing and interesting results about the emotions of protagonists in certain areas of London (Heuser, Moretti and Steiner, 2016), the mapping of fantasy children's literature set in London is far more challenging and poses far more questions and problems than solutions. More generally, literary cartography facilitates further thinking about children's fantasy literature and space at large and, as Franco Moretti underscores in his *Atlas of the European Novel*, an inquiry into space in fiction leads to a completely new interpretation of that literature (Moretti, 2015). However, while digital methods such as this allow for these digital maps to be created and geographic specificity and investment plotted, the scholar is still needed to interpret what these maps are capable of telling us.

Ambiguity and uncertainty

Literary cartography's starting point is the sometimes erroneous assumption that a large part of fiction refers to the mappable world, what Edward Soja terms 'first space' (Soja, 1996). Children's novels can refer to the physical world in a variety of ways, including the use of identifiable toponyms or the inclusion of geographically specific descriptions. Toponyms are words which refer to specific places like 'King's Cross Station' or larger areas like 'Mayfair'. These toponyms are particularly helpful as a means of mapping where characters are. As Malcolm Bradbury notes in his *Atlas of Literature*, '[a] very large part of our writing is a story of its roots in a place: a landscape, city, nation or continent' (Bradbury, 1996, p. 7). Toponyms help readers and scholars determine the locations which serve as the roots of that particular author or protagonist within both the real and the fictional spaces they inhabit. In addition to such realistically portrayed spaces, however, fantasy novels are also able to construct limitless spaces, including imaginary realms comprised of purely invented cities, countries, continents and worlds. However, the focus of this particular work is on the in between. Between these two extremes of geographic specificity lie novels set in real places which incorporate fantastical elements and locations. An excellent example of this is J.K. Rowling's Platform 9 ¾ at King's Cross Station, in which King's Cross Station is an actual useable train station but also is a location of a very popular portal to a fantastical world. Such a partly real, partly imagined space can be described and critically analysed, of course, but at the same time it can also be mapped (Piatti and Hurni, 2009).[1] Thus, this chapter digitally maps the London-based landmarks which act as doors between the real and the fantastic in fantasy youth literature.

Literary geography changes as it becomes digital. In the age of digital humanities and GIS, digital methods offer lone scholars the ability to take on larger corpora with a greater amount of precision. These systems alone, however, cannot add meaning to the maps that are created. Foundational works of literary geography such as Barbara Piatti's *Mapping Fiction: The Theories, Tools and Potentials* (2016) and Franco Moretti's *Atlas of the European Novel* (2015) argue that the advantage of this kind of digital research lies not only in the greater corpora which can be studied, but in the critic's ability to give meaning to spatial patterns, such as an analysis of the maps found in this chapter. The greater goal of my research is a synthesis of methodological innovations: the ability to code geographic information on a new scale whilst at the same time preserving the ability to understand how each landmark functions both within its unique textual environment and within the corpus at large.

A note on picturebooks

Picturebooks are not the focus of this chapter. However, it is worth noting how picturebooks set in London deal with settings, particularly landmarks, as this informs my discussion of how landmarks work in fiction for older children. Picturebooks set in London often tend to take a landmark-only approach. Two clear examples of such an approach are *Katie in London* (Mayhew, 2014) and *The Queen's Hat* (Antony, 2014). *Katie in London* tells the story of Katie and her little brother Jack riding one of the lions of Trafalgar Square around the landmarks of London. The landmarks Katie and Jack visit include St. Paul's Cathedral, the Tower of London, Tower Bridge, the Globe Theatre, the London Eye, Big Ben and Buckingham Palace. They also stop at an unnamed park near Buckingham Palace as well as Harrods to buy the lion a blanket. This story exemplifies the landmark-only approach that is a feature of picturebooks where only the noted landmarks and locations of London are visited without much variation or magical reinterpretation. Similarly, in *The Queen's Hat*, the Queen loses her hat to a brisk wind and chases after it with her soldiers around London. Her adventure begins and ends at Kensington Palace, but she also visits Trafalgar Square, the London Zoo, the London underground, the London Eye, Tower Bridge and Big Ben. Both these books only visit landmarks and do not really move into a fantasy world in terms of geography, although they do include flying and riding a lion as the way they navigate the city, and so do not adhere to street signs or trajectories, which indicates that geographically specific mapping may not be a fruitful tool for these books. These books for younger readers tend to use actual landmarks which retain their proper names and which do not act as portals to fantastical versions of London. Fantasy fiction for slightly older children and young adults, on the other hand, substitute the names of those landmarks, turn landmarks into fantastical portals and add landmarks specific to the fantasy world itself.

Methodology

Mapping children's fantasy novels yields greater rewards, as geographic specificity and investment consists of mapping the known place names each novel mentions. Fantasy novelists employ a wide range of obfuscatory techniques where setting location is concerned, for example, Holly Race's novel *Midnight Twins* changes St. Paul's Cathedral's name to Tintagel (Holly Race, 2020). Place names do very important cultural and fictional work in fantasy youth novels in particular. They join together narrative and geographic space while also calling upon and contributing to the connotations those specific London-based locations have accrued through wider media and culture. Picturebooks, too, contribute to building those sets of connotations.

The corpus of fantasy fiction used for this investigation of London place names and landmarks is derived from my greater corpus organisation in 'Finding the Fantastic in the City: Digitally Mapping Fantasy Youth Literature' (forthcoming McLeod 2022). This greater corpus only includes works of English-language fantasy fiction aimed at young people published between 1990 and 2021. In order to explore the role of landmarks within fantasy youth literature set in London, one must use the process of geo-referencing. Geo-referencing is the way in which geographic data within novels are coded based on place name as well as latitude and longitude. This duality is particularly relevant when using geographic software like ARCGIS.

In order for these searchable place names to be used within a literary corpus, every novel must be available in an eXtensible Markup Language (XML) format, which is not available for recently published novels as even purchasing them through digital means does not afford you the ability to have the XML version of a novel. Therefore, all geo-referencing and geo-parsing had to be done manually without digital methods. Geo-parsing is the use of text mining software 'to identify geographic representation of place and geographic features through matching place names' (Yuan, 2010, p. 115). Simply put, it is the technological ability to extract place names in text through natural language processing. I did not use geotagged place names in XML or Geographic Markup Language (GML) and could not then use GIS services or Keyhole Markup Language (KML) to immediately provide geographic views with maps and images of these places. Rather, I manually coded each novel for geographic language and then used ARCGIS to create the maps you see below. My ability as a literary scholar to differentiate between actual place names where the characters were and places they only referred to, to infer where they were based on their descriptions and to distinguish between things like the Duchess of Cambridge the person, the Duchess of Cambridge the pub, the University of Cambridge and Cambridge as a city are incredibly valuable. A text mining algorithm would consider all three of those instances as Cambridge the city, as it cannot differentiate between the three. This ability to differentiate is particularly helpful when exploring landmarks within London.

To find landmarks in this corpus mentioning London places, I developed a hybrid methodology that combines current excel statistical techniques with a traditional research-based approach. The excel statistics allow scholars to determine what locations occur most frequently while the research-based close reading approach allows a scholar to determine whether that location is an actual location within the map of London. From a compiled list of locations, I chose the ten most frequent landmarks to investigate for this chapter in an attempt to represent the magical portals most prominently placed in London. My list is not exhaustive, but I believe that it is broadly representative of the most magical landmarks in London. The grandeur, eternity and architecture of these landmarks give each of them a presence which has become eternal. These landmarks, like Big Ben and St. Paul's Cathedral, have come to represent not only London but also Britain and the United Kingdom to the world at large. One need only describe or show a red double decker bus and Big Ben to situate themselves in London. These particular structures in London become landmarks because the architecture of them has given each of them a presence which has become a fertile ground for magical re-imagination.

Approaches to landmark mapping

Fantasy literature has not been an important source for GIS data analysis up to now. Direct links between fantasy texts and GIS databases are just starting to become a realm of scholarly exploration. Most work being done at the moment, however, focuses on natural areas like the Lake District (Bushell et al., 2018) or on huge corpora of texts (Heuser, Moretti and Steiner, 2016). Unlike these previous studies, the goal of this work is to incorporate urban fantasy within the greater narrative of literary mapping. In order to explore youth fantasy literature set in London, I created a combination of new models and tools to extract geographic values from literary texts and populated a database with data about protagonist movement and demographics as well as the landmarks within the city they frequented.

By converting the unstructured data available in fantasy youth literature into structured GIS data for mapping and spatial analysis, I developed a new lens through which to explore these spaces. Below are three approaches to the use of landmarks within fantasy youth literature set in London.

Particularly relevant to this study is the use of geo-referencing, the use of geo-inference and, lastly, combining the two in the literary mapping of landmarks. The statistics of geospatial marking are also used to see the proliferation and use of specific landmarks within the corpus of novels and bring a new method of analysis when geo-referencing fantasy youth literature. After geo-parsing my corpus, coding each of those geographic instances and adding latitudes and longitudes, I assembled each novel into its own geographic layer. Then, I geo-parsed out the most used landmarks and coded for those landmarks based on each novel. This was then made into its own GIS layer and geographically analysed. The best way to present this kind of research is to create a series of heat maps. In the first heat map, the landmarks with a greater number of instances throughout the corpus are shown with darker shading and larger areas. In the second, the darker the shading, the more novels incorporate that particular landmark. Lastly, the third map uses circles where the greater the circle's diameter, the more instances of that landmark occur within the corpus. Each of these maps shows different underlying patterns when it concerns landmarks

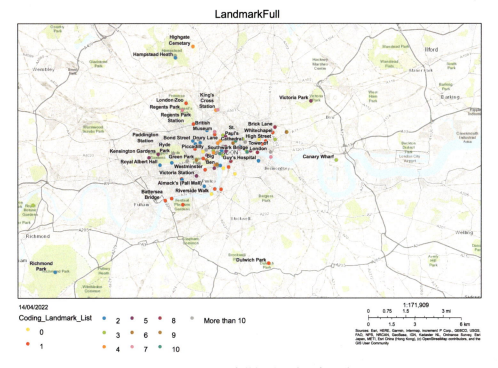

FIGURE 11.1 Map of all landmarks of London.

within fantasy youth literature set in London. Studying these maps allows me to draw a number of observations. While the dot map above (Figure 11.1) suggests that these places are spread out, the darker shading on the density map below (Figure 11.2) indicates a different underlying pattern. Instead of being more or less evenly distributed through-out London, the geography of the corpus of fantasy youth literature is shown here to be marked by areas of greater and lesser density, with clusters of references forming specific localities. These include the areas near Buckingham Palace, the Houses of Parliament and Big Ben, the area around St. Paul's Cathedral, Hyde Park and areas to the east of this, including the Tower of London, and to a lesser extent, Embankment. Interestingly, these are precisely the landmarks visited by Katie and the Queen (in pursuit of her hat) in each of their disparate picturebooks.

That these localities are the ones most frequently mentioned in this London-based cor-pus stand to reason. Each, after all, figures prominently enough in the literary and cultural history of London to remain integral to the writers' conception of literary London within fantasy youth literature. Yet, one must be mindful that these heat maps in particular need to be interpreted with care. Specifically, these London based landmark heat maps depict a generalisation of the pattern displayed in a later dot map, and that, in certain cases, don't represent certain novels which avoided landmarks altogether. For instance, *The Woven Path* by Robin Jarvis had zero landmarks within its geographic information, even though it too is set in London.

Once the corpus has been geo-parsed and coded it can then be assembled in a GIS layer; one can then begin to perform a geographical text analysis and assess the spatial dimensions

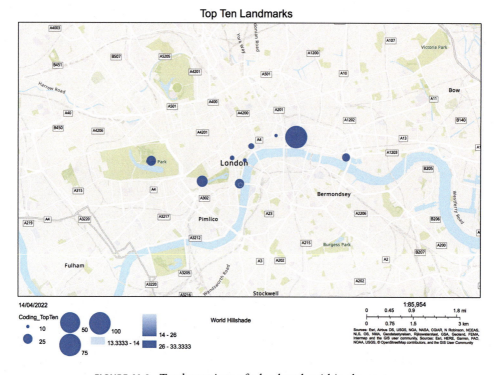

FIGURE 11.2 Total mentions of a landmark within the corpus.

of the geography that the fantastical corpus contains. The most elementary way to do this is by creating a dot map in which the referenced place names are converted into geographical dots on the map interface of the GIS. As shown in Figure 11.1, dot maps are an easy way of representing geo-referenced data; however, they are made even more fascinating when trajectories and the order of points of those dots are added.

This is, in large part, because these trajectories show the way in which protagonists can either transgress or adhere to the socio-economic boundaries of their class. When looking specifically at landmarks, though, dot maps are inadequate as a means of representing frequency because, when displaying GIS point data, GIS applications superimpose multiple placemarks in the same location (see Fotheringham et al.).[11] Consequently, a data set may contain dozens of references to a particular landmark and only one reference to a rather obscure street, but on a dot map, these places will appear in exactly the same way. An additional problem with dot maps—and one of particular relevance to this study—is that they tend to imply a lack of movement that may be misleading in terms of trajectories of protagonists.

Unlike work done by other scholars like Gregory and Donaldson (Gregory and Donaldson, 2017) or Heuser et al. (Heuser, Moretti and Steiner, 2016), in which place names do not correspond to a single, precise location, in this research place names very much correspond to single, specific, precise and mappable landmarks. To this end, consider Figure 11.2, which displays the distribution and density of the places that are referenced in the corpus and which are located at specific points in London. While the dot map suggests the places frequented by protagonists are spread around London, the darker shading and larger circles on the landmark-based map (Figure 11.2) suggest a different underlying pattern. Instead of being more or less evenly distributed, the geography of the corpus is shown here to be marked by areas of greater or lesser wealth, with clusters of references forming at specific landmarks. The data points to a specific grouping of landmarks occurring more frequently than others. And this figure allows us to see very clearly that the texts within the corpus contain a disproportionate number of references to places within specific parts of London. For example, St. Paul's Cathedral occurs in 28% of all novels and often occurs more than once in a novel. Concomitantly, it also indicates the existence of what Gregory and Donaldson refer to as 'geographies of absence: areas which are either mentioned infrequently […] or which are ignored altogether' (Gregory and Donaldson, 2017, p. 73). If we are willing to use the frequency of landmarks within the corpus as an index for the amount of interest and attention received by those landmarks, these observations mean that fantasy youth literature pays the most attention to a handful of landmarks and pays far less attention, one would go so far as to say neglects, others. The landmarks receiving the most attention are also the ones that feature in the picturebooks mentioned above.

The top ten London landmarks

Viewing Figure 11.2 gives us the sense of the most used landmarks mentioned in the corpus. It helps us to determine the number of times these landmarks are mentioned and thus, by extension, the amount of attention given to each. This, in turn, prompts investigation into why certain landmarks receive more attention than others and how these particularly popular landmarks are used throughout the various novels. Figure 11.3 shows the ten most used

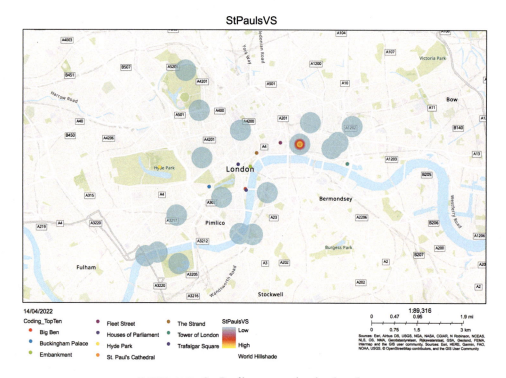

FIGURE 11.3 St. Paul's versus other landmarks.

landmarks within the corpus and each circle gets larger and darker the more that particular landmark is used.

In the first instance, simply counting and comparing the number of landmark references that occur in each novel indicates a key difference between a landmark-based approach versus a trajectory-based approach. There are 518 landmark references in total, but only 15 make up a majority of the landmark references in the corpus, which suggests that the latter are more prominent locations in the corpus than the former.

This, in itself, may be unsurprising, given that Big Ben, St Paul's Cathedral, Hyde Park and Buckingham Palace are some of London's most iconic landmarks. However, the distinction between the top 15 landmarks and the rest of the landmark list is not as great as one might expect, given that 59 of the 64 novels mention landmarks.

Prior to the COVID-19 pandemic, more tourists flocked to The British Museum than any other landmark in London, thus one might fairly expect The British Museum to be mentioned even more frequently than it is (a total of seven times).

All such inferences must be tentative, given the limited nature and scope of the corpus itself, but these findings indicate that although fewer writers discuss the East of London, those who do seem to mention the landmarks that comprise it fairly frequently. For example, *Midnight Twins* uses St. Paul's Cathedral as a base of operations and therefore that location is mentioned over 20 times (Holly Race, 2020). However, it goes by its secondary name 'Tintagel' rather than by its actual name 'St. Paul's Cathedral' in the majority of those instances. The protagonist makes it clear that the two are interchangeable when she describes St. Paul's Cathedral concurrently with Tintagel:

> We round the corner, and all sense of direction leaves me. We should be passing St. Paul's Cathedral, but all I can see is a deep moat brimming with murky water and a wooden wall beyond. 'Tintangel' Andraste says, pointing above the wall. I was wrong. There, just as it should be, is St. Paul's.
>
> *(Holly Race, p. 51, 2020)*

The corpus as a whole also corroborates this finding, as it reveals that 15 works account for most of the references to the area around Westminster.[2] By contrast, only one novel in the corpus, Charlie N. Holmberg's *The Paper Magician* (2014), references Dulwich Park and the area around it to the South of London. It can be argued that the significance of the number of references per novel may be greatly influenced by the length of the text in question. Here, however, a statistical analysis of the number of times a landmark appears in each novel is compared to the corpus as a whole (see Figure 11.2). The West End, on one hand, has 56 works with over 518 landmark instances to account for a large part of those novels' place names; the East End, on the other hand, only accounts for a small part of those novels' place names. Although East End is mentioned less frequently in the corpus overall, those novels that do mention it go into more detail about the landmarks that are a part of it.

Magic and landmarks

In maps that incorporate fantasy, other kinds of divisions occur as well. Two areas, on either side of a landmark, for example, may have completely different ways of negotiating time and space as well as magic. In *The Encyclopaedia of Fantasy*, John Clute defines a threshold as a 'gradient between two places or states of being' (Clute, 1999c, p. 945). Clute continues by listing four functions of physical thresholds which are relevant to our magical interpretations of London-based landmarks. First, thresholds 'normally form the spines of borderlands demarcating regions which borderlands join together' (Clute, 1999c, p. 945). Landmarks of London act as such borderlands as they too serve as a 'marker, resting place or toll-gate between two differing kinds of reality' (Clute, 1999a, p. 128). The second purpose of a threshold is to 'announce the presence, or intrusion, of a crosshatch', a place in which 'two or more worlds may simultaneously inhabit the same territory' (Clute, 1999b, p. 237). London's landmarks tend to act as these cross-hatches and demarcate the veil which allows for passage between those worlds. Third, thresholds 'constitute the perimeter of polders' (Clute, 1999c, p. 945). His last definition of a threshold is the most confusing as 'for those with peculiar talents, they may comprise a map of the land' (Clute, 1999c). Rather, the physical maps created in this work examine thresholds between the magical worlds and the actual world of London. Thresholds serve as a way in which we orient ourselves within London. These thresholds are particularly important to the role of magic within these narratives. Each landmark can serve as a threshold, and the more often the landmark is used, the more likely it is to be used as a threshold. This use speaks to the power of these particular buildings to elicit this kind of magical response—a response specific to the landmark itself, not the general location. Furthermore, a landmark that has acquired layers of association, not least via literature and picturebooks in particular, is a testament to its standing as a 'landmark'.

St. Paul's cathedral versus others

A comparison between the most used landmarks and those used less frequently show differences in how landmarks are used as various thresholds.

St. Paul's Cathedral is one of London's most iconic locations and serves as a very clear reminder that though a novel may include magic, portals or fantastic events, it is still very much set in London. Contrasting St. Paul's Cathedral, other landmarks and the rest of the places named in the corpus reveals that the latter are located in markedly different parts of London and as a result, have markedly different associations. Whereas the wider selection includes bridges, parks and other lower-lying landmarks, St Paul's Cathedral rises above the city of London and is visible throughout the central London area. St. Paul's Cathedral occurs not only as a place within the geographic instances of these novels, but also is a way in which characters often orient themselves in the city. For example, in *The Time Travellers*, the characters are 'walking [one evening] through the maze of narrow streets beyond St. Paul's Cathedral, they looked up [at St. Paul's], trying to get their bearings' (p. 374). While today St. Paul's Cathedral is dwarfed by other modern buildings, it remained the tallest building in London until 1963. St. Paul's Cathedral is also protected by a planning law which preserves the vista around the building itself (see *Protected views and tall buildings*, 2021). Furthermore, originally Wren designed the city of London with St Paul's Cathedral as its focal point. Fantasy novels harken to times past where St. Paul's Cathedral was the centre, the focal point and the tallest building in the city. Fantasy novels for young people in effect erase modern landmarks such as The Gherkin, the London Eye and the Shard and keep the concept of older London as somehow 'actual' London. There are many instances where characters use St. Paul's Cathedral as a way to guide themselves through the city.

This is particularly significant because it calls to mind the fact that a very visible physical landmark is often used as a secret magical threshold. A constant reminder to those 'in the know' that the magical version of London awaits.

Comparing descriptions of different landmarks

Establishing the relative amount of attention paid to historical landmarks within London is one thing, exploring *how* they are portrayed is another. Modern buildings rarely achieve the label 'landmark' as they are often historical by definition, especially in children's fantasy literature. If a modern building does become a landmark, 'modern' itself becomes history—which might indeed be argued where modernism is concerned. In reviewing Heuser et al.'s maps of geographic investment with London places in fiction, it is immediately visible that fictional London 'is remarkably concentrated' (Heuser et al., 2016, p. 30). While Heuser et al.'s research focuses on realist fiction published between 1,700 and 1,900, its findings corroborate those found in fantasy youth literature published in the last 20 years. Heuser et al.'s maps show 'a deep-rooted "gravity centre" in fictional investment centred on the point at which the City and the West End meet' (Heuser et al., 2016, p. 30). Regardless of its publication date, London-based fantasy youth literature continues to live in the past. London fantasy fictions alter its geography by compressing and centring London in the West of the city (Heuser et al., 2016). Fantasy youth literature's attention continues to distort the map of London, one whose geography is rarely impacted by the modern geography of London while still existing within a world of cell phones and computers.

To what extent does fantasy fiction aimed at children change geographically? Should we expect London's fictional geography to incorporate only 'the City' of London? The City is not only the centre of London but also the way in which London is represented across a number of other media, including movies and television. While the ambitions of this research involve resolving what Heuser et al., refer to as 'a kind of literary-historical "stuckness"' (Heuser et al., 2016, p. 30), fantasy youth literature disappointingly supports rather than disrupts this 'stuckness'. Fantasy fiction for young readers remains 'stuck' in London's past.

This is where close reading and collocation analysis become relevant. Collocation analysis is, as Gregory and Donaldson explain, 'a standard method within corpus linguistics for identifying words that appear unusually frequently or in close proximity to—that is to say, collocate with—one another' (Gregory and Donaldson, 2017, p. 76). If text mining was applied to this project, one would expect a t-score to be found indicating how often each word occurs near the search term in relation to the number of times it appears in the corpus as a whole.[3] The evaluation of a t-score alongside a collocation analysis, however, is not available here due to the corpus' recent publication dates, which means there are no text files of these novels available. Barring the t-score analysis, a collocation analysis on the basis of proximity within the quotes undertaken in the coding of each of the novels still proves fruitful. Performing this kind of collocation analysis necessitates a certain number of word 'tokens' be selected on either side of the landmark search term. Here, I have adopted a ten-token word bandwidth as a measure of proximity. In this case, each use of a landmark was recorded in the coding analysis under 'Quote' and the quotes containing the same landmarks were then compared side by side.

In order to determine the kind of language used to describe landmarks within London, I recorded whether the collocates implied positive or negative connotations (Table 11.1).

A range of aesthetic terms such as glowing, glowering, dreaded, enormous, loomed and bulk were used for these landmarks. For both St. Paul's Cathedral and Big Ben, the collocates comprise of mainly words indicative of scale, size and physical appearance such as towering, looming, bulk, above and floated. Intriguingly, the distinction between positive

TABLE 11.1 Landmarks positive and negative connotations

Landmark	Positive Connotation	Negative Connotation
Big Ben	Moon-round clock, rang, spire, chimed, clockface, glow	Towering, loomed, tolled, boomed, enormous, sentinel, base of, above, wide watchful eye, loudly struck
St. Paul's Cathedral	Dome, famous, pride, floated, hurried, sightseeing, unharmed dome, stronger for seeing it	Bulbous, hanging above, twitchy, loomed, bulk, looked up, rose into view
Hyde Park	Stroll, inside, rolls out, green expanse, walks, lovely green, verdure	Cloud, tree-shrouded, without her mama
Buckingham Palace	Invitation, poshest, Queen Victoria, like a wedding cake, set off, giant white cake, magnificent	The royal guards, summons, enormous, grand, sighted, dreaded, silent
Tower of London	Zoomed past, wandering	Down, the tower, glowering dark mass of a thundercloud, held, Traitor's gate, famous

and negative connotations of the collocated words for both of these landmarks differed from novel to novel. Some characters like Pip from *The Umbrella Mouse* see Big Ben and St. Paul's Cathedral rather differently (Fargher, 2019). Pip doesn't have much of a reaction to seeing Big Ben for the first time, 'As its bells tolled eight o'clock, she saw Big Ben for the first time' (Fargher, 2019, p. 101), which she hears before she sees it and the description of Big Ben stops there. However, St. Paul's Cathedral reassures her after a bomb has fallen on the shop that was her home: 'The great unharmed dome of St. Paul's Cathedral passed by and at once she felt stronger for seeing it standing tall above the ruins' (Fargher, 2019, p. 102). The use of 'unharmed' parallels Pip as she too is unharmed after a wartime bombing that kills her parents. The area around St. Paul's Cathedral is also destroyed during that raid, but St. Paul's remains. This provides Pip with a sense of safety as it becomes to her an element of London which is enduring and will remain constant. What is satisfying, by contrast, is that this confirms what might be expected: that—at the level of semantics—the era affects how the landmarks impact the protagonists. St. Paul's is reassuring; seeing it standing is a mainstay of London's geography and a way in which to navigate a scary, unfamiliar and, in these novels, newly magical city.

From the foregoing analyses, I can draw two conclusions: first that the area around the West End is described in more detail (and in more novels) than the East End; and second that in general the words most frequently associated with the West End and the East End can be seen to correspond to the physical, historical and geographical differences between the two areas of London. These findings affirm the merits of the digital mixed methods-based approach showcased in this chapter. Crucially, however, it does not exhaust this method's potential but is an initial foray into how and why it should be used for literary analysis. Collocation analysis, after all, can be used even more fruitfully when combined with t–scores, a larger corpus and text mining. Further, while collocation analysis may determine the words and connotations paired with a given landmark, it can also assist researchers in identifying the locations that collocate with any given search term. Rather than looking for the landmark, you can search for words to do with a certain emotion or a certain description. When combining GIS, connotation and collocation, moreover, researchers can also explore the distributions of those locations and their relation to one another. With this in mind, consider the following examples, which are based on the distribution of the landmarks that collocate with positive or negative connotations identified above.

Collocations with positive connotation

Table 11.1 displays the distribution of the landmarks that collocate with positive connotations within the corpus. As this map indicates, although the landmarks have both positive and negative connotations, each one is more strongly associated with one or the other set of connotations. Of the top five landmarks, most are associated with predominantly positive connotations, specifically Big Ben, St. Paul's Cathedral and Hyde Park. While Buckingham Palace's outward appearance is often seen to be ornate and beautiful (and described like a wedding cake on numerous occasions), a summons to the palace and the associated implications may turn it into a landmark that has largely negative connotations. The Tower of London, however, has an overwhelmingly negative connotation, so much so that when characters mention 'the Tower', they are almost always saying it with fear or trepidation. This pattern indicates that even though the works in this corpus occasionally describe buildings and landmarks as towering, huge or looming, the term is more often associated with landmarks within the central London area. These associations are due to the historical use of the buildings. However, the outlier to these descriptors is Hyde Park.

In her journey through London, Alexia in *Soulless* by Gail Carriger (2010) describes Hyde Park on a sunny day: 'the lovely green of Hyde Park, the bright hats and dresses of ladies walking arm in arm across the grass, the two plump dirigibles gliding sedately' (Carriger, 2010, p. 115). Similarly, *The Strange Case of the Alchemist's Daughter* shows Mary passing by Hyde Park and describing it as posh and green: 'verdure of Hyde Park to the left, the houses of Mayfair to the right' (Goss, 2017, p. 197). However, Hyde Park is distinct as its positive connotations invariably emphasise the green space and the promenades that occur in the park. Portrayals of Big Ben apply similarly positive descriptors, but they shift from 'verdure' and 'green' to 'glow' and 'chime'. When describing her walk through London, for instance, Lily mentions passing Big Ben and describes it as 'an approaching tower with moon-round clock faces embedded in each side' (*Cogheart*, p. 328). *The Lost Heir*'s Jake, for his part, makes note of Big Ben's glow but also describes it as 'a wide, watchful eye' (Foley, 2012, p. 253). In each of these cases, we find writers using the words like 'bulk', 'loom' and 'above' to describe the large landmarks like St. Paul's Cathedral and Big Ben seen from a position of lower elevation. This suggests that in the period represented by the corpus, the sense of awestruck wonder of these landmarks is constant and implies the appearance of a human construction towering over the protagonist. This impression is further supported by the other landmarks that make up the most used landmarks in the corpus. The Tower of London, Big Ben, St. Paul's Cathedral and Buckingham Palace are all well-known buildings, whereas Hyde Park is a very large and green space within a very bustling city. Thus, while at first it appears to be the only notable exception to this trend of using significant constructions as landmarks, it may be seen to fit when we reflect that the Park is a constructed green space.

Conclusion

What do we gain from digitally mapping the landmarks of fantasy youth literature set in London? Spatially, this research corroborates the findings of Heuser et al. and suggests that fantasy youth literature set in London suffers from spatial conservatism. However, this spatial stuckness harbours a hidden fantastical purpose. The landmarks of London act as portals and thresholds between the real and the fantastical. These public landmarks remain unchanging and it is just this stuckness which allows them to be used as liminal transition spaces over and over again.

The simplicity and precision of these very visible magical thresholds of London ultimately belies the further possibilities of digital research methods. Although these landmarks are occasionally represented as ways in which landmarks serve as doorways to magical versions of London, representations of such thresholds, when they occur, are ones which are tied to the places in London which stay constant. This speaks to the need of fantasy children's literature to stay stuck in the past, but also shows that narrative setting and specific landmarks in particular play a key role in London's fictional geography for children. Crucially, after the inception of Google Maps in 2005, geographic specificity and investment has increased in fantastical novels set in London, hinting that authors and readers alike make use of new digital tools to navigate around settings in books. Statistical and digital methods have allowed me to pinpoint which London-based landmarks occur most frequently in my corpus. Equally, reading-based methods have allowed me to do more than just digitally map these landmarks. By annotating for setting as well as threshold, I produced maps that deepen and qualify our understanding of the ways London is consciously used by authors of children's fantasy fiction. One aspect to emerge is that only a small number of buildings are used as magical landmarks in the fantasy books and that these are often the same as those that feature in the picturebooks for younger children. Despite the fact that height proved to be a factor in making a building a candidate for becoming a magical landmark, none of the buildings used as such in these books is modern. This again speaks to the need to stay stuck in the past and perhaps suggests that even in 2021, the modern simply is not magical.

Notes

1 Following the success of the *Harry Potter* books, this fictional platform now has a physical position within King's Cross station which fans of the series visit frequently.
2 Works exemplifying this point are—*A Handful of Magic* by Stephen Elboz (2001), *Bewitching Season* by Marissa Doyle (2008), *The Whizz Pop Chocolate Shop* by Kate Saunders (2012), *The Lazarus Machine* by Paul Crilley (2012), *The Lost Heir* by E.G. Foley (2012), *The Peculiars* by Kieran Larwood (2012), *Dream A Little Dream* by Kristin Gier (2015), *Flights, Chimes and Mysterious Times* by Emma Trevayne (2015), *Cogheart* by Peter Bunzl (2016), *A Shadow Bright and Burning* by Jessica Cluess (2017), *The Morphant* by Cornelius Fuel (2017), *The City of Secret Rivers* by J.S. Weinstein (2018), *The Beast of Buckingham Palace* by David Walliams (2019), *The Midnight Hour* by Benjamin Read and Laura Trinder (2020), *Midnight's Twins* by Holly Race (2020).
3 For more on text mining, see Barnbrook, Mason and Krishnamurthy (2013).

References

Antony, S. (2014). *The Queen's Hat*. London: Hodder's Children's Books.
Barnbrook, G., Mason, O. and Krishnamurthy, R. (2013). *Collocation: Applications and Implications*. London: Palgrave Macmillan.
Bavidge, J. (2006). Spatial Stories: Representing Children's Geographies, *Children's Geographies*, 4(3), pp. 319–330. doi:10.1080/14733280601005682
Blaut, J.M. et al. (2003). Mapping as a Cultural and Cognitive Universal, *Annals of the Association of American Geographers*, 93(1), pp. 165–185. doi:10.1111/1467–8306.93111.
Bradbury, M. (1996). *The Atlas of Literature*. London: De Agostini Editions.
Bunzl, P. (2016). *Cogheart*. London: Usborne Books.
Bushell, S. et al. (2018). *Geospatial Innovation: A Deep Map of the Lake District*. Available at: http://wp.lancs.ac.uk/lakesdeepmap/ (Accessed: November 8, 2021).
Carriger, G. (2010). *Soulless*. Chatham: Orbit Books.
Clare, C. (2010). *Clockwork Angel*. London: Walker.
Cluess, J. (2017). *A Shadow Bright and Burning* London: Random House.
Clute, J. (1999a). Borderlands, *The Encyclopaedia of Fantasy*. Edited by J. Clute and J. Grant. New York: St. Martin's Griffin.
——— (1999b). Crosshatch, *The Encyclopaedia of Fantasy*. New York: St. Martin's Griffin.
——— (1999c). Thresholds, *The Encyclopaedia of Fantasy*. Edited by J. Clute and J. Grant. New York: St Martin's Griffin.

Crilley, P. (2012). *The Lazarus Machine* Hoboken, NJ: Pyr Books.

Downs, D. and Stea, R. (1977). *Maps in Minds: Reflections on Cognitive Mapping*. Ann Arbor: Harper and Row.

Doyle, M. (2008). *Bewitching Season*. New York: Henry Holt.

Ekman, S. (2013). *Here Be Dragons: Exploring Fantasy Maps and Settings*. Middletown: Wesleyan University Press.

Elboz, S. (2001). *A Handful of Magic*. Oxford: Oxford University Press.

Fargher, A. (2019). *The Umbrella Mouse*. London: Macmillan's Children's Books.

Foley, E. G. (2012). *The Lost Heir*. Muse, PA: Gaelen Foley.

Fuel, C. (2017). *The Morphant*. Market Harborough: Matador.

Fonstad, K. W. (1991). *The Atlas of Middle-Earth*. Revised. Boston: Houghton Mifflin.

Gier, K. (2015). *Dream A Little Dream*. New York City: Henry Holt & Company.

Goga, N. and Kümmerling-Meibauer, B. (eds) (2017). *Maps and Mapping in Children's Literature*. Amsterdam; Philadelphia: John Benjamin Publishing Company.

Goss, T. (2017). *The Strange Case of the Alchemist's Daughter*. New York: Saga Press.

Gregory, I. and Donaldson, C. (2017). Geographical Text Analysis, in Cooper, D., Donaldson, C., and Murrieta-Flores, P. (eds), *Literary Mapping in the Digital Age*. London: Routledge, pp. 67–87.

Heuser, R. et al. (2016). Mapping the Emotions of London in Fiction, 1700–1900: A Crowdsourcing Experiment, in Cooper, D., Donaldson, C., and Murrieta-Flores, P. (eds), *Literary Mapping in the Digital Age*. Oxfordshire: Routledge, pp. 25–46.

Heuser, R., Moretti, F. and Steiner, E. (2016). *Emotions of London*, Stanford: Stanford Literary Lab: Pamphlet 13.

Jarvis, R. (2002). *The Woven Path*. Glasgow and London: Harper Collins.

Larwood, K. (2012). *The Peculiars*. Frome: Chicken House.

Mayhew, J. (2014). *Katie in London*. London: Orchard Books.

McLeod, M. (2022). *Finding the Fantastic: Digitally Mapping London in Fantasy Youth Literature* (unpublished doctoral dissertation). Cambridge: University of Cambridge.

Moretti, F. (2015). *Atlas of the European Novel*. London; New York: Verso.

Piatti, B. (2016). Mapping Fiction: The Theories, Tools and Potentials, in Cooper, D., Donaldson, C., and Murrieta-Flores, P. (eds), *Literary Mapping in the Digital Age*. Oxford: Routledge, pp. 88–101.

Piatti, B. and Hurni, L. (2009). Mapping the Ontologically Unreal: Counterfactual Spaces in Literature and Cartography, *The Cartographic Journal*, 46(4), pp. 333–342.

Piatti, B. and Hurni, L. (2011). Editorial: Cartographies of Fictional Worlds, *The Cartographic Journal*, 48(4), pp. 218–223.

Protected views and tall buildings (2021). *City of London*. Available at: https://www.cityoflondon.gov.uk/services/planning/planning-policy/protected-views-and-tall-buildings (Accessed: December 11, 2021).

Race, H. (2020). *Midnight's Twins*. Stockholm: Hot Key Books.

Read, B. and Trinder, L. (2020). *The Midnight Hour*. Frome: Chicken House.

Rogers, A., Castree, N. and Kithcin, R. (2013) landmark, *A Dictionary of Human Geography*. Oxford: Oxford University Press, Oxford Reference. Date Accessed 23 Feb. 2022 <https://www.oxfordreference.com/view/10.1093/acref/9780199599868.001.0001/acref-9780199599868-e-1032>.

Ryan, M. -L. (2014). *Space, The Living Handbook of Narratology*. http://lhn.sub.uni-hamburg.de/index.php/Space.html

Saunders, K. (2012). *The Whizz Pop Chocolate Shop*. London: Marion Lloyd.

Sharp, W. (1904). *Literary Geography*. London: Pall Mall.

Soja, E. (1996). *Thirdspace: Journeys to Los Angeles and Other Real-and-Imagined Places*. Oxford: Blackwell Publishers.

Trevayne, E. (2015). *Flights, Chimes and Mysterious Times*. London: Simon & Schuster.

Travers, P. L. (2008). *Mary Poppins*. New. London: HarperCollins Children's Books.

Walliams, D. (2019). *The Beast of Buckingham Palace*. London: HarperCollins.

Weinstein, J.S. (2018). *The City of Secret Rivers*. London: Walker Books.

Wilkens, M. (2013). The Geographic Imagination of Civil War-Era American Fiction, *American Literary History*, 25(4), pp. 803–840. doi:10.1093/alh/ajt045.

Yuan, M. (2010). Mapping Text, in Bodenhamer, J., Corrigan, J., and Harris, T. M. (eds), *The Spatial Humanities: GIS and the Future of Humanities Scholarship*. Indiana University Press, pp. 109–undefined.

12

ORDINARY CITYSCAPES AND ARCHITECTURE IN JÖRG MÜLLER'S PICTUREBOOK OEUVRE

Jörg Meibauer

Introduction

In the picturebook oeuvre of Jörg Müller, the depiction of cityscapes and architecture plays an important role. His pictures often contain ideological criticism, that is, criticism that is directed against the forces of modernity that ruin nature and make cities unpleasant places to inhabit. However, Jörg Müller avoids depicting real cities. Instead, he constructs ordinary cities and architecture on the basis of photographic documentation, leaving the judgement of what is shown to the viewer.

By the end of the 1960s, many societies faced social, cultural, and aesthetic upheavals that can only be briefly touched upon here: the international youth revolt with its antiauthoritarian attitude, the pacifist fight against the Vietnam war, the huge influence of Pop Culture, and the dominance of capitalism were sources of concern. A seminal idea was that intellectuals and artists should engage in ideological criticism, understood as the permanent and systematic effort to unveil practices leading to the oppression and exploitation of people. For instance, Western liberal democracies may only appear as tolerant, while in reality, this tolerance turns out to be repressive under a critical lens.

The dynamic development of Western post-war societies led to split attitudes. On the one hand, revolutionary ideas gained influence due to a revival of Marxism in its various shades. On the other hand, a feeling of nostalgia for the traditional, for what has gone by, was widely endorsed and part of the zeitgeist (Boym, 2001). As I will show in this article, both ideological criticism and nostalgia are concepts that play a major role in the work of Swiss picturebook artist Jörg Müller and his co-author Jörg Steiner.

In particular, my aim is to show how Müller portrays cityscapes and architecture as artefacts mirroring rapid social and cultural change. These changes may lead to widespread experiences of loss (e.g. the loss of *Heimat*) but also to political engagement and activism. While occasionally related to real cities (for instance, Berne in *Der Mann vom Bärengraben* (The Man from the Bärengraben, 1987) or Paris in *Der standhafte Zinnsoldat* (The steadfast tin soldier, 1996), Müller's drawings aim mostly at generalised pictures of cityscapes and architecture. They are realistic on the one hand (they are not fictional) yet abstract in the sense that they do not identify specific cities and buildings. In general, Müller aims to

DOI: 10.4324/9781003131755-16

depict ordinary, contemporary cities, with an eye to their past and their possible future. *Ordinariness* is an aesthetic concept (Waller, 2020) that best reflects Müller's critical stance on contemporary cityscapes and architecture.

The concept of ordinariness is twofold, since we can distinguish between formal and functional aspects of ordinariness. Formal ordinariness of a city means its structure, constituted by a network of buildings connected by streets. Often, there is a city centre and there is a periphery (suburbs). Typically, there is no agriculture in the city, just as there are no highways in the historical city centre. Functional ordinariness means that the city serves certain purposes, namely to facilitate the living and working of their inhabitants. This functionality, which also includes aesthetic pleasure, may be disrupted. For instance, when there is a lack of a playground for children or a lack of transport systems, a city is functionally disturbed. Also, a mixture of too many architectural styles may contribute to aesthetic discomfort.

I will argue that Jörg Müller's depiction of cityscapes points to the disruption of functional ordinariness. He does this through documentation but, and this is particularly important for his aesthetic programme, he does not just represent the state of the cityscapes but rather constructs them. So the critical construction of ordinariness of cityscapes and buildings is what we find in his artwork.

This chapter ties in with two strands of recent research: first the representation of the city, architecture, and building in picturebooks, be it a factual city like Milan (Campagnaro, 2017) or Berlin (Meibauer, 2021), fictional architecture and housing (Hayward and Schmiedeknecht, 2019), or recent non-fiction on architecture in general (Campagnaro, 2021); second, the contribution of picturebooks to the visual culture, that is, to the particular distribution of ideologies via literature, film, theatre, music, advertising, etc. at a given historical period. Since architecture is part of this culture, the representation of architecture in children's literature is a powerful means to shape children's 'image of the city' (Lynch, 1960).

My primary aim is not the interpretation of these picturebooks but the interpretation of the urban and architectural images as being related to the respective stories. The following topics will be dealt with in turn: the change of the city, the ordinary cityscape, the architecture of production sites, and finally, the contrast between European and African ordinariness of cityscapes and architecture.

The change of the city

It is well known that not only the bombings of cities in World War II led to the change of cityscapes but also the demolition of buildings in the interest of developers and investors. The loss of historic architectural fabric by the rapid change of the cityscape is the topic of *Hier fällt ein Haus, dort steht ein Kran und ewig droht der Baggerzahn oder Die Veränderung der Stadt* [*Here a house falls, there a crane stands and the digger's tooth is eternally threatening or The change of the city*, 1976, henceforth cited as *Hier fällt ein Haus*] by Jörg Müller. This is the sequel to *Alle Jahre wieder saust der Presslufthammer nieder oder die Veränderung der Landschaft* [*Every year the jackhammer rushes down or The change of the landscape*, 1973; henceforth cited as *Alle Jahre wieder*] that deals with landscape change. The book has a clear ideological and pedagogical mission, since it warns children and young adults who have not yet experienced such a rapid change of their surroundings not to become guilty like the ones who push this change for egotistic reasons. The exact comparison of the ongoing changes is meant to help the readers to become vigilant against such changes.

FIGURE 12.1 *Hier fällt ein Haus, dort steht ein Kran und ewig droht der Baggerzahn oder Die Veränderung der Stadt* (1976). Tableau 8, January 7, 1976, showing the final state of the change. Reprinted with permission by Fischer Kinder- und Jugendbuchverlag.

The change of a fictional city is depicted in eight large format, folded tableaus contained in a folder that correspond to temporal states between May 6, 1953, and January 7, 1976; the seven days of the week and the four seasons occur in the tableaux (Sauer, 2007, p. 22). Over the span of roughly two decades, the demolition of old buildings, the erection of new buildings, and the construction of roads and a metro cause the city to change so fundamentally that a comparison between the first and the last tableau is likely to trigger a feeling of shock in the reader for failing to recognise the original city (Figure 12.1). Such a shock might end up in a feeling of mourning about the lost surroundings and anger about the impossibility of stopping this modern development.

Indeed, anger is expressed in the preface to *Hier fällt ein Haus* by Jörg Müller and his collaborator Gerd Ledergerber. Against the backdrop of the tremendous success of *Alle Jahre wieder*, the authors insist that they do not want to be appropriated by social romanticists, monument protection authorities, and nostalgics. Nevertheless, despite the hope they place in the children and young adults at whom they have addressed their work over the course of two years, they remain furious at administrative bodies, authorities, and private developers.

Basically, the authors strive to protect the residents' habitat (*Lebensraum*). By this, they do not understand a space that organises processes like going to work, going shopping, and sleeping, but a space that enables living together, a space that is useful as well as aesthetically appealing. It is of prime importance that the city and its change is not constituted by profit-orientated action in the first place. The authors relate to Switzerland, which benefits from its neutrality in World War II, yet assume the transferability of their findings to other European cities. Thus, the impact of their work has also to do with the common stereotype of Switzerland as an intact and even idyllic country.

Jörg Müller's creative method was quasi-empirical, as he reports in an interview given to Inge Sauer in 2007 (Sauer, 2007, pp. 37–42). The drawings for the book were created on the basis of a huge photo documentation of cityscapes in Frankfurt, Hanover, Zurich, and Biel. More than 800 diapositives were made and completed with information from archives, journals, yearbooks, and photo books. The overarching goal was to construct a 'gerafft-vielseitig' [condensed and versatile] picture of a typical ordinary city (Sauer, 2007, Preface). According to Müller, using drawings is less polemical than using photographs, as it allows for the integration of narrative details like in wimmelbooks (Rémi, 2018), in order to facilitate children's identification with the city's inhabitants.

In the aforementioned interview, Müller explains that the slides were projected onto the drawing via a system of mirrors. This allowed for the repeated projection of photos up to the point where the arrangement was aesthetically satisfying. Beyond this, the drawing which had a length of 300 cm was condensed to a length of 90 cm. Apart from its progressive message, it was this unusual length that made the use of these tableaux as an element of interior design attractive. In *Der standhafte Zinnsoldat*, we find an allusion to this practice in a picture showing a tableau from *Alle Jahre wieder* as a wall decoration.

How is the change of the city shown developing over time? Indicators of change are an increasing number of colour surfaces as well as different posters, logos, and brand names which serve as indices of time. Another important indicator of change are different vehicle types. The change in architecture is depicted in accordance with authentic changes in materials, for example, brick houses versus houses made of modern materials like concrete, steel, and glass, and styles, for example, decoration of houses built during the Gründerzeit versus plain 'functional' modern facades. It is by no means suggested though that modern techniques of building will automatically lead to an austere habitat.

In order to show vistas into the streets, squares, and courtyards, Müller moved the suggested vanishing points for every object sideways. However, this did not work for the central square because it was intended to open up. Therefore, we have an optical illusion here, and Müller named the square M.-C.-Escher-Platz, honouring the work of Maurits Cornelis Escher (1898–1972), who is famous for his impossible perspectives.

In sum, then, it seems that the impression of a dense description of the changing ordinary city is due to the use of a special method, that is, the reduction of the documentary effects of photographs by drawings, leading to a reduction of complexity and pictorial information. This method leads also to the effect of double recognisability. First, the viewer will recognise the changing city despite the depicted changes. The effect is particularly striking when the first tableau is compared to the last tableau. Second, the viewer will notice similar changes in their recognition of real cities in their surroundings. It is possible to say upon visiting a city as a tourist, 'This is like in Jörg Müller's drawings'. Thus, Müller's work is an important contribution to the goal of making children (and adults) more aware of these rapid changes that seem to be steered by an 'invisible hand'.

The architecture of the ordinary city

In contrast to the two portfolios dealing with the change of the land- and cityscapes, *Was wollt ihr machen, wenn der Schwarze Mann kommt?* [What will you do when the bogeyman comes?, 1998] and *Aufstand der Tiere oder Die neuen Stadtmusikanten* [Revolt of the animals or the new town musicians, 1989] are narrative, challenging picturebooks that do not have the city and architecture as a central topic. Yet, as I will show in this section, both narratives rely heavily on the depiction of an urban background showing cityscapes with streets, squares, and buildings.

Was wollt ihr machen, wenn der Schwarze Mann kommt? tells a story of rumours spreading in a small city about a mysterious 'black man' who upsets the inhabitants. In the eponymous, well-known children's game, upon hearing the question, children have to run away as fast as possible. In Müller's version, the answer is 'ausfliegen' [fly away]. The narration is unreliable because the readers cannot decide whether the black man is real in the fiction (and the depiction) or whether his existence is only a product of the inhabitants' fantasies. However, what is important are the bad consequences resulting from this growing fear, since the community and the state react with a massive programme of surveillance. The book's lack of commercial success is no doubt also due to its sinister topic.

The urban images in *Was wollt ihr machen, wenn der Schwarze Mann kommt?* are reminiscent of the Swiss city Biel/Bienne, although the cathedral and the monument next to it are by no means exact copies of the originals. What is more remarkable is the school of the children playing the game and the surrounding streets (Figure 12.2). The school is a concrete building, with a continuous band of windows extending across its entire width. By placing large brutalist flower boxes in the middle of the façade, situated over the strip of windows, the artist chooses an

FIGURE 12.2 *Was wollt ihr machen, wenn der Schwarze Mann kommt?* (1998). The schoolyard with the playing kids is situated in a street. In the background, two large residential buildings can be seen. On the right side, the façade of the school is shown. Reprinted with permission by Fischer Kinder- und Jugendbuchverlag.

FIGURE 12.3 *Aufstand der Tiere oder Die neuen Stadtmusikanten* (1989). The high-rise office building in which the Stadtmusikanten intrude. Reprinted with permission by Fischer Kinder- und Jugendbuchverlag.

architectural device that symbolises the contrast between functional architecture and nature. The graffiti on the dirty wall ending at the school's entrance contribute to the overall impression of an ordinary, cheap, and shabby school in the suburb. The penultimate double spread shows moreover that the school is located in a dingy quarter, with an abandoned factory building and a Turkish snack stall just opposite. Along the wall of this building, which is again decorated by graffiti, a man with a suitcase is walking towards the city centre. Possibly, it is the same old man who is seen in many pictures, reading the newspaper, feeding birds, being hunted by the police, talked about at the university, and filmed by surveillance cameras. When the fear of the inhabitants vanishes like a nightmare, the children who fabricated the stories about the black man go back to boring normality and only dream of 'flying away'.

The conventional small city, with its inhabitants being concerned about security, has ordinary architecture with its typical mixture of the historical city centre, shopping streets with an unpleasant composition of architectural styles, and banal suburbs. In *Aufstand der Tiere oder Die neuen Stadtmusikanten*, the classical fairy tale of *Die Bremer Stadtmusikanten* [The Bremen Town Musicians] by the Brothers Grimm, is retold against the backdrop of the modern advertising and TV industry, which is the book's satirical target. The new town musicians are prominent advertising figures: eagle-owl, panda, crocodile, and penguin. As in the original tale, they want to break out of their daily routines and dream of having a band in

Disneyland. Following the original tale's plot, they want to attack the robbers whom they assume are in the huge high-rise office building overshadowing the city.

Like the building of the advertising company Miller Stein & Partner, from which the group fled, the high-rise office building with the sign *TV* above its entrance shows the unique traits of postmodern architecture, aiming at a playful reference to historic architectural styles. Directed against the International Style with its appeal to rationality and functionality, postmodernism revived ornamentation and the whimsical, a surprising re-arrangement of architectural elements. In Figure 12.3, such elements are depicted thus: (a) The central portico with its gothic window, like in a Medieval cathedral, (b) two structures reminiscent of a Greek temple flanking the portico, (c) the row of Art Nouveau lanterns rising up from dilapidated temple pillars, (d) the wild combination of industrial architecture (ventilation pipes) with the main body of the building, (e) the roof top hall in the style of an old glasshouse, and finally (f) the insertion of an impossible three dimensional structure into the façade, reminiscent of Maurits Escher's drawings.

Postmodern architecture has been widely criticised because of its anti-modern and irrational attitude, the weird combination of materials (e.g. marble and steel), the eclectic use of styles, and the expressive use of colour. In *Aufstand der Tiere oder Die neuen Stadtmusikanten*, this architecture symbolises the power and arrogance of the media industry. The Stadtmusikanten are not success-ful in their protest; they simply end up as protagonists that are corrupted by the media industry. Only Panda seems to escape; yet, the flicker on the picture on the back cover showing Panda with his guitar, wandering on the wet, big city street in the night (Figure 12.4), seems to indicate that even his escape is nothing but an illusion since it is a proper part of the media industry.

FIGURE 12.4 *Aufstand der Tiere oder Die neuen Stadtmusikanten* (1989). The flicker in the upper half of this picture indicates that Panda's flight is part of a movie about the Stadtmusikanten. Reprinted with permission by Fischer Kinder- und Jugendbuchverlag.

This is, of course, a dark comment on the power of the Media, although it is presented in a playful, satirical mode. The banality of postmodern architecture seems to correspond to the ordinary Western big city that is rapidly restructured, driven by big money and shareholders.

The architecture of production sites

In the 1970s, facing the renewal of socialist or revolutionary thinking, parts of society turned to reflecting labour and production conditions. The exploitation of workers, the senselessness of their work, and their low wages were topics that were widely discussed. Although Jörg Müller and Jörg Steiner's *Die Kanincheninsel* [The rabbit island, 1977] and *Der Bär, der ein Bär bleiben wollte* [The bear who wanted to stay a bear, 1976, after Frank Tashlin's *The Bear That Wasn't*, 1946] are stories about animals, that is, rabbits and a bear, they comment on factory conditions. Interestingly, the production plants have specific architectural attributes that underpin the moral of these stories. In *Der standhafte Zinnsoldat* [The steadfast tin soldier] by Jörg Müller, an adaption of the famous eponymous tale by Hans Christian Andersen, a factory in an African harbour city is contrasted with Parisian suburbs.

Already in *Alle Jahre wieder*, Jörg Müller was aware of the ongoing urban sprawl, especially that created by the establishment of commercial and industrial park areas on former arable land. The outcome of such a process, with its uncoordinated mixture of buildings serving different purposes, is impressively shown on the last tableau in this portfolio. In *Die Kanincheninsel*, two modern buildings are placed like foreign bodies in the landscape. One is the factory that produces rabbits and the other is an apartment building.

In the first picture (Figure 12.5), we see a small road leading to the factory. On the right-hand side, a cow is grazing behind an electric fence. The windowless factory building, decorated with a huge logo showing a rabbit, is surrounded by six silos. In the middle of the building, the glazed entrance area stands out. In the rabbit factory, rabbits are produced: the story begins by explaining that there are rabbit factories, just as there are chocolate factories and cannon factories.

Two rabbits want to escape their destiny, that is, to be fattened, killed, and eaten. They manage to leave the factory and run to the rabbit island. Sadly, the old, grey companion of the young brown rabbit feels overwhelmed by the newly gained freedom. He longs to return to the prison-like structures of the factory that guarantee regular food and apparent security. So, the friends decide to separate. Going back to the factory together, they come across an apartment building whose grey and functional appearance is similar to the factory. Maybe it is a factory for bigger animals, the old rabbit wonders. This is possible, the little rabbit answers. The critical observation is that some contemporary apartment houses resemble inhuman production plants.

Another repulsive production plant is shown in *Der Bär, der ein Bär bleiben wollte*. Following an idea by Frank Tashlin, the story is adapted ('nach- und umerzählt') by Jörg Steiner. Erroneously, a bear is taken for a worker in a production plant. While he was hibernating, the plant was constructed right over his cave. All his attempts to explain his true identity are in vain. In the autumn, he becomes tired and is unable to work like the other workers. Finally, he is fired because of his laziness. He wanders through the cold winter landscape, tries to rent a room in a motel, and finally finds another cave.

The viewer looks through a barbed wire fence at a scene in which the guard is commanding the bear (Figure 12.6). They are surrounded by the factory consisting of buildings, tanks or

Fabriken, in denen Schokolade hergestellt wird, sind Schokoladefabriken. Fabriken, in denen Kanonen gebaut werden, sind Kanonenfabriken.

Die Fabrik aber, von der hier die Rede ist, ist eine Kaninchenfabrik. Sie hat keinen Schornstein und macht nur wenig Lärm.

FIGURE 12.5 *Die Kanincheninsel* (1977). The rabbit factory, located in the rural landscape. Reprinted with permission by Fischer Kinder- und Jugendbuchverlag.

silos, a smoking chimney, pipes, and a letter (note that fences are also shown in Figures 12.1–12.3). The courtyard and the facades are clean, and no other people are on the scene. Thus, the picture reminds us of the kind of photorealistic paintings that were popular in the 1970s. Another possible influence are pictures in the tradition of *Neue Sachlichkeit* [New Objectivity].

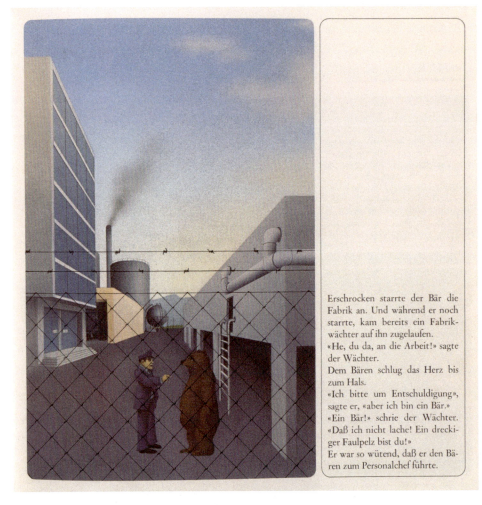

Erschrocken starrte der Bär die Fabrik an. Und während er noch starrte, kam bereits ein Fabrikwächter auf ihn zugelaufen.
«He, du da, an die Arbeit!» sagte der Wächter.
Dem Bären schlug das Herz bis zum Hals.
«Ich bitte um Entschuldigung», sagte er, «aber ich bin ein Bär.»
«Ein Bär!» schrie der Wächter. «Daß ich nicht lache! Ein dreckiger Faulpelz bist du!»
Er war so wütend, daß er den Bären zum Personalchef führte.

FIGURE 12.6 *Der Bär, der ein Bär bleiben wollte* (1976). The factory in which the bear is forced to work. Reprinted with permission by Fischer Kinder- und Jugendbuchverlag.

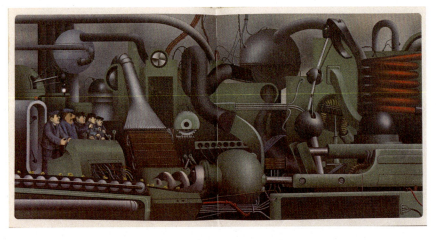

FIGURE 12.7 *Der Bär, der ein Bär bleiben wollte* (1976). Double spread showing a huge machine with workers. Reprinted with permission by Fischer Kinder- und Jugendbuchverlag.

FIGURE 12.8 *Der Bär, der ein Bär bleiben wollte* (1976). The motel in the dark winter landscape. Reprinted with permission by Fischer Kinder- und Jugendbuchverlag.

The realistic depiction of things that have no recognisable functional connection to each other is also seen in the interior design of the factory hall that is the workplace of the bear (Figure 12.7). The depiction of the huge machine producing something we do not know is reminiscent of the contemporary paintings of Konrad Klapheck (Sauer, 2007, p. 33).

The depiction of the motel in the dark winter landscape also associates the cheap, boxlike building with loneliness and despair, all the more so when the bear with his hobo-like bundle is rejected at the counter (Figure 12.8). Neither animals nor poor workers are accepted as customers. Like Edward Hopper in several of his architectural paintings, Müller succeeds in presenting the motel as a simultaneously inviting and rejecting place.

Contrasting cityscapes/architecture

Pursuing the topic of the cityscape and architecture further, *Der standhafte Zinnsoldat* provides an interesting example. Jörg Müller's picturebook of Hans Christian Andersen's famous fairy tale differs from the previous editions in two respects (Kümmerling-Meibauer and Meibauer, 2020).

First, it is a textless picturebook. Consequently, Andersen's fairy tale is not integrated into the picture sequences as text; the story is told based on the pictures alone (Bosch, 2018). As a concession to readers who may not know the original fairy tale on which the picturebook is based, the story is printed in its entirety on a separate double sheet enclosed, loose-leaf, within the book. Second, Jörg Müller has altered the original fairy tale by moving the action to the present and modifying some of the narrative strands. In Müller's version, the tin soldier and a Barbie doll meet in a Paris apartment. Thrown on the rubbish heap and washed into the Atlantic, they end up in the gut of a tuna fish. This is caught and cut up in an African fish factory. Its waste ends up in a huge rubbish dump, where the tin soldier and

FIGURE 12.9 *Der standhafte Zinnsoldat* (1976). Back cover and front cover. Reprinted with permission by Fischer Kinder- und Jugendbuchverlag.

the Barbie doll are discovered. They are made into 'ethnic toys', bought by a tourist and returned to Paris where they are exhibited in an ethnological museum.

The large-format picturebook consists of 19 double-page spreads. It contains a total of 28 illustrations, eight of which extend over a double page. The pictures are a combination of airbrush technique and gouache illustrations. All illustrations are surrounded by a narrow beige-grey frame. The same colour is found on the solid colour endpapers. The image on the cover spans the front and back of the book (Figure 12.9).

A kerb is seen in the centre with the illustrator's name, the title of the fairy tale, and the publisher's name below in black lettering. There is no reference to Hans Christian Andersen at this point. Below the block of type, the reader/viewer can see a paper boat with the tin soldier floating in the gutter. The tin soldier does not stand upright, but lies almost horizontally in the little boat, threatening to fall out. In the gutter and on the street lie crumpled paper packages, cigarette butts, and a ticket. The reader's point of view is from below, almost at the same height as the perspective of the tin soldier. Above the curb, one can see a front of houses with historicist buildings. A woman is walking on the sidewalk holding a little girl by the hand. A brown dog on a lead looks over the kerb toward the paper boat. This image does not appear in the picturebook itself and already anticipates an important moment in the plot, namely the beginning of the tin soldier's involuntary journey.

Most of the illustrations take a frog's-eye view, as if the reader were seeing things from the perspective of a miniature toy. In this way, the impression of a narrowed viewpoint is created, but it is countered by the opening up of the space to the street or the sky. The action takes place in the immediate present, recognisable, for example, in the furnishings of the apartments, the clothes people wear, and the cars on the streets. The clearest clue is a poster in the children's room showing the character Woody from the animated film

Toy Story (1995). This film was released a year before the picturebook was published. While the first as well as the last scenes are set in Europe – the newspaper clippings and the cityscape point to France and Paris, respectively – the action shifts to Central Africa in the last third.

The story culminates in the oversized garbage dump in Africa. Müller was inspired to create these illustrations by photographs of garbage dumps made available to him (Sauer, 2007, p. 92). A refuse collector takes the two figures and returns them to their original function as toys by making a car, including passengers, out of rubbish for his son. As in Andersen's fairy tale, the boy parts with the toy, here in exchange for money. There is an ironic twist at the end when this toy is brought back to Europe and given an upgrade by being exhibited in the museum. While in Andersen's tale only a pewter heart and a sequin remain at the end, in Müller's case the pewter soldier and the Barbie doll are preserved forever in a display case. Due to the lack of words in the picturebook, the viewer must reconstruct the history of these figures in their mind, suggested by knowledge of the original story.

In Müller's version of the steadfast tin soldier, the contrast between the somewhat rundown old Parisian quarter, the slum in a large African city, and the ethnological museum now play a major role.

FIGURE 12.10 *Der standhafte Zinnsoldat* (1976). The African garbage dump with the slum and the silhouette of a big city on the horizon. Reprinted with permission by Fischer Kinder- und Jugendbuchverlag.

Taking over the perspective of a bystander, we see the man transporting his finds from the dumps (Figure 12.10). The vista opens up to the huge dump in front of the slums. In the background, the harbour with a sunken ship can be seen. On the horizon, the skyline of a city is shown. In a way, the slum is a suburb of the city. The huts of its inhabitants are made from material that can be found at the dump. Like the ordinary city of Europe, the scene depicts an ordinary African city that is structured by its economy and poor social standards. This situation is normal for the people living in the slum and working on the dump, yet it is exotic and extraordinary for the tourist-voyeur.

The little boy playing with the tin soldier, Barbie, and Duplo bricks in the old building apartment is not dissimilar to the little boy tinkering with the off-road car with his father in the hut. But the further circumstances of their respective lives are opposite: the clean city, the furnished apartment, the regular work, and the abundance of toys contrast with the dirty city (the garbage dump), the poor hut, the work as a garbage collector, and the scarcity of toys. Complying with the tradition of colonialist appropriation of native art, the modern tourist donates the self-made and cheaply acquired toy artwork to the ethnological museum.

Final remarks

The critical intention of these two portfolios dealing with the change of the landscape and the cityscape has not always been understood. On the contrary, some observers used the picturebooks to demonstrate necessary civic developments. If this is true, it proves that evaluations of these changes are made on the basis of ideological conviction, including views about the beauty of a landscape, a cityscape, or a building.

In the interview with Inge Sauer, Jörg Müller is eager to explain that he does not want to polemicise or proselytise. He even wants to paint the things he detests in a beautiful way, at least to some extent ('besonders auch das, was mir zuwider ist, einigermaßen schön zu malen', Sauer, 2007, p. 21). And indeed, when we look at the last tableau from *Hier fällt ein Haus*, we can imagine that Jörg Müller does not appreciate the reflecting surfaces of the facades and the cars roaring on a motorway in the former old town, while some readers may find this scenario stylish and appealing.

The illustrator carefully avoids extremes. Pictures like the nightmarish scene with the creatures crawling out of the street and climbing up the facades, as in *Was wollt ihr machen, wenn der Schwarze Mann kommt*, are rare. Likewise, the depiction of cityscapes and architecture avoids extremes and sticks to the normal, to streets, squares, and buildings that could be found in a similar manner in every European city. It is in this sense that Jörg Müller aims at the ordinariness of cityscapes and architecture. Editions published in many different countries show that this can widely be understood, even when the architectural traditions are different.

There are, however, subtle devices that put cityscapes and buildings in a certain light or perspective. The use of photographs in an early stage of artistic work seems to guarantee a certain amount of realism. For instance, Jörg Müller used photographs of African dumps when working on *Der standhafte Zinnsoldat*. This technique is certainly inspired by photo-realism. But Jörg Müller tries to find a level of design that at the same time allows him to trigger certain emotions in the viewer. Thus, the use of brown tones in the rendering of the waste heaps in *Der standhafte Zinnsoldat* aims to trigger unpleasant feelings in the viewer. Blue tones are used to give architecture a certain look, as can be seen in *Der Bär, der ein Bär bleiben wollte* and *Die Kanincheninsel* in which the factories and the motel are associated with coolness and aseptic purity. This does not imply that these emotional values are inherent in colours, but targets conventional associations of colours with emotional responses (Papazian, 2021).

The airbrush technique used in *Aufstand der Tiere oder Die neuen Stadtmusikanten* suits the colourful postmodern architecture. Different page designs contribute to the salience of the pictures, maximised in the textless picturebooks. This is the case with the two portfolios as well as with *Der standhafte Zinnsoldat*. The latter book also uses views from below which seem to enlarge buildings. Conventionally, Jörg Müller shows cityscapes with a 'camera view', as if someone strolled through a city. In *Der Bär, der ein Bär bleiben wollte* and *Die Kanincheninsel*, however, he adds cross-section drawings in order to show the structures: the bear's cave under the newly constructed factory and the rabbits' cages in the rabbit factory.

Müller does not want the cityscapes to be identifiable as depictions of any actual city. Even when Inge Sauer states that *Der Mann vom Bärengraben* is a book about Bern – because the Bärengraben is a well-known landmark in Bern – Jörg Müller protests and argues that he has added many details of other cities (Sauer, 2007, p. 77). It is similar in *Was wollt ihr machen, wenn der Schwarze Mann kommt?* which seems to draw on the city of Biel (where Jörg Müller lived) yet does not display an exact copy of the church and the monument next to it. So, I would like to conclude that the ordinary city is also a generic city. It is this level of abstraction and close contact with reality that makes Jörg Müller's cityscapes and architectural depictions so fascinating.

References

Bosch, E. (2018). Wordless picturebooks. In Bettina Kümmerling-Meibauer (ed), *The Routledge Companion to Picturebooks*. London: Routledge, pp. 191–200.

Boym, S. (2001). *The Future of Nostalgia*. New York: Basic Books.

Campagnaro, M. (2017). Bruno Munari's visual mapping of the city of Milan: A historical analysis of the picturebook. In Nina Goga and Bettina Kümmerling-Meibauer (eds), *Nella Nebbia di Milano." Maps and Mapping in Children's Literature. Landscapes, Seascapes and Cityscapes*. Amsterdam: Benjamins, pp. 147–163.

——— (2021). Stepping into the world of houses. Children's picturebooks on architecture. In Nina Goga, Sarah Hoem Iversen and Anne-Stefi Teigland (eds), *Verbal and Visual Strategies in Nonfiction Picturebooks. Theoretical and Analytical Approaches*. Oslo: Scandinavian University Press, pp. 202–219.

Hayward, E. and Schmiedeknecht, T. (2019). Absent architectures: Postwar housing in British children's picture books (1960-present). *The Journal of Architecture* 24(4), pp. 487–511.

Kümmerling-Meibauer, B. and Meibauer, J. (2020). Jörg Müller, *Der standhafte Zinnsoldat* (1996). In Małgorzata Cackowska, Hanna Dymel-Trzebiatowska and Jerzy Szyłak (eds), *Książka Obrazkowa Leksykon. Tom 2*. Poznań: Instytut Kultury Popularnej, pp. 15–21.

Lynch, D. (1960). *The Image of the City*. Cambridge, Mass: MIT Press.

Meibauer, J. (2021). Images of the socialist city in East German picturebooks. *Stalinallee* and *Plattenbau*. *Barnelitterært Forskningstidsskrift – Nordic Journal of ChildLit Aesthetics* (BLFT) 12, pp. 1–13. [https://www.idunn.no/blft/ 2021/01/]

Müller, J. (1973). *Alle Jahre wieder saust der Presslufthammer nieder oder Die Veränderung der Landschaft*. Aarau: Sauerländer.

——— (1976). *Hier fällt ein Haus, dort steht ein Kran und ewig droht der Baggerzahn oder Die Veränderung der Stadt*. Unter Mitarbeit von Heinz Ledergerber. Aarau: Sauerländer.

——— (1996). *Der standhafte Zinnsoldat*. Aarau: Sauerländer.

Müller, J. and Steiner, J. (1977a). *Der Bär, der ein Bär bleiben wollte.* Aarau: Sauerländer.

———— (1977b). *Die Kanincheninsel.* Aarau: Sauerländer.

———— (1987). *Der Mann vom Bärengraben.* Aarau: Sauerländer.

———— (1989). *Aufstand der Tiere oder Die neuen Stadtmusikanten.* Aarau: Sauerländer.

———— (1998). *Was wollt ihr machen, wenn der Schwarze Mann kommt?* Aarau: Sauerländer.

Papazian, G. (2021). Coloring feelings: Concept books making and remaking racialized color meanings. *Children's Literature in Education* 52, pp. 357–377.

Rémi, C. (2018). Wimmelbooks. In Bettina Kümmerling-Meibauer (ed), *The Routledge Companion to Picturebooks.* London: Routledge, pp. 158–168.

Sauer, I. (ed), (2007). *Jörg Müller – Die Welt Ist kein Märchen. Skizzen, Illustrationen, Bilderbücher.* Wädenswil: Nimbus.

Waller, A. (2020). The art of being ordinary: Cups of tea and catching the bus in contemporary British YA. *International Journal of Young Adult Literature* 1(1), pp. 1–25. DOI: 10.24877/ijyal.34

INDEX

Note: **Bold** page numbers refer to tables; *italic* page numbers refer to figures and page numbers followed by "n" denote endnotes.

Aarnio, E. 120
Abercrombie, P. 169, 193, 196
Abitacolo 130, 131
About Two Squares 4, 49, 50–54, *51, 61*
acceptera 14, 27
ACME, comic magazine 77
The Adventures of Pinocchio 128
Agente Naranja, comic magazine 77
Aitchison, M. 35
Alderson, B. 33, 46n3
Alekos 75
Algorta, A. *87*
ambiguity 204–205
The Anatomy of the Architectural Book 60
Andean tropics 75
Andersen, H. C. 226, 229, 230
Andrew Jessup 101
And Tango Makes Three 170
Anglo-American children's picturebooks 167
Anthropomorphic chairs *127*
Aoyama, K. 117, *117*
ARCGIS software 203, 206
architectural: books 49; elements 20; principles of Modernism 137; representations 144; worlds 2
architecture 143; analytical framework for representations of **145–146**; as community-based democratic instance 132–135; contrasting cityscapes 229–232; of ordinary city 222–226; of production sites 226; professional knowledge of 49; representations of 144
architecture and interior design: in first half of the 20th century 126–128; history of 126; Italian

children 126–128; new cultural and social aspirations 135–140; in second half of the 20th century 128–131
Architecture Australia 98
Architecture Box LC N 1 132
Architecture for Children 45
Architecture from the Outside 171
The Architectures of Childhood 35
Ariés, P. 126
Around the World in Eighty Days 19
Art deco style (European) 84
Asquith, R. 177, 182
Atlas of Literature 204
Atlas of the European Novel 204
Aufstand der Tiere oder Die neuen Stadtmusikanten 222, 224, *224,* 225, *225,* 233
Australia 143, 163; Australian identity (mythic) 101; childhood 95; childhood mobility 101; communities 95; domestic architecture 98
Australian picturebooks 4, 95–97, 102, 163; *Bluey: At Home with the Heelers* 149, *150–151,* 151–152; discourse 105; *Max* 147; *Wren* 147, 153–154
Avant-garde designs (European) 132
Ayton, R. 4, 34

Bachelard, G. 5, 105, 111, 115, 116, 121
Bader, B. 33
Badmin, S. R. 2, 45
Baker, J. S. 192
Balbus: A Picture Book of Buildings 45
Balla, G. 127

Ball, D. 101, 102
Barbapapa's House 116
Barbican building site 41, 42
The Baron in the Trees 125
Baroux, A. 118
Basic Space 60–66, *62–64*
Baudrillard, J. 25
Baum, L. F. 128
Bavidge, J. 202
The Bear That Wasn't 226, *228,* 229, *229, 230,*
    231, 232–233
Beer, S. 153
Befreites Wohnen 55, 59, 60
Belotti, E. G. 140
Benkoz renace 85, 85–86, 88
Berenguer, J. R. 72, *72*
Bermúdez, G. 75
Berndt, W. 70
Berry, J. 4, 35
Big Ben 205, 206, 208, 210, 213–215
Billy Baggs 189, 198
Biohó, B. 85
Blair, K. 104
Blaut, J. M. 202
Blooming Season 147, *159,* 161–162
Bluey: At Home with the Heelers 147, 149, *150–*
    151, 151–154
Bogotá futuro plan 71
Bois, Y. -A. 54
The Book of Ornamentations 122
Borgström, –C.-E. 26
Boughton, J. 37
Bourdieu, P. 5
Bower, R. 196
Bradbury, M. 204
branded picturebooks 21
The Bremen Town Musicians 224
Brière-Hacquet, A. 118
British Birds and their Nests 33
British domestic architecture in
    picturebooks 105
British interwar architecture and design 190
Brooke, L. L. 113
Brunnström, L. 14
Brutalist architecture 181
Buchanan, C. 43
The Builder 33–35, 37, *39,* 39–43
Buitrago, J. 77, *80, 82,* 83, *84*
Bullen, A. 181
Bullock, N. 37–39
Burchardt, J. 31
Bygg upp 11, *12*

Caballero, A. 75
Camino a casa 79–81, *80,* 88
Campagnaro, M. 2, 5, 98
The Car Makers 41, 43, 44
Carroll, L. 125

'Casey Court' cartoons 5
Castellanos, D. 75, *76*
Castrillón, S. 75
Catalog of Children's and Youth Literature in
    Colombian 69
Celli, R. 112
centrifugal forces 125
Cervantes, M. 115–116
Chance, J. 1
Chaplin, C. 99
Chanchito 70
Charter, A. 37
child/children: aesthetics 140; books between
    1945 and 1970 74; books during the 1930s and
    1940s 21; books in Colombia 68, 71; consumer
    20–21; culture and literature 126; development,
    education and welfare 13; interpretations,
    word analysis of 88; literature 16, 26, 69, 125;
    literature scholarship 6; literature with radical
    design aesthetics 13; modern context 18; novels
    204; rhyme 75
child reader 32–34, 115, 191
children as future citizens, in Swedish
    picturebooks 11–13; child consumer 20–21;
    collage and branding 21–22; images of modern
    spectacle 22–26; modern architecture and
    space travel 13–16; world in eight days 16–20
children's fantasy fiction 201–203; ambiguity
    and uncertainty 204–205; collocations with
    positive connotation 214–215; descriptions
    of different landmarks 212–214; landmark
    mapping 206–209; literary geography *versus*
    literary cartography 203–204; magic and
    landmarks 211; methodology 205–206; note
    on picturebooks 205; St. Paul's cathedral
    versus others 212; top ten London landmarks
    209–211
Children's Literature Assembly (CLA) 170
Children's Literature: A Very Short Introduction 3
China 143, 163
Chinese picturebooks 158–162
Christian citizenship 70
'chthonicity' 152
Citroën, R. 115
city 2, 5, 36, 73, 75–77, 80–83, 86–89, 95, 116,
    119, 129, 133–137, 140, 153, 154, 157, 158,
    160–162, 195–197, 202–207, 212–215,
    220–226
The City 125
CLA *see* Children's Literature Assembly (CLA)
Clarice era una reina 81, 81–82, 88
Clark, A. 192
Clute, J. 211
cognitive map 202
collage technique 24
Collage: The Making of Modern Art 25
collocation analysis 213–215
Collodi, C. 125, 128

Colombian historiography 77
Colombian picturebooks 4
Colomer, T. 2
Comenius 3
ComicBuk, comic magazine 77
community-based democratic instance, architecture as 132–135
conservative hegemony 70
constant territorial conflicts 70
Consuegra, D. 77
contemporary authors 73
contemporary urban environments 2
Contrasts 66n5
conventional sign (word) 2, 6
Cook, D. T. 13
cooperative: architectural firm 14; brand 13, 14; picturebooks 21; retailers 23; Union 11, *12, 13*–14, *15, 17, 19, 20, 22, 24, 26;* window display 23, *23*
Coraline 125
County of London Plan 169
Crary, J. 25
Crew, G. 107
critical multimodal discourse analysis 143
Croset, P. -A. 64
Cuéllar, O. 75
'cultural capital,' Passeron and Bourdieu's concept 111

Da Coll, I. 75
Daily Mail 5–6, 190–192, 194
Daily Telegraph 194
Darling, E. 190, 195
Declaration of the Rights of the Child 129
Deleuze, G. 5, 123
Denton, T. 108n1
DePalma, R. 170, 174
Díaz, O. 71, 72
Dickens, C. 125
A Dictionary of Human Geography 203
digital humanities 6, 203
'doghouse dormers' 102
Dog In, Cat Out 96, *96,* 98–100
Dolan, M. 174
domestic: architectural design 95, 174; Australian picturebooks 4, 105; *hearth* 125; space 2, 4–5
Domus design 132, 137
Donaldson, C. 209, 213
Don Amacise 70
Donnelly, E. 101
Don Quixote 115
dot maps 209
Downing, A. J. 175
Downs, R. 202
Drac and the Gremlin 100, 101
Draper, S. 170
Drew, J. 45

Druker, E. 3–5
Duby, G. 126
Ducos, M. 120, *120,* 121
Durand, G. 115
dystopias of modernism 75–77

education 13, 32, 38, 39, 69, 70, 75, 126, 129, 135, 144
Education Act, 1944 38, 41
Eiffel Tower, in *Befreites Wohnen* 59
Eiguer, A. 111, 119
Ekman, S. 201
El edificio (The building) 82, 82–85, *83, 84,* 88
Empire State building 54, 56, 58
Enchanted Lion Books 112
The Encyclopaedia of Fantasy 211
Escher, M. C. 222
Esposito, J. 173, 174

Fajardo, D. 77
The Family Book 172–177
The Family of Fourteen Fix Breakfast 122
The Family of Fourteen on the Move 122
fantasy literature 206
Faucher, P. 112
Finding Jack 97
Fischer Kinder- und Jugendbuchverlag *223–225, 227, 228, 231*
Fogg, P. 19
'Folkhemmet' 13
Fontana, D. 54
formal ordinariness 220
Forshaw, J. H. 169
Foucault, M. 25
The 14 Forest Mice: the Autumn March 122–123; *the Dragonfly Pond* 123; *the Spring Outing* 122; *the Winter Sledding Day* 122
France or Germany 55
Franco, E. 73
Fry, M. 45
functionalist industrial facility 11

Gaitán, J. E. 73
Gastold, C. 119
gendered stereotypes 20
geographic investment 202
Geographic Markup Language (GML) 206
geographic specificity 202
geo-referencing 205–206
Giedion, S. 55
Glasheen, L. 5–6
Glendinning, M. 34, 37
GML *see* Geographic Markup Language (GML)
God is in the Detail 41
Godofredo Cascarrabias 70
Goei, G. 156–157
Goga, N. 3
Going to School 38–41, *40*

Goldfinger, E. 181
Goldilocks and the Three Bears 112
Gold, J. R. 37
Goodall, H. 97
Gooday, G. 16
Graham, B. 152
Gray, N. *106*
The Great Big Book of Families 177
Greater London Council 181
Greder, A. 125
Gregory, I. 209, 213
Grindrod, J. 37
Guattari, F. 5, 123
Guess Who Does What… An Invisible Walk 121
Guevara, S. 77

Hall, E. T. 122, 162
Hall, T. 103
Halliday, M. 144
The Hangover 33, 40, 41
Hans Andersen's Fairy Tales and *Tiny Tots Travels* 33
Haüsermann, P. 116
Haussmann's Paris 59
Havenhand, I. 43
Havenhand, J. 43
Hayward, E. 5, 105
Heather Has Two Mummies 172–179
Heidegger, M. 119
Henrietta, home decorator 117
Herbauts, A. 112, 113
Here Be Dragons: Exploring Fantasy Maps and Settings 201
Heuser, R. 209, 212, 215
'The highly modern ideal homestead,' in 'Casey Court' cartoon 187–190, *188, 189*
Hill, O. 45
A History of Private Life 126
Hixtorieta, comic magazine 77
Hoffman, M. 177, 182
Ho Lee-Ling 154
Holmberg, C. N. 211
home 34–37; and vision 197–198
Homes 34, 35, *36,* 37, 39
Homes for the People 192
Hopper, E. 229
Hornsey, R. 169
house 34–37, 111–123
housing 1, 2, 5, 21, 34, 35, 37–40, 45, 95, 100, 126, 128, 129, 134, 135, 144, 154, 157, 172, 178–182, 189, 190–198
Housing Act: 1935 189–190; 1980 180
Housing and Development Board, Singapore 154
Housing Problems 193
Housing Progress 193
How To Live in A Flat 192
Huang, H. 4
Hugo, V. 113

Hulme, T. 197
Hunt, P. 46n4
Hyde, R. 98

iconic cultural metonymies 105
iconic signs (pictures) 6
Ideal Home Exhibitions 187, 190–192, 194, 195, 197
'ideological criticism' 6
Illustrated Chips 187, *188, 189,* 191, 195, 197
'imagetext,' Mitchell's concept 3, 12
imaginaries of modernity, transformation of 69
Ina-Casa plan 134
In A Hotel 41
In my Father's Room 107, 108
'inside dwelling' 111
interior 5, 6, 19, 37, 39, 41, 44, 58–61, 86, 95, 99, 100, 107, 122, 126–131, 193
International Centre 75
Italian children's interior design: in first half of the 20th century 126–128; in second half of the 20th century 128–131
Italian picturebooks 125–126; children's culture and literature 126; community-based democratic instance 132–135; interior design in the first half of the 20th century 126–128; interior design in the second half of the 20th century 128–131; new cultural and social aspirations 135–140; representations and values in 131–132
Iversen, S. H. 3
Invisible, The 179, 181
Iwamura, K. 122

Jack, K. 97
Jacobs, J. 113
James, A. 96, *96,* 98
Jaramillo, L. 75
Jeavons, M. 104
Jerring, N. 14, 15, *15,* 16
John Brown, Rose and the Midnight Cat 99
Johnson, D. 170
Johnson, L. 33, 46n3
Johnson, M. 106
Johnson, S. 51

Die Kanincheninsel 226, *227*
Karsen, F. 72
Kartell and Danese Milano 129, *130*
Katie in London 205
Kauffman, E. 117
Keyhole Markup Language (KML) 206
Key Word Reading Scheme 32
The Kid 99
Klapheck, K. 229
KML *see* Keyhole Markup Language (KML)
Kook, C. 157
Korean domestic space/spatiality 116

Koss, M. D. 170
Kozlovsky, R. 35–36, 189, 194
Kümmerling-Meibauer, B. 2, 46

La Casa que Juan Construyó 75, 76, *76*
Laceby, L. 95–97
Ladybird books 31, 33, 38; *The Car Makers* 43;
    children in 1960s and 1970s 29; *Going to school*
    40; *Homes* 36; 'integrate young children into
    the ideology of our culture' 32; 'Ladybird
    Book of Achievements' Series 601 4, 209; *The*
    Ladybird Book of the Hangover 34; Ladybird
    Leader series 37
and modern architecture 45; modern housing
    and schools 38; modern school buildings in
    39; *People at work: On the railways* 44; 'People at
    Work' series 42; *People at work: The builder 39*;
    pictures in 41; school buildings in 38; *The story*
    of houses and homes 30; typology of 4
Ladybird by Design: 100 years of words and
    pictures 46n3
The Ladybird Story: Children's Books for Everyone
    46n3
Lakoff, G. 106
landmark mapping 206–209, *207*
landmarks: descriptions of 212–214; magic and
    211; positive and negative connotations **213**
layout 25, 37, 43, 50, 54, 55, 57, 60, 66n1, 100, 126
LC N 1 Architecture Box 133
Le Corbusier 35, 37, 55, 74, 119, 132
Ledergerber, G. 221
Lee, G. 157
Left out: the forgotten tradition of radical publishing for
    children in Britain 45
The legacy of the modern movement 77–79
Lehman, K. 153
Lemonnier, A. 119
Lenin Tribune, Lissitzky's design 52
Lewis, C. S. 203
Liberated Dwelling 55
Lissitzky, E. 4, 46, 49, 50–54, *51*, 60, 65, 66,
    66n1, 66n2
literary geography *vs.* literary cartography
    203–204
Little House on the Prairie 125
Little Red in the Hood 147, 156–157
Little Red Riding Hood 135
A little song about Per and Lisa 19, 20
Little Yellow Riding Hood 132, 135–139, *136, 139,*
    140, 141
Liu Xun *159, 160*
Lizard, home decorator 117
Löfgren, Å 26
London: architectural landmarks 6; of children's
    fantasy fiction (*see* children's fantasy fiction)
Londoño, R. 4
The Lost Heir 215

The Lost Thing 99
Lovag, A. 116
Luma Light Bulb Factory in Stockholm 3–4,
    11–12, *12*, 13, 14, 16, 17, 20, 22, 23
Lussault, M. 123

Macaulay, D. 4, 49, 54–60, *56–58*, 66
Maddie's New Neighbours 147, *149*, 154, *155–156,*
    156, 157
Magnenat, S. T. 71
Mallet-Stevens, R. 120
Man-hee's House 116
Manrique, A. 4
Mapping Fiction: The Theories, Tools and
    Potentials 204
Maps in Mind 202
Marino, R. 133
Markham, S. 115
Marples, E. 44
Martin, A. 192
Martín, A. M. 84
Marxism 219
Mason, D. 173
Mass Rapid Transportation system, Singapore 156
materialisation, international style principles
    72–75
Matless, D. 196
Max 147, 152–153
Mazetti Factory 17, *18*, 19, 20
McCulloch, D. 33
McLeod, M. 6
Meibauer, J. 6, 46
Mendoza, G. 117
Meneses, G. 77
Metaphors We Live By 106
Meunier, C. 4, 5
Midnight Twins 205, 210
The Milk Bars Book 101
The Milkman 41
Millard, F. 4, 49, 60–66, *62–64*
Minkowska, F. 115
Misia Escopeta y Polín 70
Mitchell, W. J. T. 3, 12, 22
'Modello 904' Poltrona Frau 140
modern architectural design 5
modern architecture 1–2, 6–7, 14, 22, 32, 43,
    55, 77; Ladybird and 45; light, air and vision
    192–195; and space travel 13–16
modern countryside/city invention 195–197
modern housing and schools 38
modern imaginaries, roots of 70–72
modernist 11, 35, 42, 45, 49, 54, 65, 68, 71, 162, 190
modernist architecture 5, 12–14, 20, 24
modernity 2, 3–4, 20, 22, 23, 25, 32, 41, 43, 68,
    77; in children's literature 12; emergence of 89;
    transformation of the imaginaries of 69
modern methods and materials 29

modern spectacle, images of 22
modern typographic styles 71
modus habitandi 111
Moebius, W. 32, 33, 46n1
Moffat, A. 171
Mojicón 70
Moles, A. 122, 123
Montaña, F. 77
Moretti, F. 204
The Mouse of Paris (119
Mr Plunkett's Pool 101, 108n1
Mrs Weber's Diary 179
Mrs Weber's Omnibus 167, *168*
Muller, G. 112, 121
Müller, J. 6, 219–222, 226, 229, 231–233
multimodal analysis image 148, 149
Munari, B. 5, 129–135, *136*, 137, *139*, 140, 141
Murray, K. 104
Mussino, A. 128
Mussolini, B. 133
Muthesius, S. 34, 37
My Dog's a Scaredy-Cat 101, *102,* 105
My House 115
My Uncle's Donkey 99
My Valley (*114,* 115

Nathan, M. 193
National Front (1958–1974) 73
National Law 98 75
Need A House? Call Ms Mouse 117
Nelly, E. 71
Neville, C. 195
new cultural family models *139*
Night Noises 95, 97, *97*
Nikolajeva, M. 2, 6
Nodelman, P. 1, 31, 32, 34, 45, 46n1, 46n5
No Outsiders in Our School: Teaching the Equality Act in Primary School 171
No Outsiders project 170–171
Notre-Dame of Paris / The Hunchback of Notre Dame 113
Nunca se olvida 86–88, *87*
The Nurse 41

O'Halloran, K. L. 5
Okazashiro or *The Book of Ornamentations* 122
On The Railways 41, 43, 44, *44*
Oono, Y. 65
Op de Beeck, N. 18, 25
Orbis Sensualum Pictus 3
Ordinariness 220
Osorio, M. 73, 75
O'Toole, M. 147, 149, 152
Otra vez en Lilac 72

Palace of Justice 79, 133, *134*
Palace of the Air Force 133
Paperboy 96

The Paper Magician 211
Paradox City 193, 194
Parra, R. 77
'Peacehaven' 187, 195–196
Pease, A. 192
Peckham Pioneer Health Centre 194
Peirce, C. S. 79
'People at Work' series 4, 41, 43, *44,* 45
Per and Lisa: Around the world in 8 days 16, *17,* 19, 20; *A Christmas book with holes* 24, *25; build a grocery store* 26; *journey with Lampe the tube* 14, 15, *15,* 20
Percival, T. 179
Peters, V. 77
petit small grand big 64
physical maps 211
Piacentini, M. 133
Piatti, B. 204
pictorial maps 201
picturebooks 3, 205; Anglo-American children's picturebooks 166; Australian picturebooks (*see* Australian picturebooks); branded picturebooks 21; British And American children (*see* British And American children's picturebooks); British domestic architecture in 105; children as future citizens, in Swedish picturebooks (*see* children as future citizens, in Swedish picturebooks); Chinese picturebooks (*see* Chinese picturebooks); Colombian picturebooks 4; cooperative picturebooks 21; domestic architecture in Australian picturebooks 105; Italian picturebooks (*see* Italian picturebooks); modern picturebooks 95; Singaporean picturebooks (*see* Singaporean picturebooks)
Pippi Longstocking 125
Pirellone 137
Poe, E. A. 125
The Poetics of Space 113, 119
The Policeman 41–43, 45
Ponge, F. 119
Ponti, C. *114,* 115
Ponti, G. 132, *136,* 137
Posada, M. C. 75
positive and negative connotations **213,** 214–215
postmodern architecture 225
post-war modernism 6
Powers, A. 1
Priestley, J. B. 196
product placement 13
The Proud City: A Plan for London 193
Puddle Hunters 104, 105, 108
Pugin, A. 66n5
Pullman, P. 32, 46n1
Pumarejo, A. L. 71

Queen Elizabeth Hall site 41, 42
The Queen's Hat 205
'Queenslander' 106, 107, 151

Rabanal, D. 75, *82,* 83, *84,* 89
Ramírez, A. 75
rank-based system framework 147
Ransome, A. 196
reading, as building 49–50; *About Two Squares* 50–54, *51*; *Basic Space* and *Upside Down* 60–66, *62–64*; *Unbuilding* 54–60, *58*
reading-based methods 216
representations, modern architecture and urbanism 68–69; *Benkoz renace 85,* 85–86; *Camino a casa* 79–81, *80*; *Clarice era una reina 81,* 81–82; dystopias of modernism 75–77; *El edificio 82,* 82–85, *83, 84*; imaginaries of modernity, transformation of 69; legacy of the modern movement 77–79; materialisation of the international style principles 72–75; *Nunca se olvida* 86–88, *87*; roots of modern imaginaries 70–72
Restrepo, S. M. 77
Reyes, Y. 75
Reynolds, K. 2, 3, 13, 34, 45, 198
RIBA *see* Royal Institute of British Architects (RIBA)
Rickenmann, I. 87
Riddle, T. 99
The Road Makers 41, 43–45
Robinson, B. 34, 35
Robinson, W. H. 192
Robots 130
Rodchenko, A. 59
Ródez, E. 75
Rodríguez, C. 4
Rogers, G. 106, *106*
roots, modern imaginaries 70–72
Rose, G. 195
Rosero, J. *81*
Rother, L. 72
Rowling, J. K. 204
Royal Institute of British Architects (RIBA) 1, 196
Rubino, A. 127, *127,* 128
Rubinstein, G. 96, 98, 108n1
Rudd, J. 4
Rules of Summer 99
Running Away from Home 99, 106, *106*
Ryan, D. S. 190, 191
Ryan, M.-L. 202

Saint, A. 38
St. Paul's Cathedral 209–211, *210,* 212
Salazar, G. 77
Salmona, R. 75
Samarbete insurance company 25
Samper, A. 70
sample media files *148*
Sanabria, F. M. 75
Sanchez, D. F. 77
Sánchez, R. 77

Sandes, S. 32, 46n1
San Jorge theatre *83, 84*
Sapper, R. 129
Sauer, I. 232
Scatola di Architettura LC N 1 140
Schmiedeknecht, T. 1, 4, 105
Scott, A. 107
Scott, C. 2, 6
semiotics 68, 69
Sert, J. L. 74
Shock, comic magazine 77
Shulevitz, U. 3, 32, 46n1
Silva-Díaz, C. 2
Simmonds, P. 167, *167,* 168, *168*
Singapore 143, 163; Housing and Development Board (HDB) 154; Mass Rapid Transportation (MRT) system 156; urban planning policy 158
Singaporean picturebooks 163; *Little Red in the Hood* 156–157; *Maddie's New Neighbours* 154, *155–156,* 156; *There was a Peranakan Woman who Lived in a Shoe* 157–158
The Sketch 192
Skoindustri, S. 20
Smiff, M. 189
Smith, C. 101, 102, *102*
Smith, D. S. 117
Smitty 70
social beliefs 2
social semiotic perspective 143, 144
Soja, E. 204
Soulless 215
space: domestic space 2, 4–5; Korean domestic space 116; urban space 2, 5–6
space travel 13–16
Spanish Civil War 70
Spanish hegemony 69
Der standhafte Zinnsoldat 226
Stanford Literary Lab 204
statistical and digital methods 216
Stea, D. 202
Steiner, J. 219, 226
Stenberg-Masolle, A. 14, *15*
Stephens, J. 2, 4, 112
Stina's Peculiar Birthday Journey 17, *18,* 19, 20
The Story of Houses and Homes 29, *30,* 32–35, 37, 39
The Story of Our Churches and Cathedrals 33
The Story of the Three Little Pigs 113
The Strange Case of the Alchemist's Daughter 215
Street Playgrounds Act, 1938 169
suburban landscape architecture 95
suburban modernity 191
Sundahl, E. 13, 14
Sweden: analogous ideas 21; architecture 14; Cooperative Union 11, *12,* 13; political landscape 13; welfare state and the people's home idea 13
Switzerland 6, 221
systemic functional theory 144

Tan, A. 157
Tan, S. 5, 99
'Tantibambini' 136, 137, 141
Tashlin, F. 226
Tavares, A. 60
Taylor, A. J. P. 196
Taylor, B. 25–26
Taylor, T. 116
technical and electrical culture 16
technical inventions 24
technical novelties 16
Teigland, A. -S. 3
There was a Peranakan Woman who Lived in a Shoe
   147, 157
'Third England' 196
Thomas, B. P. 35
'360°BOOK' 65
Tilly 99, 105–106
The Time Travellers 212
Tison, A. 116
TNT, comic magazine 77
Tofano, S. 128
Tolkien, J. R. R. 201, 203
Tooth, Tooth, Throw it onto the Roof 147, *159,*
   160–161
toponyms 204
Towards a New Architecture 55
Toy Story, animated film 230–231
traditional domestic architecture 98
traditional religious schemes 70
traditional research-based approach 206
'tradition and modernity' 191
Traffic in Towns 43
Treasure Hunt in Volubilis 120, *120*
Trellick Tower in West London *181,*
   181–182
Triana, E. 75, 86
The Trouble with Dogs 99
t-score analysis 213
Tudor Revival Architecture 109n6

The Umbrella Mouse 214
Unbuilding (Macaulay) 4, 49, 54–60, *56–58*
uncertainty 204–205
'Uncle Mac' series in 1945 33
United Nations General Assembly 129
Up-Down vertical metaphor 107–108
Upside Down 4, 49, 63, *64,* 65
urban 6, 20, 22, 24, 25, 35, 36, 69–71, 73–76,
   80–87, 89, 97, 128, 132–134, 136, 137, 139,
   140, 153, 154, 158, 160–162, 169, 180, 182
urban architectural aesthetics 137
urbanism 69, 71, 73, 76, 83, 90, 197
urban space 2, 5–6
useful art 73

Valencia, M. 75
Vallejo, E. 75

value added tax (VAT) 75
Vasco, I. 75
verbal maps 202
Vergara, Y. 75
Verne, J. 19
versatile homes 77, 177–182
Village and Town 2, 45
Villekulla, V. 125
Ville Radieuse 37
von Schmalensee, A. 13
von Uexküll, J. 116
Vuarnesson, B. 120

Wall, C. 41, 42
Walle, M. 16, *17*
Walmer, publishing house 166, *167*
Wang Yimei 158, 159
*Was wollt ihr machen, wenn der Schwarze Mann
   kommt?* 222, 223, *223,* 232, 233
Way, L. 5
We Are Moving! 118
Weber, W. 166, *167, 168*
We Have Fun 31
We Need Diverse Books (WNDB) 166, 170
Western liberal democracies 219
Western post-war societies 219
What Are Little Girls Made Of ? 140
What Are You Doing, Mr. Architect? 117
Wiener, P. L. 74
Wilcox, publishing house 166, *167*
Wilkens, M. 202
WNDB *see* We Need Diverse Books
   (WNDB)
Wölfflin, H. 66n5
The Wonderful Wizard of Oz 128
world of work 41–45
World War I 97, 109n6
World War II 5, 13, 31, 70, 100, 109n6, 116, 125,
   128, 134, 169, 221
The Woven Path 208
Wren 147, 153–154
Wright, F. L. 117
Wu Heng *159,* 161

Xiao Ai 158
Xiao Ai's Dragon Boat Festival 147, 158,
   159, 160
Xinchao Zhai 5

Yambo 128
Yockteng, R. 77, *80*
Yoon-Duck, K. 116

Zanuso, M. 129
Zapata, J. P. 85, 86
Zeegen, L. 31, 42, 46n3
Zelizer, V. 13
Zhang Xiaoyu 158, *159*